I'll Find a Way
or Make One

ALSO BY JUAN WILLIAMS

My Soul Looks Back in Wonder: Voices of the Civil Rights Experience

This Far by Faith: Stories from the African American Religious Experience

Thurgood Marshall: American Revolutionary

Eyes on the Prize: America's Civil Rights Years, 1954–1965

I'LL FIND A WAY OR MAKE ONE

A Tribute to

Historically Black Colleges and Universities

Juan Williams *and* Dwayne Ashley

with Shawn Rhea

Amistad

An Imprint of HarperCollins*Publishers*

All royalties from the sales of this book will be paid to the Thurgood Marshall Scholarship Fund. The Thurgood Marshall Scholarship Fund is preparing a new generation of leaders! 90 William Street, Suite 1203, New York, NY 10038. www.thurgoodmarshallfund.org.

HarperCollins books may be purchased for educational, business, or sales promotional use. For information, please write: Special Markets Department, HarperCollins Publishers Inc., 10 East 53rd Street, New York, NY 10022.

FIRST EDITION

Designed by Laura Lindgren

Printed on acid-free paper

Library of Congress Cataloging-in-Publication Data

Williams, Juan
    I'll find a way or make one : a tribute to historically black colleges and universities / by Juan Williams and Dwayne Ashley.— 1st ed.
        p.   cm.
    Includes bibliographical references.
    ISBN 0-06-009453-2 (hc. : alk. paper)—ISBN 0-06-009456-7 (pbk. : alk. paper)
        1. African Americans—Education—History. 2. African American universities and colleges—History. I. Ashley, Dwayne. II. Title.

LC2741.W55 2004
378.73'089'96073—dc22

2004046450

05 06 07 08   ❖/RRD   10 9 8 7 6 5 4 3 2

THURGOOD MARSHALL
SCHOLARSHIP FUND

The Thurgood Marshall Scholarship Fund (TMSF) was founded in 1987 to offer scholarship assistance to students attending public black colleges and universities. Since its founding, TMSF has awarded more than $50 million in scholarships and programmatic support to close to 4,500 students attending its forty-five member institutions.

The quest to start a merit-based scholarship fund to support public HBCU students was begun by Dr. N. Joyce Payne, director of the Office for the Advancement of Public Black Colleges of State University and Land-Grant Colleges (OAPBC) of the National Association of State Universities and Land-Grant Colleges, in cooperation with the American Association of State Colleges and Universities. She discovered that her alma mater, D.C. Teachers College, was not a member institution of the United Negro College Fund, which aids private HBCUs. Payne enlisted the support of Thurgood Marshall, Supreme Court associate justice, who lent his name to the effort. With a vision and Justice Marshall's blessing, Dr. Payne hit the pavement with Noel Hankin, then of the Miller Brewing Company, Al Smith, of North Carolina A & T State University, and James Parks, formerly of the Miller Brewing Company, to form partnerships with corporate executives and educators. Many in the corporate world had to be made aware of the contributions that public black colleges and universities had been making for well over a century. Seventy-seven percent of the students enrolled in a historically black college or university attend one of Thurgood Marshall's member institutions. Presently TMSF has partnerships with corporations, foundations, and organizations that provide financial support, internships, and job opportunities for deserving graduates.

TMSF has expanded its work to include students before they enter college and after they graduate. Innovative programs with groups like the New York City Summer Employment Program expose students to different career choices through interaction with TMSF corporate partners and Thurgood Marshall scholarship alumni. TMSF has also joined with the Bill and Melinda Gates Foundation to improve five low-performing high schools and create three new high schools in low-income areas. The National Test Prep Program prepares students for the GRE, GMAT, MCAT, and LSAT tests.

Ninety-eight percent of TMSF scholarship recipients graduate, and 50 percent gain entry into the most prestigious graduate and professional schools. A special scholarship is available to students attending the four historically black law schools. Many of the students who receive financial assistance from the fund would not be able to attend school without these awards.

The Thurgood Marshall Scholarship Fund is the only national, merit-based scholarship fund for students attending black public colleges and universities. As a result of the fund's support of African American education, future black leaders are being trained to enter the workforce and make a difference in their communities, the nation, and the world.

To a great American and one of the Historically Black Colleges and Universities' (HBCU) most famous alumni, Thurgood Marshall—a graduate of Lincoln University (Pennsylvania) and Howard University School of Law. A champion, an architect, and a crusader for equal access and open opportunity, Marshall led an extraordinary life dedicated to the transformation of humankind.

Because of his vision and commitment to equality and his willingness to lend his name to the founding of the Thurgood Marshall Scholarship Fund, his legacy continues to influence thousands of young men and women who aspire to walk in his footsteps.

Black classroom, Birmingham, Alabama, 1956, by Gordon Parks

CONTENTS

1 · SHACKLED MINDS · 1

The citizenship status of African Americans in the American colonies was loosely defined during the country's infancy. In colonial America, there were free blacks as well as enslaved blacks. But as the colonies began to rely on a slave labor economy, education of blacks was restricted, and even outlawed.

2 · BOOKS BEFORE FREEDOM · 31

The trumpet sounds for war. While white Americans fight over the economics of slavery, black Americans declare war on illiteracy.

3 · YEARNING AND LEARNING · 51

With the close of the Civil War, 4.4 million free African Americans embark upon an educational journey. Blacks, missionaries, and the federal government work together to create schools.

4 · VOICES OF A PEOPLE · 101

In search of self-definition, students and faculties of historically black colleges and universities begin to deconstruct the white patriarchal systems and philosophies that govern their schools.

5 · THE ART OF CULTURE · 137

As the Roaring Twenties begin, historically black colleges and universities represent the vanguard of black middle-class culture and the arts.

List of Historically Black Colleges and Universities
Profiled in the Appendix

List of Informational Sidebars

FOREWORD

Since before the days of slavery, education has been the North Star of black aspiration. It is the certain road to a promised land where black people are seen as fully human by whites—even by the racist whites who first consigned blacks to the status of subhuman slaves. Education alone has been key to the fight for black freedom in America because people who could read and write automatically became leaders among a people who had been denied schooling as a tool of racial oppression.

To be a black person without an education is to find independence and freedom always out of reach. Segregationists knew this as surely as they knew that night-riding Klansmen and indiscriminate lynching served to intimidate any black soul seeking to stand on equal ground with fellow Americans. History has revealed they were right to fear educated black people. The trained black mind is the cornerstone of institutions created to advance black freedom, ranging from black churches to black businesses, political and civic groups, and, of course, black colleges.

The principal measure of black progress over the generations is the growing number of educated black people trained and positioned to produce better black churches, businesses, and colleges.

What cannot be measured about education and black Americans is the stamp of personal prestige it offers. Yesterday and today, black people are often stereotyped as ignorant, stupid, lazy, and incapable of academic excellence. To defy that defeating assumption about an entire race, black people have had to raise high the banner of intellectual achievement. The best rebuttal for any charge of stupidity is a degree, preferably a degree that confers the title of "doctor." That designation offers deep emotional gratification to black people once derided as mentally deficient. To be an educated black man or woman is to spit in the devil's eye. It is a repudiation of all the slanders uttered by advocates of white supremacy about weak-minded blacks.

In Ralph Ellison's classic novel *Invisible Man,* the unnamed narrator and central character is a young black man who begins his life journey in search of education. He is bright and capable, but only a generation removed from slavery. He introduces himself as a man of "flesh and bone," but he immediately betrays the deep insecurity of the black psyche when he writes that he is a being who might "even be said to possess a mind." When the young narrator, just out of high school, is asked to deliver a speech to the town's leading white men, he finds himself reduced to the level of objectified lust and violence. First, he is forced to watch a naked white woman strut around and then he is ordered into a brawl with other young black men for the entertainment of the white town fathers. They don't care about his mind. And when he is finally allowed to give his speech, he does so with blood from the fight still stinging in his mouth and no one paying attention.

Rewarded with a scholarship to a black college the narrator finds himself further locked in the tyranny of white control over black educational institutions hungering for their financial support. At the heart of the campus is a bronze statue honoring the college's black founder. The narrator writes of studying the statue and pondering the sight of the founder's hand "lifting a veil that flutters in hard, metallic folds above the face of a kneeling slave; and I am puzzled, unable to decide whether the veil is really being lifted or lowered more firmly into place; whether I am witnessing a revelation or a more efficient blinding."

When the narrator shows too much of poor black life still damaged by the horrors of slavery to a white visitor, the black college president curses him as a "black educated fool" and throws him off the campus. "Why, the dumbest black bastard in the cotton patch knows that the only way to please a white man is to tell him a lie! What kind of education are you getting around here?"

The answer to that question is that education for black people involves both classroom study and an understanding of the ways of a nation and its people, traumatized by slavery and racism.

In the high-tech, information-based society of the twenty-first century, education has become even more important, an absolute touchstone for personal advancement in the United States. The civil rights movement—first against slavery, the black codes of the nineteenth century, then against Jim Crow seg-regation, and finally for equal opportunity under the law—can be interpreted as the story of black Americans seeking their right to be educated and for the equity afforded to other Americans.

During slavery, people risked their lives for education. Literacy was key to Frederick Douglass's stand as a great abolitionist. Great preachers, most often the leaders of the black community in the immediate aftermath of slavery, were the black people who could read and interpret the Bible.

From the first days of the Republic, free blacks opened schools for their children and petitioned local officials to fund public schools for blacks. The fight to make those schools equal to white schools was at the heart of the civil rights struggle of the twentieth century. When the National Association for the Advancement of Colored People (NAACP) devised a strategy to challenge seg-regation, its lawyers focused first on ending school segregation. Once they forced graduate and professional schools to open their doors, the NAACP Legal Defense Fund, under the direction of Thurgood Marshall, then struck at segregated elementary and secondary schools. Marshall, later the nation's first black Supreme Court justice, challenged segregated schools as a violation of the equal rights protections under the Constitution's Fourteenth Amend-ment. That protracted struggle led to a shock with the May 17, 1954, *Brown v. Board of Education of Topeka* decision in which a unanimous Court ruled that "in the field of public education the doctrine of 'separate but equal' has no place—separate educational facilities are inherently unequal."

The decision struck such a blow to segregation because the power of the right to be educated allowed black people to stand as equals to all others. Georgia governor Herman Talmadge, a white supremacist, predicted racial "chaos" would result from the ruling and that it marked "the end of civiliza-tion in the South as we have known it."

The fight over education continued in the South even after the Supreme Court's landmark *Brown* decision. In 1957, President Eisenhower ordered the National Guard to enforce the relatively new law of desegregation and escort nine black children into Little Rock, Arkansas's Central High School. In 1962, federal troops forced open a pathway to allow James Meredith to be the first black man to attend the University of Mississippi. And just a year later, federal marshals had to stare down Alabama's governor George Wallace as he made his infamous stand "at the school house door" of the University of Alabama in his highly publicized effort to stop two black students from enrolling there.

The struggle for the right to education and equal opportunity is a constant in black history. In the 1960s it was a matter of enforcing school integration. In the 1970s it was the *Bakke* decision, in which the Supreme Court ruled that a university could not set aside seats for black students solely on the basis of their race but could consider race as a factor for admission. The 1970s and 1980s saw major conflict nationwide over busing schoolchildren to integrate schools. Most recently, the debate over affirmative action in higher education has centered around the use of race as a factor in selecting students for admission to historically white undergraduate and law schools.

Throughout that fight the historically black colleges and universities (HBCUs) have been the major source of education for black people in the United States. They have delivered the education that produced the leaders. HBCUs are the heart of black political thinking, art and culture, and the nurture of a black intelligentsia.

Education is the dividing line and road to empowerment in black America—period. Quakers and other Protestants, Catholics, and Jews have done great work to help with higher education for black Americans, but black colleges have always been the heart of all efforts to pull black people out of a miserable history of slavery and into the light of learning.

It is now 50 years since the *Brown* decision ended legal segregation in the public schools. *Brown* held the promise of equal education for all. But today the difference between black people who prosper in this country and black people who scrape along the bottom of American life is the canyon of distance between people who have education and people who don't. Even after *Brown,* black colleges and universities continue to be the prime source of education for black people. From 1966 to 1998, college graduate rates for African Americans went from 3.8 percent to 14.7 percent. Even with white schools slowly opening their doors, most of that increase has been a result of the continuing work of black colleges.

That work is not limited to the classroom. As graduation rates have climbed, so have black incomes. Between 1980 and 2000, median income for blacks climbed (in constant dollars) from $21,418 to $30,436. According to a 2002 report from the U.S. Census Bureau, black people with "less than a high school education would earn less than a million dollars during their work-life, increasing to $1 million for workers with a high school education, $1.7 million for a bachelor's degree and $2.5 million for an advanced degree."

The million-dollar question in terms of lifelong earnings for any black person is, Did you get an education? There are several smaller questions hidden within that big one: Did you graduate from high school? Did you graduate from college? Did you earn an advanced degree? People who answer yes to at least two of those questions, whether black, white, Asian American, or Hispanic, hold the winning ticket in the American race toward "the good life." But among black people, having the right answers is a matter of survival. Those answers impact on the next generation of every black family. A 1999 study found that 60 percent of black college freshmen were the children of fathers who had a college degree.

These are the hard facts of life for black America—get an education or take a backseat. Civil rights victories ended legal segregation. Black legends led protests for voting rights and equal access to jobs, hotels, and restaurants. But without education, all of those hard-won rights are little more than window dressing. Only one set of institutions in American history has made delivering education to black people their central mission—the historically black colleges and universities.

Juan Williams

Elizabeth City cheerleaders

ACKNOWLEDGMENTS

This project would not have been possible without the shared vision of Juan Williams, a dedicated and committed custodian of Justice Thurgood Marshall's legacy. Juan endorsed the concept more than four years ago and pledged his support to bringing this important piece of American history to the forefront. He and his wife, Delise, have been partners in helping to make this dream a reality. Juan, thank you for helping to tell the HBCU story in your voice. Your belief in the Thurgood Marshall Scholarship Fund's work and HBCU's role in preparing leaders has aided us in educating the more than 400,000 young men and women who attend our schools. This work will speak for the thousands of faculty members and leaders who dedicated their lives to educating men and women who might not have had a chance at reaching their full potential.

I'll Find a Way or Make One is a fitting title for how this book came to be. Hundreds of people helped us find a way or make a way to publish this book. It would take another book to list all of you individually, but you know who you are, and we thank you all.

Among the family of the 108 HBCUs, and the Thurgood Marshall Scholarship Fund Staff and Board, I am especially indebted to members of my staff, some of whom have moved on to other positions: Tola Ozim, an outstanding assistant; Shireen Idroos, former coordinator of government and advocacy; the late Ida Simon, former vice president, development; Paul Allen; Lisa Van Putten; Beverly Colbert; Shannon Henderson; Renau Daniels; Johana Reyes; Fred Gilbert; Virginia Johnson; Damian Travier; Susan Jacob; Courtney Booker III; Roger Lord; Regina Smith; Shineaca Moore; Rebecca Briggs, and Kofi Kubi Appiah. I am also deeply indebted to Dr. N. Joyce Payne, founder of the Thurgood Marshall Fund, for her vision and steady personal support; and to all the HBCU presidents for your outstanding leadership. A special thanks to the following university CEOs: Dr. Earl Richardson, Dr. William B. Delauder, Dr. Ernest Holloway, Dr. David Beckly, Dr. Joe Lee, Dr. Thomas Winston Cole Jr., Dr. Frederick Humphreys, Dr. Priscilla Slade, Dr. Carlton Brown, Dr. James Rennick, Dr. Edison Jackson, and Dr. Ronald Mason.

Board members: David Stern, Lorraine Thelian, James Mitchell, Robert Feldman, Butch Graves, Virgis W. Colbert, and Reginald Van Lee. To Allan Baker, Brent Clinkscale, Jim Clifton, Shelia Kearney, Noel Hankin, Michael Rhodes, and all of the other board members and corporate leaders who have helped keep HBCUs strong and vibrant.

Thanks to my parents, Mary Gipson Ashley and Archie L. Clay, who inspired me to gain all I could from the HBCU experience.

Thanks also to the Marshall family: Mrs. Cecilia Marshall, John Marshall, and Goody Marshall, whose commitment to carrying on the legacy of Thurgood Marshall inspires us all. To William Hubert Gray III for his outstanding dedication to HBCUs and all the work he has done to keep them alive.

To Oprah Winfrey, Lynn Whitfield, Tommy Dortch, Earl Graves Sr., Debbie Allen, Shirley Horn, Vernon Jordan, John Thompson, Dixie Garr, Ed Bradley, and all of the other distinguished alumni of HBCUs for showing America and the world the quality products that HBCUs produce.

A special thanks to those professors and teachers at HBCUs who continue to teach in order to touch a life and not just to make a dollar—to the late Dr. George H. Chandler and to Dr. Maggie Brown Daniels; to Dr. Telly Miller and Dr. Truby B. Clayton for the lessons in life that made the HBCU experience so special.

To each of the librarians and archivists who helped us unearth a wealth of rich, compelling history on HBCUs. A warm thanks to curator Joellen ElBashir at Howard University's Moorland Springarn Research Center and reference archivist Cathy Lynn Mundale at the Atlanta University Center's Robert W. Woodruff Library. To Mitch Tuchman, whose legal knowledge of publishing kept us all sane. Mitch, thank you and the Womble Caryle Family for taking on the legal representation of this project as a donation to the Fund.

To an incredible woman whose commitment to publishing and ensuring that stories are told serves as a catalyst for writers and for this project—Adrienne Ingrum. She joined me and caught the vision! She supported and dedicated years to ensuring that this project was completed. Without her commitment to bringing this work to life and rallying the group, the reality of this project would have simply been a dream unfulfilled. She was assisted by a team of people whose efforts were heroic: the writing team. First and foremost the talented and dedicated researcher and writer Shawn Rhea; Booker Mattison, Precious Mattison, Herb Boyd, and Dara Byrne; copy editor Olivia Cloud; and photo editor Suzanne Rust.

I would also like to acknowledge those friends of the Fund who have given generously of their time to assist us in hosting various events throughout the years: Sheryl Lee Ralph, Diahann Carroll, Star Jones, Jackee Harry, Stephanie Mills, Gayle King, Anna Marie Hartsford, Roberta Flack, Gordon Chambers, Johnny Gill, Ray Allen, Shane Battier, Nancy Wilson, James "Jimmy Jam" Harris, and Terry S. Lewis.

HBCUs continue to benefit from scores of elected officials who advocate on their behalf at the federal, state, and city levels. Without their continued support, this book would not have been possible; they have helped to preserve the rich history of these schools.

A special thanks to President George H. W. Bush, President William Jefferson Clinton, and President George W. Bush, former vice president Albert Gore, and first ladies Barbara and Laura Bush, and Hillary Clinton, who have all been supporters of HBCUs. I would also like to recognize secretaries of education: Dick Riley and Rod Paige, and secretaries of labor: Alexis Herman and Elaine Chao. And finally I would like to thank and acknowledge Mayor Sharpe James of Newark.

While I cannot personally acknowledge, by name, every member of Congress (past and present) who has supported our schools, I do want to pay special tribute to all members of Congress and a few individuals who have gone above and beyond, namely: Senators Arlen Specter, Herb Kohl, Rick Santorum, Christopher S. "Kit" Bond, Charles Schumer, and Hillary Clinton.

A very special acknowledgment to the members of the Congressional Black Caucus and Representatives Jesse Jackson Jr., John Lewis, Maxine Waters, and Sheila Jackson Lee.

Thank God for friends and family who hold you up during times that try the soul. My defensive backs are always steady and this dream would not have happened without their support. Thank you Debra Ashley. Albert Mitchell, Anthony Clark, Sylvia Brooks, Chris Brown, Albert Dotson, LeRoy Walker,

Roosevelt Dorn, Rustin Lewis, Rev. Joe Ratcliffe, Rev. James Nash, Savoy Walker, Kenneth Reynolds, Rev. Ralph West, David Martin, Derrick Warren, Jennifer Jiles, Dr. Eddie Jumper, Reginald Lewis, Marcus Boyd, Larry Satterfield, Ida Callier, Jeff Thompson, Julita Vasquez, Kevin Harry, Mark Moxley, Ralph Jackson, Richard Johnson, Robert Traynham, Rondo Moses, Gerald Norde, Rodney Watson, Brent Clinkscale, Michael Fitzpatrick, Arthur Thomas, Phillip Harold, Kurt John, Bert Matthews, Larry Green, Alicia Jackson, Brenda Clay Jackson, Sharmagne Taylor, Dwight Rhodes, Harold Qualls, Ronnell Walker, Sean Johnson, Steve Manning, Terry Albert, Terry Hudson, Sherrie Thannars, Dr. James Spady, Edward H. Morris Sr., Sheila Eldridge, and Winston Jones.

My friends in the world of education and philanthropy who have also been friends to HBCUs: Dr. Deborah Wilds and Tom Vander Ark of the Bill and Melinda Gates Foundation; Sara Cobb, Allan Wright, and Willis Bright of the Lilly Endowment; Dr. Lydia English of the W. K. Mellon Foundation; Florence Davis and Gladys Thomas of the Starr Foundation; Joe Nelson and Donald Sheppard of the Houston Endowment; Marvelous Baker of the Cleveland Foundation; Michael E. Szymanczyk of Philip Morris International Inc.; Silver Esther Parker, president of the Walmart Foundation (former president of the AT & T Foundation); and Linda Testa of Microsoft Corporation.

To the brothers of Phi Beta Sigma, and the women of Zeta Phi Beta sorority, I would like to say thank you. I would also like to thank all of my Greek brothers and sisters who support HBCUs, and all of the churches and community groups who partner with HBCUs in their quest to help young men and women achieve their full potential.

And, finally, thanks to the talented staff at HarperCollins who believed in this project and helped to make it happen, especially our editors, Dawn Davis and Kelli Martin, our acquiring editor, Manie Barron, and our managing editor, John Jusino.

Dwayne Ashley, president, Thurgood Marshall Scholarship Fund

INTRODUCTION

Education has always been *the* way out. In spite of popular perception, most of us can't sing or play a sport well enough to earn a living. And before there was a Jackie Robinson in baseball, a Jack Johnson in the ring, or a Paul Robeson on stage, there were doctors, lawyers, dentists, teachers, artists, businessmen and businesswomen, and other professionals who made their way in the world because of the educational foundation forged in historically black colleges and universities.

I attended one of those colleges;, in fact, the first: Cheyney University, which was founded in 1837 as the Institute for Colored Youth. When I was there, it was called Cheyney State, one of a dozen or so state colleges that made up the Pennsylvania system of Teachers Colleges. It was the only pre-dominantly black school in the system and traditionally the lowest funded.

My grades were very good and I could have attended any number of "big-name" schools, but I chose Cheyney because of the reception I received on my first visit there during my senior year in high school. There was a warmth, a camaraderie that existed that I had never experienced before. At the time, I had not given any thought to becoming a schoolteacher. But the warmth I felt on that first visit to Cheyney made an immediate and indelible impression on me: this was the school for me. In all of the years since then, as I competed against men and women who attended prestigious Ivy League schools or other big-name universities, I was always proud of the education that came with my years at Cheyney. That education gave me the tools and honed the drive that would enable me to compete against anyone—from anywhere.

The curriculum at Cheyney was determined by the state, and that curriculum was not designed to teach us about *our* history. But there were always professors at Cheyney who skirted the system and explored tangents that would lead students deep into the dark shafts where we could find the history of black people in this country and beyond. For example, you wouldn't find the story of Crispus Attucks in the state-supplied textbooks, but Professor James Stevenson, my football coach as well as history professor, pointed us to the library. He charged us with finding out what we could about Crispus Attucks and to report back on what we found. And, of course, that led to a much wider discussion of black people in America. There were many more trips to the library to find out what wasn't in those state-supplied textbooks. And that's how we learned our history.

It was a history filled with restrictive laws and people who wanted to keep blacks illiterate. If slaves couldn't read, they wouldn't know a better world was out there. And if they couldn't write, they couldn't forge travel passes that would allow safe passage to freedom. Literacy—education—was a way to escape slavery. Back then it was a way out, and today education is *still* the best way out.

Mainstream universities are more integrated than ever, but they are still closed to many. HBCUs provide the extra nurture that some black students need. At Cheyney, there were always professors who would encourage students to do better; professors who would demand more. And there were so many who encouraged you to be the best you could be. They drilled in us the idea that we had to work harder because, for us, the climb up the economic ladder would be different; there would be rungs missing from that ladder. Our climb up would be harder because we were minorities. But, as difficult as that trip could be, we were always encouraged to do more so that we could achieve more.

Today, there are still so many young black men and women who choose to attend a historically black college or university because they are reservoirs of our culture, tradition, and opportunity. HBCUs still provide a door to the future, to a better life, to a better people.

Those of us who graduated from a historically black college or university have an obligation to keep those doors open; an obligation to give back to the system that nurtured us. It can be done by example, by mentoring and by financial support.

There is a new generation seeking a way out, and with an education from and HBCU, they will find a way or make one.

Ed Bradley

I'll Find a Way or Make One

SHACKLED MINDS

The citizenship status of African Americans in the American colonies was loosely defined during the country's infancy. In colonial America, there were free blacks as well as enslaved blacks. But as the colonies began to rely on a slave labor economy, education of blacks was restricted, and even outlawed.

HISTORICALLY BLACK COLLEGES and universities (HBCUs) and their graduates and educators have played an essential role in defining the cultural and political atmosphere of this country and the world. Schools like Morehouse, Howard University, Tennessee State University, and Lincoln University (Pennsylvania) educated people who defined genius: actor Samuel L. Jackson, author Toni Morrison, media personality Oprah Winfrey, and Kwame Nkrumah, the first democratically elected president of present-day Ghana. HBCUs count Nobel Prize winner Martin Luther King Jr.; the first black Rhodes scholar, Alain Locke; the first African American Supreme Court justice, Thurgood Marshall; the first African American billionaire, Reginald Lewis; Detroit mayor Kwame Kilpatrick; gospel singer Yolanda Adams; actress Lynn Whitfield; recording artist Sean "P Diddy" Combs; and media mogul Keith Clinkscales among their alumni and faculty.

Aaron Douglas, lithograph *Study for God's Trombone.*

Cheyney University, the nation's first HBCU, was founded in 1837. Humphreys Hall, shown here in 1903, was named after founder Richard Humphreys. The structure was originally used as an industrial building.

More than 167 years after the founding of this country's first HBCU (Pennsylvania's Cheyney University in 1837) and fifty years since the Supreme Court's landmark school desegregation ruling, *Brown v. Board of Education of Topeka, Kansas,* HBCUs still graduate 70 percent of all black physicians and dentists and half of all black engineers in the United States. Tuskegee University alone produces 80 percent of the African Americans practicing veterinary medicine, while Florida A&M University has outranked Harvard in the number of National Achievement scholars among top black high school students that it has recruited and enrolled. And while only 20 percent of college-bound African American students initially choose to attend HBCUs, nearly one-third of the bachelor's degrees awarded to black graduates come from traditionally black schools. In addition, a number of HBCUs have integrated over the past two decades, expanding their immediate influence beyond the black community. These facts alone reveal the importance of black colleges. Even more compelling, however, is the indispensable role the HBCUs played in the creation of the U.S. public education system and its massive network of institutions of higher learning.

W. E. B. DuBois once wrote, "Public education for all at public expense was, in the South, a Negro idea."[1] His statement is a direct reference to the fact that, following the end of slavery, it was African Americans who, more than any other group, saw education as the great social equalizer. And it was African Americans who pushed for a truly universal system of government-supported education. Prior to the Civil War, education was a privilege afforded mostly to wealthy and middle-class white men. The vast majority of poor white Americans were illiterate, and teaching that population to read was not a priority of the government, especially in the southern states. A survey of army troops in French-controlled New Orleans in the early 1700s found that 60 percent of soldiers were illiterate. It was only when the desire for literacy among newly freed blacks became an urgent, insistent demand that the public school gospel of northern reformer Horace Mann took hold in the South. If blacks were going to be educated, so too were poor whites.

W. E. B. DuBois, who viewed education as the great equalizer, once wrote, "Public education for all at public expense was, in the South, a Negro idea."

From the outset, black schools were designed to offer more than basic literacy and math skills; most also provided training in social and trade skills. The educators and abolitionists who designed these schools determined early on that there was a need to create black institutions of higher learning because southern whites—and to a large degree northern whites—did not want black people in their schools. They wanted to maintain separate, race-based societies and U.S. law allowed this racial segregation. This meant blacks would not be accepted into most universities even if they qualified. The move to establish black colleges immediately after the Civil War highlights the significant role that advanced education was beginning to play in American society.

HBCU GRADS HAVE BECOME MEDIA SUPERSTARS

Some of the most popular media personalities in television and radio today are the products of HBCUs. Far from being here today, gone tomorrow novelties, Ed Bradley, Tom Joyner, Oprah Winfrey, and Ananda Lewis have established themselves as not only commercially viable, but also politically astute, and even trendsetting and cool. Interestingly, only one of this distinguished group majored in journalism or communications while in college.

Ed Bradley, a graduate of Cheyney, was an education major who didn't consider a career in broadcasting until Philadelphia WDAS radio personality Georgie Woods visited the teacher's college to talk to students about strategies for reaching youth. Bradley developed a relationship with Woods and the popular DJ invited Bradley to tour the radio station. Although his interest was piqued, Bradley continued on his original career path and took a teaching position after graduating in 1964. A teacher by day, Bradley would go to WDAS and volunteer at night. Del Sheilds, another DJ at the jazz-formatted station, encouraged Bradley to focus on news since that was where the opportunities were. When the riots of 1965 broke out in Philadelphia, Bradley covered the events by calling in stories from pay phones. Impressed by Bradley's work ethic, the station put him on the payroll. Balancing teaching and radio soon became too cumbersome so Bradley started applying for broadcasting positions, landing employment at WCBS radio in New York. When Bradley was hired he was the only black person on the air in the New York radio market. Ed Bradley has remained a part of the CBS news team where he has garnered numerous awards on the popular *60 Minutes* news magazine television show.

Tom Joyner's ascent to radio superstardom was as unorthodox as Bradley's. Joyner, a third-generation HBCU graduate, claims to have black college in his blood. His grandfathers attended Tuskegee and Meharry; his mother and father attended Tennessee State and Florida A&M, respectively. A sociology major at Tuskegee, Joyner was told by a friend about a radio position in Montgomery, Alabama, immediately after he graduated in 1970. Although Joyner started his career in a small market where it would be difficult to make a national name for himself, he soon moved into larger markets in Memphis, St. Louis, and then Dallas. For several years he was the morning DJ on a station in Dallas and the afternoon DJ on a station in Chicago. Joyner flew between the two cities for eight years, thus earning the nickname "Fly Jock." ABC radio then offered him a syndicated show that consistently has been ranked number one in several of the ninety-five markets it serves.

Joyner has raised millions of dollars for HBCUs through his UNCF/Tom Joyner Black College Scholarship Fund. He also uses his platform to inspire his 5 million listeners to action for social and political causes. Joyner's two sons, both of whom now work for him, continued the family's legacy by attending HBCUs.

The tools that Oprah Winfrey used to rise to stardom were shaped and developed in the speech communications and performing arts departments of Tennessee State University.

Staying true to her commitment "to use position, power and money to create opportunities for other people," she established ten scholarships at her alma mater and wrote personal letters to each recipient, encouraging some to pull up their grades. Oprah has become a household name whose giving also extends to other HBCUs. She has donated more than $1 million to Morehouse College and Spelman College.

Ananda Lewis planned to teach school after graduation from Howard. She prepared for this by teaching youth leadership and conflict resolution courses to teens during summer vacation. Upon graduation, however, Lewis had a change of heart and determined that she wanted to pursue a career in entertainment. She drew the ire of family and friends, but her change in plans was not completely baseless. She had attended performing arts school in her native San Diego, so entertainment was an early passion that was rekindled after she graduated cum laude with a B.A. in history.

Lewis quickly landed her first job as a host on BET's *Teen Summit*. After the ratings increased, Lewis moved to MTV and became one of the network's most popular VJs. Lewis added versatility to the talk show circuit when CBS added *The Ananda Lewis Show* to its daytime roster. Even though *People* magazine rated Lewis one of the world's most beautiful people in 2000, her hard work and HBCU-nurtured intelligence have been responsible for her early rise to national attention.

Black Education in Colonial America

Until the nineteenth century, a college education was primarily reserved for aristocratic men and the clergy. Churches, especially in the New England territories, did provide some education for average citizens to gain basic literacy.

Erudite advancement and reasoning were not the goals of colonial education, however. Early American settlers valued their views of Christianity above all things, and they left Europe in a determined effort to freely practice their various interpretations of the Bible. Ministers wanted the members of their churches to be able to read the Gospel. By 1647 Massachusetts legislators had passed a law requiring that towns with fifty or more households appoint an educator to teach children "to read and understand the principles of religion and the capital laws of the country."[2]

Under these early New England laws, even indentured servants and slaves were sometimes taught to read, as it furthered the colonists' efforts at religious indoctrination.

The first enslaved Africans came to North America in 1619, when Dutch :lers brought twenty black workers to Jamestown, Virginia. Slavery played elatively small role in the initial development of the United States, however, and the status of blacks was loosely defined. While they were captives ho, unlike their European counterparts, had not chosen to exchange servi- ude for passage to the colonies, many were freed after a number of years. In addition, slave owners were sometimes required by law to educate their ser-

 **Debbie Allen**, actress, producer, director, dancer, and choreographer, got her start at Howard University.

 Florida A & M alumnus **Kwame M. Kilpatrick**, is Detroit's youngest mayor and the first African American in Michigan history to lead any party in the legislature.

 Howard alumna **Shirley Clarke Franklin**, Atlanta's first woman mayor, graduated with a B.A. in sociology.

 **Ananda Lewis**, former MTV VJ and talk show host, graduated from Howard University in 1995.

 Social activist **Stokely Carmichael** (aka **Kwame Touré**) shown here during his days at Howard University.

Antebellum Negro classroom.

vants. A 1642 Massachusetts law required parents and masters of indentured servants to ensure that the children in their households became literate, while a 1674 New York law dictated a similar requirement but referred only to "servants," making no distinction between slaves and indentured.

As slave labor became more integral to economic development, however, many colonists began to view black education as a threat to their ability to control and manipulate enslaved Africans. Beginning in the 1660s, the colonies, now mostly under English rule, began passing laws that strictly defined the status of African Americans. One statute required that enslaved blacks and the children of slave women would be servants for life. But even with their freedom denied, African Americans continued to struggle to acquire whatever limited education they had access to. Education of enslaved blacks was not illegal during the seventeenth and early eighteenth centuries. Furthermore, it was always legal for free northern blacks to pursue education, although it often proved extremely difficult and dangerous.

In the southern states, where the planter class was much more dependent on slave labor for the growth of its agricultural enterprises, the education of blacks and poor whites (who provided cheap labor) was greatly discouraged. Many of these states passed laws that directly prohibited the education of blacks, or at least made education very difficult to acquire. In 1680, Virginia legislators enacted a law prohibiting blacks from meeting en masse; this was the first of many Black Codes. In Maryland, where a comparable ordinance existed, a teacher was forced to pay 1,000 pounds of tobacco for assembling black students. Other southern states enacted laws that specifically disallowed the education of enslaved African Americans. In 1740 South Carolina made it illegal to teach blacks to write, though they still were allowed to read. Georgia passed its own law forbidding the education of black Americans in 1755.

Introduction of slavery.

Document of Act Number 39, May 10, 1770, declaring it illegal to teach slaves to write in the state of Georgia.

Education of Free Blacks

The War for Independence set off a great debate about the morality of slavery. The framers of the Constitution argued the issue extensively and ultimately agreed to let individual states decide whether to uphold or abolish slavery. By 1787, all the northern states had abolished slavery. As a result, African Americans in the North were more readily able to obtain education than those in the South.

Some northern black children attended schools with whites in the colonies, but most of those schools remained segregated. Black parents had to fight for their own city-funded schools or create privately funded academies. Whether in the North or the South, black and white churches took the lead in providing educational opportunities for blacks.

In New York City, the Anglican and Quaker Manumission Society opened the New York African Free School in 1787. The primary school was totally self-funded until 1796, when it, along with six other charity schools, began receiving money from the city. The African Free School was the only city-funded black school for many years. By 1809 the school had 141 pupils, the largest student body of any New York City school. The predominantly black faculty had educated more than 2,300 students by 1814. Renowned theologian and author Alexander Crummell and celebrated actor Ira Aldridge were among the students educated at the African Free School. The curriculum focused on literacy and math, but also provided training in navigation, as New York City was a major seaport.

AFRICAN HIGHER EDUCATION

When historically black colleges and universities were opened in the United States, they continued the tradition of scholarship and higher education begun in Africa. This greatly contrasted with the misconceptions that slaveholders, and even many abolitionists, held about blacks' capacity to learn. Even after slavery was abolished, champions of African-American education, such as General S. C. Armstrong, John T. Slater, and Anna T. Jeanes, felt education that included mathematics, writing, geography, and history was important for African Americans.

The ancient West African empire of Mali, which covered a large portion of the upper Niger River region (current-day Mali, Senegal, Gambia, southern Mauritania, eastern Guinea-Bissau, and eastern Guinea), gave birth to the city of Timbuktu, a legendary center of Islamic learning that thrived between the fourteenth and eighteenth centuries. At its pinnacle, Timbuktu housed approximately 150 Quranic schools that offered formal elementary and advanced studies. Students and scholars came from all over the Islamic world to study and teach in Timbuktu. Today, several private libraries survive in Timbuktu, the largest of which features some 700 volumes.

While historians previously claimed that the sub-Saharan (black African) city's tradition of scholarship was imported from North Africa by Arab Muslims, recent research disputes this assertion. Historian Elias Saad argues that Islam was already entrenched as the leading religion and culture within the Mali (and later Songhai) Empire. In short, the city's primary scholars and students were simultaneously black and Muslim. "The scholars of Timbuktu who were predominantly of non-Arab background continued to utilize that language [Arabic] in their scholarship, legal procedure and commercial correspondence," writes Saad.

It should be noted that because Mali's schools existed in the empire's urban centers, education was a skill gained almost exclusively by city dwellers. In addition, women of royal lineage were most likely the only women to be literate. But among the men, education was not reserved exclusively for the wealthy. Tradesmen and artisans were often literate, as Mali was known for its considerable trading ports and markets. Commerce required that even the common man obtain a basic level of education so that goods could be measured and traded based on a set standard.

A large number of the Africans who were captured and enslaved came from the territory encompassed by the Mali Empire. While the majority of enslaved Africans were indeed stolen from the brush areas, where tribal languages and oral traditions prevailed, it is highly probable that more than a few of Mali's educated citizens ended up victims of the slave trade. Family infighting, political battles, and property disputes were sometimes settled when one of the feuding parties conspired with slave traders and sold the enemy into bondage. Once shackled, indigenous literacy and education were the first of many skills rendered useless by the horrors of the slave trade.

Nevertheless, the slaver's whip, the auction block, and the barrel of a gun were not strong enough to break these black forebears' desire for education. It was that desire, passed down through generations, that inspired slaves to risk life and limb to learn to read and write.

AFRICAN FREE SCHOOL

The African Free School was started by the New York Manumission Society in 1787. The society, comprised mostly of slave owners, was begun in 1786 in response to the illegal slave trading that continued in New York City despite the 1785 ban on the importation of slaves for sale. John Jay, a man of contradiction who was both a slave owner and an advocate of black education, was the first president of the society. Eventually, he would become the state's governor and sign New York's gradual emancipation act into law in 1799.

The first class at the African Free School consisted of forty students. Resistance to the school from a large part of the New York community was swift, but despite the opposition, by 1807 enrollment had grown to sixty students. The curriculum was rigorous and students were instructed in math, reading, writing, astronomy, geography, and navigation. In a report issued in 1830, the society boasted that not a single student educated at the school had been convicted of a crime in New York courts.

By 1814 the school, which had become overcrowded because of increased demand, was destroyed in a fire. The city gave society trustees a 50-square-foot lot where a new brick building was constructed for a capacity of 200 students. By 1820 the Free School had outgrown this space and the second African Free School, which could hold 500 students, was opened. Rapid growth continued, and by the time the city of New York took over the school in 1834, the African Free School had seven locations.

A quality education was not enough to lift many graduates from the mire of menial labor, however. Racism complicated students' efforts in finding apprenticeships. Those fortunate enough to land an apprenticeship were then faced with the obstacle of finding a company that would hire a skilled black worker. There were, however, a number of African Free School alumni who defied the odds and excelled in their chosen professions. Some of these include abolitionist and clergyman

The New York African Free School, founded by the Anglican and Quaker Manumission Society in 1787.

Henry Highland Garnett; Ira Aldridge, the first black actor to perform at the Royal Coburg Theatre in London College; and Charles L. Reason, who went on to become the first black professor at a predominantly white college in New York. Reason left this post to become the first African American president of the Philadelphia Training School, which later became Cheyney University.

Across the North, in cities such as Philadelphia, Boston, and Newport, Connecticut, African Americans endeavored to gain education. In 1787 black Bostonians petitioned state legislators for a school, saying that their children received "no benefit from the free schools" attended by whites. The African American community petitioned the state on two other occasions to no avail. A private school was finally opened for black children in 1803 in the home of Primus Hall. The school found a permanent location in 1806 in the basement of the African Meeting House on Boston's Beacon Hill. Several years later, the school finally began receiving city funds and became a public school.

Yet even when blacks won their battle for public funding or were able to open their own schools with the help of private dollars, the resulting schools were often poorly subsidized. Many of the supporting northern benevolent societies and foundations consistently gave fewer dollars to black schools. The Peabody Fund, for example, donated a third less in financial support to African American schools, opining that it "cost less to maintain schools for the colored children than the white."[3]

Educating the masses of African Americans was indisputably a multiracial crusade, however, and it would have failed miserably without the complete commitment of both black and white educators who pushed aside any fear they may have had for their own safety and followed their moral convictions. Yet even the most determined educators sometimes failed in their efforts to educate African Americans.

In 1829 Samuel Cornish, editor of the New York–based African American newspaper *The Rights of All,* and Simeon Jocelyn, a white minister who pastored a black Congregationalist church in New Haven, joined forces in an attempt to establish the first college for African Americans. The two men envisioned a mechanical and agricultural arts school, referred to as Negro College, that also would provide classical studies. Jocelyn had briefly attended Yale, and he believed that the high educational atmosphere of New Haven made it a natural location for the proposed college. In 1831 Cornish, Jocelyn, and renowned white abolitionists Arthur Tappan and William Garrison attended the First Annual Convention of the Free People of Color in Philadelphia to rally support for the school. Tappan had already purchased land for the college, and he committed $1,000 to a building fund. The conference-goers enthusiastically agreed to raise the additional $19,000 needed to erect the school.

But if the free blacks gathering in Philadelphia were vociferously supportive of the proposed Negro College, the white residents of New Haven—particularly several influential alumni, faculty members, and administrators at Yale University—were equally opposed to the idea. After learning of plans for the school, Mayor Dennis Kimberly, a Yale graduate, put together a committee to block Negro College. Mayor Kimberly called a town meeting on September 10, 1831, so citizens could vote on the resolutions prepared by the committee. If passed, the resolutions would ban the school from the town.

Rallied by anti—Negro College campaigners and a recent newspaper editorial that questioned the moral integrity of black students, saying that they might feel more at home attending school in a nearby town renowned for prostitution, New Haven residents packed the small city hall meeting room. The first of the two resolutions argued that Negro College would be detrimental to the financial interests of Yale and other schools in the community, while the second claimed that it would be a tacit disregard of the rights and interests of slave states. The proposed Negro College hardly stood a chance in light of such powerful opposition. Residents upheld the resolutions in a vote of 700 to 4. Cornish and Jocelyn were shocked by the rejection, and while they made plans to seek another location for the proposed college, the effort lost all support.

Other Connecticut townspeople were equally resistant to the idea of blacks being educated. Quaker abolitionist Prudence Crandall was met with violent protest after she allowed black student Sarah Harris to enroll in her Canterbury, Connecticut, school for girls in March 1833. When townspeople threatened to shut down the school if Crandall continued to integrate, the educator turned it into an academy for black girls. The move angered citizens even more, and residents began a full-fledged assault on the school, Crandall, and her students. Under pressure, state legislature passed a law forbidding out-of-state blacks to attend school in Connecticut. Crandall lost the bulk of her students, who were from Philadelphia and New York. The remaining young women were harassed regularly and the school was vandalized. Crandall was finally forced to shut down the school in 1834 after a mob set fire to it while she and the students were inside the building. Crandall was also briefly jailed and fined for violating the earlier legislation.

In August 1835 angry Canaan, New Hampshire, residents shut down Noyes

Prudence Crandall, a Quaker abolitionist who enrolled blacks in her school
for girls.

Academy, which admitted both black and white students, after only five months of operation.

Despite the obstacles, northern blacks and supportive whites did make strides in providing educational opportunities for African Americans. In 1837
Cheyney University, the nation's first HBCU, was
founded in Pennsylvania. Originally named the African
Institute and renamed the Institute for Colored Youth,
Cheyney was founded through a $10,000 donation
from Quaker philanthropist Richard Humphreys.

In 1829 a growing number of mob attacks against
blacks occurred, and Humphreys—who had long
been concerned about the difficulties African Americans faced finding employment and accessing education—was moved to will money for an academy
committed to "the benevolent design of instructing the
descendants of the African Race in school learning."[4]

Humphreys died in 1832; five years later the Insti-
tute for Colored Youth (the original name of the school) opened 7 miles outside of Philadelphia. Initially, residents were resistant to a secondary school
for African American boys in their community, and landowners refused to
sell property to the trustees. Eventually, a 133-acre farm was purchased.
The school taught a primarily liberal arts curriculum, but it also provided
some agricultural and trade training. It was open to both boys and girls, and
during its first decade, the school was run by three different teams of
husband-and-wife educators.

Strides were being made elsewhere as well. The 1850 census revealed
that four-fifths of urban free African Americans were literate. Ninety percent
of the black population of Boston could read, as could 96 percent of blacks in
Providence. In addition, there was a small but growing group of college-educated
African Americans. Among them were: Dr. James Hall, a graduate of the Medical College of Maine (1822); Edward Jones, who received his degree from
Amherst (1826); the outspoken abolitionist John Russworm, who graduated
from Bowdoin College (1826); and Jane Patterson, who later became the first
African American female to receive a degree when she graduated from Oberlin

(1862). While these individuals were able to gain admission to white schools, the vast majority of educational institutions in the North did not admit people of color. Nevertheless, African Americans were legally free to pursue education in the North, and some communities were funding, if minimally, public schools for that purpose. The South, however, was altogether another story.

Black Education in the South

Southern blacks' access to education was at the discretion of the white aristocracy, and that discretion often was influenced by three factors: the importance of slave labor to the economic welfare of a particular southern state (or city, for that matter); the European country governing the territory; and the free or enslaved status of southern blacks themselves. Baltimore and the District of Columbia, for example, were cities influenced as much by East Coast as by southern

Fanny Jackson Coppin was the first female principal of the Institute for Colored Youth, the original name of Cheyney University. She went on to form Coppin State.

culture. Urban whites tended to own far fewer slaves than plantation owners. In addition, most urban slaves worked as house servants, and since house servants interacted with the ruling class more frequently and managed important aspects of the household, urban whites often preferred to afford enslaved blacks some level of education. While the city governments did not provide for the education of African Americans, a number of churches, both black and white, established schools for this purpose.

In New Orleans, which vacillated between French and Spanish control until the Louisiana Purchase in 1803, the intermingling of French, Africans, Spaniards, and Native Americans created the Creole culture and a resulting color-caste system that blurred the line between free, quasi-free, and enslaved persons of color. Moreover, French and Spanish enslavers were inclined to recognize the children that they fathered through liaisons with their African American mistresses, and were more likely to educate and take financial responsibility for those children. As a result, the octoroon, quadroon, and mulatto

SUNDAY AMUSEMENTS IN NEW ORLEANS—A CREOLE NIGHT AT THE FRENCH OPERA-HOUSE.—SKETCHED BY OUR SPECIAL ARTIST, A. R. WAUD.—[SEE FIRST PAGE.]

New Orleans Creole culture: "Sunday amusements in New Orleans—a Creole night at the French opera," *Harper's Weekly*, July 21, 1866.

castes (as they were identified) were more financially secure than biracial blacks in other states. In *Upon These Shores*, William G. Shade writes that in New Orleans, "wealthy urban mulattoes established their own schools, and . . . the Catholic Church provided for the education of some black children."[5]

In other southern cities like Charleston, South Carolina, and Mobile, Alabama, the vast majority of free blacks were literate, and nearly three-fourths of free African Americans in Savannah, Georgia, could read. In contrast, two-thirds of free blacks in Richmond, Virginia, remained illiterate even though Thomas Jefferson was a pioneer of public education in Virginia. A slave owner, Jefferson had advocated abolition during the early constitutional debates.

In the North and South, enslaved African Americans did find ways to become literate. In the slave-dependent agricultural state of Missouri, for example, Baptist missionaries, who stressed literacy for the purpose of Christian conversion, held a great deal of influence. In an 1825 report missionary John Mason Peck wrote, "I am happy to find among the slave holders in Missouri a growing disposition to have blacks educated, and to patronize Sunday schools for the purpose."[6]

In most rural southern areas, however, slave masters either did not provide for or strictly forbade the education of enslaved blacks. There was a feeling among many that education fueled slaves' dissatisfaction with their subservient status. Even more specifically, many slave owners feared that literate slaves would read and be influenced by literature promoting the growing abolition movement. Despite the risks, courageous African Americans continued to find ways to educate themselves and to pass on the torch of literacy, while some compassionate whites educated enslaved blacks in secret.

The great abolitionist Frederick Douglass was first exposed to reading as an 8-year-old, when his master's sympathetic wife, Sophia Auld, began teaching him the Bible. Even after Auld's husband demanded that she end the lessons, saying that Douglass "should know nothing but the will of his master," the bold youngster continued teaching himself by sneaking books from the Aulds' library. When he was 12, Douglass bought his first book, *The Columbian Orator.*

The patriotic tome lit fire to his developing abolitionary beliefs and emboldened him to share his knowledge. Before escaping slavery at the age of 20, Douglass held clandestine classes where he taught twenty to thirty other enslaved young men to read.

Revolutionary preacher Nat Turner was another slave who secretly learned how to read. His master's son taught him as a young boy. For Turner, as for most Americans of his time, literacy was linked to a need to read and understand Christian doctrine. But Turner and other enslaved blacks often adopted a very different interpretation of the Bible than the one promoted by southern slave owners. Slave masters often quoted Ephesians 6:5, which admonished slaves to be obedient to their earthly masters, in an effort to reinforce and justify their exploitation. African Americans, however, identified with the biblical story of Moses who led the Hebrews out of Egyptian bondage, and with Galatians 3:27–28 in the New Testament: "For as many of you as have been baptized into Christ have put on Christ. There is neither Jew nor Greek, there is neither bond nor free, there is neither male nor female, for ye are all one in Christ Jesus."

It was biblical stories of radical activism that emboldened freedom seekers like Turner. His exposure to education enabled him to pass his interpretation

Renowned abolitionist Frederick Douglass was taught to read by his master's wife, Sophia Auld. Douglass then shared his knowledge by offering secret classes to groups of slaves.

of Christian doctrine on to other enslaved African Americans. As a preacher who traveled from church to church, his ability to read maps gave him the information necessary to plan and mount a rebellion. On August 22, 1831, Nat Turner led the bloodiest slave revolt in U.S. history. The action began on the Southampton, Virginia, plantation owned by Turner's master, Joseph Turner. Just after midnight Turner and four recruits killed everyone in the home. They then moved about the community, taking over one plantation after another and killing slaveholding families. The rebel brigade eventually numbered seventy men, and they killed fifty-seven people. The revolt went on for three days before a militia, which executed more than one hundred blacks, defeated the group. Nat Turner escaped but was finally captured on October 31, 1831. He was tried and hanged on November 11.

In the minds of many whites and blacks, Turner's rebellion solidified the belief that education could be used as a tool of revolution and freedom. For black and white abolitionists the beacon of education took on a brighter glow. For supporters of slavery, education became an even more subversive and dangerous tool in the hands of blacks. The southern black rural population significantly outnumbered the southern white rural population by the early 1800s, and that added to white fear of educating blacks. In response, southern states passed even more draconian slave codes, which placed greater restrictions on enslaved and free blacks alike. By 1835 most southern states had passed laws making it illegal to teach a slave to read as well as write. In Virginia, where Turner and his gang rebelled, legislators even outlawed the education of free blacks. Tougher anti-gathering laws were passed and slaves were forbidden to assemble in groups larger than five without the presence of a white person. This ostensibly ended church gatherings for enslaved blacks, and as church was the primary educational institution for African Americans, the law greatly inhibited their efforts toward literacy.

Newly enacted pass laws required free blacks to always travel with papers verifying their status, while enslaved blacks were only allowed to travel alone by written permission from their masters. This last law necessitated that blacks be denied access to education because literate blacks could forge freedom papers or travel passes that would allow safe passage to freedom.

Nat Turner's ability to read and interpret biblical passages of radical activism helped inspire him to lead the bloodiest slave revolt in U.S. history on August 22, 1831.

In 1856 the Reverend H. P. Jacobs, a slave from Natchez, Mississippi, formulated an escape plan that took advantage of just such an opportunity. As a child, Jacobs was assigned to care for a man who was insane, yet literate. Even as a youngster Jacobs realized the value of learning and convinced the man to teach him how to read and write. Some years later, Jacobs used his secretly acquired education to flee slavery. He wrote a travel pass and, after stealing a wagon, horse, and money from his master, escaped to Canada with his wife, three children, and brother-in-law. Jacobs returned to Natchez following the Civil War to help found an HBCU—Jackson State University.

Story after story documents blacks who used literacy as a means to escape slavery. And equally as many stories reveal literate blacks who had the means to leave, but continued to reside under the tyrannical, oppressive slave culture of the South so they could teach other African Americans to read. Even after the majority of southern states passed laws outlawing education of enslaved African Americans, efforts to teach slaves continued. The lessons came at great danger to both students and teachers. A reporter for the *New York Observer* wrote that he knew of eight Sunday schools for slaves in one southern city, and that the students at each were taught to read. He wisely chose not to print the names of the schools or of the city for fear that the students and teachers would be punished. Another story tells of a slave named Scipio who was hanged when it was discovered that he had taught his grandson Jamie how to read. Enoch Golden, a slave who secretly taught many others to read

and write, was said to have related on his deathbed that he had been responsible for the "death o' many a nigger," because he educated them.[7]

Interestingly, a number of southern white women quietly participated in
the effort to educate blacks. Rebelling against the stereotype of southern women
as small-minded, they secretly taught enslaved blacks to read, knowing that if
they were caught, they were not likely to suffer the worst of fates. One Louisiana
mistress, for example, admitted as late as 1840 that she continued to teach
slaves on her plantation to read, even though it was "not a very popular thing
to do."[8]

Freeing Minds, Then Bodies

Southern mistresses who taught blacks to read were not always simply
rebelling against their own oppression. Some truly were opposed to slavery
and the willfully imposed ignorance of African Americans. Unable to own
property, vote, or control their own finances, however, these southern white
women often had to marry slaveholding men simply to ensure their own survival. Their clandestine efforts to educate enslaved blacks were, for some, strikes
against patriarchy as well as slavery. In the case of Virginia matron Margaret
Douglass, she and her daughter Rosa were arrested and prosecuted in a Norfolk, Virginia, Circuit Court in 1853 for daring to teach free blacks. Douglass,
who previously had owned slaves when she lived with her estranged husband
in South Carolina, was found guilty and convicted to jail. During her trial
she pointed out the hypocrisy of the men who had charged her, noting that
some were the biological fathers of the very children attending her school.

Women like Douglass were not alone in their sentiments. By the 1830s
the abolition movement had begun picking up steam. Northern Presbyterian,
Methodist, and Baptist congregations had embraced the early Quaker conviction that slavery was a moral sin. Black and white abolitionists banded together
through religious and missionary organizations such as the American Missionary Association (AMA), the Freedmen's Aid Society of the Methodist Episcopal Church, the African Methodist Episcopal Church (AME), the Colored
Methodist Episcopal Church, and many others to intensify educational efforts.

Members of these organizations believed that educated, assimilated blacks
would be the best rebuttal to white supremacist rhetoric and the strongest

weapon in the antislavery battle. These organizations employed covert and overt means of educating African Americans. Missionaries were sent south under the auspices of opening churches, and once there they secretly taught blacks to read. In the North, organizations focused on funding schools in areas where the local government simply refused to provide public education to blacks.

African American abolitionists were among the most active educators. Samuel Cornish, an AMA board member, became director of the African Free School in New York City from 1830 to 1834. Enrollment doubled during his tenure. Mary Ann Shadd Cary spent years teaching free and fugitive blacks at schools she started in Delaware and Ontario, Canada, prior to the Civil War. Cary later became the first African American female lawyer when she graduated from Howard University law school in 1871.

Southern mistresses often taught blacks to read.

A Crack in the Floodgates

Four additional HBCUs had opened by the conclusion of the Civil War in 1865. Surprisingly, all of these schools were not located in the North. HBCUs were opened in the slave-holding territories of Tennessee and the District of Columbia, while the remaining two were located in Pennsylvania and Ohio— border states immediately north of the Mason-Dixon line.

Miner Normal School became the seed for the University of the District of Columbia (UDC) in 1851 when Myrtilla Miner started her normal school for African American women.

As a young woman Miner attended the Young Ladies Domestic Seminary in Clinton, New York, a school that admitted both black and white students. After teaching in a Mississippi school for wealthy young white women and observing the horrors of slavery firsthand, Miner became determined to open a teacher's college for black women in the South. No longer able to tolerate the slavocracy culture in Mississippi, Miner left the school in 1847

Myrtilla Miner founded a school for African American women in 1851. Named the Miner Normal School, it was the seed institution for the University of the District of Columbia.

and began raising money and support for her proposed normal school. She decided to open it in Washington, D.C., reasoning that if the men who ran the capital could be shown that African Americans were capable of intelligence and industry, they might advocate for black schools throughout the Union.

Securing support was not easy. Miner wrote letters to and met with Frederick Douglass, renowned abolitionist Henry Ward Beecher, and numerous other black and white clergymen and educators. All advised her that the current political atmosphere made it unwise for her to attempt to open a school, but Miner was undeterred. An uncompromising and highly dramatic woman, Miner saw herself as a martyr for a noble cause. "My hand trembles & refuses to serve me well, as I here transcribe the offering I make of myself upon the antislavery altar of my country; but my spirit is strong, & I sincerely hope it may be accepted," wrote Miner to fellow abolitionist Gerrit Smith in 1850.

The determined educator raised funds for four years before scraping together enough money for the venture. She arrived in Washington in the fall of 1851 with only $100 and rented a 14-foot-square room from a black woman whose former master had willed her the home. Six students showed up for the first day of class, but the number quickly increased to forty. The curriculum included spelling, reading, geography, composition, moral philosophy, and analysis of authors. Teaching the last subject was especially important because Miner discovered that while a good number of her students could read, few had a good grasp of comprehension. If these young women were going to teach the rest of their race, they needed to master critical thinking as well as the three R's—readin', writin', and 'rithemetic.

Miner and the students quickly encountered many of the problems that her advisors had predicted. A mob threatened to attack the school, and a male neighbor hit and cursed at several of the young women when they were leaving school. The neighbor, a lawyer, went so far as to petition the court for closure of the school. The challenges of remaining open were so extensive that

Miner had to shut down in 1861. But the school was not without supporters. Facing tough opposition, in February 1863 Senator Henry Wilson of Massachusetts, J. W. Grimes of Iowa, and Senator Lot Morrill, author of the Morrill Act, pushed a bill through Congress that incorporated the school "for the education of colored youth in the District of Columbia."

It would be fourteen additional years, however, before the school would actually reopen as Miner Normal School (which merged with Wilson Teachers College in 1955 and became the University of the District of Columbia).

Other brave educators also opened schools at the height of the struggle between the North and South over the slavery issue. John Miller Dickey, the white pastor of Oxford Presbyterian Church in Oxford, Pennsylvania, founded Ashmun Institute in 1854 "for the collegiate and theological education of Negro young men."[9] He opened the school when protégé John Amos was rejected because of his race from both Princeton Theological Seminary and a Philadelphia Presbyterian Seminary. Ashmun changed its name to Lincoln University in honor of assassinated President Abraham Lincoln in 1866.

The Methodist Episcopal Church opened the doors of the Ohio African University in 1855. Ohio governor Salmon P. Chase, a renowned abolitionist who eventually became President Lincoln's treasury secretary, helped raise seed money for the school. The school was forced to close in 1863, however, due to mounting debt and declining enrollment. Many of the young male students were joining the Army in an effort to end slavery. The university was taken over by the AME Church that same year and chartered as Wilberforce University.

The church paid $10,000 for the college, and the Reverend Daniel Alexander Payne became the first black college president in the United States. From its beginnings, Wilberforce admitted both men and women, and its first students were a mixture of free and enslaved blacks. Wilberforce conferred its first baccalaureate degree in 1857, fully four years before the start of the Civil War.

A Union Army nurse named Lucinda Humphrey cultivated the beginnings of LeMoyne-Owen College in 1862. An attendant at Camp Shiloh in Tennessee during the Civil War, Humphrey began teaching the contraband freedmen to read by candlelight. The camp school grew and was moved to Memphis in

Rev. Daniel Alexander Payne, president of Wilberforce University and the first black college president in the United States (Wilberforce University).

1863 and named the Lincoln School. The school was burned down during a race riot in 1857, but quickly rebuilt. Still, the school faced significant financial troubles until AMA member Dr. Francis Julian LeMoyne gave a $20,000 endowment. The school was renamed LeMoyne Normal and Commercial School in 1871. (It merged with Owen Junior College in 1967.)

These early educational efforts, both legal and illegal, reached only a limited number of blacks, but they went a long way in stirring the desire for education in the hearts of African Americans. More important, the efforts ensured that there would be black teachers to take up the cause of educating other blacks.

The truly important role that education played in securing the emancipation and advancement of African Americans would only begin to be revealed during and after the Civil War. The war shook the foundation of slavery and allowed educated blacks to emerge as leaders. In *Between Church and State,* author James Fraser writes that black abolitionists like Frederick Douglass, politicians like Louisiana's first black lieutenant governor, P. B. S. Pinchback, and such religious leaders as Henry M. Turner, Isaac Land, and Lucius H. Holsey all secretly began their pursuit of education during slavery.

Wilberforce University. The oldest building on campus (1856) was originally a resort hotel.

Early photograph taken at Jackson State, founded by the American Home Baptist Mission Society in 1877.

NORMAL SCHOOLS

Although today's public schools are a part of every city's municipal budget, the same could not be said about the southern United States before the last quarter of the nineteenth century. Many white Southerners were adamantly opposed to publicly supported education in general, but most especially public education for blacks. There had been no tradition of paying taxes to support schools, and education was one of the prerequisites of belonging to the privileged class. The scions of wealthy planters were trained by private tutors in their homes or sent to Europe to receive their education.

Even when taxes to support public education were implemented in the South, the monies were difficult to collect and complaints were frequent. An even deeper fear was that mixed schools would come on the heels of a publicly financed school system. Because of the way that education had been structured in the South, there were not many

Southerners who were trained to run a school or to provide teacher training. Northern missionaries who came to the South after the war filled this vacuum and operated under the auspices of the Freedmen's Bureau and other northern aid societies to start common schools and universities for freed blacks.

Once the Freedmen's Bureau was shattered in 1873 and funds from wealthy Northerners were exhausted, education for African Americans suffered a severe setback. Many of the schools begun by the Freedmen's Bureau and the aid societies were taken over by the states. These "universities" were changed to normal and industrial institutes to focus more on teacher training and trades rather than the classical education favored by northern missionaries. Manual arts and domestic science curriculums were more in line with what state governments and their white constituents approved for blacks. Since these were the jobs available to normal school graduates, it was thought that African Americans needed this type of training more. As the southern states began to move away from an exclusively agrarian economy, manual education became the exclusive domain of black normal schools.

Despite the low expectations that society had for normal schools, they provided instruction beyond the grammar school level, and most had a high school department. Some of the more progressive normal schools included four-year college prep courses to prepare students to go on to college. Because there was a general shortage of teachers in the southern states, this increased the need for black teachers in the South. In 1871, for example, black teachers in Mississippi who had been educated while they were enslaved or in Freedmen's schools made up about 13 percent of the teaching force. In South Carolina in 1873, the state started a normal school to train teachers, and more black students were enrolled than whites.

Not all whites were proponents of the domestic education being offered in the normal schools, however. William T. Harris, the U.S. commissioner of education, argued before the National Education Association in 1872 that an intellectual education was the way to prevent blacks from returning to their "former lower stage of spiritual life."

By the early 1900s normal schools had already begun teaching classical education, offering courses in the sciences, geography, and mathematics. The normal and industrial mantle was used as a cover when wealthy white funders visited. Private black schools fared much better and received more support from philanthropists when they offered normal and industrial education. As the normal schools expanded, southern whites were ensured that social equality would not occur between the races since whites controlled the schools. The issue of control would become a flashpoint for black students in the 1920s, as they demanded more control of the institutions that were created to educate them. By the 1940s, black schools began to drop the normal school distinction and openly pursued accreditation.

Hampton, Lincoln, Cheyney, and Tuskegee Universities all started as normal schools. HBCUs still train a great number of black teachers; Alabama State produces more teachers than any other college in the entire state of Alabama. Great universities have emerged from humble beginnings. They have endured opposition and neglect and have established a tradition of academic excellence.

ALPHABET OF SLAVERY.

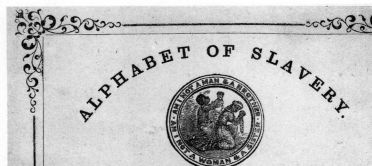

A Is an AFRICAN torn from his home.

B Is a BLOODHOUND to catch all that roam.

C Is the COTTON PLANT Slaves pick and hoe.

D Is the DRIVER who makes their blood flow.

E Is for ENGLAND which Slaves long to see,
Her daughter, fair Canada, whither they flee.

F Is a FUGITIVE—hide him by day!
The North Star at midnight will show him the way.

G Is for GAMBLER both drunken and wild,
Stakes money and bowie-knife, mother and child.

H Is SLAVE HUNTER with horses and gun,
The ugliest monster that's under the sun.

I Is for INFANT at mother's breast found,
Was sold at an auction one guinea a pound.

J Is the JOURNEY when many Slaves die,
Their grave the deep waters, their shroud the blue sky.

K Was a KIDNAP' who stole a poor man,

L Was the LAWYER who joined in the plan,

M Was the MERCHANT who bartered for gold,

N The poor NEGRO like pig or horse sold.

O Is OHIO, the train starts from here
Of that underground railway the slaveholder's fear.

P Are some PREACHERS with Slaves like the rest,
They buy them, and whip them, then pray to be blest.

Q Stands for QUAKER, who helps the poor slave,
A hero of hero's both peaceful and brave.

R Is the RICE SWAMP, a sickening place,
Where ague and fever soon finish the race.

S Is for SUGAR—Slavegrown—and shrewd sages
Declare 'twould be better if Negros had wages.

T Is TOBACCO—I don't like the weed—
To sow it and dress it the Negros oft bleed.

U Is that UNION of stripes and of stars,
The Slaves get the stripes, yes! and plenty of scars.

V Is VIRGINIA where Uncle Tom's wife
With Children and home were the joy of his life.

W Is the WHIP, which with paddle and chain,
Stocks, thumbscrew, and bell give them terrible pain.

X Ends the REFLEX of every ones mind,
The better for all men when gentle and kind.

Y Is for YOUTH, and wherever you be
Z ealously labour to set the Slaves free

Leeds, July, 1856.

J. Kershaw and Son, Printers.

2

BOOKS BEFORE FREEDOM

The trumpet sounds for war. While white Americans fight over the economics of slavery, black Americans declare war on illiteracy.

THE MOVEMENT TO better educate black people began to grow in the 1830s. But it was not until the 1850s that the issue reached critical mass and the country was forced to move to resolve it. By 1850 the United States consisted of thirty-three states, which were split nearly equally between free and slave areas. Settlers in numerous western territories were applying for admission into the Union, and the question of whether they would enter as free or slave states was driving the country toward war. By midcentury economics rather than morality was at the center of the battle to abolish slavery. The slave economy had given southern white farmers and businessmen a substantial advantage over those in free states. The free labor allowed southerners to make goods and products that were more affordable and available in greater quantities.

The argument intensified when northerners fought to reduce the economic impact of slavery by preventing its expansion into new states. Southerners, fearing the power of the growing abolition movement, campaigned for indi-

Alphabet of slavery.

President Abraham Lincoln was a strong
and outspoken critic of slavery.

vidual state choice. A compromise was reached in 1850 that helped maintain the tenuous economic balance of the Union. Included in the agreement, however, was the controversial Fugitive Slave Law that obligated Northerners to return escaped slaves. Though Congress made the agreement in an attempt to avoid a split of the Union, it actually further entrenched supporters on both sides of the issue. The debate became so intensely divisive that the newly formed Republican Party rose to prominence and won the 1860 presidential election when their candidate, Abraham Lincoln, promised that his administration would not allow the Union to split.

While Lincoln had not advocated abolition throughout the Union, he was an outspoken critic of slavery. Perhaps because he had grown up in poverty on the Kentucky frontier, and had struggled to gain his own education, Lincoln's sympathies ran toward limiting the suffering of African Americans. As a boy Lincoln worked on a farm, where he split rails for fences and learned how to read, write, and do arithmetic in his spare time. "When I came of age I did not know much. Still, somehow I could read, write and cipher . . . but that was all," he wrote in a campaign speech.[1] Those sympathies made Southerners extremely leery of the new president, and in January 1861, two months before Lincoln's inauguration, South Carolina became the first state to secede from the Union. By June, ten other states—Mississippi, Florida, Alabama, Georgia, Louisiana, Texas, Virginia, Arkansas, Tennessee, and North Carolina—had seceded and joined together to form the Confederacy.

Ironically, South Carolina, the first state to leave the Union, provided a germinating ground for the mass advancement of education among African Americans and, ultimately, the growth of HBCUs.

Just one month after taking office, Lincoln ordered supplies sent to Fort Sumter in Charleston, South Carolina. Believing that federal troops were attempting to take control of the state, General Pierre Gustave Toutant Beauregard demanded that Union soldiers surrender to Confederate troops. When the battalion refused, Confederate soldiers opened fire, sparking the first battle of the Civil War. In November, General Thomas Sherman of the Union Army ordered a blockade of ships along the South Carolina coast. The plan was to take over the tiny yet highly fertile row of Sea Islands, which included Hilton Head, Port Royal, St. Helena, and Ladies. Here, cotton was king, and the plantation owners whose livelihoods depended on selling the crop got rich off the backs of slaves who toiled in the fields free of charge. The federal government intended to confiscate the crops, sell the cotton, and use the cash to shore up Union coffers and support northern troops. Sherman surmised that Union soldiers could move in from the inner shoreline and advance on other parts of South Carolina.

The ships arrived at the South Carolina coast at 9:25 on the morning of November 7. Huge cannons fired on the islands, sending black and white residents alike into panic. There would be no ground combat, however. The rifles and handguns that residents possessed were no match for the large artilleries of the Union ships. Plantation owners all over the islands began evacuating. Nearly all of them threatened, begged, lied to, and pleaded with enslaved blacks to leave the islands and remain in their service. Few were successful. Although most blacks on the islands were unable to read the abolitionist propaganda that predicted emancipation, they had been informed by the literate few, or by others who were simply reliable sources of information. The vast majority of Sea Island blacks stood in direct defiance of their fleeing masters and chose to take their chances with the invading soldiers, whom their masters claimed would "sell them to Cuba."[2]

Willie Lee Rose, author of *Rehearsal for Reconstruction: The Port Royal Experiment,* writes that years after the Civil War, former slave Sam Mitchell recalled the day that his parents refused to help their master, John Chaplin, escape Ladies Island. When Chaplin ran into the yard and ordered Sam's father to serve as an oarsman for his journey over to Charleston, Sam's mother hollered out, "You ain't gonna row no boat to Charleston, you go out dat back door and keep a-going."[3]

The black residents who did leave the islands most often left to join the Union Army or find family members who were on other plantations. The ones who stayed, however, were among the first newly freed men and women to gain access to education.

The Port Royal Experiment

An estimated 10,000 African Americans remained on the islands, and education was among their immediate priorities. In December, fearful that the cotton crops might not be harvested and that unscrupulous soldiers might exploit or even sell off the newly freed blacks, Treasury Secretary Salmon Chase sent abolitionist and Boston attorney Edward Pierce to the Sea Islands to "look into the contraband situation."[4] On February 3, 1862, Pierce issued a report to the federal government on the situation at Port Royal, the island that served as the Union Army's base of operation. In his report, Pierce noted an eagerness for education among the freedmen, writing that on St. Helena and Ladies Island, "No school, it is to be regretted, has yet been started, except one on Sunday, but the call for reading books is daily made by the laborers."[5] On Port Royal Island, however, the recent arrival of a Massachusetts minister and three black teachers (one identified as John Milton) had greatly inspired the islanders. "[The minister] has established a school for the children, in which are sixty pupils, ranging in age from six to fifteen years. They are rapidly learning their letters and simple reading. . . . A visit to the school leaves a remarkable impression."[6]

The Port Royal experiment, as the early emancipation and education project came to be called, greatly inspired Pierce. Chief among his efforts to help former slaves attain a life of true freedom was providing them with educational opportunities. But as author Rose conveys, Pierce wisely realized that while the government was willing to pay blacks to continue as laborers in the cotton fields, federal officials likely would not be inclined to pay for books and teachers to establish schools for the black islanders, especially under the uncertainty of war. Asking only that Secretary Chase approve the arrival and pay for the passage of missionary teachers to the Sea Islands, Pierce issued an appeal to religious organizations, benevolent societies, and abolitionist groups asking that they donate teaching supplies and, most important, money for teachers' salaries. Locating books was of considerable importance to the effort since Lieutenant Colonel William H. Reynolds, the officer in charge of the island troops, had taken it upon himself to pack up the library at Port Royal and ship the books north for sale.

Arriving on the Sea Islands shortly after Pierce was the Reverend Manfield

French, a New York City Methodist minister who was associated with the American Missionary Association—the abolition-minded missionary group that originally banded together in support of the *Amistad* captives' fight for freedom. French had also served as president of the Ohio-based Xenia Female Seminary, an AMA-sponsored school. The two men immediately agreed to join forces in the educational effort. Pierce would head the recruitment and funding efforts in Boston, while French would lead the activities in New York. By early February, both men had returned to their respective cities and were hastily orchestrating funding for the team of fifty-three missionary teachers who would ultimately pioneer the educational effort.

In Boston, Pierce engaged the assistance of the Reverend Jacob Manning, a dyed-in-the-wool abolitionist who had connections with several prominent Bostonians. Manning helped garner support from some of the wealthiest and most committed abolitionists in Massachusetts. Many of the younger abolitionists were convinced that slavery was as much an economic evil as it was a moral one. Edward Atkinson was one such supporter. A businessman, Atkinson was an agent for six northern cotton-manufacturing companies, and he had gained prominence by authoring books that argued the unfairness of the southern slave economy. But Atkinson was also morally opposed to slavery and had helped raise money for the 1859 raid on Harpers Ferry executed by John Brown.

Reverend French's New York recruitment efforts were also proceeding well. Here, the AMA began soliciting funds and interviewing potential volunteers. Within three weeks the efforts were complete, and each man had secured funding for the mission through their respective committees—the General Committee of the Education Commission in Boston and the New York National Freedmen's Relief Association in New York. Working together the two committees reviewed one hundred and fifty applicants and from those chose thirty-five persons from Boston and eighteen from New York. Twelve of the teachers chosen were women. Among the lot were Harvard, Yale, and Brown graduates, divinity students, New England schoolmarms, doctors, lawyers, and secret agents of the Underground Railroad. Some were volunteers, while others were paid between $25 and $50 monthly for their services.

On Monday, March 3, 1862, the *Atlantic* steamer set sail from Canal Street Pier in New York City. Among the passengers were the fifty-three educators, all of disparate backgrounds, but united in their conviction that once blacks had proven themselves to society by gaining education and becoming self-sufficient, "no government could ever be found base enough to turn its back upon them," as Pierce had previously written.[7] At the close of their three-day voyage to Port Royal, Pierce called a meeting aboard ship and, writes historian Willie Lee Rose, "warned them that their work would be extremely hard and that they might be shocked by what they saw."[8] Pierce impressed upon the missionaries the importance of treating the former slaves with respect and dignity despite their condition. He cautioned that they would most likely see individuals who, at the hands of neglectful, cruel enslavers, had become "very dirty" and "even vermined."[9] Finally, Pierce issued a prophetic directive that would become a hallmark of early black educational efforts. He advised the missionaries to instill in the freedmen an appreciation for New England values, which advocated stringent views on cleanliness, religious piety, and manners. (These views would govern the social codes on black college campuses for the next half-century and eventually would become a major bone of contention between the black student bodies and the mostly white administrations.)

Teaching in the Trenches

It took several weeks to assign the teachers to various islands and to begin setting up schools. Almost immediately Pierce, French, and their band of educators met with resistance from white Union soldiers, who were often illiterate themselves and resentful of the idea of blacks gaining formal education. Despite these challenges the work forged ahead. By April, teachers from Philadelphia began to arrive on the islands. Charlotte Forten, granddaughter of wealthy African American abolitionist James Forten, was among this group and one of only a handful of black educators who taught at Port Royal.

For obvious reasons, black educators were few in number. Teaching blacks had been restricted or outlawed by individual southern states, beginning with the 1740 South Carolina law that made it illegal to teach enslaved African Americans to write. While free southern blacks could legally pursue education, violence against black schools by white-supremist organizations such as the Ku Klux Klan made it dangerous for them to attend school.

THE FORTEN FAMILY

The Forten family was one of the most important African American families in the country for two generations. Their support of abolition and education for African Americans provided a foundation for free men and women and the schools that would be developed to teach them.

James Forten Sr., the family patriarch, was born free in Philadelphia in 1766. He was educated at a Quaker school for colored children run by abolitionist Anthony Benezet. At 8 years of age, he started working with his father as a sail maker in the sail loft of Robert Bridges. After the death of his father, young James started working to support his mother and sister. By the time he was 15 he had joined the Continental Army and served as a powder boy on the privateer ship *Royal Lewis*. During a sea battle with three heavily fortified British frigates, the crew of the *Royal Lewis* was captured and Forten imprisoned when he refused to join the Royal Navy. He served his sentence and survived the squalid conditions of the notorious prison ship HMS *Jersey* before he was set free and returned to his native Philadelphia.

Forten returned to Robert Bridges's sail loft, and when Bridges retired in 1798, Forten took over the business. He eventually became one of the wealthiest sail makers in Philadelphia and used his fortune to support abolition and women's suffrage. In 1800 he wrote a letter to Massachusetts congressman George Thacher, thanking him for being the sole member of Congress who sought to repeal the Fugitive Slave Law of 1793. Years later this letter would be praised and circulated, eventually making its way to England. In 1813 Forten addressed his "Letters from a Man of Colour" to the Pennsylvania Senate in response to a bill that would prevent blacks, slave or free, from migrating to Pennsylvania. It also would require black residents of the state to be registered, taxed to support the black poor, and sold if they committed crimes.

Forten started a school for black children in his home. He helped fund William Lloyd Garrison's abolitionist paper the *Liberator*, and his

Charlotte Forten, grand-
daughter of wealthy African
American abolitionist James
Forten, was one of the
teachers assigned to establish schools in Port Royal.

daughters and granddaughters submitted articles and poetry to the publication. His zeal
was transferred to his wife, Charlotte Vandine
Forten, and their three daughters Margaretta,
Harriet, and Sarah. In 1833, while James Forten
was supporting the Pennsylvania Anti-Slavery
Society, the Forten women were helping to
establish the Philadelphia Female Anti-Slavery
Society. All three daughters were active, serving
in various capacities. They served on the
governing board, cochaired events, and even
participated in drafting the society's constitution. James Forten's death in 1842 brought
about the demise of the family business, but his
legacy continued for three more generations.

Following the example of her father, daughter Margaretta opened a
private school for black children in 1850 that developed a reputation
for academic excellence as far away as Charleston, South Carolina. Harriet married Robert Purvis, who was raised for much of his life in the
Forten home. The couple established themselves as noted abolitionists
in their own right. Robert Purvis and Harriet Forten Purvis bought
an estate a few miles outside of Philadelphia that became a gathering
place for abolitionists and suffragists from the United States and abroad,
such as Susan B. Anthony, Elizabeth Cady Stanton, and Sallie Holley.
They constructed a special room on the property that they used as a
stop on the Underground Railroad. Robert and Harriet were involved
with numerous women's rights and antislavery groups through the
years, including the American Equal Rights League, the National
Women's Suffrage Convention, and the Pennsylvania Anti-Slavery
Society. Once the Civil War broke out, Robert recruited black troops
for the Union Army and fought for commissions for black soldiers.
Harriet took up the fight to have Philadelphia's streetcars desegregated
even though as a woman of privilege she had her own carriage.

The Purvises' older daughter Harriet also joined the fight to abolish slavery and achieve equal rights for women begun by her grandfather James Forten. She was involved with the Philadelphia Female Anti-Slavery Society, the Woman Suffrage Association, and the National American Woman Suffrage Association. She and niece Alice (James Forten Sr.'s great-granddaughter) once traveled to London with Susan B. Anthony to attend a meeting held by the International Council of Women.

James Forten Sr.'s youngest son, William, would establish himself as a venerable black politician in Philadelphia. In 1855 he and his older brother Robert, along with five other black men, petitioned the Philadelphia legislature to demand that black men be counted as citizens because of the role that blacks played in the War of 1812. To strengthen their appeal they recounted the exploits of their father, James Forten, who had by this time become a legend of sorts. William unsuccessfully lobbied his friend Senator Charles Sumner to have the wording of the Fifteenth Amendment changed so that it would not mention color or slavery. He was active in mobilizing the black vote and, in 1874, pushed for passage of a civil rights bill. William's older brother, Robert Bridges Forten, was also an ardent abolitionist. He abhorred the proslavery stance that many American churches held and once locked horns with Frederick Douglass, debating whether the Constitution was a proslavery document. In 1859 Robert migrated to England and joined the London Emancipation Committee. Once the Civil War broke out, he returned to the United States to serve in the Union Army. He quickly advanced in rank, becoming a sergeant major before he died of typhoid fever in 1864. He was the first black man in Philadelphia to be buried with military honors.

Robert Bridges Forten was the father of Charlotte Forten. After Charlotte's mother died, she spent much of her childhood in the home of her aunt, Harriet Forten Purvis. In 1854, when Charlotte was 16, her father sent her to an integrated school in Salem, Massachusetts, so that she could be with girls her own age. Charlotte excelled in Salem, and after graduating from Salem Normal School she became the first

African American in Massachusetts history to teach white students. Because of failing health, however, she was forced to retire at the young age of 20. Charlotte returned to Philadelphia, where she taught in her aunt Magaretta's school. In 1862 she joined the Port Royal experiment in the Sea Islands of South Carolina, becoming one of the few black teachers on the island. After the Civil War ended, she worked for the Freedmen's Aid Society in Boston. At the age of 41, she married Francis Grimké, nephew of the Grimké sisters, who were well-known white abolitionists.

Angelina and Sarah Grimké had abandoned their privileged southern lifestyle, migrated north, and became actively involved in the antislavery movement. Angelina discovered that she was related to Francis while he and his brother Archibald were attending Lincoln University. The two brothers fled the South after their father, Henry Grimké, who was the slave-holding brother of the Grimké sisters, died. Francis and Archibald's white half brother attempted to put them to work in his house rather than set them free as Henry Grimké had stipulated in his will. Francis was captured and sold and didn't obtain his freedom until the end of the war. Charles Purvis, Charlotte Forten's first cousin (and James Forten Sr.'s grandson), was teaching at Howard Medical School during Francis's brief stint at Howard's law school. Purvis introduced Francis to Charlotte and they were married in 1878.

Although the Forten family legacy began almost a century before the founding of the first HBCU, the family's work to abolish slavery, educate black youth, and gain equal rights for women prepared the way for the establishment of schools that would train and develop generations of African Americans.

As previously illustrated, even northern blacks met with financial and safety challenges when endeavoring to start or attend schools. As a result, the African American community produced few teachers. Those who were skilled enough to teach most often were weighed down by the educational demands of their own communities. For them, the South Carolina Sea Islands simply represented one more black community desperately in need of education.

Charlotte Forten's presence on the Sea Islands brought an unexpected element to teacher-student relationships at Port Royal. As a black woman, she could readily identify discrimination and snobbery when she encountered it, but she could not have anticipated the deeply entrenched caste system used by slave owners to suppress and divide African Americans. The culture gave preference first to whites and second to fair-skinned blacks, often house servants who were led to feel superior to darker-skinned blacks and field hands. But no matter how elevated an African American became within southern slave culture, he or she would never be considered equal to even the least achieved white person. To the newly freed black Sea Islanders, Forten's familiarity with whites on the island, along with her obvious education, must have flown directly in the face of all that they had come to accept about the station of blacks in southern society. While blacks on the islands addressed white missionaries as "Massa" and "Missus," even after being told that the titles were unnecessary, Forten was often referred to as "dat brown gal."[10] Over time, however, she won the trust and respect of the islanders.

Forten was deeply moved by the efforts of the freedmen to learn, and by the parents who insisted that even the youngest of their children take advantage of the opportunity to gain literacy. But she also admitted to being overwhelmed by the challenge of teaching them. "Part of my scholars are very tiny—babies, I call them—and it is hard to keep them quiet. They are too young even for the alphabet, it seems to me. I think I must write home and ask somebody to send me picture books and toys to amuse them."[11]

Educators Laura Townes and Ellen Murray started the Penn School on St. Helena Island, which in coming years would become the educational center of the Sea Islands. In 1901 the Penn School was rechartered as the Penn Normal, Industrial, and Agricultural School, becoming, for a short time, a state-sponsored HBCU. The school closed in 1948 and has since become the Penn Center, a research and community resource center.

As the Civil War raged, African Americans living on the islands and the visiting missionary teachers devoted themselves to the business of learning. "Where the [Army] superintendents met stubborn and passive resistance, the teachers were joyfully accepted everywhere," writes Willie Lee Rose. "The Negroes evinced an eagerness to learn."[12]

Despite the fact that few blacks knew how to read, they demonstrated an overall appreciation for the power of education. For many it held a promise of independence that could not be taken from them even if the North lost the war. Although the black Sea Islanders had been more isolated from educational opportunities than their land-bound counterparts, the community was not without literate persons of color. Children like Suzy King Taylor had learned to read by attending a secret school taught by a free African American woman in Savannah, Georgia. Another slave girl had learned to read while playing with her master's daughter. Still others, such as the plantation drivers and foremen, had been illegally educated by masters who found it far too problematic to have illiterate men keeping track of their crop production.

By the end of 1863 as many as 1,700 Sea Island children were regularly attending classes. Furthermore, a significant number of adults attended night school after working in the fields all day. Others pushed aside issues of pride and allowed themselves to be tutored by their own children. But gaining education was not without its challenges. One teacher noted that while the children were anxious to learn and made steady progress, they were often hampered by the northern reading primers, which used words and colloquialisms that were clearly unfamiliar to the Sea Island residents.[13] The blacks who inhabited the Sea Islands were descendants of Africa's Mende, Kissi, Melinka, and Bantu tribes, and their isolation from the North American mainland allowed them to maintain and merge many of their tribal traditions. The merged African cultures were called Gullah, and the enslaved blacks even spoke Gullah, a blend of African and European tongues. For black Sea Islanders, learning from the northern primers was tantamount to learning in a foreign language.

In other cases, the children were so burdened with responsibility that it was nearly impossible for them to concentrate on learning. One such case was that of 13-year-old Hector, who was forced to watch his younger brother and infant sibling during class and often fell behind in the lesson or was forced to leave school if the baby began to cry. Students also endured loud, overcrowded classrooms and traveled inordinately long distances to attend school. Despite the challenges, young and old remained committed to education.

South Carolina was not the only state where newly freed blacks and abolitionists banded together to begin the arduous and still dangerous process of education during the war. All across the South groups of driven educators followed in the wake of Union Army victories and established schools for Negroes. Camp Nelson in Jessamine County, Kentucky, drew one of the largest contingents of refugees fleeing their enslavers. Missionaries set up schools there and attempted to teach, feed, and clothe more than 3,000 freedmen. John G. Fee, founder of Berea College (est. 1866), helped lead the effort. Among the freedmen soldiers was A. A. Burleigh, who met Fee at the camp and later became the first student to graduate from Berea.

PENN CENTER, FORMERLY PENN NORMAL, INDUSTRIAL, AND AGRICULTURAL SCHOOL

When Union troops took over Port Royal Sound in 1861, the white plantation owners of the Sea Islands in South Carolina fled their homes, land, and property. Part of the abandoned property was 10,000 black men, women, and children. St. Helena Island became the proving ground to test the question black and white abolitionists had been debating for decades: "Is the Negro educable?" Laura Towne and Ellen Murray set out to settle the question once and for all when they founded the Penn School in 1862, six months before the declaration of the Emancipation Proclamation and three years before the end of the Civil War. Named to honor Quaker activist William Penn, the school was the first learning institution in the South for freed black slaves. Classes initially were held in a back room of the Oaks Plantation House.

The freedmen's interest in learning multiplied and soon one room could no longer accommodate the demand. The next stop for the school was across the road at the Brick Baptist Church. October 1862 brought about an unusual occurrence at Penn for both faculty and students. One of the school's few black teachers, Charlotte Forten, arrived on the island. Forten became deeply involved with the blacks on the island, teaching students after school hours in her home, making dresses for some, and distributing Christmas gifts to still others. The school soon outgrew the Brick Baptist Church. In 1865 the Philadelphia Port Royal Relief Commission donated money to purchase 50 acres of land to build the school's first permanent building.

The Penn School was devoted to the enlightenment of both its students and the other black residents of the island. Penn offered classes in carpentry, wheelwrighing, basket making, harness making, cobbling, and mechanics—courses uniquely suited to prepare students for professions in and around the islands. The school also offered midwifery and teacher training for its female students. In 1900 Penn undertook the normal school curriculum that had proven so successful at Tuskegee Institute. An influx of black teachers arrived at the school in 1915 and ushered in an unprecedented tradition of excellence that would last for more than three decades.

Two major factors contributed to the demise of the Penn School. The Great Migration of blacks to the North drained enrollment, and the boll weevil epidemics of the 1940s wreaked havoc on the indigenous crops of the island. In 1948 the school was changed to Penn Community Services Center to continue to meet the needs of the Gullah people of the Sea Islands. The site was designated a National Historic Landmark in 1974. The significance of the Penn School in African American history is best expressed in the St. Helena hymn written by John Greenleaf Whittier at the request of Charlotte Forten a month after her arrival to the Sea Islands in 1862:

> Oh, none in all the world before were ever glad as we,
> We're free on Carolina's shore
> We're all at home and free.

The Freedmen's Bureau was established by the Lincoln administration in 1865 to address the various concerns of the newly freed African Americans. It was a key element in providing funding and guidance for black schools. General Oliver Otis Howard was appointed as head of the bureau.

The Freedmen's Bureau Steps In

Undoubtedly, the Port Royal experiment set the stage for black schools to be developed on a broader scale following the defeat of the Confederate Army. The impact of the effort began to become manifest during the latter part of the Civil War. By Christmas 1864—nearly a year after Lincoln issued the Emancipation Proclamation, which freed enslaved black Americans—Union troops finally gained control of South Carolina.

Thousands of refugees from the coastal areas of Florida, Georgia, and North Carolina streamed into Port Royal, as the White House had designated

Beaufort, the island's main city, as the location for handling the host of problems faced by displaced and often destitute African Americans.

It became apparent very quickly that the private aid societies and missionary organizations, which were then the primary means for assisting freedmen, were not equipped to handle the needs of the masses of former slaves being directed into the region. The various organizations had sent nearly 800 teachers into the region, but they were no match for the estimated 40,000 blacks settling throughout the South Carolina coastal islands. The aid societies banded together and petitioned the Lincoln administration to establish a government agency to address the freedmen's concerns. They had been lobbying for such an agency since 1863, the year Lincoln issued the Emancipation Proclamation. On March 3, 1865, Lincoln signed a bill for the creation of the Bureau of Refugees, Freedmen, and Abandoned Lands.

Most referred to the agency as "the Freedmen's Bureau." While the Bureau was established to address the multiple concerns of African Americans, it clearly was most effective in providing funding and assistance for the establishment of black schools. During its six years of existence, bureau officials directed $5 million in federal funds toward education.

The creation of the Freedmen's Bureau could not have been timelier— just one month before the end of the Civil War. Now came the daunting task of bringing education and self-sufficiency to millions of former slaves.

The Emancipation Proclamation helped open the gates of education to African Americans.

THE FREEDMEN'S BUREAU

The Freedmen's Bureau was established on March 3, 1865, when Congress established the agency to address all matters concerning refugees and freedmen within the states under reconstruction. In the South, resistance to the education of African Americans remained strong even after the last shot of the Civil War was fired in 1865. With the end of the war, 4 million slaves had become free, and young and old alike hungered for education and training.

On May 12, 1865, less than a month after the assassination of Abraham Lincoln, President Andrew Johnson appointed General Oliver Otis Howard as commissioner of the Bureau of Refugees, Freedmen, and Abandoned Lands. Commonly thought of as a clearinghouse of government funds for freed slaves, the Freedmen's Bureau was conceived as a far-reaching agency that functioned much like a government. Its assistance extended to both blacks and whites who had suffered loss during the war. At various times the bureau distributed food and clothing, made laws and executed them, set and collected taxes, punished crime, and even maintained and used military force. Despite the gross mismanagement and corruption that eventually brought about its demise, the Freedmen's Bureau helped found Howard, Fisk, Hampton, and Atlanta Universities. In its first year alone, the bureau helped to establish schools that educated more than 100,000 blacks.

The Freedmen's Bureau also served as an intermediary between these new black schools and northern aid societies. Northern teachers would be recommended to the bureau, who in turn would consult with the freedmen regarding whom to hire. The bureau distributed money to HBCUs for the construction of buildings, classroom furnishings, maintenance and repairs, and textbook purchases.

The primary source of income for the Freedmen's Bureau was supposed to be the sale and rental of lands confiscated during the war, but President Andrew Johnson eliminated that revenue stream in 1866 when he declared that all land be returned to pardoned Southerners.

By 1868, the bureau was beleaguered by attacks from southern and border states that considered the sweeping authority of the agency unnecessary and unconstitutional during a time of peace. Meanwhile, southern apathy toward the bureau was growing and financial mismanagement was coming to light. By the time the bureau ended operations in 1872, over $20 million had been expended. In 1874, General Howard was court-martialed to give an account of the many abuses that occurred under his watch. Although the investigation uncovered no direct wrongdoing on Howard's part, his management of the bureau was called into question as even some of his handpicked appointees were exposed in the scandal.

Though the Freedmen's Bureau was mired in controversy for much of its short life, the contributions it made to African American education were significant and worthy of recognition. All black colleges established between 1865 and 1872 either were founded by or received aid from the Freedmen's Bureau.

3

 .

YEARNING
AND LEARNING

With the close of the Civil War, 4.4 million free African Americans embark upon an educational journey. Blacks, missionaries, and the federal government work together to create schools.

IN 1869, THE head of the Freedmen's Bureau's education desk in Missouri and Kansas grew frustrated:

> I find among the colored population persons . . . whose ancestors have been free . . . [and who] possessing the means to provide adequately for . . . their own families hold themselves apart from all efforts for elevation of the race. It is with me, a problem how such men are to be reached, and brought into sympathy with their less fortunate brethren. If they cannot see that their own social position is defined by the condition of the race; that as long as the avenues to distinction and elevation are shut to the rest they are also closed to them; that as long as the mass of colored men are only "niggers" they will be comprehended in the same significant catalogue; if they cannot be influenced by these considerations, I do not see what will stimulate them.

Though the vast majority of emancipated slaves were illiterate, these, for example, child students and their teachers, placed a high value on obtaining some form of education.

On April 9, 1865, on the battlegrounds of Appomattox, Virginia, the Union Army dealt the final blow to the Confederacy, thereby ending slavery. For the first time, all of the 4.4 million blacks living in the United States now stood as free people. With emancipation came the right for blacks to legally pursue education. But with 80 percent of African Americans living south of the Mason-Dixon line, the vast majority of blacks were illiterate and the task of educating them was overwhelming. Despite the challenge, forward-thinking Americans of all colors understood the vital importance of the task. As one Freedmen's Bureau agent aptly observed, the social elevation and equity of even the most educated African Americans were anchored by the status and suffering of the least learned and underprivileged of the race.[1] Fortunately, the desire among educated African Americans to share their knowledge and lend assistance to their less fortunate conterparts far outweighed the oppressive mentality of a small segment of elitist blacks.

Edmonia Highgate was one of the black educators who went south during Reconstruction to help educate the newly freed men and women. Highgate was just 19 years old when she became principal of a school for blacks in Bingham, New York. A radical abolitionist before the war, she went south after the Union's victory and taught in Norfolk, Virginia, New Orleans, and other such cities. In several cases, she publicly challenged racist city officials. In New Orleans, her battle with the school board prompted one unidentified citizen to fire shots at her students as they were on their way to school.

The danger that Highgate experienced was not unusual. After the Civil War, southern whites often used violence to assert control over free blacks. Black-owned businesses, homes, and farms were burned. The Ku Klux Klan beat and lynched countless numbers of African Americans, and threatened and attacked northern white missionaries. Part of their campaign of intimidation included trying to stop black schools from opening. Yet the freedmen were undeterred in their pursuit of education. In many cases, former slaves who had gained the fundamentals of education took on the responsibility of opening schools. Freedmen planted the seeds for what would become Talladega College (est. 1867), Atlanta University (est. 1867), and Morehouse College (est. 1867), to name a few. In many cases they were directly responsible for the educational initiatives that prompted AMA missionaries and Freedmen's Bureau representatives to send teachers, money, and supplies.

Class of 1590.

With the aid of the Freedmen's Bureau, the American Missionary Association founded Atlanta University in 1867. By the 1870s the school was awarding bachelor's degrees. Pictured are students from the class of 1890.

Educational Roadblocks

Immediately following the Civil War, the Freedmen's Bureau dispatched field representatives to assist former slaves in their efforts to find homes, gain employment, and establish schools. These representatives often witnessed or were the victims of heinous attacks from Confederate loyalists. In an 1868 report to the Freedmen's Bureau, a Texas field representative listed a litany of crimes perpetrated against educators.[2] For example, in Williamson County, a school under the direction of a young black woman named Laura Eggleston was destroyed by fire in the middle of the night. In Red River County, the Ku Klux Klan vandalized a black school and chased the Presbyterian minister right out of the state. A group that was opposed to educating African Americans murdered a teacher in Falls County.

Talladega College was founded in 1867 by William Savery and Thomas Tarrant with the aid of General Wager Swayne and the Freedmen's Bureau. Shown here are normal graduates from 1884.

In Kentucky, one bureau agent was chased out by mobs in at least three different cities as he toured the state to inquire about the need for black schools. During his visit to one town, a white Methodist preacher became enraged when the agent suggested that his church work with the black citizens to start a school. "[He said] that it would not be safe for me to undertake any such thing, for the people there did not want any abolition Yankee to come among their Negroes to make them discontented. They did not need education . . . they had already high notions enough in their heads. With this he threw open the door and walked out of the room without ceremony, muttering as he went on the street."[3]

Government officials also participated in obstructing the development of black schools. In an 1869 report from the chairman of the Board of Trustees of Color Schools in Washington, D.C., W. Syphax details his difficulty in getting city officials to pay for needed repairs in black schools. He writes that "if the Mayor of Washington were not so backward in his compliance with the laws in reference to the support of colored schools," then funding for the repairs would have been approved long before.[4]

Despite the roadblocks, the number of schools for blacks grew swiftly, in part because of Freedmen's Bureau money and the power of the federal government. Some white missionary organizations also continued to help.

Credit for the work cannot be given to any one agency or group, however. It was an egalitarian effort whose success depended on all involved. Notwithstanding the obvious veil of racism that still blanketed the country and the hostilities expressed by some citizens regarding African American education, the task of building black schools may be the most cooperative peacetime effort undertaken by U.S. citizens. Americans—rich and poor, black and white—worked together to open schools to educate newly freed blacks.

In the five years following the Civil War, 4,239 schools for African Ameri-

cans were opened and more than 9,300 teachers were employed. The new
schools were flooded with more than 247,300 new students. African Americans were responsible for starting and sustaining 1,304 of these institutions,
and they purchased 592 schoolhouses. The Freedmen's Bureau donated 654
school buildings to the effort. Religious and missionary organizations made
significant contributions. The AMA, for example, established ten HBCUs,
including Fisk University (est. 1867) and Dillard University (est. 1869), and the
AME Church funded fourteen schools, among them Wilberforce University
(est. 1856) and Morris Brown College (est. 1881). The American Baptist Home
Missionary Society also created schools, while philanthropic organizations such
as the Slater Fund and Peabody Fund gave continuing support.

Dillard students just before the turn of the century. The school's mission was "to develop graduates who are broadly educated, culturally aware, concerned with improving the human condition,
and able to meet the competitive demands of a global and technologically advanced society."

CHRISTIAN DENOMINATIONS WERE IMPORTANT HBCU FOUNDERS

Black Clergy Leaders

Black ministers traditionally have been among the most visible and vocal leaders in the black community. Often founders and early leaders of HBCUs were members of the clergy.

When the Reverend H. P. Jacobs was a slave he was too small to work in the fields, so his job was to attend to a white man who was under his master's care. Jacobs used his time with the man to learn how to read and write. His craftiness paid off in 1856, when he escaped to Canada with his family in tow. Moreover, Jacobs accomplished this remarkable feat without using the Underground Railroad. Jacobs remained in Canada until the end of the Civil War and returned to Mississippi in 1866 to assume the pastorate of Pine Street Baptist Church in Natchez. (See page 21.)

The first annual Saint's Baptist Missionary Association convened on July 12, 1870, at King Solomon Baptist Church in Vicksburg, Mississippi. Jacobs was elected president at this first convention. He believed that a school was needed to educate black ministers who would then reeducate African Americans, who had been taught a perverted form of Christianity. He blamed the carnage and strife of the Civil War on the ignorance of white people who "were educated to believe that they were the peculiar and favored work of God's hands, and that the poor African race was born to be their slaves. That made them [white people] believe that a Negro had no rights that a white man was bound to respect." Jacobs's reference to blacks having no rights in the eyes of whites was taken directly from the Dred Scott decision of the Supreme Court in 1856.

For the next five years the Saint's Baptist Missionary Association continued to support the idea of opening a school to train ministers and teachers, but the task of raising the money was daunting. By 1875, the association had raised $1,547.08, which was kept in the Freedmen's

Bank. Even though the goal of Jacobs and the other black ministers of the convention was black self-sufficiency, a decisive blow was dealt to their dream of starting a school without the assistance of whites when the Freedmen's Bank defaulted amid the corruption of the Freedmen's Bureau. The $287.62 that was left was not enough to start a school, so Jacobs made the decision to join forces with northern Baptists. This union enabled the Saint's Baptist Missionary Association to unite with the American Baptist Home Mission Society, which by 1876 was successfully operating eight schools throughout the South. The American Baptist Home Mission Society contributed the $5,000 necessary to buy an abandoned U.S. Marine hospital that served as the first location of Natchez Seminary in 1877. The seminary eventually became Jackson State University. Because Jacobs was the guiding force behind the vision to start the school he is credited with being the founder of what is today one of the largest HBCUs.

Mordecai Johnson and Benjamin Mays were a part of a new generation of black ministers who were not only well versed in the traditions of the black church, but also trained theologians with stellar academic credentials. Johnson and Mays were also great leaders and administrators whose influence reached beyond the ivory towers of HBCUs and into the public sector and the international community.

Mordecai Johnson's mother said that God gave her the name Mordecai, after the man in the Bible who saved his people from annihilation in a hostile land. Later, when Johnson read the story in the Book of Esther he was inspired and felt that the Lord would use him to serve his people in a mighty way.

Johnson was a second-generation minister. By the time young Mordecai was born in 1890, his father was the pastor of Mount Zion Baptist Church in Johnson's hometown of Paris, Tennessee. His parents were firmly committed to Johnson obtaining a Baptist education. When Mordecai's Baptist high school burned down in 1904 his parents bypassed three other schools in Tennessee because they were affiliated with other churches. Lane College was Methodist, Knoxville College was Presbyterian, and LeMoyne was Congregationalist.

They instead chose Atlanta Baptist College, where Johnson would complete his high school and college studies, graduating with honors in 1911. Atlanta Baptist eventually would become Morehouse College. The year after Johnson's graduation John Hope, the first black president of Morehouse, hired Johnson as a teacher. Johnson was a quarterback on the football team, played on the first varsity basketball team at Morehouse, and wrote the words to the first school song. After receiving his call to the ministry, Johnson applied to Newton Theological Seminary in Massachusetts. He was denied admission because of his race, however. He settled instead for Rochester Theological Institute. During his time at Rochester, he became pastor of Second Baptist Church in Mumford, New York.

Johnson obtained his master of divinity degree at Harvard where he was given the esteemed honor of speaking at the commencement exercises of 1922. His rousing speech on "The Faith of the American Negro" put the world on notice that Johnson was a star on the rise. After the commencement address, Johnson turned down lucrative, high-profile positions to continue preaching at the First Baptist Church in Charleston, West Virginia, where he had become pastor. Among those extending him offers was Julius Rosenwald, who wanted to sponsor Johnson and send him around the country on speaking tours. Howard University also came knocking with the offer of the presidency, but since Johnson did not intend to leave the pastorate he did not want to be considered for the job. But the search committee, which included Colonel Theodore Roosevelt, drafted him because of his academic record, his leadership skills, and his status as an outsider who could mend some of the internal strife that had been developing at Howard. Johnson accepted the position, becoming the school's first African American president. During Johnson's legendary tenure at Howard he transformed "his law school" into a legal training ground that produced graduates who would change the legal landscape of race relations in

America. During Johnson's presidency, the university hospital at Howard produced 50 percent of all black doctors in the United States. Donations to the university from Congress and philanthropists skyrocketed. Johnson also recruited world-class faculty who themselves would make their mark in American history. One such individual was Benjamin E. Mays.

Johnson hired Mays as the dean of Howard's divinity school soon after Mays earned his Ph.D. from the University of Chicago's divinity school in 1934. Like Johnson, Mays was denied admission to Newton Theological Seminary despite being a Phi Beta Kappa graduate of Bates College in 1920. By the time Mays arrived at Howard, he had served as pastor of Shiloh Baptist Church in Atlanta for three years while he was teaching math, psychology, and religion at Morehouse. He had published *The Negro's Church* with fellow minister Joseph W. Nicholson in 1933. When Mays arrived at Howard the divinity school was not accredited. Under his leadership, in 1939 Howard became the second HBCU to have an accredited divinity school through the American Association of Theological Schools. When Mays left the divinity school to become the president of Morehouse College, the physical plant and the size of the faculty had greatly increased.

Mays spent twenty-seven years at Morehouse College. When he arrived in 1940 Morehouse was on the brink of financial ruin. Always prepared to rise to a challenge, Mays proclaimed during his acceptance speech that he would "serve this institution as if God Almighty sent me into the world for the express purpose of being the sixth president of Morehouse College." And serve he did, transforming Morehouse from a school that had no control of its own budget into a fully accredited institution that produced an alumni roster that rivaled that of Howard.

By 1944, during World War II, the enrollment at Morehouse was rapidly declining because of the draft. Mays devised and secured funding for a program that would allow gifted high school students to enter Morehouse as freshmen. Included in this class was Martin Luther King Jr. Coretta Scott King stated that King's acceptance of the call into ministry was due in large part to the example of Mays and how he used ministry as an intellectually respectable instrument of social change. When Mays spoke to the World Council of Churches Assembly in 1954, he testified, "It will be a sad commentary on our life and time if future generations can write that the last bulwark of segregation based on race and color was God's church."

Mays balanced preaching at small rural congregations with advising heads of state. President Jimmy Carter called Mays "my personal friend, my constructive critic and my close advisor." He conducted the Easter service on the campus of South Carolina State, where he graduated from high school, for twenty-five years. It was Mays who presided over the funeral of his former protégé Martin Luther King Jr. on the Morehouse campus in 1968. Mays was a great leader who built Morehouse into one of the best colleges in the United States. He once stated that "if Morehouse is not good enough for anybody, it's not good enough for Negroes." Most importantly, however, Mays was a man inspired by God to help people. His life mission was best expressed by the title of his last book, published when he was 86 years old, *Lord, the People Have Driven Me On.*

The Catholic Church

The Catholic Church's commitment to education in the United States can be traced back to 1789 with the founding of Georgetown University in Washington, D.C. Some 126 years later, that same commitment would extend to African Americans when Mother Katherine Drexel founded the only Catholic HBCU, Xavier University. (See page 427.)

Drexel and her two sisters helped start and fund schools for Native American children in the West from a hefty inheritance left by their father, Francis, and her sister and brother-in-law built a school for African American teenage boys near their order in Philadelphia. But Drexel wanted to do more. She joined a convent and devoted her life to helping Native Americans and African Americans. This calling was so strong that she was led to form a congregation of sisters who would help her in this quest. The order became the Sisters of the Blessed Sacrament, founded in December 1892 in Philadelphia. The sisters went south to build a school for African American teenage girls in Virginia. Drexel and her order also helped black parishes in Chicago, New York, Boston, and Columbus, Ohio, start schools.

Their work caught the attention of the archbishop of New Orleans, who invited her to come to Louisiana to open a school for African American youth. In 1915 Drexel bought an old college property. She named the future high school Xavier Academy in the hopes it would become a college where teachers would be trained to educate black children in Louisiana and throughout the South. Within two years Xavier became a normal school, and by 1925 Xavier had changed its name to Xavier University.

American Missionary Association

The American Missionary Association was founded in 1846 in Albany, New York, with goals of educating the masses, fostering equality of the races, and spreading a liberalized, tolerant form of Christianity. Among the organization's notable contributions is the creation of more than 500 schools and institutions of higher learning for African Americans. HBCUs founded by or with assistance from the AMA include Atlanta University, Avery Institute (now closed), Berea College (no longer considered an HBCU by the Department of Education because only 12 percent of its students are African American), Dillard University, Fisk University, Hampton University, Howard University, Huston-Tillotson College, LeMoyne-Owen College, Talladega College, and Tougaloo College.

The American Missionary Association's seed was planted in 1839 when several of its future founders banded together to secure the freedom of the illegally captured West Africans brought to the United States aboard the Spanish ship *Amistad*. The founders officially came

together at an 1845 missionary convention. They were staunch abolitionists who relinquished memberships with more influential missionary
organizations to establish one that vigorously engaged in antislavery
activities. Though the AMA was primarily white, blacks sat on the board
and worked to execute many AMA programs. Among the founding
leaders were New York City merchant and former *Amistad* committee
member Lewis Tappan; renowned abolitionist George K. Whipple;
Samuel Ringgold Ward; and the Reverend James Pennington, founder
of the Union Mission Society, a black benevolent organization.

The AMA was among the first benevolent societies to support
schools for the newly freed blacks in Port Royal, South Carolina, during
the Civil War. The organization worked to establish an educated black
leadership who could teach and uplift the masses of African Americans.
By 1879, AMA normal school and college graduates were educating
more than 150,000 southern black students. The organization had created 7,000 black teachers by 1888.

All of the AMA's primary and secondary schools were either taken
over as or absorbed by state government schools by the mid-1940s.
AMA-founded Fisk University and Talladega College became, respectively, the first and second black institutions of higher learning to
receive A ratings from the Southern Association of Colleges and Southern
Schools.

Throughout its history, the AMA also conducted large-scale educational and missionary efforts among Native American and Asian American immigrant communities. In 1987 the United Church Board for
Homeland Ministries of the United Church of Christ absorbed the AMA.

African Methodists

In November 1787, former slave Richard Allen, Absalom Jones, and
several other black Christians were praying in St. George's Methodist
Episcopal Church in Philadelphia when they were forcibly thrown out
because the area where they were praying was a whites-only section.

This incident led to a chain of events that resulted in the formation of a number of black Methodist Episcopal denominations that would found numerous historically black colleges and universities.

Since its founding in 1816 the African Methodist Episcopal Church concerned itself with providing housing for the poor and education for all black people. Although many within their own ranks were not educated, AME Church leaders knew that education would be the key to advancing the race as well as firming up the church's foundation. Educator Bishop Daniel Payne became instrumental in shaping those goals. He was the first bishop in the AME Church to have a formal education and was therefore inspired to ensure that all AME ministers had a firm educational foundation. To make this possible, Payne helped establish what would later become a required course of study for all AME Church ministers as an alternative to a seminary education, which he hoped all pastors would eventually obtain.

Payne founded Wilberforce University in Ohio in 1856. Not only was Wilberforce the first college owned and operated by African Americans, it was the first college in the world to be headed by an African American. Payne served as the school's president for the first sixteen years. Wilberforce was but the first of several colleges the AME Church would establish. AME schools still in existence include Morris Brown College, Allen University, Paul Quinn College, Shorter Junior College, and Edward Waters College.

The African Methodist Episcopal Zion Church was known as the "Freedom Church." Like the AME Church, the denomination was born out of the racial inequality embedded in the white-controlled Methodist Episcopal Church. Officially founded in 1820, the AME Zion Church counts many in its membership who openly fought against slavery. Some of these trailblazers were Sojourner Truth, Harriet Tubman, and Frederick Douglass. These and many others laid the foundation for equality as well as for educational liberation. The AME Zion Church founded two junior colleges: Hood Theological Seminary and Livingstone State University.

The black community within the United Methodist Episcopal Church wanted the freedom to worship in a way that celebrated their culture. It is this spirit that inspired Dr. Harry Van Buren Richardson to found the Interdenominational Theological Center (ITC). Richardson originated the idea for a theological hub while he was serving as president of Gammon Theological Seminary. Since the existing black seminaries each represented a single denomination, this idea was unprecedented. The purpose was to create an environment that raised Christian leaders to think globally and use their skills to help develop solutions to address social and moral crises. In 1958 Richardson's vision was realized with the chartering of ITC. Four denominations helped make this a reality— Baptist, United Methodist Episcopal, African Methodist Episcopal, and Christian Methodist Episcopal. Richardson served as the school's first president from 1959 to 1968. ITC now represents twenty-one denominations, including six core ones: Disciples of Christ (Christian Church), United Church of Christ, African Methodist Episcopal Zion, Lutheran, Episcopal, and Roman Catholic, as well as students who are nondenominational. Besides ITC, the black Methodist Church helped found the following schools: Bennett College, Bethune-Cookman College, Philander Smith College, Clark Atlanta University, Dillard University, Meharry Medical School, and the Gammon Theological Seminary.

Baptist Founders of HBCUs

The oldest black church in North America was a Baptist church begun by George Liele in Savannah, Georgia, in 1777. Although Liele started the First African Baptist Church under the auspices of the white Baptist denomination, the establishment of this church predated the worship services held by Richard Allen and the Free African Society in Philadelphia by fourteen years. A strong missionary fevor has always been preeminent among Baptist denominations. One of the most active groups involved in starting schools was the American Baptist Home Mission Society. The society was founded in 1832 to spread the gospel message in the new territories as the frontier moved west. This group took an interest in the condition of southern blacks at the beginning of the Civil War and became deeply committed to educating and evangelizing them. It was this drive that motivated Baptist organizations like the American Baptist Home Mission Society to found and support several historically back colleges and universities.

The year 1865 saw the death of legal slavery in the United States. That year two educational institutions opened for blacks with the assistance of the Baptist Church. Shaw University holds the distinction of being the first black college started in the South. The church provided aid to Henry Tupper, a white New England missionary, to train emancipated slaves to read and interpret the Bible. Several years after its founding as Raleigh Institute, the school was renamed after Minister Elijah Shaw, who contributed significantly to the school.

Also in 1865, on a site that was formerly a slave jail located in the former capital of the Confederacy, the American Baptist Home Mission Society, along with Dr. J. G. Binney, started training black students at the newly founded Richmond Theological Institute. The institute later merged with Wayland Seminary in Washington, D.C., Hartshorn Memorial College of Richmond, and Storer College of Harpers Ferry, West Virginia, to form the union of these schools in and around Virginia. Since its founding, Virginia Union has made a lasting impression on the spiritual life of African Americans. The seminary at Virginia Union alone is responsible for educating 10 percent of all blacks currently serving in ministry.

Baptists were busy in Georgia also. In 1867 the Augusta Institute opened its doors to a handful of young black men. Baptist minister William Jefferson White held classes in the basement of Springfield Baptist Church. Former slave Richard C. Coulter and the Reverend Edmund Turney, who also started a seminary in Washington, D.C., assisted Rev. White in teaching the students to read, write, and live according to the word of God. The school relocated to Friendship Baptist Church in Atlanta in 1879 and changed its name to Atlanta

Baptist Seminary. The school was renamed Morehouse College in 1913 to honor Henry L. Morehouse, corresponding secretary of the Atlanta Baptist Home Mission Society.

In 1870 the American Baptist Home Mission Society founded Benedict College in South Carolina, the seat of the southern states' rebellion. The school was named after Mrs. Bathsheba Benedict, who purchased a former slave plantation and converted it into a campus to educate freed slaves in Christian faith, academic excellence, and black heritage.

Florida Memorial College came about after the merger of two private black Baptist schools, Florida Baptist Institute, founded in 1879, and Florida Baptist Academy, established in 1892. The two institutions were committed to producing Christian leaders to make a positive impact on society. By the time the two schools merged in 1941 they had been fulfilling their missions successfully for more than half a century.

Spelman College is the lone institution started by Baptists for women. Initially a seminary, Spelman like its AU Center neighbor Morehouse was begun in the basement of a Baptist church. Two female missionaries sponsored by the Woman's American Baptist Home Mission Society came up with the idea to start a college for women after they conducted a study on the condition of former slaves in the South. Sophia B. Packard and Harriet E. Giles devoted much of their time to raising funds for the fledgling institution. In 1882 Packard and Giles met John D. Rockefeller Sr. at a church meeting while on a fundraising trip to Cleveland. Rockefeller emptied his wallet to support their cause and assured them of future support if they made good use of his donation. Three years later, on the third anniversary of the school's founding, Rockefeller appeared with his wife and mother-in-law, Lucy Henry Spelman, to observe what was made of his investment. Impressed with what he saw at the seminary, Rockefeller paid off the outstanding debt on the school's property.

Some of the most prominent HBCUs were founded through the missionary efforts of the Baptist Church. These schools have continued to produce great leaders both within the church and in the larger society.

Presbyterian Founders of HBCUs

The Presbyterian Church's commitment to education is inspired by a Bible verse that states, "And you should teach these things diligently to your children" (Deuteronomy 6:7). Presbyterians were one of the first denominations to have large numbers of members in the colonies. Usually the Presbyterian minister was appointed as schoolmaster. Education was considered essential to having a public that would fulfill its civic duties, exercise astute political responsibility, and adhere to devout religious allegiance. This philosophy led to the founding of schools and colleges. The first Presbyterian college was the College of New Jersey founded in 1746, which later became Princeton University.

By the nineteenth century, the Presbyterian Church established missions to reach out to African Americans. This included not only evangelical outreach but also the establishment of educational institutions. John Miller Dickey, pastor of Oxford Presbyterian Church in Oxford, Pennsylvania, had tried to get a black man into two different white theology schools only to be rejected by both. It was his lack of success with the white seminaries that led Dickey and his wife, Sarah Emlen Cresson, to found Ashmun Institute in 1854 under the auspices of the Presbyterian Church. The school was intended to contribute to "the elevation of an intellectual elite, divinely ordained, through whom would be exercised on the lower classes among their fellows, the saving grace of God's plan for redemption." The school was later renamed Lincoln University, one of only two antebellum HBCUs in the United States. Dickey, who was well respected and had considerable influence in the Oxford community, fell out of favor with local residents after founding the school. After two years of controversy, Dickey resigned his pastorate in 1856.

Issues of race, particularly slavery, would eventually fracture the Presbyterian Church and breed offshoot denominations. Nevertheless, the work of founding schools for African Americans continued despite the divisions that had sprung up. However, it wasn't until after the Civil War that another Presbyterian-sponsored HBCU was founded.

Two years after the conclusion of the Civil War two Presbyterian ministers, S. C. Alexander and W. L. Miller, founded Biddle Memorial Institute in North Carolina. Biddle would later become Johnson C. Smith University. That same year in Alabama, the Reverend Luke Dorland founded Scotia Seminary to prepare black women for careers in education and social work. In 1930 Scotia Seminary merged with Barber Memorial College and became Barber-Scotia College.

The Reverend Dr. Charles Allen Stillman petitioned the general assembly of the Presbyterian Church in 1874 to start a male counterpart to Scotia Seminary to educate the black men of Alabama for the ministry. The result was the creation of Stillman College. Although a charter was issued in 1874 the school didn't begin classes until 1876. Within those two years the Presbyterian Church in Tennessee founded another HBCU, Knoxville College, in 1875.

All of these institutions, with the exception of Lincoln, are still affiliated with the Presbyterian Church. The Presbyterian Church and donations from church members have kept some schools afloat in the midst of financial crises. Alternate ways of fundraising will become increasingly important, however, as revenues from the Presbyterian Church continue to decline.

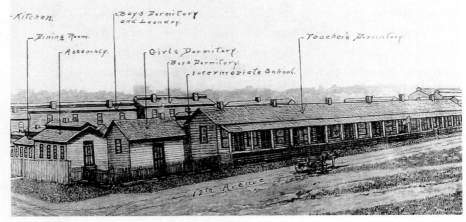

An early illustration of the Fisk School campus in 1866.

Higher Learning

One of the more lofty goals set by educators and African American communities themselves was the development of new institutions of higher learning for black students.

It is, however, difficult to separate the development of public preparatory and secondary schools from that of colleges and universities during the two decades following the war. There are two primary reasons for this. First, the Freedmen's Bureau was mandated to lend assistance to the various private organizations—churches, missionary groups, benevolent societies, philanthropists, and black communities themselves—that were starting up schools. The support and backing of a federal agency was particularly important because even with the defeat of the Confederacy, Southerners clearly were not going to acquiesce to integration. Also, segregation was still the norm among many private northern institutions; therefore, if African Americans were going to have any meaningful access to education, schools for their benefit would have to be created. Second, the vast majority of African Americans were not prepared for college-level instruction in 1865. In fact, only 5 percent of black Americans were able to read or write. In most cases, the black schools with "college" or "university" included in their names opened offering preparatory, secondary, and normal school training and added college courses as students progressed toward higher learning levels.

A Cooperative Effort

There is no one model of development for the multitude of HBCUs that began to spring up during the post–Civil War era, but the case of Talladega College highlights the way many schools depended on the combined efforts of the freedmen, missionary organizations, and the federal government for their beginnings. In November 1865, seven months after the war had ended, freedmen convened in Mobile, Alabama, to begin addressing the needs of former slaves.

Talk quickly focused on creating educational opportunities, and when convention attendees William Savery and Thomas Tarrant, both former slaves, returned home to Talladega they immediately set about opening a school for black children. After some planning, the black townspeople decided that classes would be held in the home of David White Sr. and taught by Leonard Johnson.

An undated photograph of Anderson Anatomical Hall on Meharry Medical College's South Nashville campus. The college, established in 1876, was made possible through the generous donations of the Meharry family.

The school quickly outgrew White's home, however, as the student body comprised black children from nine surrounding counties. To accommodate the students, a small group of African American residents pooled their money and purchased a site that housed an old carpentry shop. The shop was demolished and a school was constructed on the site. Shortly thereafter, residents requested that the Freedmen's Bureau help them locate a more qualified teacher. The bureau consulted the AMA, which in turn sent Mrs. C. M. Hopson, a white missionary from Cleveland, to take up the charge of educating the children.

By 1867, the students had outgrown their quarters again, so the AMA and the Freedmen's Bureau joined together to purchase an abandoned schoolhouse that originally had served as a white Baptist high school for males. Ironically, slaves had been used to construct the school in 1852 and it had served as a prison for Union Army soldiers during the war. The building was renamed Swayne Hall, in honor of Freedmen's Bureau officer General Wager Swayne.

Over the next two years, plans to officially charter a college evolved. The charter was completed in 1869 under the leadership of Rev. Henry Edward Brown, the first principal of Talladega.

Although it was labeled a college, most of the students attending Talladega during the first five years were mastering elementary-level skills. The curriculum allocated six months just to learning the alphabet; only then did students move on to the primary readers. While the process was unusually slow, Brown and the teachers at Talladega College had a very rational reason for their approach—many of the young people who attended the school returned home to teach family members and neighbors. The educators had seen how well-intentioned teachers with limited abilities had, through no fault of their own, passed along poor grammar and reading skills to large groups of students. The educators at Talladega were determined that their students would pass on proper knowledge.

The curriculum continued to evolve, however, and by 1880, Rev. Henry Swift Deforest was appointed president of the college. Under his guidance, Talladega implemented collegiate-level courses. The normal school preparatory department was phased out and the curriculum of the normal school was made more efficient. Curriculums within the Industrial Department (i.e., agricultural, printing, and domestic skills) were revamped, placing more emphasis on practical experience. Through this method, students were also able to work to pay for their tuition and board. Talladega conferred its first collegiate degrees in 1895.

A Federal Mandate

While Talladega College was started through the grassroots efforts of newly freed African Americans, Howard University (est. 1867) had a different sort of start. It was founded through the efforts of the all-white, AMA-affiliated First Congregational Society. Additionally, where Talladega is an example of an elementary-level school that evolved into a four-year college, Howard was conceived as a place of higher education for African Americans. The thirty society members who gathered in mid-November 1866 to discuss starting a theological seminary and normal school for freedmen had their sights set on higher education. This was made apparent quickly when the group trashed its original plan and began work on a university charter that offered broader studies. The new plan included a four-year college curriculum, a theological curriculum, and a medical school. By January 1867, a fifteen-member board was elected. The draft charter stated that the school would be named Howard University in honor of the Freedmen's Bureau commissioner, Oliver Otis Howard.

Because Howard would be located in the nation's capital, the charter had to be approved by Congress. That approval was hardly a given. As President, Andrew Johnson consistently blocked the efforts of liberal-leaning Republicans who tried to ensure the civil rights of African Americans. The charter prevailed, however, and on March 2, 1867, Howard University was established.

General Howard was appointed president and the school received a large portion of its funding from the Freedmen's Bureau.

GENERAL OLIVER OTIS HOWARD

Born November 8, 1830, Oliver Howard earned a degree in 1850 from Bowdoin College, located in Brunswick, Maine. In 1854 he graduated from West Point Academy in West Point, New York. Called the "Christian soldier," General Howard was a decorated military veteran who was awarded the Congressional Medal of Honor for losing his right arm in battle during the Civil War.

General Howard had a significant hand in the affairs of African Americans following the Civil War. He served as head of the Freedmen's Bureau from 1865 to 1872. As a founder and the third president of Howard University, the general was an industrious leader and tireless fundraiser who used his influence and life experience to establish the Washington, D.C.–based university as one of the preeminent institutions of higher learning for African Americans after the Civil War. It was as a Union general that he received the inspiration to start the school. Before fighting alongside General William Tecumseh Sherman during his infamous "march to the sea," Howard visited the Sea Islands off the coast of South Carolina. He witnessed firsthand the strides that had been made in the education of freed slaves through the Port Royal experiment.

In 1867 Howard enlisted the help of the Freedmen's Bureau, of which he was commissioner, and the First Congregational Church, where he was a member, to purchase land to start the university. Because of the unique challenges that faced a university for freed slaves, Howard continuously had to raise funds from organizations and northern philanthropists to construct buildings for classrooms and cover tuition for students who arrived on campus without the ability to pay. He devised creative ways to raise money, once working out an agreement with the inventor of the American building block. In the agreement, the new, cheaper, less sturdy brick would be made on campus, allowing students to work to pay their tuition and buildings to be constructed cheaply. Undeterred by financial challenges, Howard continued to be the fledgling university's greatest advocate and accepted the presidency in 1869 while still serving as commissioner of the Freedmen's Bureau. He relocated the bureau's headquarters from downtown Washington to the Howard campus to bring in rent for the school.

Drawing on his army experience, Howard brought military training to the university and trained students in the disciplines of West Point. As he guided the school through its difficult early years, Howard ensured that high academic standards were not compromised and that students were of high moral character. The General O. O. Howard house still stands on the university campus, serving as a monument to the general's mission and his commitment to academic excellence.

Overcoming Financial Hardships

The Freedmen's Bureau played an indispensable role in the founding of many schools for blacks, both large and small. But in April 1870, General Howard, who was simultaneously in charge of the bureau and president of Howard University, was brought before a congressional committee on charges that he had mishandled a large portion of the nearly $13 million in federal funds that had passed through the Freedmen's Bureau. Eventually, the general was cleared of any wrongdoing, but the end of the hearings did not spell the end of trouble for the Freedmen's Bureau.

The overarching goal of the bureau was to move newly freed African Americans toward self-sufficiency. In an effort to help reach this goal, the bureau established the Freedmen's Bank, a federal depository that held the receipts for numerous HBCUs, black-owned businesses, and individual accounts. The bank had branches in twenty cities, including Charleston, South Carolina, New Orleans, New York City, and Washington, D.C. That meant the banks' problems became problems of black businesses and schools.

In Jackson, Mississippi, a group of prominent black Baptist ministers from across the state convened in 1869 and began planning for the establishment of Natchez Seminary, a theological school that would prepare black Baptist ministers. Heading the group was the Reverend H. P. Jacobs, a literate former slave who, in 1856, forged a "pass" that allowed him and his family to escape to Canada. Jacobs was an extremely capable leader, but the process of raising money for the proposed school moved slowly. Most of the black Baptist congregations were extremely poor, and members were seldom able to donate to the building fund. There were also a number of setbacks in their fundraising efforts. In December 1871, for example, the group of ministers convened again to discuss location and funding proposals for the school. Jacobs represented the ministers who wanted to see the school built in Natchez, while the Reverend William Gray represented the ministers who wanted it located in Greenville. The Greenville proposal, which offered to give a half-acre of land and $1,000 to the building fund, was chosen. A year later, however, the Greenville group had failed to deliver on its promise.

The disappointed ministers immediately appointed a building committee and assigned the Reverend M. B. Black the task of collecting contributions for the school fund from the various churches. The ministers were again disappointed when on December 12, 1872, less than a week after being appointed to his post, Rev. Black informed the group that he had used the collected money to seek medical care for a sick family member. Black was removed from his post and the ministers decided to open an account with the Freedmen's Bank in Vicksburg, Mississippi.

Over the next two and a half years, all donations were deposited into the Freedmen's Bank. Jacobs and the other ministers felt confident that their dream for a school was within reach. In July 1875, however, the ministers discovered that Freedmen's Bank had defaulted. The group lost nearly $1,300 in savings. This third setback stalled the school efforts for another two years. Ultimately, the American Baptist Home Mission Society, an all-white northern missionary group, provided the ministers with enough money to finance the school. The ministers implemented a name change, and chartered the school as Jackson College. The college opened in 1877, the same year that marked the end of Reconstruction.

Reconstruction

Despite many obstacles facing black institutions of higher learning, 83 of the 108 HBCUs in existence today had opened their doors by the turn of the century. An even greater testament to the strength of HBCUs is the fact that fifty of those eighty-three schools were chartered following the close of the Freedmen's Bureau in 1873. Thirty-eight of those came into existence after the premature ending of Reconstruction. Among the schools founded before the termination of Reconstruction are Virginia Union

Thomas DeSaille Tucker was the first president and principal of Florida A & M (1887).

(1865), the all-male Morehouse College (1867), Fisk University (1867), Hampton University (1868), Meharry Medical College (1876), Huston Tillotson College (1876), and Florida A & M (1877).

In retrospect, the end of the Reconstruction period—with federal support for the freed slaves—probably had an even more devastating effect on the development of black colleges and universities than the closing of the Freedmen's Bureau. While it is true that the bureau was assigned the specific task of assisting and advocating for black schools, the federal government was still engaged in ensuring the civil rights of African Americans following the bureau's close. Additionally, black students were studying law in greater numbers, and the presence of African Americans in elected state and federal offices meant there were politicians representing the interests of black citizens. In South Carolina, for example, black representatives comprised the majority of the legislature in 1872. Five years later, however, the Republican Party abandoned Reconstruction as a part of a presidential election deal, and the civil rights of African Americans were essentially forfeited as a result.

The 1876 presidential election was a hotly contested run between Democratic candidate Samuel J. Tilden and Republican candidate Rutherford B. Hayes. The race ended in a tie, but in a bid to retain control of the White House, Republicans made a compromise with southern Democrats to motivate them to concede the election. Hayes would pull federal troops out of the South and give the former slave states more autonomy in handling their race issues.

No longer under the microscope of federal lawmakers, many southern congresses began to invoke state's rights claims, passing "separate but equal" segregation legislation. Under these new laws, institutions that received state funds were in danger of losing their appropriations if they either unwittingly or knowingly violated the legislation. This is exactly what happened during an 1887 conflict between Atlanta University and the state of Georgia.

Founded in 1867, Atlanta University began receiving an annual appropriation of $8,000 from the Georgia legislature in 1871. In conjunction with the funding, special committee inspectors were dispatched annually to review the school. During a visit in 1887 several of the inspectors took notice of what had always been the case—children of the university's white professors and administrators attended the school. The inspectors claimed that the presence of whites was a violation of state funding laws, because the university's annual appropriation was reserved for schools with student bodies that were exclusively black. Not only did Georgia lawmakers revoke the funding, state representative W. C. Glenn introduced a bill that sought to punish university trustees, officers, and teachers for misuse of funds. The proposed legislation requested a fine of $1,000 or six months' jail time for the university official. The bill passed the house and went to the senate. The senate modified the measure, linking funding to stringent segregation rules. Ultimately, neither version of the bill was ratified, but the action of the Georgia Congress was a sign of a swiftly spreading Jim Crow sentiment.

Vocational classes were an important element of the early training at HBCUs. These Voorhees students are learning how to wait tables (circa 1900).

When the federal government abandoned Reconstruction, it removed the buffer that had been erected between hostile southern legislatures and black citizens. The civil rights and educational gains of the previous two decades rapidly evaporated. Missionaries who had promoted the ideas of liberal arts education and equality for African Americans soon fell out of favor with federal government officials. Worse yet, the church funds that had helped to establish numerous HBCUs were dwindling. As a result, black colleges and universities were forced into a new phase of survival.

As white Southerners began to exert more influence among federal lawmakers, federal funds were increasingly awarded to HBCUs that promoted vocational training over liberal arts education. Northern philanthropists and foundations such as the Slater and Peabody funds funneled their money toward vocational schools like Hampton (est. 1868), which advertised in its brochure that "no classics are taught," and Tuskegee (est. 1881). Foundation administrators reasoned that it was better to support southern whites' limited vision for black education than to destroy all possibility for it by force-feeding a liberal philosophy to the powers that be. In addition, many of the northern foundations that were tied to big industry saw an advantage in supporting schools with industrial and mechanical curricula over those focusing on liberal arts. After all, they would be investing in the training of laborers who might one day work for their companies.

The industrial school philosophy was a major shift from the classic liberal arts curriculums that had been promoted and instituted by northern missionaries and abolitionists. These early pioneers of black education, especially those who were black, did not accept the idea that African Americans

Young men learning a trade in the broom-making department of Prairie View State Normal and Industrial College in Texas.

Talladega sweing class, 1928.

The auto-mechanics class at Prairie View, early 1900s.

At Central State University, many young women learned millinery skills.

The machine shop of Langston University, circa 1900.

were inherently inferior. They believed that, given the chance, oppressed African Americans would prove themselves as capable intellectually as white Americans.

The powerful political arm-twisting following the demise of Reconstruction forced even the most broad-minded HBCU presidents to develop industrial programs at the expense of the liberal arts curriculums at their schools. This agenda was pushed despite the fact that the vast majority of black college students chose liberal arts and professional majors over technical pursuits. Students in the technical curriculums were taught the fundamentals of reading, writing, and mathematics, but the bulk of their educational efforts were spent learning vocational skills such as agriculture, animal husbandry, domestic care, laundry services, tailoring, or metalwork.

PRODUCING SCHOLARS AND
PUBLIC INTELLECTUALS

Since the dawn of this nation, African Americans have been viewed as intellectually deficient. In *Notes on the State of Virginia,* Thomas Jefferson declared that blacks were "in reason much inferior . . . and that in imagination they are dull, tasteless, and anomalous." The concept of black inferiority was etched into the United States Constitution when, for the purpose of population counts for elections, each black was to be counted as three-fifths of a person.

The black university has traditionally been the center of intellectual activity. Almost from their inception, HBCUs have produced scholars and intellectuals who have shaped public opinion and showcased their cognitive prowess despite the dominant culture's insistence that such a concept could not exist. Any factual discussion of the scholars and public intellectuals that came from black colleges must begin before the abolition of slavery. Blacks' ability to learn, think, and speak for themselves was one of the greatest weapons used by opponents of slavery to demonstrate the inherent equality between the races.

Samuel Eli Cornish was a man of means and an early example of African American ability. He shaped public opinion as the founder and pastor of New York's first African American Presbyterian church in 1822 and cofounder of the nation's first black newspaper, *Freedom's Journal,* in 1827. Cornish and partner John Russwurm used *Freedom's Journal* to offer an alternate view of the misconceptions of African Americans being propagated in the New York press. This was a matter of life and death—in antebellum America race riots could be sparked in response to negative stories about blacks in white newspapers. *Freedom's Journal* served as a veritable clearinghouse of black intellectualism with its editorials and special features, such as James Forten's "Letters from a Man of Colour." But it was Cornish's work as an officer of the American Missionary Association that connected him to HBCUs. Cornish's ideas help shape the mission of the AMA, which founded eleven black colleges.

W. E. B. DuBois's intellectual and scholarly achievements did much to dispel doubts about the veracity of the black mind. DuBois was valedictorian of his integrated high school in Massachusetts in 1844. Unable to attend Harvard, he accepted a scholarship to Fisk University and almost immediately began to demonstrate that the pen was mightier than the sword. One of his earliest essays of note was written while he was still a student at Fisk. Written in 1887, "An Open Letter to the Southern People" came at a time when the gains of Reconstruction were being systematically dismantled through government legislation and violence. The essay was a vociferous attack on Jim Crow laws. It called for whites to exercise civilized conduct and end the barbarism directed toward blacks. DuBois's experiences in Nashville while attending Fisk forever changed his perspective on race relations and shaped his lifelong commitment to the eradication of racial and economic oppression of colored peoples the world over. After graduating from Fisk, DuBois went on to become the first African American to earn a doctorate from Harvard.

Alain Locke, who studied at Harvard, Oxford, and the University of Berlin, was the first African American Rhodes scholar. Locke chaired the philosophy department at Howard for almost forty years, until his retirement in 1953. With the publication of *The New Negro* in 1925, Locke was responsible for changing the way the world viewed African American literature and art. Locke was the foremost interpreter of the Harlem Renaissance and considered himself a "philosophical midwife" to black artists and intellectuals. Locke was also a leader of the adult education movement, working with the American Association for Adult Education and the Carnegie Corporation. He served as president of the American Association for Adult Education from 1946 to 1947. Locke undertook all of these laudable intellectual achievements while balancing his work as a professor and department chair at an HBCU.

Mordecai Johnson, chosen to become Howard's first black president in 1926, inherited a faculty that included some of the great minds in the African American intellectual community. Many of these men were not allowed the academic freedom that they desired under the leadership of Howard's white presidents, but flourished under Johnson's leadership. Carter G. Woodson, the Harvard-educated founder of Negro History Week (which evolved to Black History Month in the 1970s), author of *The Education of the Negro Before 1861* and founder of the *Journal of Negro History*, became a dean at Howard in 1919. Now hailed as the father of black history, Woodson resigned a year later, when the president, the Reverend J. Stanley, did not allow him to teach a course in African American history.

This same president had denied Locke's earlier request to teach a course in race relations. Johnson was determined not to make the same mistakes. He oversaw the development of the law school from a "dummies retreat" into a world-class department that, under the leadership of Charles Hamilton Houston, produced esteemed alumni like Thurgood Marshall. Johnson also brought in intellectual heavyweights such as William Leo Hansberry, the father of African studies.

Hansberry developed a course of study in ancient African history that was diametrically opposed to the scholarship of his contemporaries. Prevailing wisdom in the ivory towers of American colleges was that African culture was not worthy of serious academic examination. Hansberry, who received his M.A. in history from Harvard, never obtained a doctorate because no schools offered doctorates in African studies. He started the country's first African studies program in 1954. Hansberry remained at Howard until his retirement in 1959. As a result of Hansberry's work, African studies is one of the most popular majors for black students at predominantly white institutions.

Horace Mann Bond spent time at five different HBCUs, serving as president of two. His tenure as president of Lincoln University, Pennsylvania, was groundbreaking, as he was the school's first black president and an alumnus of the class of 1923. Bond was president of Fort Valley State from 1939 to 1945. He also taught at Fisk and Dillard and chaired the education department at Atlanta University. For over thirty years, he was a champion for equality in education for black students. Like his predecessor, Booker T. Washington, Bond was responsible for increasing donations to black schools from wealthy philanthropists. Much of Bond's scholarly research examined the economic and sociological factors that affect academic performance. His published works included *The Education of the Negro in the American Social Order* and *Negro Education in Alabama: A Study in Cotton and Steel*. In 1946 during his second year as president of Lincoln, Bond awarded an honorary degree to Albert Einstein. Bond's autobiography is appropriately titled *Black Scholar*.

Sufficient mention of every scholar and public intellectual who has graced an HBCU campus would fill volumes. Names like Aaron Douglas, the Reverend H. P. Jacobs, Benjamin Mays, and Nathan B. Young come to mind, to name a few. History has demonstrated that black colleges and universities consistently have produced some of the best and brightest intellectuals of the last two centuries.

A Powerful Voice for Industrial Training

The movement toward better funding of vocational colleges did not hurt all HBCUs, however. In the case of Tuskegee University, founder and educator Booker T. Washington had long emphasized industrial and vocational training over liberal arts curriculums. In his renowned Atlanta "Compromise" speech, Washington warned blacks, "Our greatest danger is that in the great leap from slavery to freedom we may overlook the fact that the masses of us are to live by the productions of our hands, and fail to keep in mind that we shall prosper in proportion as we learn to dignify and glorify common labour and put brains and skill into the common occupations of life."[5]

Washington's appeals to black educators pleased benefactors and influential white Southerners who believed that blacks should aspire to nothing more than agricultural, domestic, and skilled-labor jobs. This ideal—known as the Hampton-Tuskegee model because the two schools pioneered the HBCU industrial education curriculum—became the educational barometer against which all other HBCUs were compared when benefactors and politi-

Dillard students in home economics class, 1907.

cians considered which schools to fund. Those with curriculums closest to those of Hampton and Tuskegee received the greatest amount of funding.

A good deal of Washington's public rhetoric may well have been espoused for the express purpose of increasing the endowment at Tuskegee. For example, though Washington promoted the virtues of working the land and earning a living through manual labor, he also admitted that Tuskegee was not sending students out into the world simply to become laborers. What he endeavored to create were teachers who could go among the masses of uneducated blacks and, through example and training, impart basic life and trade skills. In fact, the first name given to the school highlighted teaching, not a vocational curriculum: the university was originally called the Normal School for Colored Teachers at Tuskegee.

Privately, Washington made it clear to his students that he did not expect them to end their higher education pursuits upon leaving Tuskegee. One former Tuskegean recalls the educator telling students that "This school, while I live, is not for professionals [or] high learning. This school will teach you a trade

Shown here with students, celebrated scientist George Washington Carver joined Tuskegee as head of the agriculture department in 1896.

and help you to go to the higher learning schools [and] get a higher education, because you will have a skilled trade to earn it with." In some ways, Washington was ahead of his time as an educator and college administrator. Under his guidance, Tuskegee became the first HBCU founded solely by African Americans, as well as the first to employ an all-black faculty and administration.

As a young man, Washington was shaped by an education based on manual labor ideology. Determined to enroll at Hampton Institute, in 1872 Washington left his home and his job in the coal mines of Malden, West Virginia, and walked nearly 500 miles to Hampton, Virginia. He arrived at the school hungry, extremely dirty, and, as he was broke, uncertain how he would pay his tuition if admitted. He pleaded his case, and after some consideration, headmistress Mary F. Mackie assigned him a custodial job and admitted him to the institute. It was there that Washington, like many other newly freed men, learned the basic life skills that had been denied him as a slave.

"The matter of having meals at regular hours, of eating on a tablecloth, using a napkin, the use of the bath-tub and of the tooth-brush, as well as the use of sheets upon the bed," were all new concepts that Washington encountered during his days at Hampton.[6]

In developing the curriculum at Tuskegee, Washington relied heavily on what he had learned as a student and during his subsequent years teaching at Hampton under the direction of its founder, President Samuel Chapman.

Washington arrived in Tuskegee, Alabama, in June 1881, at the request of the black townspeople who recently had secured a $2,000 annual appropriation from the state to hire instructors to teach their children. While Washington's name and educational philosophy became almost singularly linked to the school's founding, it was the political savvy and educational desires of the black residents that secured the initial financing for Tuskegee.

In 1880 Wilbur F. Foster, a former Confederate colonel, was running for state senate on the Democratic ticket. He faced a tight race against his Republican opponent, yet Foster became convinced he would win the race if black voters cast their ballots for him. This was a safe prediction since the black residents of Macon County outnumbered whites by nearly three to one. But most blacks were inclined to vote Republican. It was, after all, the party of Abraham Lincoln. Foster reached out to Lewis Adams, a prominent African American leader and member of the Republican Negro Congress, and asked how he could win over black voters. Adams told Foster that the black residents needed a school. Adams promised to help deliver the black vote if Foster promised to secure funds for black schools once in office. Foster won, and the following year the Alabama state legislature approved an annual appropriation.

The state appropriation could be used only to cover salaries, however, so when Washington arrived in town he also was given the task of finding a location for the school. The educator found a run-down shanty, which was located near a dilapidated church owned by black Methodists. Initially, the buildings were in such disrepair that whenever it rained the pupils were drenched by water coming in through the roof.

The conditions under which Washington and his students labored were typical of the circumstances that many freedmen faced during the early days of black education. But in each case, both the students and the instructors persevered. The story was no different at Tuskegee. On the day that the school opened, a large crowd of hopeful students gathered outside the schoolhouse. Washington accepted only about thirty pupils. His prerequisites for admission were that the students had to be at least 15 years of age and possess some amount of previous education. Many of the students he chose were public school teachers hoping to improve their skills.

Three months into his new educational endeavor, Washington discovered that a nearby plantation was for sale, but the black community of Tuskegee had no money with which to buy the property. Purchasing the property would put Washington and the black citizens of Tuskegee one step closer to their goal of building a first-class industrial school, however, so the educator wrote Hampton Treasury General J. F. B. Marshall and requested a personal loan of $250. Marshall agreed and the money was used as a down payment on the property. The school was promptly relocated to the plantation.

Although the new campus did not yet possess the physical plant, livestock, or equipment necessary to implement the industrial curriculums that Washington envisioned, the educator began introducing his students to the program in small ways. To begin, he employed some of the students to turn the cabins into classrooms. Others he assigned to clear the land and prepare it for crop planting. From this first effort, Washington began implementing the industrial, agricultural, and vocational curriculums that made him and Tuskegee famous among some circles and infamous among others.

As the school grew, Tuskegee students were taught shoe making, carpentry, saw milling, cooking, and brick making, among other vocations. The work provided students with a means to earn their $10 annual tuition. Some of the enterprises were successful enough to produce income for the school. Brick making was one such business, and the money earned from that effort was used to expand the facilities and curriculums at Tuskegee.

Students did more than simple labor, however. They were expected to learn how to run the business aspects of their respective vocations. They also learned how to keep account of expenditures and receipts, as well as how to purchase the correct equipment and keep it operating properly. Of course, basic reading, writing, and arithmetic were also part of the curriculum.

The Tuskegee Machine

By 1893, Tuskegee had grown from a school of thirty students and one teacher to 600 students and thirty-eight professors. In addition, the state had increased

Booker T. Washington, the founder of Tuskegee, was a staunch supporter of vocational training.

its annual appropriation to $3,000, and the Slater Fund had given a restricted grant of $1,000 for the development of the industrial program. Most impressive was that the school had amassed 1,400 acres of land, twenty buildings, and substantial amounts of livestock, equipment, and property totaling $180,000 in value. The quality of the faculty was also improving, with a good number of the teachers graduating from Hampton and Fisk. Prominent scientist George Washington Carver joined the faculty in 1896.

As head of the agriculture department, Carver elevated the curriculum to scientific study. He and the students introduced many trailblazing techniques to the field of agriculture. Carver and Washington also lobbied the state congress to designate the agriculture department as a research center.

By the beginning of the twentieth century, Tuskegee had become one of the most renowned and best-funded HBCUs, and Washington had become so powerful that his endorsement or disapproval could prevent individual educators from receiving philanthropic grants or entire universities from being

W. E. B. DuBois was a strong advocate of a liberal arts education for African Americans.

funded by top foundations. John Hope, the first African American president of Morehouse College (then Atlanta Baptist Seminary), discovered the power of the "Tuskegee Machine." Hope, who assumed the presidency of Morehouse in 1906, inherited a substantial challenge: the college was on the verge of financial ruin.

The college president solicited financial support from Andrew Carnegie, John D. Rockefeller, and other philanthropists who had long supported HBCUs. All of them denied his request. In dire straits, Hope spoke with Booker T. Washington and asked him to intercede on behalf of Morehouse. Washington agreed and donations began to pour in "as if by magic."[7] The financially challenged school even received funding for Sale Hall, a new academic building.

For many HBCU educators and administrators, the situation at Morehouse clearly signaled that the industrial training philosophy had become the only black educational bandwagon upon which many philanthropists and legislators were willing to ride. Neither Tuskegee nor Washington was free from criticism, however. Both were squarely attacked by a number of African American intellectuals. Chief among these critics was W. E. B. DuBois.

Staunchly rejecting the philosophy put forth by Washington, DuBois argued that African Americans should not be limited to one type of education. DuBois believed in "the higher education of a Talented Tenth who through their knowledge of modern culture could guide the American Negro into a higher civilization." He believed that without such erudite leaders African Americans would always be at the mercy of whites.

DuBois, who was teaching at Atlanta University when Hope appealed to Washington, was outraged by the Tuskegee president's power-mongering and even angrier at the Morehouse leader for setting the power play in motion. He vehemently denounced, both in writing and in speeches, the Hampton-Tuskegee model. He was particularly concerned that so many HBCUs seemed to adopt the model in the name of expediency. In his paper *The Negro Artisan,* DuBois listed ninety-eight HBCUs that offered industrial curriculums by 1900.

HBCU-TRAINED SCIENTISTS

From the fields of Alabama to the edges of outer space, HBCUs have played a major role in fortifying great minds that have contributed to numerous developments in the sciences. Botanist George Washington Carver, astronaut Ronald McNair, and physicist Julian Earls defied the odds and refuted the notion that science is an Achilles' heel for African Americans.

Perhaps the most well known black scientist associated with an HBCU is George Washington Carver. Before he arrived at Tuskegee, where he would become internationally known, Carver already had established himself in plant pathology and mycology as an assistant botanist at Iowa State University. Carver was Iowa State's first black student and its first black faculty member. When Carver joined the Tuskegee faculty in 1896 he brought with him a wealth of information that he used not only to educate his students but also to improve the agrarian Alabama economy while training local farmers in modern methods of agricultural efficiency. He developed new ways to improve soil and increase crop yields. Carver paid particular attention to nitrogen levels in soils, which led to the work he pioneered with the cow pea and the peanut. Although this work would ultimately make Carver famous, eminence could not have been further from Carver's goal of improving people's lives through science and education. Carver created over 100 products from over a dozen plants native to the South. These products created alternative revenue streams from crops other than cotton, which in turn helped to improve the economic vitality of the region.

A standout athlete in high school, Ronald McNair turned down a football scholarship to Howard to attend North Carolina A & T in 1967. His reasons were threefold. First, his brother attended A & T; second, A & T offered physics; and third, he was afraid to stray too far from his native South Carolina. His inclination to stay close to home is ironic given that he would one day defy gravity, soar through the earth's atmosphere, and become only the second African American in space.

From 1967 to 1971 McNair was a presidential scholar at North Carolina A & T. More than a priggish academic, McNair was an accomplished saxophonist who played in campus clubs to earn spending money. He pledged Omega Psi Phi fraternity, and in his junior year he earned a black belt in karate. All of his extracurricular activities caused his grades to slip, but his academic advisor saw promise in McNair and challenged him to do better. McNair reluctantly partook in a physics exchange program at MIT during his junior year. In 1978, just seven years after graduating magna cum laude from A & T, McNair was chosen for the astronaut program at NASA. Tragically, after logging 191 hours in space, McNair died in the space shuttle *Challenger* explosion in 1986.

McNair's colleague at NASA Dr. Julian Earls began his road to distinction on the campus of Norfolk State University in 1960. When he and fellow Norfolk State student Zenobia Gaines got married after their sophomore year, Earls didn't have a permanent job, a car, or money in the bank. Nevertheless, his meager beginnings did not deter him from his studies or his desire to innovate. At the end of his junior year Earls and nine other students chartered Norfolk State's first chapter of Kappa Alpha Psi fraternity. He graduated with honors with a degree in physics in 1964.

Since leaving Norfolk State Earls has committed to creating opportunities for black students majoring in science and technology and for research programs at the black colleges that train them. In 1983 he and a group of black scientists and technology professionals founded the Development Fund for Black Students in Science and Technology. Each member commits to contributing a minimum of $1,000 per year for life, which will result in a scholarship endowment of $1 million for black students who are enrolled at HBCUs. One of the group's primary objectives is to demonstrate its commitment to black schools and black students in the sciences.

Earls also has used his position at NASA to direct lucrative research grants to black colleges. His advocacy has created opportunities for future black scientists and increased the stature of black science and technological programs at historically black colleges and universities.

Baptist missionaries Sophia B. Packard and Harriet E. Giles opened a school for black women in the basement of an Atlanta church in 1881. This modest start was the seed for Spelman University, sister school to Morehouse.

Another Model for Learning

Despite the pressures for HBCUs to adopt industrial or agricultural curriculums, some colleges were able to solicit substantial sponsorship while developing a liberal arts curriculum. Spelman University, the sister school to Morehouse, was one such institution. Founded in 1881 as the Atlanta Baptist Female Seminary by Baptist missionaries Sophia B. Packard and Harriet E. Giles, Spelman furthered the cause of liberal arts education even though the school opened well after the end of Reconstruction. When the school opened in the basement of the Friendship Baptist Church in Atlanta, eleven young women showed up for the first day of classes.

Like most HBCUs, Spelman had extremely humble beginnings. Packard and Giles began the school with just $100 to finance their endeavor, but almost immediately they gained a staunch ally and financial supporter in John D. Rockefeller.

The philanthropist emptied his pockets for the school at an Ohio fund-raiser in 1882 and once the school acquired a campus, he paid off the property debt. Black supporters contributed more than $5,000 to help satisfy this debt as well. Rockefeller later brought his wife (a Spelman at birth), sister-in-law, and mother-in-law to visit the campus. Rockefeller's mother-in-law, Mrs. Lucy Henry Spelman, made several significant contributions to the school. In 1884 the name of the school was changed in honor of his wife's family, longtime abolitionists and supporters of the Underground Railroad. In 1887 the Rockefellers donated $40,000 to finance the construction of Rockefeller Hall. The Slater Fund was also a significant contributor, underwriting the cost of curriculum and department development.

Meanwhile, most other liberal arts HBCUs—including Spelman's brother school Morehouse, which never received significant support from the Rockefellers—were struggling to get a small percentage of the philanthropic support that Spelman attracted. The fact that Spelman is a college for women may have helped the school attract donors. Apparently, educated African American women did not present the same perceived threat to white society as black men.

A Bridge Between the Two

Educator and activist Mary McLeod Bethune founded the all-girls Daytona Educational and Industrial Training School in 1904, now Bethune-Cookman College.

By the turn of the century, most of the benevolent societies, churches, and missionary organizations that had provided financial and human resources to help establish HBCUs had ceased opening new ones. While a handful of religious organizations such as the AME Church and the AMA were still closely affiliated with their schools, most were relinquishing their involvement to private boards of trustees or state educational boards. Individual missionaries were still committed to the cause of higher education for African Americans, however. Educator-activist Mary McLeod Bethune was one such person. In 1904 Bethune founded the all-girls Daytona Educational and Industrial Training School for Negro Girls (now the coeducational Bethune-Cookman College) in Daytona Beach, Florida. The school was the only

Girls enrolled in a sewing class at the Daytona Educational and Industrial Training School for Negro Girls, which later became Bethune-Cookman College in 1931.

educational institution founded by an African American woman to evolve into an accredited four-year college. The incredible vision and drive of the devoted educator were almost single-handedly responsible for the success of the college.

Bethune's desire to become a missionary educator was first nurtured during her time as a student at the Presbyterian Missionary School in Mayesville, Florida. It was later solidified by her experiences as a student at both the Scotia Seminary in Concord, North Carolina, and at the Moody Bible Institute in Chicago. But by the time Bethune was ready to start the Daytona Educational and Industrial Training School, the religious-based funding sources that she might have relied on for support were no longer available. Corporate philanthropists and foundations had become the new sources for funding. This change presented two caveats for Bethune. First, philanthropists and foundations were much more hands-off in the school charter and development process than the missionary boards had been, but they were often much more restrictive and dictatorial about how their donations could be allocated. Second,

The Talladega Women's Rifle Club, 1895.

Bethune had spent a good portion of her life in the company of missionaries, but she had no personal relationships with philanthropists or foundation trustees.

What Bethune did possess, however, was the ability to realize grandiose dreams through practical hard work. And she could inspire people of any background to see the possibilities of her vision. Her plan for opening a school and developing it into a successful liberal arts and vocational college was rooted in big dreams, hard work, and inspiration.

In many ways the approach used by Bethune at Daytona Educational shifted the missionary-HBCU paradigm. Instead of receiving assistance from missionaries, the school and its African American students became missionaries to the surrounding community. In that sense, through them the work of the early northern missionaries had come full circle. Through Daytona Educational they had realized their belief that the standards of Christian thrift and compassion could become governing values among former slaves and their children. The new paradigm would serve Daytona Educational—soon to become Bethune-Cookman College—well. The school would be a stabilizing force for the Daytona African American community as the United States entered and recovered from World War I. Among its many activities, the school administration would lead a dangerous yet successful voters' rights campaign. The activism exhibited by Bethune, her staff, and her students was typical of the political activism sparking on HBCU campuses throughout the country in the years following World War I.

LEGISLATIVE INITIATIVES

The National Land Grant Colleges Act, commonly referred to as the first Morrill Act of 1862, revolutionized American higher education. It was one of the first congressional acts to benefit from the amendments passed in the years following the Civil War. With federal funds being distributed to the states for the purpose of making higher education available to everyone, especially freed slaves, blacks expected to reap some of the benefits. Because the states did not admit black students to these new land-grant institutions, however, blacks would have to wait another twenty-eight years before they could partake in state-funded educational institutions. Alcorn State University was the lone exception. Founded in 1871 in Mississippi, Alcorn was the only black school started under the first Morrill Act.

As Reconstruction came to a close and wealthy planters regained control of local and state governments and the lands seized during the Civil War, federal funds intended to be used to educate all of the South's residents were funneled to whites-only institutions. The Supreme Court ruled in 1882 that the Civil Rights Act of 1864 was unconstitutional and that the Fourteenth Amendment could only be violated if a state directly discriminated against individuals.

The Morrill Act of 1890 sought to redress the failings of the first. This second act required states to provide land-grant institutions that benefited both races in the segregated educational system. Nineteen HBCUs were founded as a result of this legislation, although the black schools that were started did not grant college degrees. The U.S. Bureau of Education undertook a study in 1915, revealing that of the thirty-three black schools providing college-level curricula, a sizable amount of the instruction at these schools was at the elementary and secondary school level. These institutions were designed to be social equalizers that would give blacks the opportunity to rise above the vestiges of two and a half centuries of slavery, but the funding required to make them a vital link to the economic prosperity of the nation continues to be a struggle to this day.

Although the traditional mission for land-grant institutions has been teaching, research, and cooperative extension, these schools have evolved to include agricultural engineering, landscape architecture, and research in the natural sciences, among many other fields of study. To ensure that land-grant institutions and HBCUs in general benefit from the federal programs and research that have made schools like Ohio State and MIT great, every administration includes a White House Initiative on Historically Black Colleges and Universities, which is designed to serve as a liaison between the executive branch and HBCUs. The president appoints a President's Board of Advisors on Historically Black Colleges and Universities, which is composed of sitting presidents from HBCUs, business and financial leaders, representatives of other higher-education institutions and private foundations, and secondary school administrators. The White House Initiative is administered through the Office of the Secretary of Education, who under the Bush administration is Rod Paige. An alumnus of Jackson State University, Paige served as dean of the College of Education at Texas Southern University before assuming the role of secretary of education.

Although Executive Order 13256, signed by President George W. Bush, states that the goal of the White House Initiative is "to strengthen the capacity of historically black colleges and universities to provide the highest quality education, and to increase opportunities for these institutions to participate in and benefit from Federal programs, as do other colleges and universities," serious inequities between HBCUs and majority institutions remain. According to Dr. N. Joyce Payne, director of the Office for the Advancement of Public Black Colleges of the

National Association of State Universities and Land-Grant Colleges, "the Initiative has failed to treat inequality as a deliberate and systematically applied aberration in the distribution of Federal funds. And, most importantly, it has failed to create a progressive agenda designed to radically transform black colleges and the communities they serve as instruments of social and economic change."

Black state institutions continue to receive significantly less than their white counterparts. Although *Brown v. Board of Education* struck down legal segregation half a century ago, the uneven distribution of wealth continues to plague state and federal governments when it comes to resourcing historically black colleges and universities.

4

❧ · ❧

VOICES OF A PEOPLE

In search of self-definition, students and faculties of historically black colleges and universities begin to deconstruct the white patriarchal systems and philosophies that govern their schools.

BY THE TIME THE United States entered World War I in 1917 ninety-five HBCUs had come into existence. These schools were quickly creating a black middle class, which boldly began rejecting the white patriarchal system that controlled most HBCUs. W. E. B. DuBois vehemently rejected the premise that African Americans should be relegated to vocational training, opining that the educational plan promoted by Booker T. Washington was "unnecessarily narrow," and that Washington represented "in Negro thought the old attitude of adjustment and submission."[1] DuBois's uncompromising conviction became a battle cry for many educated blacks, who began demanding that they receive a greater voice in defining the curriculums and the social and cultural atmospheres of their schools.

In addition to the liberal arts versus vocational education debate, several other themes drove African Americans to demand greater control of their schools. Many blacks began to question why, in the wake of an increasingly educated population, more African Americans were not being appointed to

Elizabeth City University, Class of 1900.

W. E. B. DuBois vehemently rejected the premise that African Americans should be relegated to vocational training. Here at Cheyney, students read in the library room in 1905.

Although DuBois did not believe in a solely vocationally based curriculum, Booker T. Washington stood behind it. Here students at Cheyney work in an industrial arts class in the early 1900s.

tenured faculty positions and high-ranking administrative jobs.

Students also began to challenge the long-held belief that black youth were more sexually promiscuous than their white counterparts and thereby in need of stringent rules to police their social interaction. This misguided belief was undoubtedly a product of the greater number of single black mothers as compared to the number of white ones. Hardly considered was that many black single-parent households were the product of employment discrimination that kept black men out of work and unable to support their families, or the unchallenged rape of black women by white men.

Students demanded that administrators lift the ban on dancing, dating, and stylish dressing that existed on many HBCU campuses, a holdover from missionary days. And students, black faculty, and alumni alike vehemently protested the practice of on-campus Jim Crow, which was observed at numerous HBCUs when white benefactors visited.

Though there were not many African American educators in powerful positions, even at black schools, Bruce Jones was vice president of Langston University in the 1920s.

Radicalized Minds

The demands for these changes hit an all-time high following World War I. Throughout the North and South, HBCU students, alumni, and in some cases black faculty members launched forceful campaigns to gain control over their institutions. These individual battles amounted to a long-term war that found courageous blacks going toe-to-toe with the Ku Klux Klan, police troops, white administrators, and members of the press. The war for black autonomy culminated in revolts on no fewer than eleven black college campuses during the 1920s. Unsettling, sometimes violent uprisings were sparked at Fisk, Howard, Tuskegee, Lincoln (Missouri), Morehouse, Florida A & M, Hampton, and numerous other campuses.

HBCU BENEFACTORS

Wealthy individuals who financed the development and growth of HBCUs have been involved with black institutions of higher learning since their inception. Early philanthropists include Quaker Richard Humphreys, who in 1829 established a $10,000 trust for the founding of Cheyney State, the first HBCU. International investor George Peabody created the Peabody Fund in 1867 for the express purpose of educating newly freed slaves. Textile tycoon John F. Slater established the Slater Fund in 1882, while John D. Rockefeller and his wife, Laura Spelman Rockefeller, were supportive of a wide range of well-documented educational initiatives devoted to HBCUs. Beginning in the late 1800s the couple made significant contributions to schools such as Atlanta University and Spelman College (named after the Spelman family). In 1904 Rockefeller established the General Education Fund Foundation and in 1918 the Laura Spelman Memorial Fund. The funds later merged into the larger Rockefeller Foundation.

Sisters Olivia Egleston Phelps and Caroline Phelps Stokes established the Phelps-Stokes Fund, which made significant contributions to black schools, and wealthy northern businessman Julius Rosenwald set up the Rosenwald Fund, which provided seed money for many HBCUs.

Black philanthropists as well have been key to the development of HBCUs. In his book *The Big Sea,* Langston Hughes writes of a Washington, D.C.—based numbers runner who during the 1920s was shunned by the city's black elite, but who used a good portion of his profits to provide scholarships for black college students. In 1969 Boston-born community activist Ruth Batson founded the Ruth Batson Foundation, which during its first two decades made over 160 grants to HBCUs and their students.

As black wealth has grown, so have the contributions made by African Americans. Media mogul Oprah Winfrey has endowed several chairs at her alma mater, Tennessee State University, and has given more than $6 million to Morehouse College. Actor-comedian Bill Cosby and his wife, Camille, made a historic $20 million gift to Spelman College, while music mogul P Diddy (Sean Combs) gave $500,000 to his alma mater, Howard University, in 1999. With this gift, he established the Sean "Puffy" Combs and Janet Combs Endowed Scholarship Fund to assist students pursuing careers in business arts. Nationally syndicated radio DJ Tom Joyner created a foundation that provides matching fundraising dollars to one HBCU each month, as well as scholarships to students attending HBCUs. Comedian Steve Harvey created an annual scholarship at Southern University, Baton Rouge, that provides books for freshman students.

Financiers and entrepreneurs also have made generous contributions to HBCUs. Wilmington, Delaware, businessman James H. Gilliam recently gave $1.5 million to his alma mater Morgan Sate, while late Wall Street tycoon Reginald Lewis often donated to his alma mater Virginia State. In 1991 Florida-based attorney and entrepreneur Willie Gary donated $10 million to his alma mater, Shaw University, and has since made numerous other contributions.

Corporations such as Microsoft, Procter & Gamble, and Coca-Cola USA also provide ongoing scholarships and seed money for the creation of technology and other curriculum-oriented projects.

But one of the most impressive philanthropic donations ever made to an HBCU came when a retired southern housekeeper willed her life savings, totaling more than $100,000, to an HBCU. The donation was in the grand tradition of some of the earliest contributors to HBCUs— most of whom were hardworking African Americans with limited education but an unlimited quantity of faith in the transformative power of education.

ABOVE: Fayette Avery McKenzie became the president of Fisk in 1915.

BELOW: World War I: soldiers in the 369th Regiment.

In 1917 the United States entered World War I. For two years, African Americans participated in the war effort and endured extreme racism and segregation in the U.S. Armed Forces so that the rest of the world could be made "safe for democracy."[2] Fisk University took a leading role among HBCUs in the war effort.

Male students and alumni were called to duty, and the school's administration, under the direction of Fayette Avery McKenzie (who became president in 1915), worked diligently to convince black Americans to set aside their immediate demands for racial equality and sacrifice for the greater need of the country. University-issued pamphlets implored African Americans to remember that they were countrymen first, promising that there would

Educators were prominent among the burgeoning black middle class. These young Spelman women are graduates of a teacher's professional course.

be time enough to address the critical issues of racial inequities and segregation after the war was won.

But in 1919, black soldiers who had fought against ethnic genocide in Europe returned to an America that was even more racially polarized. Between 1900 and 1918 at least 325 African Americans were lynched and six race riots broke out across the country. During 1917, the year the United States entered the war, eighteen black soldiers were hanged for participating in a riot against the white citizens of Houston, Texas. In the Red Summer of 1919, the war against racism and genocide was about to spark inside American borders. Twenty-six race riots occurred between April and October. Cities such as Charleston, South Carolina, Chicago, Longview, Texas, and Washington, D.C., were devastated by violence between blacks and whites. Seventy-six lynchings took place that year.

It was not only returning African American soldiers and the black working class who were made more militant by blatant discrimination, however. The burgeoning black middle class was also fighting to destroy racist institutions and traditions that placed limits on their professional and social aspirations. Segregation was still the status quo in southern states, and it prevented blacks—no matter how educated and accomplished—from enjoying the full fruits of their labors.

Even more disheartening for many HBCU students and alumni was witnessing and experiencing this same type of oppression and discrimination on their own campuses.

An Uprising at Fisk

Fisk was one of the first campuses to feel the rumblings of revolution, particularly in the arena of social life. As early as March 1918, student B. J. Farnandez wrote President Fayette McKenzie, a white man, about the growing restlessness with the administration's policies, especially as they related to student social life. "For some days I have been wondering if you still feel with sufficient assurance the loyalty of the student body to you and the administration, to which they pledged themselves three years ago at your inauguration," observed Farnandez. "When there are numerous regulations covering every possible chance of contact between men and women in the University . . . you can not but expect that some of them will be violated as a matter of course. . . . It occurs to me that not a student in the University is unaware of the existence of Constituted Authority, which they must ultimately obey, but I believe that when there occur so many occasions for its demonstration, there is obviously some fault in the management."[3]

While McKenzie's official response to the letter was a curt acknowledgment and dismissal of the complaint, his own personal notes—penned at the bottom of Farnandez's correspondence—reveal that the president was not a man who took criticism well or gave up authority easily. "I feel it my obligation and right to observe things at any and all time and in all places without any imputation of error from anybody. The whole situation is unhealthy because of the thought that there is a possibility of change in the substantial elements of the policy of the university on sex relations," he wrote.[4]

To some extent, it may have been dogged determination and inflexibility that helped McKenzie and his administration raise an unprecedented $1 million endowment for Fisk. By the time the Pennsylvania-born sociologist took over, the liberal arts school's financial support from the AMA was dwindling. McKenzie believed that in order for Fisk to prosper, administrators had to convince southern whites and northern contributors that the school embraced the Hampton-Tuskegee model—if not in scholarship at least in terms of social segregation and white superiority.

Fisk, however, had produced some of the most outspoken and liberal scholars in the United States—most notably W. E. B. DuBois. McKenzie knew that many Fisk students were the children of such alumni, and that he would have to suppress the wave of discontent that was sure to surface once he implemented the policies necessary to satisfy contributors. Early in his administration,

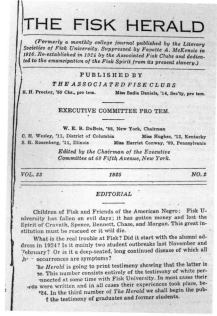

A portion of an editorial from the Fisk *Herald* addressing the troubles at the school. Early in his administration, controversial President McKenzie stopped publication of the college's paper to impede students from commenting on the heated debates going on at the time.

McKenzie disbanded the student government, giving students no voice in the policy-making process at the university and no official channel for making complaints and requesting change. He ceased publication of the student newspaper, the Fisk *Herald*, effectively ending any medium for students to comment publicly on the climate of the university. In an attempt to quash any appearance of radicalism, McKenzie refused to allow a chapter of the NAACP on campus and had librarians censor portions of the organization's official publication *The Crisis*.

McKenzie also instituted a tyrannical student code of conduct. And while the rules partially addressed the belief held by many whites that blacks were not able to exercise control over their sexual urges and social behavior, they also satisfied McKenzie's own puritanical sense of propriety. By limiting social interaction, especially between the sexes, McKenzie believed that he also limited the opportunity for students to act inappropriately. As a result, the university athletic program was cut, male-female interaction was strictly limited, and fraternities and sororities were not permitted on campus.

The college president also required that faculty or administrators supervise all student activities; set up a strict meal, study, and lights-out schedule; establish a stringent student dress code; and only allow administration-approved student social functions on Friday evenings. Most unacceptable to Fisk students, alumni, and the vast majority of the African American community in Nashville was that McKenzie, in an effort to satisfy southern whites and benefactors, practiced a system of Jim Crow at university events both on and off campus. According to historian Raymond Wolters, the president of Fisk's board of trustees also endorsed segregation as "the only solution to the Negro problem," and advocated that whites contribute to black colleges that encouraged their students to embrace racial division and build a separate black society.[5]

Off campus, McKenzie was accused of segregating the audience at a performance given by the Jubilee singers in a downtown Nashville theater. Black and white faculty who worked together daily were forced to sit in separate sections of the theater, and even to buy their tickets from a different box office window. When Isaiah Scott, a well-respected bishop from a black Nashville church, unwittingly tried to buy a ticket from the "whites-only" window, he was insulted by the attendant and refused service. McKenzie was also charged with compromising the integrity and endangering the safety of young women in the Glee Club when he led them down a dark alley, through the back entrance of a men's club, and into the basement where they sang for a group of southern white men who laughed, smoked, and talked throughout their performance.

The tactics of the Fisk president placated enough southern whites and philanthropists to ensure the university's $1 million endowment. But by spring of 1924, his treatment of the students for whom the school was created had incensed enough members of the black community to spark a defiant response. It came in the form of Fisk alumnus W. E. B. DuBois who, outraged by reports that he had received, spoke out against the administration during a commencement week address to fellow alumni on June 2, 1924.

DuBois, who was present for his daughter Yolanda's graduation, had been following the developments at Fisk for some years. He knew from accounts given by his daughter and visiting alumni that Fisk students were feeling oppressed both academically and socially. In his commencement day speech DuBois said that there was "a shadow . . . across this institution," and that the trend toward industrial education for blacks was lowering the academic standards at Fisk. He openly stated that he had "come to criticise" Fisk for its treatment of its students and the black community at large. DuBois insisted that a desire for money had driven the university administration to give in to the demoralizing beliefs that blacks were inferior and should be relegated to second-class citizenry. "Of all the essentials that make an institution of learning, money is the least," DuBois stated.[6]

The renowned scholar went on to denounce "the pall of fear which envelops the student body" at Fisk. He insisted that the regulation placed on every aspect of students' lives had created an environment of mistrust and suppressed the natural atmosphere of self-expression and experimentation that defined college life and helped give birth to independent thinkers. DuBois accused McKenzie of attempting to turn young black men and women into "docile animals."[7]

Initially, DuBois's speech received mixed responses. Students and some alumni—those who had been discouraged by the atmosphere at Fisk during their visits—heartily embraced DuBois's challenge to Fisk supporters to publicize what was happening at the university, organize an effort to rescue the school, and demand an alumni presence on the board of trustees. Others, however, ran to the defense of McKenzie and his administration. The trustees issued a statement that they "earnestly and vigorously" supported McKenzie, and they insisted that the faculty be "united and loyal" in carrying out his policies.[8] Numerous alumni, in particular a group of ex-patriots living in London, sent the president letters of support. Carl James Barbous wrote saying, "I am indeed very sorry that you have to endure so much for my ungrateful people."[9] L. D. Collins wrote that, "If the address were as it has been pictured to me, I am very sorry that the jack ass was allowed to kick at all at Fisk."[10]

McKenzie made no official response to the challenge issued by DuBois. He most likely believed that the controversy would die out over the summer months, and that his success in securing the endowment would buffer him

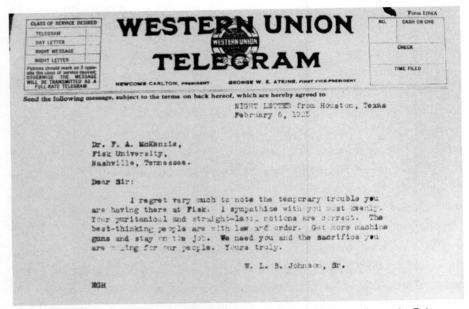

A sympathetic telegram sent by W. L. B. Johnson Sr. to President McKenzie during the Fisk controversy.

from the slings and arrows of student discontent and alumni accusations. But the college president woefully underestimated the resolve and anger of Fisk students and alumni and overestimated his own authority.

DuBois immediately set about gathering testimonies that would support his charges. Former Fisk professor Alphonse D. Philippse complained that academic structure was being neglected under McKenzie. He said that the administration made no distinction between the secondary-school and college-level curriculums. "We have students of college standing taking high school subjects. We have high school scholars in college classes." Philippse also lambasted the strict rules that governed personal lives of students as well. "A girl and boy could be sent home for walking together in broad daylight, on the sidewalk from Livingstone to Jubilee Halls."[11]

In her letter of criticism, Abigail Jackson—a former Fisk matron and a niece of the school's founder and first president—wrote that the problems at Fisk were so frustrating that "if the school were not so important in its relation to the whole problem of education of the colored race, one might be content to shun it and forget." Jackson also revealed that the dress code, which required young women to wear uniforms, cotton tights, and plain outerwear, was not enforced equally. While some coeds were being expelled for the most minor infractions, others were allowed to blatantly disregard it. "On one occasion, I was sent to interview a very pretty girl who was wearing a fur-trimmed plush coat. She showed me a letter from the President to her father giving her permission to wear the coat." Most outrageous, offered Jackson, was an incident in which McKenzie "brought to Chapel men who had no idea of social service or training, who knew and spoke of the Negro only as 'niggers.' "[12]

DuBois repeated these and other complaints during his visits to Fisk alumni associations across the country. By the fall of 1924, many of the associations had abandoned their support of McKenzie. But it was the students themselves who finally turned the tide against the president. Frustrated that their requests for more social and extracurricular freedom had gone ignored, the students decided to act. They strategically chose a date in November 1924 when the board of trustees was scheduled to arrive at Fisk for its annual meeting. The trustees were greeted by a throng of 100 protesting students (about one-sixth of the student body), who stood at the gates, banged on tin pans, and shouted, "Away with the czar!" and "Down with the tyrant!"[13] The trustees also found student grievance lists placarded on doors and bulletin boards throughout the campus.

The demonstration continued until the trustees agreed to a meeting with the protesters. A committee of seven students was formed and developed a list of requests. The committee spokesmen requested that the administration allow a student council, permit sororities and fraternities on campus, establish an athletic association, allow a student publication, give seniors off-campus privileges, modify the dress code, relax the rules regulating male-female interaction, hire more qualified faculty, appoint an alumnus to the board, and discontinue preferential treatment of white visitors and contributors.

Following the meeting, the board's president, Paul Cravath, said he was "deeply impressed and pleased with the fair and manly way in which the students conducted their case."[14] The board members guaranteed that there would be no reprisals against the students, and suggested that a student-faculty committee meet to reach a compromise on the requests. Over the next three months, students and faculty worked at reaching an agreement. McKenzie,

IS IT FAIR?

Fisk students did not RIOT, nor SHOOT UP the campus, nor THREATEN Dr. McKenzie's life or the lives of his faculty. Why then, these unjust persecutions? The men suspended were not even accused of being in the demonstration. They were "undesirable" because they had the courage to tell Dr. McKenzie that he was not PLAYING FAIR. The students elected leaders in their movement. Dr. McKenzie and his intimates opposed this movement. The opportunity came for him to avenge himself upon these defenseless youths. He did so, under the false colors of law and order.

Is It Fair?

A flyer distributed by Fisk students contesting the alleged "riot" on campus.

however, remained uninclined to grant many of the suggestions made by the committee. Though he initially agreed to allow a student council, an athletic association, and some minor adjustments in the dress code, he dragged his feet on implementing the promises. He flatly refused to relax the student code of conduct or allow fraternities and sororities on campus. Students became so frustrated with the president's flagrant dismissal of their requests that during the first week of December they staged two boisterous, postcurfew demonstrations where they pounded on trash cans and chanted DuBois's name.

McKenzie reacted to the protests by digging in his heels and declaring that the real root of the controversy was that certain alumni and students were intent on deposing him so that a black man could be put in charge of Fisk. The true goal of DuBois and his rebel-rousing contingent, insisted the president, was "to get rid of white participation in Negro education, not [only] at Fisk but in all similar institutions."[15] Both DuBois and the students vehemently denied the charge, saying that while they looked forward to the day that black presidents would serve Fisk and other black colleges, they specifically were fed up with McKenzie's administration. The situation on campus became so heated that both the black and the white press in Nashville began reporting on the troubles at Fisk. Then, according to DuBois, on January 31, 1925, McKenzie "returned . . . in high feather" from a New York City trustee meeting and "announced to reporters that 'a complete ignoring of the charges made against the administration will be the policy of the Board of Trustees of Fisk University.' "[16]

Pushed to their limits, on February 4, the students launched a demonstration and strike that polarized the campus for nearly ten weeks. The trouble began shortly after a chapel address, during which McKenzie criticized students for disregarding the Fisk code of conduct. Angered by the scolding, about 100 students living in the male dormitory at Livingstone Hall broke the 10:00 P.M. curfew and created a two-hour-long disturbance, breaking lights and windows and overturning chapel seats. Around 11:00 P.M. the crowd of demonstrators filed onto the campus, sang loudly, and chanted, "Before I'll be a slave, I'll be buried in my grave!" Although the young men assured the two white matrons living in the dormitory that they would not be bothered, the fearful women locked themselves in an office. One exaggerated news report claimed that the students fired twenty-five to fifty pistol shots. The young men insisted, however, that there was no gunfire.[17]

By midnight, McKenzie had gotten wind of the demonstration, and he summoned police to quell the activity. Fifty motorcycle patrollers descended upon the campus, and a searchlight-equipped helicopter was sent to scan the grounds. By the time the police reached Livingstone Hall, however, the demonstrators had returned to their rooms and were in bed. Although McKenzie had not witnessed the demonstration, he identified the seven students who had met with the trustees in November as the ringleaders. Police were able to locate only five of the young men, whom they arrested for inciting to riot.[18]

McKenzie most likely calculated that his get-tough stance would quell the campaign. But it actually galvanized alumni, parents, and members of the black Nashville community to support the students and call for the Fisk president's resignation. Many believed that McKenzie's insensitive decision had come too close to endangering the lives of the black college students. In fact, several of the young men claimed to have seen police clubbing two students during the arrests.

"No man, white or black, who knows anything about the South and southern attitudes could help but know that such a move would bring . . . trouble and lots of it," said A. L. Jackson of the Chicago Urban League. "Better to have a few broken window glasses than broken heads at the hands of bullying police officials."[19] "Mac, you went crazy!" opined a *Chicago Defender* writer.[20] NAACP Field Secretary William Pickens said, "When [McKenzie] called in those cops he could not have done better to alienate the regard of the colored people."[21]

The arrested students were arraigned in court on the following afternoon, February 5. But when the judge asked McKenzie to offer proof that the arrested young men had been involved with the disturbance, the president admitted that he had no actual evidence. It was even revealed that two of the seven students originally named were not on campus at the time of the demonstration. The judge dropped the felony charges against the students, but found them guilty of disorderly conduct and gave each a $50 suspended fine. Despite his lack of proof, McKenzie dismissed five of the seven students. Among them was George Streator, who was off campus at the time of the demonstration. After learning of the expulsions, two-thirds of the student body gathered inside Livingstone Hall Chapel and voted to boycott classes until their demands had been met and the five students readmitted to the college. On Saturday, February 7, the striking students drafted a petition that called for McKenzie's resignation. More than 100 students signed the petition.

Meanwhile, the prosecution and expulsion of the students so outraged the black community of Nashville that over 2,500 citizens gathered at St. John's AME Church to organize a campaign to oust McKenzie. Initially, a reconciliation committee was formed in an effort to get McKenzie to recognize and grant the students' requests, but when the black citizens invited McKenzie to attend a February 9 meeting, he failed to appear. Speaking on behalf of McKenzie, Dr. W. W. Sumlin, a black citizen, told the audience of 1,000 that "the trouble at Fisk is an acute attack of smart alexitis. It's all right for these students to get out and pop off a lot of hot air, but we other folks have got to live here."[22] Expelled students George Streator and Charles Lewis also spoke, accusing McKenzie of intimidation and operating a spy system against the students. The meeting closed with black residents and Fisk alumni drawing up a resolution that condemned McKenzie and asked the trustees to launch a full investigation into the students' grievances.

The unequivocal support that McKenzie received from Nashville's white citizens and press undoubtedly lulled him into believing that he would survive the scandal. But the African American community was determined that McKenzie had to go. Fearful that the campus had become unsafe, parents began to wire their sons and daughters to return home. A large number of students attempted to transfer en masse to Howard University, but McKenzie tried to block the transfers. Ten weeks later, however, the students remained united in their classroom strike, and the trustees had begun to waver under pressure from the black community and press. Alarmed, perhaps, by the number of student withdrawals and transfer requests, the board agreed in April 1925 to assemble a committee to investigate the entire controversy and reach a compromise. Realizing that he had lost the support of the trustees, and believing his authority had been compromised, McKenzie tendered his resignation on April 16.

The students viewed McKenzie's resignation as a major victory. The expelled classmates were readmitted, and the incoming president, Thomas Elsa Jones, a Quaker pacifist and doctoral candidate at Columbia University, granted many of the requests originally made by the students. DuBois praised the victory, and declared brave the student "who hits power in high places, white power, power backed by unlimited wealth."[23]

The Spreading Flames of Revolution

Even before the lengthy battle at Fisk began, students, alumni, and faculty at other HBCUs had begun fighting for change on their campuses. In October 1923, Florida A & M students launched a boycott in an effort to oust their

The Florida A & M class of 1907. Students slowly began to resent the rules and regulations that the schools often imposed on their social lives.

president, W. H. A. Howard. Though Howard was black, students maintained that he was unqualified to run the school because he did not possess a college degree. They also believed that he supported a plan to turn the college away from academics toward vocational pursuits. Nearly one-third of the student body withdrew from the college, and it was rumored that striking students were responsible for fires that burned down three campus buildings and destroyed three others. The students won their battle, and in May 1924, the board appointed a new president.

Students at Lincoln University in Missouri launched a brief strike in October 1927. Protesters broke windows and damaged other property in defiance of the governor's ousting of university head Nathan B. Young. President Young had long been the target of disgruntled faculty members who were threatened by his efforts to raise the standing of the university through increased faculty degree requirements and academics that were more rigorous. Although the student protest was a flash in an ongoing effort to reinstate Young, it did draw national attention to the dispute and ultimately helped the ousted president regain his appointment.

On October 11, 1927, Hampton students initiated a classroom boycott in response to an oppressive, racist culture that tolerated on-campus segregation and employed professors who were known Ku Klux Klan members. School policy also barred everything from card playing to dating to fraternities and sororities. The student body developed a list of seventeen concerns. Among them was a demand to improve the academic curriculum and faculty, both of which the students felt lacked rigor. Two days later, however, Principal James Edgar Gregg declared a student lockout and shut down the university for twelve days. He suspended sixty-nine students and placed hundreds of others on probation. While Gregg was successful in ending the strike without addressing student demands, a climate of protest prevailed. Resentful students frequently disregarded university rules, and one even had a physical confrontation with his professor. In light of a declining state of affairs at Hampton, Gregg decided to leave the school in May 1929.

Fisk alumnus DuBois did not play as prominent a role in the uprisings at fellow HBCUs, but he did serve as an influential voice of support. His editorials for *Crisis* often praised the rebellious groups and criticized HBCU administrators.

An African American President for Howard

The theme of black control of black universities had been downplayed during the Fisk uprising, but it spoke with a clear voice during the multifactioned battle waged against the administration at Howard University.

As early as 1874, following the resignation of the university's founder and president, General Oliver O. Howard, students, alumni, and prominent leaders such as Frederick Douglass pushed for the trustees to elect a black man to head the school. The call for an African American president continued with each successive appointment, but by 1925, not one had occupied the position. Historian Raymond Wolters observed that Howard's presidents typically found their powers mitigated by the presence of several autonomous African American deans who often circumvented the administration when making decisions about their respective schools. Among those deans were Kelly Miller, head of the College of Liberal Arts, and George Williams Cook, who ran the commercial department. In addition, African American professors held roughly two-thirds of the teaching positions at Howard by the late 1800s. Renowned historian Carter G. Woodson and Rhodes scholar and Harlem Renaissance figure Alain Locke could be counted among the faculty. Furthermore, prominent blacks had always sat on Howard's board, although they comprised a minority of the trustees. Frederick Douglass was

James Stanley Durkee was appointed president of Howard University in 1918.

among the earliest African American trustees, while Jesse E. Moorland, Bishop John Hurst, and Dr. C. Sumner sat on the board during the 1920s. In essence, an African American did not control the reins at Howard officially, but blacks clearly were among its power brokers. But the tenuous power dance came to a screeching halt when the board appointed James Stanley Durkee to the presidency in 1918.

Durkee soon recognized that in order to be effective he had to restructure the chain of command at Howard and move key figures outside of the power loop. The Boston-bred, white minister began his campaign by convincing trustees to approve a restructuring plan that, among other things, called for eliminating the commercial department and splitting the College of Liberal Arts into junior and senior divisions with their own respective deans. By doing so, Durkee essentially removed Dean Cook from his seat of power and considerably weakened the influence of Dean Miller. Early in his tenure, the president's actions threw the Howard community into an ongoing battle against his administration and the board of trustees.

The faculty vehemently challenged the restructuring efforts. A special committee comprised of ten professors called a private conference with the president and advised him to abandon his plan. They characterized it as "expensive and unsuitable for the resources, financial and academic of Howard University."[24] But Durkee maintained that his strategy would improve the university's academic structure.

Over the next several years, some of the more outspoken faculty members became entangled in a variety of public disagreements with the administration. Carter G. Woodson resigned in 1923, after the board refused to approve his plan to develop a black history course and later reprimanded him for inviting public school teachers to black history seminars on campus. Science professor Thomas W. Turner—a member of the committee that opposed the restructuring plan—quit in 1924 after getting into a physical altercation with Durkee, who refused to approve a $500 purchase of laboratory equipment. When Durkee revealed that he suspected the equipment was for Turner's personal use, the argument became heated. The president ordered Turner out of his office, to which he replied, writes Alain Locke, that he would leave in his own way.[25] According to DuBois's account of the incident, an angry Durkee then grabbed Turner by his shoulders, and yelled, "Well, then I'll put you out." He then pushed Turner over chairs and toward the door.[26]

Dean Miller also experienced an infamous, albeit murkily detailed, confrontation with the president when Durkee, at the behest of the board, called the professor out of class and criticized him for writing a newspaper editorial about a controversy involving the D.C. superintendent of black schools. Angered by Durkee's attempt to curtail his right to comment on public issues, Miller responded that he felt "like smashing [Durkee] in the face." The incensed president fired back, calling the dean a "contemptible pup."[27]

Durkee's tendency to micromanage the faculty must have seemed insulting to Howard professors, accustomed to greater autonomy. Faculty members were not alone in running afoul of his administration, however. Students also threatened regular strikes and protests. In 1922, for example, a number of students were suspended for accumulating more than eight unexcused absences from daily noon services. Howardites promised to strike if mandatory attendance was not repealed. They plastered the campus with posters declaring that "Compulsory Chapel Must Go," and a large contingent wrote letters promising to withdraw unless the rule was abolished.[28] Albeit reluctant to do so, Durkee convinced the trustees to waive the rule. The board's decision may have been forced, in part, by faculty support for the students' demand. Dr. Locke, for instance, had gone on record as being against mandatory chapel after Durkee criticized him for nonattendance. The faculty at large charged that compulsory chapel violated the Constitution's separation of church and state, and they threatened to raise the issue when Congress next convened to consider annual appropriations for Howard. The student council also threatened a strike if the administration didn't give the council a role in handling disciplinary cases. Again, Durkee relented.

While students and faculty were often supportive of each other's efforts, the two groups were not always allied in their battles. That became evident in the spring of 1925 when students and faculty became embattled over an ROTC attendance policy.

On May 7, exactly three weeks to the day that Fayette McKenzie resigned from Fisk, Howard students launched their oft-threatened strike. Angered by the suspension of five students who had incurred twenty absences from compulsory ROTC, students announced that they would not return to school until their classmates were readmitted and the ROTC attendance policy repealed. The motive for the strike had been raised more than a year earlier when, in March 1924, the student council made a recommendation that the administration end compulsory military training. The student newspaper reported that the council "bitterly condemned" the forced training. And in a statement that surely spoke to blacks' growing postwar radicalism— which often found African Americans questioning whether they should risk their lives for a country that continued to regard them as second-class citizens—students argued that mandatory ROTC was "a breeder of war" that "encourag[ed] Howard students to sell their birthright because a few are receiving money from the government."[29]

Council members also made several other far-reaching requests, including the firing of six "old fogey" faculty members whom students deemed to be doing not more than "drawing salaries." Finally, the student leaders requested that the administration hire a "Negro Dean of Men . . . who can freely mingle with the large number of male students and really know their yearnings and aspirations."[30]

Durkee had been inclined to negotiate and grant the students many of their requests in previous years, but in 1924 he and the board had become enmeshed in an ongoing war with faculty members who were demanding pay increases and a standardized salary grade based on seniority and scholastic achievement. Unlike his prior disagreements with professors—generally one-on-one skirmishes—Durkee found himself pitted against a large contingent of highly respected faculty members. A group of sixty-seven professors joined forces in 1921 and, after electing Locke secretary of their salary committee, submitted a written raise request to the board of trustees. As both a member of the board and university president, Durkee held great influence in determining salaries. Principal among the group's complaints was that the president persuaded the board to assign salaries based on his personal opinion of individual faculty members. The group noted cases where new professors (some handpicked and hired by Durkee over the objections of the deans under whom they would work) earned salaries equal to professors who were tenured. The board initially denied the raises, but the professors submitted their request on two additional occasions. Finally, in 1924 the trustees allocated an additional $15,000 to the faculty salary budget.

Not only were the professors disappointed by the small amount allotted for pay increases, they were also outraged by the arbitrary manner in which the raises were given. Once again allegations of favoritism surfaced. In response, in November 1924 Locke composed a statement that, among other things, noted, "Of the $15,100.00 allotted by the board of trustees for increase of salaries . . . little over $5,000.00 was assigned to the sixty academic teachers who signed the original memorial."[31] The letter was signed by fifty-three faculty members and sent to the press.

The black press immediately endorsed the cause of the faculty. Durkee,

unfortunately, found little support for his position outside of the board of trustees. Strategically, he may have hoped that the student strike
against the faculty-enforced ROTC policy could
help sway public opinion in his favor. He most
likely reasoned that critics would begin to question whether faculty members deserved raises in
light of the student unrest. The president also had
a practical reason for insisting on compulsory
ROTC, however. Located in Washington, D.C.,
Howard University had no source of state funding.
Consequently, the university received annual congressional appropriations, and Durkee feared that
ending compulsory ROTC would jeopardize this
funding.

Commandment and student cadet officers at
Voorhees College pose in regulation uniforms in the 1920s.

Durkee's strategy failed. Instead, the black press
and alumni asserted that if Durkee was unaware
that the ROTC policy would cause tension between
students and faculty, then he was unfit to run the
university. Still others accused Durkee of passing
the buck to the faculty. In a letter to DuBois describing the catalyst for the
students' strike, Locke insisted that "the [ROTC] issue fell between the student body and the faculty, but the real cause was Durkee." He explained that
without consulting the faculty, the president had convinced the board to pass
a four-year compulsory physical education requirement that included two
years of ROTC training for male students. "For two years the program worked
because it was laxly administered . . . due . . . to inadequate teaching personnel and . . . gym facilities," wrote Locke.[32] Saddled, however, with enforcing
attendance and realizing that the majority of male students were not attending
ROTC, the faculty passed a twenty-cut suspension rule at the beginning of
the spring term, 1925. Notices promoting the new rule were not posted until
midsemester, and by that time students had accumulated numerous absences.

The student council filed exceptions to the new rule, calling the policy
"oppressive and retroactive." But shortly thereafter, on May 5, the faculty suspended Norris Cuney, George Dabney, John George, Owen Edwards, and

Gilbert Edwards for excessive ROTC absences. In response, the student council called a mass meeting, and students voted to strike unless their fellow class-mates were reinstated. Durkee advised the teachers to stand firm in their ruling, but when faculty members who were sympathetic to the students questioned the veracity of the attendance records, it was discovered they were inaccurate at best. The inaccuracies were further confirmed when several students who had not been suspended admitted to never having attended ROTC classes. Faced with these facts, the faculty decided to reinstate the five students. Durkee and the faculty also agreed to adopt an unofficial policy of disregarding ROTC attendance for the rest of the semester. Unaware of this arrangement, however, and concerned that other students would soon be suspended, the student council extended its strike threat and demanded that mandatory ROTC be abolished altogether.

Flabbergasted by the students' attempt to force academic policy, the faculty refused to consider eliminating compulsory ROTC. Even if they were inclined to do so, the teachers were in no position to change the attendance policy without the president's approval, and Durkee had hopped a train for Boston immediately following the May 6 meeting. The Howard president was scheduled to preside over the annual graduation ceremony at the Curry School of Expression—a small oratory school of which he was also president, and for which he was receiving a merciless barrage of criticism because the school did not accept blacks. (To Durkee's credit, he had accepted the Curry School position with the stated purpose of integrating the school.) With the president away and the faculty and students at an impasse, the students employed the promised strike. On the morning of May 7, faculty and administrators were greeted by demonstrating students and signs reading "Who is president of Howard University, Durkee or Colonel Howard?" and "Military training or academic, which?" Protest slogans were written on sidewalks, parked cars, and the sides of buildings. More than 600 students signed the student council petition, and even ROTC band members joined the effort, providing music for students who danced "the latest in fox trots" on the campus yard.[33]

HBCU MARCHING BANDS

The Florida A & M College Band.

For many fans attending a football game between rival HBCUs, the real action does not begin until the "fifth quarter." The pageantry and showmanship exhibited by black college marching bands at halftime has become synonymous with the black college experience.

Bands first started to show up on black college campuses in the late 1800s. Most were not sponsored by the institutions, and the few that existed were made up of students who owned their own instruments. Extracurricular activities that did not generate revenue were few and far between at the poorly funded schools.

Tuskegee Institute was the first HBCU to have a band. In 1890, N. Clark Smith, the first band director, wrote the music to the Tuskegee school song and brought in Paul Lawrence Dunbar to write the lyrics.

Other schools would follow suit, and in 1900 William C. Handy would take over leadership of the Alabama A & M band. Creative differences with the school president led Handy to resign. He sought to include the ragtime rhythms in the band's repertoire that would later dub him "father of the blues."

Dr. William Foster is credited with creating the high-stepping, precision marching and intricate dance steps for which HBCU marching bands have come to be known. When Foster arrived at Florida A & M in 1946, the band included sixteen members—and they were rarely used except to march students to chapel. The first FAMU dance routine was not planned, however. It happened at a practice when the band was playing "Alexander's Ragtime Band" and doing steps and high knee lifts to the music. Foster later brought in a physical education teacher from the school to help include more dance steps and polish the new act. It was an instant hit with band members and fans, and soon other schools abandoned corps-style marching for horn swinging, hip swaying, and rocking.

In 1955 Tennessee State University took its high stepping from the gridiron into the living rooms of a national television audience. They were the first black college band to play during the halftime show of an NFL football game. Tennessee State achieved another first when it played at John F. Kennedy's inaugural parade.

By the late 1970s several HBCU bands had toured the world, appeared in television commercials, and recorded for major recording labels. Virginia State toured Europe in 1972; Grambling, known as "the world's most televised band," toured Asia; and members of Southern University's band did 140 shows at Radio City Music Hall with the Rockettes for the musical *Black Tie*. This standard of excellence remains at battle-of-the-bands competitions that take place each year during black college football rivalries in every conference. This continued into the 1980s and 1990s, with FAMU receiving the highest honor a college band can receive, the Sudler Intercollegiate Marching Band Award, in 1985. It was the first time the award had gone to a historically black college or university. In 1992 *Sports Illustrated* named FAMU's Marching 100 the nation's best marching band.

Music and dance have traditionally been used by African Americans to uniquely express their creativity. The black college marching band blends these two elements, creating an extravaganza that can be experienced best on a Saturday afternoon during the fifth quarter of an HBCU football game.

For two days the protest boasted a more festive than confrontational mood, but by the weekend Durkee had returned and the Washington, D.C., Alumni Association had appointed a committee to investigate the strike. On Sunday, a group of six local alumni met Durkee in his office and offered to arbitrate the strike. The president declined and made light of the protest, calling it an "exuberance of youth." He assured the alumni members that he would resolve the matter within a day, but his meeting with student leaders later that evening failed to end the strike. On Monday, Howardites were standing firm on their cause. In a mass meeting at Lincoln Theater, the council added seventeen grievances and four additional demands to their initial petition, which they sent to the president. The list demanded that all students be reinstated without penalty; that the physical education requirement be reduced to two years; that the council control all student social activities; and that student representatives be placed on the academic council.

An overwhelming number of students supported the strike. One reporter wrote, "Rival fraternities and sororities, male and female students, junior and senior colleges—all formed a big orderly group and fought for their principle."[34] Even those who did not support the protest found it impossible to attend classes because strikers were blocking entryways. One student complained that two young men had hit him when he attempted to get past their blockade. Fearful that the strike might take on a more unpleasant tone, Durkee threatened that he would "maintain order at all costs, even if police reserves must be called." Congressman Thomas L. Blanton (D-Texas) sent the president a letter urging him to maintain "strict order," but both the faculty and trustees—no doubt in light of the Fisk fiasco—urged Durkee not to call in the police.[35]

The faculty proffered a mixed response to the student demands. While the vast majority of professors felt that negotiating would usurp their authority, some supported the students. Dean Miller encouraged the strikers to "stick together," noting that, "the new Negro is learning that the race must hang together or hang separately."[36] The faculty finally issued and posted an ultimatum on May 12. In a letter delivered to student council president A. M. Brady, the faculty demanded that students cease striking and return to class by May 14, or risk suspension. In response, students launched a loud but orderly campuswide protest during which they were heard yelling, " 'Are we scared?' followed by an explosive 'No!' "[37]

With the faculty and students at an impasse, both the alumni and the trustees feared that the constant barrage of newspaper reports and uncontrollable rumors would threaten the financial welfare of the university. All involved knew there was a small yet vocal group of congressmen and senators who could be counted on to protest the annual appropriations. The continuing strike would be ammunition for their fight. Members of the local alumni association set up a reconciliation committee and reached a settlement after two days of nonstop negotiations. The students agreed to return to class on May 14 in exchange for the faculty's promise to reinstate the five expelled students, grant amnesty to the strikers, and place a moratorium on mandatory ROTC attendance. A special committee would be appointed to study the physical education requirement. Ultimately, the committee decided to reduce the physical education requirement from four to two years, with ROTC being one of many options.

While the battle with the students had ended, the trustees and Durkee still had to settle their fight with teachers who were demanding raises. With the alumni and faculty threatening to go to Congress and charge the administration with the misappropriation of the $15,000 that had been allocated for raises, Durkee was anxious to put the controversy to rest. He sought to quash it by dismissing a number of the most vocal faculty members. With trustee approval, he fired Professors Locke, Alonzo Brown, Metz T. P. Lochard, and Orlando C. Thornton. He forced Professor Cook (the former commercial department dean) into mandatory retirement and attempted to banish Dean Miller by sending the popular educator on a yearlong public relations campaign to raise money for Howard's endowment.

Ostensibly, the firings and reappointment were a part of a university-wide reorganization, but all involved understood that his actions were linked to the raise request and past squabbles with critical deans and faculty members. Alumni and the black press demanded that the fired professors be rehired and that Dean Miller be reappointed as head of liberal arts.

Convinced that Durkee's continued presidency would do the school more harm than good, a key group of alumni launched a concerted campaign to oust the embattled president. Meanwhile, the black press kept up its barrage of anti-Durkee stories. Many critics latched on to Durkee's dual presidencies, noting that his work for the Curry School not only took him away from Howard at a critical moment, but also compromised his relationship with the black community and made him supremely unfit to lead a black university.

Durkee resigned from the Curry School in the summer of 1925, but his critics were not satisfied. Howard students, alumni, and faculty demanded his resignation. In a desperate attempt to gain alumni support, Durkee and the board persuaded renowned writer and Howard alumna Zora Neale Hurston to write literature supporting the administration. No doubt the administration viewed this as a major coup, since Hurston was a protégée of Locke.

Few were swayed by the gesture, however, and the General Alumni Association demanded a hearing to investigate eight charges of misconduct that they planned to proffer against Durkee. The administration refused, so in September the alumni association followed through on its threat to take their charge of misappropriation to Congress. The alumni asked Congress to investigate the charges and to postpone voting on the Crampton Bill—pending legislation that would make Howard's annual appropriation a federal budget line item—until after the investigation. The trustees were able to head off the investigation, but they realized they could no longer disregard the hearing request. In December 1925, the trustees agreed to a hearing and the General Alumni Association submitted its charges. Chief among them was that Durkee had circumvented traditional university policy on hiring and dismissing faculty; that he had verbally and physically assaulted faculty members; that he diverted half of the $15,000 appropriated for teachers' raises to hire new instructors of his own choosing; and that he compromised his commitment and effectiveness as president of Howard by accepting the presidency of the Curry School.

Forty-seven professors testified during the hearing and most expressed their belief that Durkee's continued presidency would be injurious to Howard. The board exonerated the president following the trial, noting, "Durkee was merely implementing policies of the board itself."[38] Like McKenzie, however, Durkee knew that his effectiveness as president had ended. He tendered his resignation in March 1926 after accepting an offer to pastor the Plymouth Congregational Church in Brooklyn.

Determined HBCU students and alumni had come together again to define the leadership and culture of their school. But the most significant outcome of the Howard uprising came after Durkee's resignation. Convinced that the time had come for a black administrator to lead Howard, alumni and students kept pressure on the trustees until they agreed to search for and hire a black president. Howard supporters were not content simply to have a black man at the helm of the university, however. They insisted that the board hire a qualified administrator whose fortitude and commitment would put the welfare of the university ahead of the idiosyncratic bidding of the board. When word got out that the board was considering appointing one of their own members, Jesse E. Moorland, to the presidency, alumni made it clear that they felt Moorland, a former YMCA secretary who lacked a college degree, was not qualified for the job simply because he was black.

Finally, in June 1926, the Howard board elected 36-year-old Mordecai W. Johnson, a Baptist minister with degrees from Morehouse, the University of Chicago, and Harvard, as the institution's first African American president. Of the ousted professors, only Alain Locke returned to his position. Nevertheless, Johnson, who remained at Howard until 1960, would lead the university through a period of prolific growth.

Locke's return to Howard gave him a bully pulpit from which to help guide the rapidly growing Harlem Renaissance movement. Historically black colleges and their students would play a major role in defining and contributing to this burgeoning black arts and culture movement.

MARY MCLEOD BETHUNE

While schools like Howard and Fisk were struggling to have black presidents at their helms, a black woman was founding her own school.

With a personal philosophy to educate the "heads, hearts, and hands" of the masses, Bethune founded Daytona Educational and Industrial Training School for Negro Girls in 1904, which in 1923 merged with the all-boys Cookman Institute to become Bethune-Cookman College. Bethune was president of the college until her retirement in 1948. Bethune-Cookman College is the only school founded by an African American woman to evolve into a fully accredited four-year institution of higher learning.

A true Renaissance woman, Mary McLeod Bethune's efforts to improve the lives of African Americans was hardly limited to her work with Bethune-Cookman College. Born July 10, 1875, Bethune did not begin her formal schooling until age 10. Educated at Presbyterian Missionary School in Mayesville, Scotia Seminary in Concord, North Carolina, and Moody Bible Institute in Chicago, Bethune was president of Carter G. Woodson's Association for the Study of Negro Life and History, vice president of the NAACP and the National Urban League, and founder of the National Council of Negro Women, among other organizations. She was also a member of Delta Sigma Theta sorority, winner of the Spingarn Medal, and an advisor to three presidents—Calvin Coolidge, Herbert Hoover, and Franklin D. Roosevelt.

Bethune proved herself an able fundraiser as well as an educator. From its inception Daytona Educational and Industrial Training School, the root of Bethune-Cookman College, grew slowly but steadily during its first decade of existence. Bethune began the school with five young female students in a dilapidated house with missing floorboards. By 1908 she had hired three teachers, opened a night school for the black adult population of Daytona, and started construction on a new campus. By 1911 Daytona Educational had 200 students, many of whom constituted the first high school–level class to matriculate at the school.

Bethune was a diplomat who picked her battles wisely. Though she could be tolerant of petty racism that did not stand in the way of her resolve to educate her people and improve their lot in life, she was known to risk her own life to defend her cause. Her face-off with the Klan is one such example.

When the Ku Klux Klan marched on Daytona Educational's campus and threatened to burn down the school if Bethune didn't stop leading the effort to get black voters to the polls, she stood her ground. Bethune had long felt frustrated that women in the United States could not vote, but by late summer 1920, the suffrage movement had prevailed, and women had won the ballot. The educator was determined to help southern blacks exercise their right to vote as well, so she made a plan to get as many as possible of her county's eligible black voters to the polls. With the power to vote, Bethune believed that Florida's black population had the power to elect politicians into office who would support black educational institutions and address issues that affected her people.

Bethune taught classes to prepare eligible black voters to pass the state's stringent literacy and civics test. She hit the dirt roads of Daytona's black community and went door-to-door encouraging would-be voters. She implored poor families to make whatever sacrifices necessary to come up with the $1.50 poll tax that each adult had to pay in order to vote. "Go without food if you must," she told them. Her work paid off. The night before the election, nearly 100 blacks had qualified to vote, including 11 of Bethune's own teachers. But Bethune's efforts angered more than a few of Florida's white supremacists, and they meant to keep her and every other black person in Daytona from casting their votes, even if it meant using force.

It was a moonless November night in Daytona Beach on the evening before the 1920 elections. Mary McLeod Bethune had heard from reliable sources that the Klan was stirring up trouble. Just the night before, while she was out of town, a group had marched through the campus, circling Faith Hall and White Hall. They had promised to return, and Bethune meant to face them. She stood on her front porch with the lights from the brightly lit dormitory illuminating the night. The sound of the older students at choir practice calmed her as she waited. Then she saw it: a line of torches and flailing white sheets headed up the road straight toward White Hall. Eighty Klansmen had come by foot and horseback to threaten and terrorize a school filled with women and girls. Bethune steadied herself and did not budge when the lead night rider stopped in front of the dormitory and shoved a large wooden cross into the ground. Several other men walked toward the porch; one was carrying a kerosene can. "We hear you're teaching colored folks around here to vote," one shouted. "We've just come to warn you about filling niggers' heads with such ideas." Then she heard the words that strengthened her resolve: "If you go on teaching it, we'll be back and we won't stop till we burn every building here to the ground."

She stared intently at the Klansmen. Any fear that she had felt was now replaced by anger. She resented these hateful men threatening everything she and the rest of the black community had worked so hard to establish. She was indignant at the thought that ignorance and racism might destroy a vital place of learning. Bethune did not mince words when she opened her mouth. "If you must burn my buildings, then go ahead," she responded. "But let me tell you. Once you burn them, I'll build them back again. . . . And all the while . . . I'll be troubling Heaven about your dark and evil deeds, and I'll pray so hard that neither you nor any of your offspring will have any peace by day or night." Her words cut through the night air, and to her own surprise the night riders turned—first one by one, then in larger numbers—and retreated, leaving the cross unburned.

Early the next morning nearly 100 African American voters gathered outside the same dormitory that the Klan had threatened to torch only hours before. Bethune led the procession off the campus of the Daytona Educational and Industrial Training School, across the bridge, and straight to the voting polls.

UNORTHODOX FUNDRAISER:
MAKING PIES AND PHILANTHROPISTS

Educator and activist Mary McLeod Bethune on the campus of Bethune-Cookman in the 1930s.

One of the primary issues that has threatened the survival of every HBCU has been money. Those determined to secure the future of the schools they founded or invested in were willing to do whatever was necessary in order to survive. To raise money for the school she had envisioned, Mary McLeod Bethune made sweet potato pies, which she sold at nearby resorts during the vacation season in and around Daytona Beach. It was at one of those resorts that she met James N. Gamble, a forefather to Procter & Gamble, who became one the college's most important benefactors. Bethune used her visits to promote the Daytona Educational and Industrial Training School, and possibly interest wealthy vacationers in making donations.

She encountered Gamble on numerous occasions, and he always became engrossed in their conversations about the challenges that African Americans faced in gaining education. Bethune told the philanthropist of her desire to build Faith Hall, a redbrick building that would house a chapel and classrooms. She described in detail her vision for a library and science laboratory. One day, while standing and talking with Gamble outside the sun-drenched beach resort, Bethune asked the wealthy businessman if he would be willing to become the first trustee to Daytona Educational. While Gamble did not make an immediate commitment to the school, he made periodic donations and continued to visit with Bethune during his vacations. By the summer of 1908, Gamble was ready to invest more of his time and money to help Bethune realize her dream for expanding Daytona Educational. Equally as important, he had convinced a few other philanthropists to join him in forming an official board of trustees for the school. Sewing-machine tycoon Thomas White was among them, and together they helped finance Faith Hall, a chapel, and White Hall dormitory, among other ventures.

Bethune lobbied the wealthy white community to support the school, but she also called upon those in the black community of lesser means to contribute. She called on a disparate mix of supporters to ensure the success of her school. Teachers from the schools that Bethune formerly attended sent books; many of the men who took night classes at Daytona helped construct and maintain the campus buildings; students tended the fields that provided food for the school; and donations came in from wealthy benefactors.

Bethune employed the same amount of savvy in providing learning opportunities for her students. Upon her arrival to Daytona, the educator set up several missions. One served the black townsmen who worked in the turpentine camp and lived in the surrounding shanties. Bethune required her students to work at the missions. Young women who were training to become teachers taught there three months each year, while nursing students treated the sick. Bethune created an educational curriculum that was rooted in practical experience and community services.

❦ . ❧

THE ART OF CULTURE

As the Roaring Twenties begin, historically black colleges and universities represent the vanguard of black middle-class culture and the arts.

HISTORICALLY, BLACK COLLEGE students of the 1920s were anxious to invoke change on their respective campuses and were willing to employ confrontational activities to do so, but their activism rarely extended to challenge the pervasive racial inequities that kept large numbers of African Americans undereducated and mired in poverty. In fact, much of the protest initiated by students during this era revolved around their desire to dismantle the antiquated campus codes that prevented them from indulging in decidedly bourgeois social activities such as secret societies, coed social events, pop-culture pursuits, and high-fashion dressing.

Social climate was not the only condition to change at HBCU campuses during this period, however. As American educational standards increased, black colleges and universities were forced to modify and upgrade their programs in order to keep pace. Issues such as accreditation, student enrollment, and curriculum improvement took precedence. A movement was afoot to modernize education at HBCUs.

Jackson State University students looking sharp in 1925.

Several occurrences set the stage for the sweeping social and educational changes that took place on HBCU campuses during the 1920s. Within the social realm, the proliferation of black Greek societies gave birth to traditions and social caste systems that would shape and define student life for years to come. More attention was being given to fine arts training, both in the classroom and through extracurricular activities.

The success of Negro spiritual ensembles such as the Hampton Singers and the Fisk Jubilee Singers—who in 1871 raised more than $70,000 during an international tour and used the proceeds to finance the construction of Jubilee Hall—accelerated the growth of artistic pursuits on HBCU campuses. Debate clubs and literary societies were also very popular, and gave rise to theatrical and creative writing groups. The popularity of college athletics grew during this era as well. In 1912 the Colored Intercollegiate Athletic Association (CIAA) was formed, and intramural sports gave way to intercollegiate programs.

Inter-Collegiate Debate

MOREHOUSE COLLEGE *vs.* TALLADEGA COLLEGE

April 13, 1917

QUESTION : Resolved, That pensions should be paid out of the public funds to needy mothers of dependent children.

DECISION : Majority for the affirmative.

N. B.—The Inter-Collegiate Debate is triangular in nature, involving Knoxville, Morehouse and Talladega Colleges. The affirmative remains at home in every case.

"Not until human nature is other than it is, will the function of the living voice, the greatest force among men, cease. I advocate, therefore, in its full extent, and for every reason of humanity, of patriotism, and of religion, a more thorough culture of oratory."—Henry Ward Beecher.

Debate clubs were very popular. Shown here is an intercollegiate debate between Morehouse and Talladega in 1917.

Track meets, baseball, and especially football games brought together HBCU students from various campuses. High-society sports such as tennis and golf also developed a following. Surprisingly, a coach from Tuskegee, a school whose administration had championed working-class educational curriculums, started a number of the intercollegiate tournaments for these upscale sports.

On the educational front, beginning in 1897, W. E. B. DuBois used his Atlanta University teaching post to organize an annual economics and sociology conference that defined and addressed the conditions of African Americans. These conferences sparked an interest

Women in their tennis whites at Florida A & M.

in sociology among black educators. In 1928 Fisk hired renowned African American sociologist Charles S. Johnson and planted the seed for what would become one of the top-ranked sociology departments in the country. HBCUs also began to phase out lower-level curriculums while increasing their offering of college-degree programs. The movement toward full-fledged college curriculums forced HBCUs to seek accreditation of their undergraduate and graduate schools. To meet these standards, emphasis necessarily shifted from developing industrial programs to improving the liberal arts curriculums that had been championed by early missionaries.

It is hardly coincidence that both the social and educational evolutions of HBCUs occurred after the death of Booker T. Washington in 1915. With the voice of the "Tuskegee Machine" silenced, other branches for HBCU development were able to flourish. Under the leadership of Robert Russa Moton, who succeeded Washington, even Tuskegee began to offer a liberal arts curriculum by the early 1920s.

In fifty years' time the effort to educate African Americans had produced some significant achievements. The illiteracy rate had fallen, and prominent African American families such as the Churches, Grimkés, Fortens, Bonds, and Lockes could claim two or more college-educated generations. What is more,

their ranks were expanding. Between 1920 and 1928 there was a 115.5 percent increase in the number of undergraduate degrees earned in this country.
Among African Americans that figure increased an unparalleled 296.9 percent,
with over 85 percent of black graduates earning their degrees from HBCUs.
Educated African American communities were growing in both size and wealth,
and they needed doctors, nurses, lawyers, insurance experts, and bankers as
well as teachers and preachers to service their needs. Black colleges had to get
busy creating these professionals.

The movement to satisfy these needs was clearly at work during the 1924
General Conference of the AME Church. The AME organization was one of
few religious entities that maintained control over the HBCUs it founded,
and during the conference church officials split over the issue of school consolidation. One group was in favor of merging some of the smaller schools so
that more financial and teaching resources could be directed toward preparing
successful schools like Wilberforce and Morris Brown to pass accreditation.

The opposing camp was concerned that consolidation would facilitate the
education of fewer African Americans. In his passionate address to delegates,
the AME commissioner of education observed that "Our universities and col-

This 1905 Cheney English class was part of the growing emphasis on liberal arts training.

leges are called, and they must respond to this new spirit; this modern notion in the history and life of education. . . . We live in a day of standards and we cannot live alone."[1]

Several HBCUs did receive accreditation during this era. Meharry Medical College, the first HBCU to become accredited, received a class A rating from the American Medical Association in 1923, while Fisk also received an A rating from the Southern Association of Colleges and Secondary Schools in 1926.

African American students of the 1920s heartily embraced the rising standards that expanded their educational opportunities. The broadened agenda exposed students to new career opportunities, and they were not as limited in their professional choices as previous generations. As their personal options grew, so too did the students' quest for social status and pleasure. In many ways, the experiences and desires of black students began to resemble those of white students: they were as concerned with developing their personal lives as they were with developing their minds and Christian spirits. For HBCU students of this era, education was not just a tool to become literate and functional in society; it was a means to gain material comfort and social standing. This new culture created an undercurrent of social competition among some students, but it was also an indicator that the African American middle class was growing in size, strength, and security as a result of the educational opportunities provided by black schools.

FISK JUBILEE SINGERS

An early portrait of the celebrated Fisk Jubilee Singers, who traveled worldwide raising funds for the school.

In 1871, six years after the dismantling of that "peculiar institution," eleven black singers, nine of them former slaves, rode the wings of their talent to the height of musical acclaim. During their ride, the Fisk Jubilee Singers gave the world their first experience with African American music. And as they exposed this genre, the Jubilee Singers met their goal: "To sing money out of the hearts and pockets of the people."

The Jubilee Singers started as the Fisk school choir under the direction of George T. White, who also served as Fisk's treasurer. White was a Northerner who had come South to work with the newly freed slaves. The singers, some barely out of their teens, were students at Fisk. Still a fledgling institution barely in its fifth year of existence, Fisk was on the brink of bankruptcy. White decided to take the most talented students from the choir on a tour of the North to raise money. White met resistance from the faculty, the school's founding patron, the American Missionary Association, and the parents of the choir members. It was the height of Reconstruction and violence against blacks was a common occurrence. But in October 1871, declaring that he was "relying on God," White took the last $40 from the Fisk treasury and embarked on the first tour, which lasted five months.

The choir's repertoire consisted of traditional ballads, with a few slave spirituals as encores. These were sacred to blacks and performing them publicly to entertain whites was unthinkable. The choir's initial concerts at churches, in halls, and on street corners barely made enough to cover expenses. The students were not discouraged; they were driven by their desire to make sure "Fisk would stand." It was during a concert at Oberlin College in Ohio that the group found its niche. During one of the encores, the audience was spellbound by this new style of singing. Singer Ella Sheppard, who sometimes served as the choir's director, was charged with the task of learning as many of the slave spirituals as she could to make them the focus of the performances. Word quickly spread about the choir from the colored college, and demand for the group skyrocketed.

The choir refused to perform for segregated audiences. George Pullman, inventor of the Pullman sleeping car, attended the Jubilee Singers' concert at Library Hall in Lexington, Kentucky—the first integrated performance at the auditorium. He was so moved by "Gospel Train" that he chartered one of his parlor cars to take the choir to their next concert. He determined that all of his railcars would be integrated.

In 1874 Queen Victoria invited the group to England. They would successfully tour Europe and bring home $20,000 to settle the debt on Fisk's land and build Jubilee Hall. Though success had come, it was not without a price. The constant touring began to take its toll on the singers. One suffered a stroke and another collapsed several times on the group's final tour of Germany.

With Fisk no longer in financial trouble, the group disbanded in 1878 after three successful tours. Their résumé included performances for President Ulysses S. Grant and numerous heads of state.

The Jubilee Singers demonstrated to the world that talent and artistic excellence was being developed at HBCUs.

An Educated Black Middle Class

Black colleges were often hubs for African American communities, with black-owned businesses springing up to serve the students, faculty, administrators, and families making their homes around the schools. The U Street district bordering Howard University, for example, was a center of black social life in Washington, D.C. The campus district was home to a bevy of black-owned businesses. Following Sunday church services residents often hit the campus district for a bite to eat, but mostly just to stroll or drive around the area, to see and be seen. Mondays brought new movies to the Lincoln and Republic theaters, and along with the motion pictures came lines of well-dressed blacks determined to catch the latest offering from Hollywood. Young Howard men and male professors caught up on the latest goings-on while getting haircuts at Greg's Barber Shop, and the cafe-set crowd relaxed over drinks at Harrison's Café.

Even with its primary focus on industrial training, Tuskegee Institute also became a hub for upwardly mobile African Americans in Alabama. Black doctors at the VA Hospital often got together with professors, administrators, and black businessmen for a round of golf on the university course.

Blossoming communities, such as those surrounding Howard and Tuskegee, were duplicated around Fisk in Nashville, Tennessee, and in Atlanta, Georgia, which was home to the Atlanta consortium: Clark-Atlanta University, Morehouse, Spelman, and Morris Brown. Other HBCUs, such as Lincoln University in Pennsylvania, were located in rural settings where the campuses became virtual stand-alone towns. These vibrant, self-contained communities shielded students from the constant barrage of racial insults that the average African American encountered in daily life, but there were occasions when students were slapped in the face by Jim Crow laws. In 1928, Thurgood Marshall, then an undergraduate student at Lincoln University, went into nearby Oxford, Pennsylvania, with a group of friends to catch a Saturday-afternoon western at the local movie house. It was only after they had bought their tickets that an usher told the group they had to sit in the colored-only balcony. The students decided to leave the theater and demanded a refund. When the usher refused, the enraged young men yanked down the theater's curtains and broke the entryway door in protest.

Ironically, Marshall and some of the students present at the movie-house incident recently had taken a poll to determine whether Lincoln students supported integrating the school's entirely white faculty. Marshall was among the majority of students who voted to keep the existing faculty, reasoning that the white faculty and administration took a hands-off approach to governing extracurricular activity, whereas HBCUs with black faculty and administration did not. As a result, Lincoln had developed a reputation for being a party school where rival fraternities, particularly members of Alpha Phi Alpha (Marshall's fraternity) and Omega Psi Phi, ran the campus and engaged in outlandish pranks against one another.

Celebrated poet Langston Hughes (right) graduated from Lincoln University in 1929.

Fellow Lincolnite and celebrated writer Langston Hughes, who helped conduct the poll, took Marshall and others to task for their racial shortsightedness. Marshall, of course, went on to successfully argue *Brown v. the Board of Education of Topeka, Kansas,* the Supreme Court case that desegregated American schools. But during his first few years at Lincoln, Marshall, like many HBCU students, was more concerned with ensuring a lenient campus atmosphere than challenging racism. Writers for student newspapers did occasionally pen articles protesting the embarrassing nature of Jim Crow laws that forbade them to eat at certain restaurants or prevented them from trying on clothes in local department stores. These objections, however, primarily addressed social slights that kept the burgeoning black middle class from enjoying the leisure activities that, through education and upward mobility, they were more readily able to afford. Apparent in students' indignation over such slights was a clear undercurrent of thought: education had possessed the black middle and upper classes with a sense of preeminence and entitlement. Many thought themselves to be socially and intellectually superior to the whites who championed segregation.

By the 1920s a good number of black undergraduates came from homes where college attendance was not the product of bootstrap efforts, but the natural and expected progression of the educational process. In his book *The Negro College Graduate,* social scientist Charles S. Johnson (who chaired Fisk's renowned Department of Sociology from 1928 to 1947) writes that while

Morehouse men in 1925.

"the majority of matriculants still come from lowly homes . . . [t]here are, however, increasing numbers and proportions of graduates who, in the security of good incomes and familiarity with the routine of learning, look upon college as simply a normal phase of the development of children."[2] Johnson notes that while previous generations of black students viewed college as a means to social and economic elevation, moving them from the ranks of the lower class to the middle class, college students of the 1920s often already defined themselves as middle class.

For these students advanced social status was often more nuanced and competitive. Prestige was defined by acceptance into particular social clubs and Greek-letter organizations, as well as family wealth and educational history, athletic ability (for men), exposure to cultural activities, and even skin color.

The manifestation of these growing class distinctions could be seen in the assuming nature of many HBCU students. College quickly was becoming a place were career and social connections were made, spouses were found, and the folly of youth was encouraged—if not by the faculty and administration, then certainly by the students themselves. Academic achievement was but one of many—and often not even among the most important—criteria that determined social standing and future success.

Johnson's book offers an example of one HBCU graduate who was an admitted slacker and spoiled rich kid during his early school days.

Students from Jackson State's 1903 graduating class.

"I entered Bishop [junior high and high school] when I was twelve, played all the time, never studied, was all the time in minor troubles during the entire six years of my stay there. I didn't get a diploma from the academy because I was caught stealing . . . my father was funny; he spent too much money on me. When I was just a kid at Bishop he bought me tailored suits, flannel vests, diamond studs and diamond stik pins [sic]. I had a checking account out in the city, and those old heads around the school thought my daddy was white."[3]

Though less than focused during his early school years, this HBCU graduate completed his high school work at Hampton, received his bachelor's degree from Howard, and then went on to Meharry for his dental degree before opening a very successful practice. His achievement flew in the face of previous generations of black college graduates who, had they not seriously focused on advancement from the earliest opportunity, were likely to remain uneducated and poor.

Extracurricular activities on the campus of Pennsylvania's Lincoln University during the 1920s illustrates how some students perceived college life as merely a time for youthful indulgence. Despite its Presbyterian roots, the college was widely regarded as a party school, and the existence of Prohibition hardly discouraged the flow of alcohol on campus.

On one occasion in 1927 the campus bootlegger threw an all-night party, which became so rambunctious that five students were expelled. Perhaps because it was an all-male school, extracurricular life at Lincoln received little policing from the faculty and administration. Young men regularly sneaked coeds from nearby Cheyney College into their rooms, and the level of alcohol

Dillard students posing in front of a car, circa 1918.

consumption prompted one theological professor to angrily refer to the students as "libertines and lickerterians."[4]

If the first two decades of the twentieth century were about solidifying the existence of HBCUs, then the next forty years would be about establishing the mores, language, and lifestyle that characterized the growing black middle class being nurtured by the schools. Prior to the emergence of black fraternities and sororities, student-founded black-and-tan societies appeared on some campuses. Much to the dismay of school administrators, these social clubs were often exclusive to light-complexioned blacks. In an interview for the Black Women Oral History Project, Atlanta University alumna Norma Boyd recalled the Owls and the Wolves, two all-male society clubs. "We noticed the top students were the Wolves on campus . . . most of the lighter boys went to the Owls . . . they weren't the top students . . . [but] they had to have something to set them aside so . . . most of them were lighter skinned."[5]

SOCIOLOGISTS

Because of the innumerable social issues that African Americans have faced in this country, it is no surprise that a robust group of black sociologists developed out of the black colleges and universities. The impact they had would not only change the way white society viewed African Americans; it would also change the way blacks viewed themselves.

Fisk alumnus W. E. B. DuBois is credited with writing the first sociological study of blacks in this country with the publication of *The Philadelphia Negro* in 1899. DuBois wrote the book while he was teaching at Atlanta University. His tenure there was marked by numerous sociological studies. While at Atlanta, he also edited the annual *Studies of the Negro Problem* and published some of his most renowned literature, including *The Souls of Black Folk, Black Reconstruction in America*, and *Dusk of Dawn*. DuBois left Atlanta University in 1911 only to return more than two decades later to chair the Department of Sociology from 1933 to 1944.

After completing his undergraduate training at Virginia Union University, Charles Spurgeon Johnson studied under sociologist Robert Ezra Park at the University of Chicago, which pioneered social research at the university level. Johnson completed a study of the causes of the Chicago race riots of 1919 and presented its findings to the governor of Illinois. As a result of this work, he was appointed associate executive director of the Chicago Race Relations Committee and in 1922 published *The Negro in Chicago*, based on his research.

Johnson moved to New York, where he directed research for the New York Urban League. During his time at the Urban League, Johnson founded *Opportunity: A Journal of Negro Life,* which provided a voice for many of the well-known artists and intellectuals of the Harlem Renaissance.

In 1928 Johnson relocated to Nashville to head Fisk's Department of Sociological Studies. Even as a teacher and administrator Johnson's sociological endeavors continued. He was the first black sociologist to be named vice president of the American Sociological Association in 1937. When Fisk's renowned Institute of Race Relations was created in 1944, Johnson was the natural choice to lead it. He brought in the best sociologists from around the country to address the various nuances in the relationships between blacks and whites. He became Fisk's first black president in 1946. After World War II, Johnson was involved in planning the reorganization of the Japanese educational system.

E. Franklin Frazier studied the problems affecting black America by examining the attitudes as well as the economic, social, and political structures of the communities in which they lived. An alumnus of Howard and Clark University, Frazier taught sociology at Morehouse and organized the Atlanta University School of Social Work. His book *The Pathology of Race Prejudice* created a firestorm of controversy that resulted in his departure from Morehouse in 1927. Charles S. Johnson recruited him to Fisk, where he taught from 1929 to 1934, before returning to Howard to teach. Frazier was elected president of the American Sociological Association in 1948. He expanded his influence to an international audience when he became the director of the United Nations Educational, Scientific and Cultural Organization's (UNESCO) Applied Social Sciences Division from 1951 to 1953.

Abram Harris was a trailblazer whose most famous publication was *The Black Worker,* cowritten with political scientist Sterling Shapiro in 1931. In 1935 he was the main author of the *Harris Report,* which urged the NAACP to become more active in race relations. His book *The Negro Capitalist* came a year later, in 1936. He helped organize the Social Science Division at Howard and was an intellectual leader there until moving to the University of Chicago in 1945. Harris underwent a philosophical metamorphosis in Chicago and began to focus less on race and more on class and economics. After this change he wrote *The Social Philosophy of Karl Marx-Ethics* in 1948 and *Economics and Social Reform* in 1958.

Horace Mann Bond did groundbreaking research on subjects never before studied from a black perspective. His research on academic achievement, intelligence, aptitude testing, and black doctorates provided insight into the black psyche from an intellectual and sociological perspective. A Lincoln alumnus, Bond became Lincoln's first black president in 1945. After his tenure at Lincoln, he became the dean of the School of Education at Atlanta University in 1957.

As a result of the work of the many sociologists connected to HBCUs, the nation as a whole was given an opportunity to learn about the capacity of the black mind. These researchers proved that blacks were indeed capable of abstract thought, analysis, and critical thinking.

Men of distinction at Livingstone College, circa 1920.

The Flourish of Black Greeks

Black Greek-letter organizations were active on a number of campuses by the 1920s, and students affiliated themselves with fraternities such as Alpha Phi Alpha and Omega Psi Phi, and sororities like Alpha Kappa Alpha and Delta Sigma Theta, among others. Black Greeks had emerged on college campuses shortly after the turn of the century.

In 1906 seven African American male students founded Alpha Phi Alpha on the campus of Cornell University. They created the fraternity to be a system of support and brotherhood for the black students who were systematically locked out of the Ivy League institution's social networks and existing Greek-letter organizations. The incoming black freshmen were determined to create a means for survival, yet the six blacks who had entered Cornell in 1905 were so ostracized that they did not return in the fall of the following year.

Like its white counterparts, Alpha Phi Alpha soon became a secret society where membership requires an initiation period during which pledges learn confidential codes and subjugate themselves to existing members. The Greek-letter movement quickly caught on among black college students, and by the following year, the Alphas had organized a second chapter at Howard University. Other black Greek organizations soon followed.

Alpha Kappa Alpha, the first black sorority, was founded in 1908 at Howard University. The Black Mecca (as Howard is affectionately known) also gave birth to Omega Psi Phi fraternity in 1911. Delta Sigma Theta sorority was created at Howard University as well, in 1913. Phi Beta Sigma fraternity was founded there also, in 1914, followed by Zeta Phi Beta in 1920.

Kappa Alpha Psi fraternity planted its roots at Indiana University in 1911, but quickly started chapters on HBCU campuses. Sigma Gamma Rho sorority also founded its first collegiate chapter at a predominantly white school, Butler College, in 1922.

More than a half century after the first black Greek organization was begun, in September 1963, three weeks after the historic March on Washington, twelve friends from Morgan State University founded Iota Phi Theta fraternity.

Greek organizations were intended to promote brotherhood and sister-hood between black college students and counter racist exclusion by whites, yet from the beginning they were marked by rivalry, clannishness, and, to some extent, a color caste system. "You had to be from a wealthy family, a famous athlete, a brilliant scholar, or very light-skinned to join a fraternity," offered Howard University graduate Dr. William Allen in John Henry Little's Princeton dissertation *The Black Student at the Black College*. The color caste was even more prevalent among sororities. While light-complexioned women had no trouble being accepted, "a black or brown-skinned co-ed had to come from a well-to-do family, have a better than average scholastic record, be beautiful and posses 'a vivacious and pleasant personality' before she could join a sorority," writes Little.[6]

Despite, or perhaps due to, their exclusive nature, fraternities and sororities quickly became the governors of campus social life and extracurricular activities. Greek organizations co-opted the student debates, which had traditionally attracted a diverse campus audience and involved people on the basis of individual talent. Fraternities and sororities barred nonmembers from joining their own debate teams, however, and the events were often less about oration and more about rivalry between the Greeks. Fraternity- and sorority-sponsored debates became more popular than their university-sponsored counterparts, partly because the Greek organizations held dances and social hours after their events.

A young woman's undergraduate popularity often rested upon whether she received invitations to screening events known as sorority smokers. An invite meant she was being considered for membership not only into a particular sorority, but also into the upper echelons of campus society. Fraternity men took note of which freshmen women were pursued by the sororities and often voted these ladies as sweethearts of their own organizations. Delta and AKA women consistently won the homecoming and campus queen titles.

HBCU GREEKS

Alpha Kappa Alpha

In 1908 three institutions were begun on the campus of Howard University. The law department of Howard officially became the School of Law; the university's Freedmen's Hospital opened; and Ethel

The Alpha Upsilon chapter of Delta Sigma Theta at LeMoyne-Owen (then known as LeMoyne).

Hedgeman Lyle conceived the idea of creating a sorority. Alpha Kappa Alpha holds the enviable title of being the first Greek-letter organization for black women in the United States. Only Alpha Phi Alpha fraternity preceded AKA's founding. In 1913, AKA became the first black sorority to be incorporated.

Hedgeman, who was a junior when she decided to start a sorority, wanted a group that would be "an instrument for enriching the social and intellectual aspects of college life by providing mental stimulation through interaction with friends and associates."[7] From this goal grew a commitment of service to all humanity accomplished by distinguished women of character with high ethical standards. From its humble beginnings in Miner Hall on the Howard campus, the sorority has grown to include over 170,000 women in chapters throughout the United States, the Caribbean, Europe, and Africa.

The sanctuary of Andrew Rankin Chapel on the Howard campus boasts a stained-glass window dedicated to the founding members of the sorority. AKAs from all over the world make the pilgrimage to the chapel to see this breathtaking work of art done by Soror Lois Mailou-Jones Pierre-Noel, which was dedicated at the 1976 national convention.

Several famous HBCU alumnae are members of AKA, including Phylicia Rashad, Toni Morrison, and Lynn Whitfield—all from the Alpha chapter at Howard.

Alpha Phi Alpha

Alpha Phi Alpha fraternity, the oldest Greek-letter fraternity organized by African Americans, was founded on the campus of Cornell University in 1906. Since black students were segregated and confronted with racial prejudice at Cornell, the need to have closer social and educational contact with other black students was a practical reason for its creation. Skeptical of clandestine activities among blacks, many whites and some blacks were opposed to secret Greek-letter fraternities for black students. Nevertheless, the seven founders forged ahead with their desire to create a fraternity that would join the struggle for social, educational, economic, and political equality for African Americans.

Soon after being established at a white institution, Alpha Phi Alpha spread to HBCUs. The brotherhood has since become an indelible part of black college life. Even though Alpha wasn't founded at a black college, its links to HBCUs date back to the fraternity's early days. The first general convention was held at Howard in 1908. During that gathering the fraternity stated that "the influence of Alpha Phi Alpha would reach every [African American] college and university in the land."[8]

Through the years, members of the fraternity have been active participants in the struggle for black equality. Fisk's W. E. B DuBois, Martin Luther King Jr. from Morehouse, Thurgood Marshall from Lincoln (Pennsylvania), and Andrew Young from Howard were all Alpha men. The fraternity's relationship to HBCUs was demonstrated when the fraternity chose to house the Alpha Phi Alpha archives on the campus of Howard University.

Delta Sigma Theta

In January 1913 twenty-two female students on the campus of Howard University came together to found Delta Sigma Theta, the second oldest Greek-lettered sorority for African American women. The vision that bound these women, some of whom were members of Alpha Kappa Alpha, was a desire to create an organization focused on academic excellence and helping people in need.

At the time of Delta's founding, women were agitating for a constitutional amendment that would give them the ballot. Recognizing the importance of this issue, the members of Delta Sigma Theta participated in the women's suffrage march in Washington, D.C., on March 3, 1913—just two months after their creation. During the parade, they were forced to march in the back because the parade organizers felt that the votes of southern congressmen would be jeopardized if blacks were involved in the struggle. Violence marred the parade when bystanders attacked the marchers. Army troops were called in to stop the violence as over 200 marchers were injured. This courageous move on the part of the Deltas typifies the type of women who have joined their ranks.

Several notable HBCU alumnae are members of Delta Sigma Theta, including founding members Osceola Macarthy Adams, one of the first black actresses on Broadway, and Sadie T. M. Alexander, the first African American woman to earn a doctorate in economics and the first admitted to the Pennsylvania bar. Texas Southern alumna Barbara Jordan was the first African American from the South to serve in the U.S. Congress since Reconstruction. Artist and sculptor Elizabeth Catlett pledged Delta at Howard and went on to teach at Prairie View, Dillard, and Hampton. Delta Sigma Theta's ranks also include Johnetta B. Cole, the first woman to serve as president of Spelman College, and poet and literary icon Nikki Giovanni.

Today, Delta has a membership of over 200,000 women, with over 900 chapters in the United States, Japan, Germany, Bermuda, the Bahamas, Korea, and the U.S. Virgin Islands.

Iota Phi Theta

Founded in September 1963, Iota Phi Theta fraternity was the vision of twelve friends from Morgan State University. Many of them were older than the average college student, however; three were veterans, and three were married with children. Most of them had full-time jobs, so they brought a more mature perspective to Greek life. The fraternity's purpose is "The development and perpetuation of scholarship, leadership, citizenship, fidelity, and botherhood among men." Although the newest member of the National Pan Hellenic Council, Iota Phi Theta is the fifth largest black fraternity. Iota has remained true to its motto, "Building a tradition, not resting upon one."

Within five years of its founding, Iota had established chapters at Hampton University, Delaware State, and Norfolk State University, respectively. On November 1, 1968, Iota Phi Theta became a national fraternity under the laws of the state of Maryland. Today, Iota Phi Theta has 198 chapters, spread across forty states and the District of Columbia. Its reach has extended beyond the United States into the Bahamas.

Distinguished Iota men who attended HBCUs include Hampton alumnus and former *Good Morning America* weatherman Spencer Christian and Raymond Grady, president and CEO of Evanston Hospital in Evanston, Illinois.

Kappa Alpha Psi

Kappa Alpha Psi fraternity was founded on January 5, 1911, on the campus of Indiana University. Because of the challenges that black students at Indiana faced as they attempted to assimilate into the mainstream of campus life, Elder W. Diggs, Byron K. Armstrong, and eight other students formed the fraternity. It is the only Greek-letter organization founded at Indiana University. Although Kappa Alpha Psi's name is well known on HBCU campuses, the initial name of the fraternity was Kappa Alpha Nu. The name was changed officially on April 15, 1915. The first three expansion chapters were founded at white schools, but the fourth and fifth chapters were established at two of the oldest HBCUs in the country, Wilberforce and Lincoln University in Pennsylvania.

Kappa Alpha Psi's fundamental purpose is achievement. Although

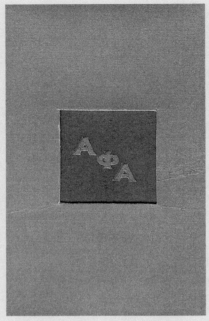

Nu Chapter
of
Alpha Phi Alpha

Lincoln University

Entertains in honor of
visiting brothers

Friday evening
November twenty-sixth
Nineteen Twenty Five

Nine to One o'clock
Clavers Auditorium
12th and Lombard Streets

A 1925 invitation to a gathering of visiting brothers of the Alpha Phi Alpha fraternity's Nu chapter at Lincoln University.

Kappa Alpha Psi is a predominantly black fraternity, its constitution has never contained language to exclude people on the basis of race.

Well-known Kappas who have attended HBCUs are magazine publisher Keith Clinkscales from Florida A & M, civil rights activist Ralph Abernathy from Alabama State, writer and publisher Lerone Bennett, and the Reverend Calvin Butts from Morehouse.

Omega Psi Phi

Omega Psi Phi was the first fraternity for black men to be founded on an HBCU campus. In November 1911, Edgar Love, Oscar Cooper, and Frank Coleman founded the fraternity on the campus of Howard University. The faculty advisor who assisted them, biology professor Ernest Just, would become a member in 1941. The Omega Psi Phi name came from the initials of the Greek phrase "Friendship is essential to the soul." This became the motto of the fraternity, while manhood, scholarship, perseverance, and uplift were chosen as cardinal principles.

In March 1912 the Howard University faculty council rejected the fraternity's constitution and offered Omega Psi Phi recognition as a local organization. But the founding members had larger ideas in mind and opted to refuse the council's offer. Although it took almost two years, the faculty council withdrew its rejection in 1914. Omega Psi Phi was incorporated on October 28, 1914, and the beta, or second, chapter was established at Lincoln University (Pennsylvania) the following February.

Some of Omega Psi Phi's most famous members would join the ranks of the fraternity in its early period. Honorary member and Howard professor Carter G. Woodson made a speech at the Nashville Grand Conclave in 1920, urging the establishment of a week to observe the history of African Americans. Langston Hughes pledged Omega Psi Phi's beta chapter at Lincoln University. In the 1930s Howard medical school professor Charles Drew wrote part of the Omega hymn "Sweet Omega."

Omega Psi Phi is an ardent supporter of historically black colleges and universities. The fraternity donates an annual gift of $50,000 to the United Negro College Fund, and each year exposes high school students to the finest black institutions of higher learning on their Black College Tour. In 1981, Omega Psi Phi created the Omega Faculty Chair, an endowed professorship. Rust College in Holly Springs, Mississippi, was the first HBCU to benefit from this endeavor.

Several well-known HBCU alumni are members of Omega Psi Phi fraternity. Jesse Jackson Sr. and astronaut Ronald McNair (who was killed in the space shuttle *Challenger* explosion) both pledged at North Carolina A & T. *Black Enterprise* publisher Earl Graves pledged at Morgan State, and Virginia's first elected black governor, Doug Wilder, pledged at Virginia Union.

Although political activism was growing stronger on HBCU campuses, Greek organizations continued to thrive. Wilberforce AKA sorority girls in 1931.

Phi Beta Sigma

When Phi Beta Sigma was founded on the campus of Howard University in 1914, skin color provided a line of demarcation within the black community. Some of the fraternities and sororities that had been founded up to this point rarely pledged members who were darker-skinned, who were from less-affluent family backgrounds, or whose hair was coarse. The divisiveness of such thinking inspired A. Langston Taylor, Leonard Morse, and Charles Brown to organize a fraternity that would truly adhere to the concepts of brotherhood, scholarship, and service.

Shunning exclusivity and determining to use the skills they were learning at Howard to empower the communities from which they had come, the founders developed the motto, "Culture for Service and Service for Humanity." Phi Beta Sigma holds the distinction of being the first fraternity to have presidents of other countries as members. Nnamdi Azikiwe, former president of Nigeria, and Kwame Nkrumah, Ghana's first president, both pledged Sigma at Lincoln University (Pennsylvania). The Sigmas were also the first fraternity to establish a chapter south of the state of Virginia before 1915. The Alpha Beta chapter of Phi Beta Sigma was the first Greek-letter organization for African Americans chartered in the state of Mississippi.

Other notable HBCU alumni who pledged Sigma include NBA Hall of Famer Willis Reed, who attended Grambling; the NFL's leading receiver Jerry Rice, who is a Mississippi Valley State alumnus; and civil rights activist Congressman John Lewis, who graduated from Fisk.

Sigma Gamma Rho

Sigma Gamma Rho was the first African American sorority founded on a predominantly white campus. Because black students could not join white sororities at Butler University, seven schoolteachers, led by Mary Lou Allison Little, joined together and founded the sorority on November 12, 1922. "Greater Service, Greater Progress" became the motto of the sorority, and it was initially open to teachers only. Recognizing that teaching could take place in many other places besides the classroom, membership was soon opened to intelligent women of good character, regardless of their discipline.

By the end of the 1920s the sorority began to expand to HBCUs, one of the earliest chapters being chartered at Virginia Union University on January 29, 1930, one month after the sorority was incorporated as a national organization. After the Great Depression began to take its toll on black college campuses, the sorority held book showers for cash-strapped HBCUs. This creative idea was eventually made into a national program.

Sigma Gamma Rho now has over 400 chapters in the United States, Bermuda, the Virgin Islands, the Bahamas, and Germany.

The Bela Psi chapter of the Omega Psi Phi at Clark University. Many fraternities and sororities grew more socially aware during the 1930s.

Zeta Phi Beta

"The Zetas," as they are known on HBCU campuses, were founded on January 16, 1920, at Howard University. The Five Pearls (founders) of Zeta Phi Beta sought to set themselves apart from other black sororities by placing greater emphasis on community service rather than the elitism and socialization that some members of other sisterhoods promoted. The Zetas' motto is "Scholarship, Service, Sisterly Love, and Finer Womanhood."

Zeta's expansion was quite different from the expansion of other Greek organizations. Rather than starting chapters at white schools, their goal was to establish chapters at other HBCUs. Zeta Phi Beta wanted to pour the skills and training they were learning at Howard back into black communities. Zetas braved the dangers of the South during a time when black secret societies of any kind were frowned upon. The first two expansion chapters were established in Georgia, at Morris Brown College, and Maryland, at Morgan State College. Three years after Zeta Phi Beta was founded, it established the first black sorority in the state of Texas, at Wiley College. Creating chapters at HBCUs and in other areas of the South continued to be a goal of the sorority even after chapters had been established at majority schools.

Zeta Phi Beta is a sorority of firsts. In 1937 it became the first black Greek-letter organization to hold its national convention south of the Mason-Dixon line. Staying true to their commitment to empower the black community, the Zetas held their convention in the black business section of downtown Houston. Because there were no restaurants or hotels that served blacks in the area, the YWCA provided catering for the event and the Zetas received their lodging through the black community. In 1948 Zeta Phi Beta established the first Greek-letter organization in Africa, when a charter was granted to establish a graduate chapter in Monrovia, Liberia. Famous HBCU alumnae who are Zetas include Zora Neale Hurston, who was one of the sorority's earliest pledges at Howard, and Esther Rolle, who attended Spelman.

The pressure to gain social status was so great during this period that academic achievement tended to take a backseat to popularity for a number of young women. This fact was well illustrated in the April 1929 issue of the Howard University student newspaper *The Hilltop*, where student journalist Ivan Earle Taylor recognized outstanding members of the senior class. Senior men such as Glenwood Jones, Baxter Goodall, Theodus Conner, and Charles Manney were cited for their leadership of the student council, the football team, or their dogged career focus. The women, however, were praised for their physical charms. Taylor praised "Lil" Johnson as being "pretty and from New Haven. . . . So gentle, so lovable." He wrote that Harriet Ferguson was the "striking exception to the rule that beauty and brains don't mix." And of Cozette Walker, who had won second place in Howard's popularity contest that year, Taylor wrote, "We have never been able to explain the reason for her popularity, except that she is so genteel and pleasing." Of the eight women mentioned in the article, only two, honor student Norma Parks and senior class officer Gladys Harris, were cited for their academic or leadership efforts.[9]

Fraternity members were particularly notorious for their eyebrow-raising

Clark College homecoming queens Irene Burch Williams and Lithia Bailey Clark, 1928.

campus hijinks and sometimes dangerous hazing of pledges. In his autobiography, *The Big Sea*, Langston Hughes recalled his experience pledging Omega Psi Phi fraternity. "Fraternity initiations occasionally sent agonized howls into the darkness around the countryside." Although he was already a well-known poet when he entered Lincoln, Hughes's Omega brothers were determined not to let the young bard off easily. They paddled him so often and so hard that he could "scarcely walk for a week." In one paddling episode, the Harlem Renaissance artist recalled his big brothers chiding him endlessly.

"A New Negro, huh?" Wham!

"The boy poet, heh?" Wham!

"So nobody else'll beat you, heh?" Wham!

"Letting you slip by easy, are they?" Wham! Wham! Wham![10]

Hughes was not the only famous frat brother to recall his college experience. Alpha man Thurgood Marshall built a reputation for coming up with some of the most dreaded hazing activities. One such antic involved having the pledges place a pickle between their buttocks and race around the room. After the preserves had fallen to the floor they would be placed in a bowl, swished around, and the pledges had to choose one to eat.[11]

Sororities and fraternities were not without significant redeeming value, however. Unlike their white counterparts, black Greek organizations created multiple chapters throughout the country and maintained ongoing relationships with their members after graduation. This network often proved invaluable when a fraternity or sorority member moved to a new town where he or she had no family or needed a network to find social, career, or educational opportunities.

Greek organizations also proved to be among the few student-run campus groups that engaged in continuous social service and political activities. Delta Sigma Theta was less than two months old when sorority members joined the women's suffrage movement, participating in a massive march on Washington in March 1913. Zeta Phi Beta was

Langston Hughes writes about his college days in his autobiography, *The Big Sea*.

founded in 1920 for the express purpose of combating the elitist nature of existing Greeks organizations. Community service was among the tenets of its mandate, and it was the first Greek organization to embrace pan-Africanism by chartering chapters in Africa. Omega man Carter G. Woodson gave birth to National Achievement Week at the fraternity's 1920 conclave, and it was through the continued efforts of other Omegas that the event became the nationally celebrated Black History Month. The Alphas conducted a national Education Week during which fraternity members visited schools and churches to encourage young black students to complete their education. They also provided schools and churches with books when possible. The Kappas mentored young men through their Guide Right Movement, which helped put them on a path toward college or vocational careers.

From Intramural to Intercollegiate

The growth of intercollegiate sports also helped to build the social network linking HBCU communities. Not only did sports events allow African American students to connect with counterparts attending other HBCUs, they also

provided opportunities for alumni to connect with current faculty, administrators, and students. Intercollegiate sports truly broadened the HBCU
community by creating traditions—and the resulting colloquialisms and affec-
tations—that were embraced and celebrated throughout the black college
universe. To be sure, the rivalry between teams was real, but the social opportunity that these events provided was far more important than a win or a loss.

Satellite events such as fraternity- and sorority-sponsored parties, tailgating
celebrations, and campus step shows were spawned, giving HBCU sports a
unique culture. These events allowed alumni to honor the schools that prepared them for success, students to feel that they were a part of a thriving,
elite community, and faculty and administrators to celebrate the fruits of
their labor.

In *The Black Student and the Black College*, Little writes that intercollegiate
sports did not exist on HBCU campuses during the earliest days because schools
could not afford to purchase equipment and enrollment was too sporadic to
field permanent teams. Nevertheless, most schools did provide intramural
competitions, and baseball was initially the most popular sport. By the end
of the nineteenth century both endowments and enrollments had grown, and

One of the famous Lincoln versus Howard football games. The game was long considered a premier event of black college life. Lincoln won this game, played on Thanksgiving Day 1945, 6–0.

schools began expanding their sports programs. The first football game between two HBCUs was played in 1892, when North Carolina–based Johnson C. Smith University (then known as Biddle College) produced a 4–0 victory over nearby Livingstone College. In 1896 Atlanta University, Clark College, Morehouse, and Morris Brown College took advantage of their close proximity and formed the first baseball league. The first intercollegiate football game was played on New Year's Eve 1897, when Atlanta University and Tuskegee competed.

Football rapidly became a popular sport, and by the early 1900s campus newspapers and alumni publications were providing extensive coverage of the games, with writers giving attention to the renowned

Coach Cleve "Major" Abbott was a key figure in increasing intercollegiate HBCU sporting events.

alumni and popular students in the stands as well as the game itself. In a November 1910 issue of the *Athenaeum*, a joint quarterly publication issued by Morehouse and Spelman students, seven pages were given to football coverage, with the writer reporting on games that Morehouse played against Talladega, Montgomery State, Fisk, Tuskegee, and Atlanta University. The journalist also wished a speedy recovery to then–Morehouse student Mordecai Johnson (future president of Howard University), who was injured during a game.[12]

Intercollegiate sports of all kinds grew after the creation of the Colored Intercollegiate Athletic Association in 1912 and the Southern Intercollegiate Athletic Conference in 1913. But by 1920 football had clearly become the most popular sport, and several "classics" were begun. The annual competition between Tuskegee and Morehouse and the Thanksgiving Day game between Lincoln University, Pennsylvania, and Howard were among the biggest draws, with alumni attending from around the country.

Coach Cleve "Major" Abbott, who arrived at Tuskegee the year after the death of Booker T. Washington, played a significant role in increasing intercollegiate HBCU events. Among the sports that Abbott coached were tennis, golf, track, baseball, and football. In 1927 he created the Tuskegee Relays, which became the third largest track event in the country. A number of future Olympians got their start training under Abbott and competing in the relays. The coach also created intercollegiate golf and tennis tournaments, which were held simultaneously with the relays. While these tournaments drew only a fraction of the supporters that football and track meets did, the events introduced an entire generation of HBCU students to the high-society sports of tennis and golf long before the Williams sisters or Tiger Woods demonstrated that African Americans can and do play them well.

HBCU SPORTS AND ATHLETES

The popularity of college sports was on the rise. This is a portrait of an early football star from Langston University in 1920.

Black colleges traditionally have turned out some of the world's greatest athletes. For over a century, HBCUs have fielded competitive athletic teams whose members have participated around the globe, from the dusty playing fields of rural southern campuses to capacity crowds in Helsinki and Japan.

Atlanta, Georgia, was the scene of one of the earliest black intercollegiate sporting events when Atlanta Baptist (now Morehouse) took on Atlanta University on a baseball diamond in 1890. The teams made their own bats and manicured the baseball diamond themselves. Two years later, Biddle University (now Johnson C. Smith) and Livingstone College played a "match game of ball" on a snow-covered field in North Carolina in the first black college football game. Most teams were "coached" by students; players made their own uniforms and stadiums were nonexistent. In the Livingstone-Biddle matchup, the Livingstone team pooled its resources to purchase a leather football specifically for the game. Cash-strapped HBCUs of the late nineteenth century did not spend money on fun and games. Sports took a back seat to the economic realities of the day. It was not unusual for classes and

Just after the turn of the century, sports became a popular distraction at HBCUs. The Atlanta University baseball team posed for this photograph, circa 1900. James Weldon Johnson is seated in the bottom row, third from the left.

sporting events to be suspended during planting and harvesting seasons, as well as during the vacation season of rich white Northerners, so that students and athletes could obtain work.

It wasn't until football and baseball began to draw large crowds during the early 1900s that schools took over control of athletic teams. In 1912 the first black college conference was formed. Colored Intercollegiate Athletic Association (CIAA) members included Virginia Union, Lincoln (Pennsylvania), Shaw, Hampton, and Howard. There were persistent problems with the early games, however. It was common for professional athletes to compete with and against college athletes: playing on black professional teams during summer breaks was more dignified work than washing dishes or shining shoes. Although the CIAA issued statements condemning professional participation in black college athletics, administrators turned a blind eye to the practice because the publicity that schools received from sports teams was the only way for them to gain recognition outside of their local areas.

The 1906 Cheyney baseball team takes a break.

Track and field started to increase in popularity in the 1920s. Tuske-gee's athletic director, Cleveland Abbott, created the Tuskegee Relays in 1927. His inclusion of women's events was monumental for women's sports. He hired Amelia C. Roberts to coach the Tuskegee women's team, and in 1937, they won the Amateur Athletic Union (AAU) Nationals, the highest honor for a track team. During his storied career at Tuskegee, Abbott also coached the football team, which won five Southern Intercollegiate Athletic Conference (SIAC) titles. This con-ference, created in 1913, included Florida A & M, Alabama A & M, Albama State, and Morris Brown. Black college coaches, unlike their counterparts at white schools, usually coached several different sports teams and taught classes as well.

While Abbott was dominating the SIAC, Morgan State's Edward Hunt was creating a dynasty in the CIAA. Coach Hunt, like most black college coaches, was a mythic, larger-than-life figure. From the late 1920s through the 1930s, Hunt coached some of the most dominant football and basketball teams in black college history. Morgan State's football team won seven CIAA football titles and had fifty-four consecutive victories from 1931 through 1938, a black college record. And the basketball teams of the Hunt era were considered as good as professional teams.

After World War II, baseball declined in popularity and basketball was beginning to rival football as the most popular sport on black college campuses. Despite the growing popularity, however, professional athletes continued to plague black college sports into the 1940s. Virginia Union's "dream team" won the CIAA title in 1940 and 1941, but the CIAA did not recognize their titles because they had played the Harlem Globetrotters.

When Althea Gibson arrived on the campus of Florida A & M in 1950, she had already won the American Tennis Association (ATA) singles title for three consecutive years. Before her graduation from FAMU in 1953, Gibson broke two color barriers. She was the first

The Langston University football team, seen here in 1925.

The Jackson State University baseball team as they were in 1925.

African American to compete in the National Grass Court Championship, and in 1951 she became the first African American to participate in Wimbledon. Gibson went on to become the first African American to win the French Open, Wimbledon, and the U.S. Open.

Tennessee State became the first black college team to win a national championship against a white school in 1957 when it won the National Intercollegiate Athletic Association (NIAA) championship in basketball. Coach Johnny B. McClendon's team repeated the feat in 1958, and again in 1959. McClendon left Tennessee State in 1961 to become the first black professional basketball coach for the Cleveland Pipers.

Track dominance transferred from Tuskegee, Alabama, to Nashville, Tennessee, where Tennessee State track coach Ed Temple and his Tigerbelles took their talents to the world stage. Temple coached Wilma Rudolph, who earned the title "the fastest woman in the world." She won three gold medals at the 1960 Olympics, a first for a female

Olympian. The 1964 women's Olympic team included three Tiger-belles, who brought home five medals. Crediting some of his success to his wife's support, Temple once remarked that his wife was the only woman he knew who condoned her husband spending time with "fast women."

While Temple was traversing the globe with his Tigerbelles, Clarence "Big House" Gaines was making history at Winston Salem State University. He was the first black coach to win an NCAA Division II championship in 1967. This team was led by the legendary Earl "The Pearl" Monroe. With 822 victories, Coach Gaines has the second most wins in college basketball history.

By the 1970s, women's basketball at black colleges was coming of age. Vivian Stringer started her coaching career at Cheyney State in 1971. During her eleven-year career, she had an impressive record of 251 victories and 51 losses. Stringer took the Cheyney women to the first Women's National Basketball Championship in 1982. Cheyney lost a hard-fought battle against perennial power Louisiana Tech, 76–62.

The 1970s also brought a shift in focus from dominant coaches to dominant players. This was the era of Walter Payton, Doug Williams, and Edwin Moses at Jackson State, Grambling, and Morehouse, respectively. During Walter Payton's playing days the Jackson State University signs that greeted visitors to the campus were covered up with signs that read "Payton's Place." By his junior year in 1973, Payton was named to five different all-American teams and led the nation in scoring with 160 total points. Never before had a player from a Division II black college attracted so much national attention. One writer from *Sporting News*

Although Morehouse is an all-male college, these young women proudly show their support by holding up a school pennant in 1925.

The Fisk football team in an undated photograph.

predicted that Payton, though a long shot, would be the first player from a black college to win the Heisman Trophy. All of the hype made for an electrifying atmosphere on the Jackson State campus in the fall of 1974. Before the season was over Payton would set nine different school records, rushing for 1,069 yards, scoring nineteen touchdowns, one field goal, and five extra points. He set a Southwestern Athletic Conference record for most points in a game and shattered the NCAA scoring record by producing 464 career points. Though he came in fourth in the Heisman Trophy race, his consolation prize was being the Chicago Bears' first pick in the 1975 draft.

When Doug Williams was recruited to attend football powerhouse Grambling State in 1973, head coach Eddie Robinson was already obsessed with the idea of a quarterback from his program becoming the first black chosen in the first round of the NFL draft. Williams picked apart opposing Southwestern Athletic Conference defenses. He was unstoppable in 1976 and was named Black College Player of the Year. Grambling and Morehouse became the first American colleges to play in Japan that same season. During his senior year Williams passed for a school record 3,286 yards. He came in fourth in Heisman Trophy voting and was named Black College Player of the Year once again. Williams's remarkable season earned him first team all-American honors, a first for a black college player. Coach Robinson got his wish when the Tampa Bay Buccaneers chose Williams in the first round of the 1978 NFL draft.

Twenty years after making history as a player, "Mother Grambling" called Doug Williams home to succeed his former coach Eddie Robinson in 1998. Robinson still holds the record for most victories in college football history and has sent 106 players to the NFL.

Edwin Moses was called the "Bionic Man" while a student at Morehouse. Moses was at the college on an academic scholarship, and although Morehouse had a track team, it did not have a track on which to practice or compete. Still, Moses won his first gold medal and set an Olympic world record in the 400-meter hurdles as a sophomore in the 1976 Olympics. Moses would later bemoan the fact that training for the Olympics caused his grade-point average to drop to 3.57. His amazing ten-year, 122-consecutive-win streak in the 400-meter hurdles began in 1977, a year before his graduation in 1978.

The greatest wide receiver in NFL history played college football at Mississippi Valley State. Jerry Rice still holds the black college record for most receiving yards and total receptions. Rice and quarterback Willie Totten produced one of the most lethal offenses in black college football history in 1984 when Totten set the single season record for most touchdown passes with sixty-one, and Rice set a single season record for most touchdown receptions with twenty-seven.

The heir apparent to Willie Totten was Alcorn State's Steve McNair. By the time McNair retired in 1994, he had set black college records for most career passing yards and total offensive yards. McNair has since enjoyed a successful career in professional football.

Black college athletes have continued to make their marks as players and coaches on both the college and professional levels. Halls of Fame of every sort are filled with the names of graduates of historically black college and universities' most illustrious sports alumni.

The "New Negro" Movement

At the very moment that HBCUs were giving birth to a black middle class, the schools were also giving rise to a phenomenon that would have definitive affects on American culture for decades to come. It was the "New Negro" movement, better known as the Harlem Renaissance. While the literary, music, and visual arts offerings of the Harlem Renaissance are widely celebrated, little attention is given to the role that HBCUs played in facilitating the movement. New York City, with its Broadway theaters, publishing houses, and Prohibition speakeasies, may have been the gathering place for the brilliant minds contributing to this cultural renaissance, but HBCUs were the incubators of its talent as well as the germinating points for much of its activity.

Alain Locke, W. E. B. DuBois, sociologist Charles S. Johnson, and writer-educator Jessie Fauset are most often cited as the elder statespeople of the "New Negro" movement. Unlike her three male counterparts, Fauset never held a professorship at an HBCU. She did, however, occupy a teaching post at the prestigious Washington, D.C., Dunbar High, a feeder school for Howard and other top HBCUs.

The debating team at Talladega, circa 1920.

Crisis magazine was an influential literary source during the Harlem Renaissance.

Locke's contribution and leadership of the Harlem Renaissance originated from his post at Howard, while DuBois, who left Atlanta University in 1910 to head up the fledgling National Association for the Advancement of Colored People, worked from New York City. Locke edited such definitive publications as the March 1925 issue of *Survey Graphics* magazine, which focused exclusively on the blossoming arts and culture movement in Harlem, and the 1925 anthology *The New Negro*. DuBois, along with Fauset, was editor of *Crisis* magazine, a quarterly publication of the NAACP that was a primary outlet for Harlem Renaissance writers and artists. Johnson, who eventually would head the sociology department at Fisk, spent part of the Harlem Renaissance as editor of the Urban League journal *Opportunity* and also was responsible for publishing many important literary and sociological works by black authors and scholars.

The pivotal role that HBCUs played in facilitating the Harlem Renaissance cannot be overstated. After years of teaching and sending young minds out into the world, both Locke and DuBois no doubt recognized that the time was ripe for these critical voices to be heard and seriously considered en masse. The artistic, cultural, and sociological statements that these young men and women were making about modern-day African American life had the power to reframe the debate about "the Negro problem," race in America, and the value of liberal arts education among blacks. To that end, the vast majority of the acknowledged literary voices of the Harlem Renaissance were college-educated, and almost all attended or received their degrees from HBCUs. Others became teachers at these institutions.

Among the most celebrated literary artists of the Harlem Renaissance were writers Zora Neale Hurston, who attended Morgan State and Howard universities; Langston Hughes, a graduate of Lincoln University, Pennsylvania; Nella Larson, who was a student at Fisk; and Claude McKay, who briefly attended Tuskegee. Painter Aaron Douglas, who taught at Fisk, was largely considered the movement's most prolific visual artist, but Howard graduate turned art professor James A. Porter was also among the ranks.

E. Franklin Frazier, who graduated from Howard and taught at Tuskegee, Morehouse, and Fisk before returning to his alma mater to teach, was a prolific writer of definitive sociological texts. So, too, was Horace Mann Bond, who graduated from Lincoln University, Pennsylvania, and taught at his alma mater Dillard University and several other prominent HBCUs before serving as president of Fort Valley State College and Lincoln.

Much of what coalesced during the Harlem Renaissance was in fact organic, but it is irrefutable that DuBois and Locke positioned themselves as the main arbitrators of the artistic and intellectual offerings of the period. For DuBois, the New Negro movement was the realization of his call for a talented tenth—a group of educated African Americans who would be the "leaders of thought and missionaries of culture among their people"—nearly two decades earlier.[13] DuBois believed that young men and women like Hughes, Frazier, Hurston, and Larson were critical thinkers whose eloquence and diversity of thought represented the capacity of the black race. They were to serve as examples, inspiring the masses of African Americans to embrace education and convincing white Americans that blacks could indeed be their intellectual equals.

For Locke, the Harlem Renaissance was an undoing of the myth of the "Old Negro," an objectified being who was not intelligent enough to be a man but too emotional to be an animal: "A creature of moral debate and historical controversy," wrote Locke in his 1925 *Survey Graphics* essay "Enter the New Negro." The revered educator argued that the "Old Negro" was a false creation spawned by white oppression and blacks' inferiority complex. He was "something to be argued about, condemned or defended, to be 'kept down,' or 'in his place,' or 'helped up,' to be worried with or worried over, harassed or patronized, a social bogey or a social burden."[14]

Opinions vary about when the Harlem Renaissance began and ended, but historians concur that the movement reached its pinnacle during the 1920s. Among the activities during the initial four years of that decade were the debut of *Shuffle Along*, the first Broadway musical written and performed by

The Duke Ellington Band with the chorus line at the Cotton Club in 1929 performing "Black and Tan Fantasy." Although African Americans were not allowed in as guests, the Cotton Club was the showcase for black entertainers.

African Americans, the opening of the legendary Cotton Club, and the publication of a multitude of black literary works in journals such as *Crisis, Opportunity*, and *The Messenger,* as well as seven major tomes by African American writers.

For Locke the cultural groundswell signaled that black America had "enough talent now to begin to have a movement—and to express a school of thought," as he wrote to a friend in the early 1920s.[15] The talent of which Locke spoke had been nurtured on the campuses and inside the classrooms of black colleges.

The early spiritual ensembles, which brought considerable fame and finance to numerous black schools, opened the door for musical training to flourish at HBCUs. While most of the instruction offered was in the realm of classical and traditional spirituals, beginning in the 1920s students put together jazz ensembles that were popular among their peers and the larger community. Fisk, for example, had the Fisk Collegians, fronted by musician-composer Jimmie Lunceford, who, after graduating in 1926, organized the internationally celebrated Gentlemen of Swing. Alabama State had the 'Bama State Collegians, led by Erskine Hawkins, who became a renowned trumpeter known as the "twentieth-century Gabriel."

These student-organized groups got their start by playing at campus events, faculty parties, and local haunts. In many cases, they planted the seeds for the acclaimed jazz programs later developed by some HBCUs.

Cultural pursuits were alive and well at HBCUs. Shown here is the Morehouse Orchestra and Glee Club in 1926.

HBCU ART COLLECTIONS

Some of the largest collections of African American and African art are in the museums and galleries on historically black college and university campuses. In addition to artists from the African diaspora, artworks from diverse cultures from around the world are featured in these valuable collections.

The Hampton University Museum is the oldest African American museum in the United States. The museum is located in a renovated historic 1903 beaux arts–style building that was formerly the university library, with 12,000 square feet of gallery space housing a collection of over 9,000 objects that feature African, Native American, Native Hawaiian, Pacific Island, and Asian art in ten different galleries. The permanent collection features the work of Joshua Johnson, the earliest African American painter whose work is still in existence.

Hampton's museum includes the work of Henry O. Tanner (*The Banjo Lesson*), Jacob Lawrence, Elizabeth Catlett, and Hampton alumnus John Biggers. The African art collection at the Hampton Museum is by far the most substantial collection at any African American museum or university in the country. The Native American art featured in the museum is a testament to Hampton's legacy of educating Native American students. Photographs depicting Hampton's early years show Native American students wearing and using some of the artifacts that are on display. The museum publishes the only periodical devoted to African American visual art, the *International Review of African American Art* (IRAAA).

Although Hampton has collected art, artifacts, photographs, and documents since it was founded, the board of trustees at Howard University established the first permanent gallery on an HBCU campus in 1928. Under the direction of James V. Herring, the Howard University Gallery of Art was housed on campus in the basement of the Andrew Rankin Memorial Chapel. One of the first works acquired by the gallery was Henry O. Tanner's *Return from the Crucifixion,* his last completed work before his death in 1937. In 1955 the gallery received a substantial contribution from the estate of Alain Locke. This contribution included 365 pieces and forms the centerpiece of the gallery's classical African art collection. In 1961 the Howard University Gallery of Art moved into larger quarters in the new fine arts complex, which features three interconnecting galleries. Works of art in the collection date from as far back as the early eighteenth century. Other highlights in the collection by African American artists are Charles White's *Progress of the American Negro* and Archibald Motley's *Carnival*. The Howard University Gallery of Art's collection has grown to over 4,500 pieces and features works from artists from around the world, including Renaissance and Baroque paintings donated by the Kress Foundation and the Irving Gumbel collection of European prints from the sixteenth through the nineteenth centuries.

Like Hampton, Fisk has collected art and artifacts dating back almost to the school's founding. Many of the faculty and staff who were active in the American Missionary Association, one of Fisk's founding patrons, were responsible for some of Fisk's earliest acquisitions. They sent back art and artifacts from their missionary journeys to Africa in the 1870s. In 1871, after the Fisk Jubilee Singers' successful European tour, which included a performance for Queen Victoria of England, the school received a life-size portrait of the Jubilee Singers as a gift from the queen. In 1949 Fisk received a gift from artist Georgia O'Keeffe from the estate of her late husband, renowned photographer Alfred Stieglitz. This acquisition of 101 paintings included several works by Pablo Picasso, Pierre-Auguste Renoir, Paul Cézanne, and O'Keeffe, as well as photographs by Alfred Stieglitz. When O'Keeffe came to the campus to select a space for the collection to be housed, she chose the old gymnasium, which was renovated and became the first permanent gallery on the Fisk campus. These works are now housed in the gallery named after Carl Van Vechten, writer and cultural critic who was a friend of O'Keeffe, and Fisk's first black president, Charles S. Johnson. Van Vechten facilitated the transfer of the works to the school. The Fisk University galleries also feature a gallery named after Aaron Douglas, the notable African American artist who formed Fisk's art department and chaired it for over thirty years.

The Clark Atlanta University Art Galleries include a permanent collection that features paintings, murals, sculpture, works on paper, and ethnographical artifacts. Muralist Hale Woodruff, who started the art department in 1931, spearheaded the creation of the permanent collection at Clark Atlanta. Woodruff's sweeping, six-paneled mural series, *The Art of the Negro*, greets visitors to the galleries and introduces a dynamic collection that features African American, African, and contemporary American art. Some of the most valuable pieces of African American art showcased at Clark Atlanta University Art Galleries were acquired during the now historic *Exhibition of Paintings, Prints and Sculpture by Negro Artists of America,* sponsored by Atlanta University from 1942 to 1970. Alain Locke gave the opening address at this first exhibition, which was nothing short of radical. Never before had an "all-Negro" show in the visual arts been exhibited. Although initially panned by white art critics, sometimes with racist commentary, the shows did much to expose the work of African American artists and engendered a general appreciation for black subject matter in the visual arts. Paintings and sculptures were acquired from artists who were then relatively unknown, but who are now considered masters—Jacob Lawrence, Elizabeth Catlett, Charles White, John Biggers, Lois Mailou Jones, and Roy DeCarava, among others.

In 1999 the Addison Gallery of American Art and the Studio Museum in Harlem put together a touring exhibition, *To Conserve a Legacy: American Art from Historically Black Colleges and Universities*. This exhibition featured some of the finest art from the galleries of Hampton, Howard, Fisk, Clark Atlanta University, Tuskegee, and North Carolina Central. This was a monumental event for African American artists and the black colleges that exhibit their work as part of their collections. The project also included a conservation training program for minority students and a book. The exhibition premiered at the Studio Museum in Harlem in March 1999 and made stops at the Addison Gallery of American Art in Massachusetts and the Art Institute of Chicago. The exhibition also toured the galleries of HBCUs that contributed the art in conjunction with such galleries as the Corcoran Gallery of Art in Washington, D.C., the High Museum of Art in Atlanta, and the Chrysler Museum in Virginia.

Although housed in the Barnes Foundation, 50 miles from the campus of Lincoln University, Pennsylvania, the Barnes collection is by far the most valuable art collection controlled by an HBCU. Considered one of the world's most significant private art collections, it boasts 181 Renoirs, sixty-nine Cézannes, several Matisses and Picassos, African sculpture, and thousands of other pieces estimated to be worth billions of dollars. Lincoln assumed control of the collection after millionaire Albert C. Barnes died in a car accident in 1951. Barnes and Horace Mann Bond, Lincoln's first black president, had become friends five years earlier and Barnes's intention for the collection was "to weld Lincoln and the foundation in an education enterprise that has no counterpart elsewhere."[16]

The Barnes collection has been mired in controversy in recent years as a series of legal challenges have been waged to wrest control of the collection from the school. The Barnes Foundation and some wealthy Philadelphians contend that the school has not been a good custodian of the collection. But Lincoln is committed to fighting to maintain the relationship between Barnes and Bond that has joined Lincoln and the Barnes collection together for almost half a century.

Among the ranks of visual artists, the contributions from HBCU-affiliated talent were equally as strong. Famed Tuskegee scientist George Washington Carver was also an acclaimed artist. Carver painted compelling canvases of the plants and flowers he bred, and they were displayed at a small campus gallery. For many students, Carver's paintings were their first exposure to fine art in an academic setting.

Painter James Amos Porter obtained his art degree from Howard in 1927. Porter (who later returned to Howard to teach) created a wealth of highly prized work, including *Woman Holding a Jug,* which won the 1933 Arthur Schomburg Portrait Prize. Aaron Douglas was commissioned by Fisk president Thomas Jones in 1929 to paint a mural in the new library. Douglas designed a didactic piece, which conveyed how African Americans went from free Africans to slaves in the New World to their current state of freedom and educational triumph. The artist hired three Fisk students, none of whom had ever painted, to assist him with the project. Douglas also taught an art class there.

The existence of theater on black college campuses was a direct outgrowth of the popular debate and oratory clubs that began to appear on HBCU campuses prior to the Civil War. Founding missionaries encouraged these clubs because they were an important element of the liberal arts curriculum and because they provided future ministers with opportunities to hone their presentations and persuasive powers. One of the first such clubs was Giddings Lyceum at Wilberforce, where students debated subjects such as repatriation to Africa, coeducation, and temperance laws. Rhetorical competitions, which added theatrical elements to oration and debate, and theater groups soon followed. In 1915 Talladega showed its growing commitment to theater arts when it converted a campus barn into a theater. The administration also began an arts lecture series in 1922, bringing nationally known musicians, vocalists, and entertainers to the campus. Professor Leonard Drewry directed the college theater, and in 1929 he, along with the students who formed the Talladega College Little Theatre Players, mounted a major original production that reenacted the history of the school.

THEATER AT HBCUs

Black involvement in American theater can be traced back as far as 1769 when a black character named Raccoon appeared in Thomas Forrest's play *The Disappointment*. The stage has always had a place for the black performer, though the roles made available were often less than desirable.

After years of emphasizing normal and industrial training, HBCUs slowly started to shift their focus to liberal arts education. This opened the door for formal training in the dramatic arts. Although black theater groups had been operating in the United States since as early as 1820, dramatic courses would not be offered for academic credit at an HBCU until the early 1900s.

In 1909 biology instructor Ernest Everett Just and a group of students at Howard University founded the College Drama Club and started giving performances at the Howard Theatre. The shows staged were so financially successful that they were able to donate a clock to the Andrew Carnegie Library on the Howard campus. In 1919 the College Drama Club was changed to the Howard Players, and that same

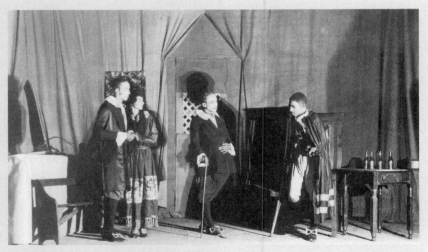

The Talladega College Little Theatre Players.

year T. Montgomery Gregory took over the speech department and began to offer courses for academic credit in drama.

In 1949 the Howard Players became the first college drama group to go on an international tour; they toured Norway, Sweden, Denmark, and Germany under the direction of Anne Cook. Alumni from the Howard Players are a veritable who's who in African American film and television. They include Ossie Davis, Roxie Roker, Debbie Allen, Phylicia Rashad, Lynn Whitfield, and Isaiah Washington.

Students and faculty members at Tougaloo College in Mississippi attempted to convey the civil rights struggle dramatically on stage. The Free Southern Theater (FST), whose name approximated the Freedom Schools, was founded by Doris Derby, Gilbert Moses, and John O'Neal in 1964. From its inception, the purpose was to deliver performances to sectors of the state, and ultimately throughout the South, that had not experienced the theater. The group toured extensively in the rural regions of Mississippi, Alabama, and Georgia before establishing its headquarters in New Orleans in 1965.

Over the years theater departments have emerged at other HBCUs. Notable programs include Prairie View A & M, Spelman, Morgan State, and North Carolina A & T. The drama department at Morehouse produced Bill Nunn and Samuel L. Jackson. Two other prominent film and television actors who attended HBCUs, although they did not study drama, are Tim Reid, who majored in business at Norfolk State University, and Michael Clark Duncan, who studied communications at Alcorn State University.

Wilberforce drama students in 1970.

WRITERS

Storytelling has been an ineradicable part of black life. Griots from Africa preserved tribal histories and established the pattern of passing down stories orally from generation to generation. Displaced Africans arriveing on American shores continued to tell stories orally out of necessity—because learning to write could bring severe punishment, or even death.

There were blacks, however, who did learn to write, and a few even got their work noticed before the abolition of slavery. Jupiter Hammon was the first African American to have his writing published; his poem "An Evening Thought" went to press in 1760. Phillis Wheatley's *Poems on Various Subjects,* the first book published by an African American, came thirteen years later in 1773.

Historically black colleges and universities have produced an impressive number of successful writers who carry on the long tradition of African American storytelling. This is particularly striking since creative writing programs are nonexistent on HBCU campuses. Lincoln University produced one of the best-known African American writers in Langston Hughes. Ralph Ellison is a product of Tuskegee, and James Weldon Johnson graduated from Atlanta University.

Author Tina McElroy Ansa was thankful she chose to attend Spelman College because it was there she was introduced to the writings and scholarship of Zora Neale Hurston, whose presence during the Harlem Renaissance has been widely documented. "I took a course from Gloria Wade Gayles," she recalled. "I had never heard of Zora Neale Hurston, and at the time *Their Eyes Were Watching God* was being reprinted, sort of just being rediscovered." Discovering Hurston, who attended Howard University, was a blessing to Ansa, and she admits that her own books and stories owe much to Hurston's influence.

Ansa says, however, that writing wasn't a popular career choice in the 1960s and 1970s on HBCU campuses, and it wasn't encouraged by her professors. This is ironic, given that during this time African American writers won more Pulitzer Prizes and National Book Awards than in any previous period of American history. Pulitzer Prize–winning authors Alice Walker (Spelman) wrote *The Third Life of Grange Copeland,* James Alan McPherson (Morris Brown) wrote *Elbow Room,* and Toni Morrison (Howard) published *The Bluest Eye*.

Morrison, the first black woman to win the Nobel Prize for Literature, changed her name from Chloe Anthony Wofford to "Toni" when she was an undergraduate at Howard because she thought her birth name was too difficult to pronounce. After obtaining her master's degree at Cornell, she started her teaching career at Texas Southern University. After two years, she returned to her alma mater, where she taught in the Howard English department. It was during her time on the Howard English faculty that she began writing fiction. Howard also produced writers Zora Neale Hurston and Omar Tyree.

In 1966 John O. Killens founded the first Fisk Black Writers Conference, which drew writers such as Amiri Baraka, Margaret Walker, Ron Milner, and Haki Madhubuti. Nikki Giovanni, a student at Fisk at the time, took advantage of this seminal event and immersed herself in the workshops. The fire expressed in Giovanni's early work was clearly influenced by the theme of art as social change, which pervaded the writers' conference at Fisk. Giovanni since has written over twenty books in a career that has spanned more than thirty years.

Gwendolyn Brooks, the first African American to win a Pulitzer Prize, in 1950, attended the second Fisk Black Writers Conference in 1967. Her experience at Fisk revolutionized her writing and transformed her treatment of black subject matter in her work.

Other writers of note who attended HBCUs are Nella Larson (Fisk), Lerone Bennett Jr. (Morehouse), Iyanla Vanzant and Gloria Naylor (Medgar Evers College), and Nathan McCall and Curtis G. Bunn (Norfolk State).

Almost every HBCU campus had multiple literary groups by the 1920s. Atlanta University had the Phyllis Wheatley Literary Society, while Howard University had the Stylus Club, a national organization founded by Alain Locke. The Stylus Club was created for the "encouragement and development of original literary expression," and competition for membership was stiff. Students wishing to join the group submitted creative writing samples, and writers of the best-judged samples were admitted into the club. Countee Cullen and Atlanta University graduate James Weldon Johnson were among the national members who judged the submissions.[17]

Locke's assertion that there was enough talent for an artistic movement that expressed black culture and thought was clearly based on his intimate knowledge of the creativity on black college campuses. In early 1925, he was given an opportunity to showcase some of that talent. Locke was approached by *Survey* magazine, a journal read primarily by academics, intellectuals, and sociologists, and asked to edit an illustrated "Graphics" issue focusing on the New Negro. The educator used his Howard professorship as a bully pulpit for gathering an impressive array of submissions. *Survey Graphics* hit the stands in March and HBCU alumni and faculty were strongly represented among the featured writers, with Claude McKay, Langston Hughes, W. E. B. DuBois, Howard University professor Kelly Miller, Charles S. Johnson, and James Weldon Johnson all contributing. The hugely successful edition became the best-selling issue in the history of the magazine.

Jamaican immigrant Claude McKay, who attended Tuskegee in 1912, emerged as the premier young voice of the New Negro movement when his work appeared in *Seven Arts,* making him the first African American writer to be published in a white avant-garde literary magazine. McKay's patois poetry and revolutionary sonnets cast him among the initial stars of the New Negro movement.

Zora Neale Hurston, another celebrated Harlem Renaissance literary talent, arrived at Howard University in 1920 and immediately caught the attention of Locke. The professor was notoriously preferential to male students (it was rumored that he began the first day of classes by telling his female students that the majority would receive C's), but he took an uncharacteristic interest in Hurston, whose outrageous wit and highly colorful yarns were irresistible. She gained a coveted membership in the Stylus Club, and some of her work was featured in the organization's publication.

ZORA NEALE HURSTON
AUTHOR OF THEIR EYES WERE WATCHING GOD

MULES AND MEN

"Simply the most exciting book on black folklore and culture I have ever read."   —Roger D. Abrahams

Writer Zora Neale Hurston was one of the literary giants of the Harlem Renaissance. *Mules and Men* was one of her successful titles.

Hurston had a down-to-earth intelligence and was filled with anecdotes remembered from her childhood growing up in the all-black town of Eatonville, Florida. Those experiences found their way into her writing, and Locke was the first to recognize that her work could provide an authentic literary connection to black folk life. In Locke's view, it was an imperative connection that gave voice to a shared African American experience. No matter their particular standings, the majority of African Americans had roots in southern rural life, yet most literary representations of this lifestyle had been distortions offered by racists or well-meaning white abolitionists. By contrast, Hurston's work was an authentic portrayal of southern black life and an important piece of the African American cultural puzzle that Locke and others were trying to construct through the New Negro movement. Locke helped Hurston build a bridge between the world of her youth—which provided fodder for future works such as *Mules and Men, Spunk,* and most notably her classic novel *Their Eyes Were Watching God*—and the literary world.

It was Lincoln University, Pennsylvania, that nurtured the literary talents of Langston Hughes. The young literary talent—who had published his poetry collection *The Weary Blues* as well as his signature missive *The Negro Speaks of Rivers*—was already a successful poet by the time he arrived at the school in 1926. But he would write his first novel at Lincoln—*Not Without Laughter.* Administrators at Lincoln supported the young poet's work by allowing Hughes to remain in the dormitory free of charge during the summer months of his junior and senior years.

The encouragement that Hughes received while at Lincoln was the antithesis of what he had experienced upon his arrival as a freshman at Columbia University in New York City three years earlier. There, a school administrator had tried to prevent his admittance into the dormitory. Hughes finally was admitted, but only to be snubbed consistently by his white dorm mates. He was also prevented from participating in all but the most requisite of extracurricular activities at the Ivy League institution.

At Lincoln, the already famous poet fell easily into college life, evidenced by a letter written to his close friend Carl Van Vechten shortly after his arrival at the school. "I like the school out here immensely," penned Hughes, who went on to describe the scenic rural landscape, rolling hills, and trees surrounding the campus. "Life is crude, the dorms like barns but comfortable, food plain and solid, first bell at six-thirty, and nobody dresses up,—except Sunday." At Lincoln, Hughes found what so many other black college students before and after him would continue to discover: HBCUs offer up a safe but intellectually challenging space for young African Americans to begin to explore, express, define, and reflect on their culture and experience.

While the artists of the Harlem Renaissance concerned themselves with reflecting African American culture, HBCU graduates and sociologists such as E. Franklin Frazier and Horace Mann Bond were busy defining and qualifying the experiences that shape black people and their communities. Their contributions to the Harlem Renaissance were as important as the artistic ones because they presented an entire social and cultural context from which to view the artistic movement. The work presented by Frazier and Bond ensured that the artistic offerings of the Harlem Renaissance were not viewed in a vacuum, and they helped white America see that blacks were indeed a crucial part of the American experience. Their text also defined the spirit of the New Negro. In an essay for *The Annals of the American Academy of Political and Social Science,* Bond wrote that he and his peers were imbued with a "novel attitude [whose] spirit . . . frees itself from a provincial and subjective view of race and its problems." Frazier's analysis spoke clearly of the militancy and cultural arrogance that black college students of the 1920s wholly embraced.

The HBCU-trained artists and intellectuals who converged in the 1920s and produced works that became synonymous with the Harlem Renaissance were the bountiful harvest over a half-century in the making. The stock market crash of 1929 ushered in the depression, and the difficult financial years that followed forced HBCU administrations, faculty, and students to shift their focus. Where social status, cultural chic, and artistic endeavors had been stage front during the postwar boom, financial stability, civil rights, and concern over a brewing second world war would become the order of the day during the coming period. Nevertheless, a cultural and artistic legacy had come into its own during the 1920s, due in large part to the educational efforts and influence of HBCUs. That legacy would continue to expand and evolve during the coming decades.

A music professor interacts with his students at Fort Valley State University.

MUSICIANS

HBCUs have served as a vast conservatory of black musical talent. Some of the biggest names in jazz, opera, and rhythm and blues have studied at historically black colleges.

Leontyne Price was inspired to sing when she was 9 years old after hearing African American opera singer Marian Anderson perform in 1936. Price received a full scholarship to Central State College, where she trained to be a music teacher. She discovered her true vocal range while she was in the college choir. Price was accustomed to singing alto, but after a piano instructor asked her to sing a song in the lyric soprano range, she broadened the reach of her vocal talents. After graduating from Central State in 1948, she attended the Juilliard School in New York. Not long after finishing Juilliard, Price landed the role of Bess in *Porgy and Bess.* In addition to mesmerizing audiences around the world with her voice, Price was the first opera singer to receive the Presidential Medal of Freedom, from President Lyndon B. Johnson, in 1965. She influenced a generation of African American opera singers, including Grammy Award–winning Jessye Norman, a Howard alumna who graduated cum laude in 1967.

HBCU alumni also impacted the jazz world. Nat and Julian "Cannonball" Adderley attended Florida A & M, Erskine Hawkins attended Alabama State, and Billy Eckstine attended Howard for one year before striking out on his professional career.

A good number of contemporary artists attended HBCUs, including Erykah Badu (Grambling), Toni Braxton (Morgan State), Sean Combs (Howard), Terry Ellis (Prairie View), and Brian McKnight and Take 6 (Oakwood).

6

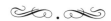

SEASON OF THREAT

HBCUs faced a new threat as the Great Depression, a new world war, and sweeping political changes unsettled the nation. The continued growth and existence of many HBCUs was jeopardized. The major challenge came from the stock market crash of 1929, which ushered in a thirteen-year economic depression. Fewer African Americans can afford college, and HBCUs struggle to keep their doors open in the face of falling enrollments.

B Y THE END of the 1920s, HBCUs had established themselves as invaluable contributors to the idealistic and lofty educational goals of the United States. Black colleges had grown substantially during the first two decades of the twentieth century. Schools like Fisk, Howard, Morehouse, Spelman, Atlanta University, Hampton, and Tuskegee had become the darlings of philanthropic organizations, and large-scale donations had allowed these schools to build beautifully landscaped and architecturally impressive campuses. Black college libraries acquired valuable literary collections and archives, and faculty members developed ambitious graduate programs. In addition, a number of schools had gained or were in the process of gaining accreditation.

Bread lines and unemployment lines were a common sight following the 1929 stock market crash.

Howard University's Founders Library.

Yet even during the prosperous postwar era, black colleges experienced neither the levels of prolific growth nor the financial security of their white counterparts. Amid the heady, prosperous days of the Roaring Twenties, many HBCUs struggled to keep their doors open. With the major source of funding for black schools shifting from religious groups to corporate-affiliated philanthropic organizations, HBCUs found themselves being held to the strict curriculum and faculty standards of these entities in order to qualify for financial support. Many philanthropic organizations were only interested in funding schools with technical curriculums, however, leaving liberal arts colleges desperate to identify sources of financial support. In many cases, liberal arts schools that called themselves colleges, but were actually no more advanced than high schools, closed because of a lack of funding. The number of black institutions of higher learning went from an all-time high of 217 schools in 1920 to 130 by 1930. The AME Church–affiliated Turner College in Tennessee and Lampton

College in Louisiana were among the schools that closed. The specific causes of the closings varied, but nearly all could be attributed to a lack of government or private funds to hire teachers, purchase books, or maintain school buildings.

D. O. W. Holmes wrote in a 1933 issue of the *Journal of Negro Education* that little of the money donated by philanthropic foundations during the postwar era had been earmarked as endowment funds—contributions set aside for financial growth, asset acquisition, and investment. That fact would prove to be particularly troublesome to black colleges during the coming decade as the nation entered an extended period of financial downturn.

The End of Prosperity

On October 21, 1929, the American stock market began a rapid, devastating descent that quickly plunged the rich into financial uncertainty, the middle class into poverty, and the poor into destitution. Brought on by unbalanced distribution of wealth and aggressive stock market speculation, the Great Depression lasted nearly thirteen years. At its most acute point in 1933, unemployment reached nearly 25 percent nationwide, customers made runs on banks out of fear that they would lose what little money they had tucked away, and colleges saw swift declines in enrollment.

What the general population suffered as a result of the depression, black Americans suffered doubly. African American unemployment stood at 50 percent for more than two years; the number of black-owned banks dropped from 134 in 1929 to only 12 by 1938. Beginning in 1933, many white Americans were able to find jobs through President Roosevelt's New Deal programs, but black Americans were often denied employment. A 1935 report from the *Journal of Negro Education* noted that in Dallas County, Alabama, blacks comprised 75 percent of the population but only 69 young black men had been given jobs at federal government–sponsored work camps, while 155 young white men had found employment at the camps. Additionally, black agricultural workers lost jobs when farm owners—most of them white—were paid by the federal government to reduce crop production.

The declining economic security of African Americans had a grave effect on black colleges. A 1933 survey by the *Journal of Negro Education* reported

In 1923 Daytona Normal and Industrial Institute merged with Cookman College to form Bethune-Cookman.

that 60 percent of HBCUs experienced an enrollment drop of between 1 and 40 percent. That same report also noted that the median annual family income of black college students was approximately $1,559.52—less than half of the $3,129.05 annual median family income of white college students. Unable to afford school, many young blacks who normally might have entered college after high school left home in search of employment rather than education. Errol Lincoln Uys writes in his book, *Riding the Rails: Teenagers on the Move During the Great Depression,* that some blacks jumped boxcars, rode the rails, and picked up odd jobs wherever they could. By mid-decade, 98 percent of black youths were unemployed, compared to 85 percent of white youths.

Not only did schools lose tuition money as a result of falling enrollments; donor contributions also decreased and HBCUs were forced to tap into their meager, often fledgling endowments in order to stay afloat. Desperate times demanded that HBCU administrators employ creative, uncommon methods to stabilize enrollment and cut expenses.

Before and during the depression, a number of HBCUs combined their assets through mergers and consortiums so that they could focus resources on raising standards and remaining open. Daytona Normal and Industrial Institute merged with Cookman College in 1923 to become Bethune-Cookman

College. In 1929 newly appointed Atlanta University president John Hope—the school's first black president—negotiated a consortium between his college, Morehouse, and Spelman. The agreement called for the schools to share faculty and curriculum resources and limited Atlanta University to graduate degrees, while Morehouse provided undergraduate degrees to African American men and Spelman to black women. (Morris Brown and Clark, now Clark Atlanta University, joined the consortium in 1972.) In 1930 New Orleans College, which was founded by the Methodist Episcopal Church, and Straight College, established by the AMA, merged to form Dillard University. In what was undoubtedly an effort to draw financial support from the Slater Fund, school administrators named the new college after the fund's president, James H. Dillard.

The issue of consolidation was not always looked upon favorably, however. During the AME Church's 1932 general conference members once again vigorously debated the need to merge or close smaller, less viable schools so that larger schools such as Wilberforce and Morris Brown could prosper. The financially desperate times made resolution of the debate even more urgent. By this time, Wilberforce was experiencing an annual budget shortfall of roughly $25,000. The support that the school received from the church—whose donations had dwindled as a result of the depression—fell from $41,481.74 in 1929 to just $12,793.63 in 1932.

On the one hand, predepression monetary challenges like the lack of endowment funds and a small pool of philanthropic donors—many of whom only gave to black technical and agricultural colleges—meant that HBCUs felt the financial squeeze brought on by the market crash more sharply and sooner than many white institutions of higher learning. On the other hand, black schools—well versed in financial belt tightening and alternative methods of generating income and receiving compensation—were already armed with many of the skills needed to survive the financial crisis. HBCU administrators devised ingenious tactics that kept their doors open and allowed young black students to continue their education. In the end, however, it was the united, selfless determination of administrators, teachers, and students that ensured the survival of black colleges during the Great Depression.

HBCUs Tighten Their Belts

As tuition funds decreased, HBCU administrators employed a number of measures to reduce expenses. Similar to their presidential counterparts at white colleges, black school presidents cut staff travel expenses, publicity costs, and expenditures on entertainment, sports teams, and campus events. They also eliminated paid teaching sabbaticals. Numerous HBCUs also shut down their elementary and secondary schools, which received little by way of foundation financing.

Reducing expenditures on campus and physical plant maintenance was one area where HBCU administrators felt they could cut costs with minimal negative effect on faculty and students. But there needed to be some level of continued care given to the properties or many of the new buildings and assets that had been purchased just prior to the stock market crash would decline in value. Taking cues from their schools' pasts, HBCU administrators instituted work-study programs where students labored on campuses as gardeners, janitors, cooks, farmers, handymen, maids, and more. The arrangements helped HBCUs maintain the value and good condition of school property and fulfilled the service needs of the university populations. In exchange, determined students were able to earn money toward their tuition. One school president estimated that his university's work-study expenditures were in the range of $1,000 per month. The expense was a steep outlay given the financial times, but it was one that many HBCUs struggled to cover so that deserving students could continue their education.

"The colleges this year were faced with an army of eager youth, in the midst of their college careers, standing at the doors and asking a little time to pay, and a chance to go on," wrote D. O. W. Holmes in the January 1933 issue of the *Journal of Negro Education*. HBCU administrators stretched the boundaries of accommodation in an effort to answer that urgent need. Some schools accepted farm products in lieu of cash for tuition payments. Others reduced housing expenses and allowed students to prepare their own meals instead of requiring them to pay for mandatory meal plans as they had in previous years.

A few schools even managed to increase the number of scholarships and loans that they were able to provide students.

"A drive for scholarships was put on and some secured," wrote one HBCU administrator in response to the *Journal*'s inquiry about depression-era strategies. "We are offering 100 scholarships worth on the average $50.00 and 30 more of less value."[1]

While HBCU presidents were highly reluctant to do so, many were forced to cut faculty and reduce teachers' salaries in order to balance school budgets. Not wishing to add to the already high unemployment rate among African Americans, most administrators opted for across-the-

Administrators and faculty at Voorhees in the early 1930s.

board salary cuts instead of layoffs. Roughly 40 percent of HBCU presidents answering the *Journal*'s 1933 survey reported that they had let go of faculty, while 60 percent estimated a 2 to 30 percent reduction in the salaries of teachers.

"Our State Fund of $140,000 a year for teachers has been reduced 20 percent," wrote one HBCU president. "This $28,000 reduction was absorbed in the reduction of the salaries of our workers. When teachers are poorly paid to start with, a reduction in the amounts which they receive is always depressing. To date, we have not been forced into a reduction in personnel. In spite of the reductions in salaries, our teachers have to date maintained a fine spirit."[2]

The willingness of faculty members to accept salary reductions was undoubtedly a sign of the financial times. Though blacks suffered dispropor-tionately, the depression had left its mark on the vast majority of Americans. Black teachers with jobs were simply happy to be employed and knew that if they complained of salary cuts, other equally qualified teachers would gladly accept their positions.

Black educators' readiness to share the financial burden not only allowed HBCU administrators to maintain their curriculum standards during a volatile financial period; it also allowed them to focus on maintaining enrollment and keeping their schools open. In the rare instance that schools were able to hire new faculty, HBCU administrators found that they were able to pick from a large pool of highly qualified educators who were willing to work at reduced salaries. "All of the new teachers we employed this year hold graduate degrees from standard colleges of the North and West. Some of them have advanced work toward their doctorate," noted one black college president.[3]

Government funding provided state-financed HBCUs with better security than their privately financed counterparts. In addition, a few state-funded black colleges were pleased to report that their appropriations had been reduced by the exact same percentage as white schools. Two schools even revealed that they received smaller reductions than other state-financed institutions slated for similar cuts.

"Even though budgets from other institutions outside of colleges were cut, the institution appealed to the legislature and was fortunate enough to operate as in the old budget," wrote one HBCU president.[4]

Black Students Struggle

Black college students also made tremendous sacrifices and endured hardships in order to remain in school. A study of Howard University students conducted between 1929 and 1931 found that the average student scraped by on roughly two-thirds of the ideal minimum annual support, which was estimated at $800 for men and $850 for women. Whereas 24 percent of white college males and just fewer than 6 percent of white college females were the sole sources of their tuition payments, nearly 69 percent of African American college men and 10 percent of African American college women were solely responsible for earning their own tuition.

Students clocked long hours in order to pay for school, some working as many as twelve hours a day. Parents of black college students, whose earnings averaged just $1,560 annually (less than half of what the average white college students' parents earned), also made significant sacrifices to keep their children in college. Despite their best efforts to do so, a large number of HBCU students were unable to complete their education as a result of the depression. Responding to the *Journal of Negro Education* survey in 1933, one HBCU president wrote that he expected second-semester enrollment to be substantially less than the first semester. "I dictated a letter yesterday to twenty-five students asking them to withdraw because of their inability to pay their expenses," wrote the president. "Many of our students are self-supporting, and they were unable to secure work last summer so that they may remain in school during all of this school term."[5]

HBCUs Press On

Even in the face of financial devastation, not all of the news was bad for HBCUs during the depression era. At Lincoln University, Missouri, the number of students pursuing graduate studies climbed to 23 percent between 1929 and 1938, due in part to a state assistance program that paid Lincoln graduates' tuitions.

In this period of economic downturn, Fisk University completed a $400,000 library, while Howard continued construction on its university plant, estimated to be worth $20 million. The financing for this venture came in 1932 when Mordecai Johnson managed to secure money from Congress for a twenty-year university development plan that called for the construction of three dormitories, a chemistry building, a new library, and a classroom building. The plan was funded through the Cramton Bill, which was passed in 1928 to ensure permanent annual federal appropriations for the university. It was during the 1930s that Howard's library also became a nationally recognized clearinghouse and center for the study of black history.

Meanwhile, Fisk continued development of its sociology program, which, under the leadership of Charles Johnson, became one of the most recognized programs on any university—black or white. The success of Fisk's program spurred extensive sociological studies of African American communities by professors at a number of HBCUs and the first comprehensive visions and voices of black America written and researched by black Americans began to emerge.

In 1929 Johnson and his staff launched a massive effort to interview and record the life stories of former slaves in Tennessee, Kentucky, and Alabama. Southern University professor John B. Cade began a similar project in Louisiana that same year, and in 1934 Kentucky State University professor Lawrence Reddick secured support from the Federal Emergency Relief

Fund to begin his own survey of freedmen in Kentucky and Indiana. Unemployed African American college students were hired as surveyors. In 1934 W. E. B. DuBois returned to Atlanta University as chairman of the Sociology Department.

A First-Class Law School Is Born

It was also during the depression era that many of the legal minds who would play key roles in forthcoming civil rights cases began their law training. Not long after taking over the presidency of Howard, Mordecai Johnson began a campaign of evaluating and, where necessary, revamping the curriculums of key schools so that they all met accreditation standards. After meeting with accreditation officials, he quickly learned that the Howard law school fell woefully short of meeting the standards of the American Association of Law Schools. Johnson used his connections to secure a meeting with Supreme Court Justice Louis D. Brandeis, who invited Johnson to his home to discuss his concerns about the school. During their meeting Johnson posed a very simple, but key question: "If you were President of Howard University, Mr. Justice, in what way would you proceed to build up a first-class law school?"[6]

Johnson sat quietly as Brandeis set out the clear and direct path of development that ultimately put Howard on the path of creating some of the most successful and respected civil rights attorneys in the history of the United States. "Dr. Johnson, if I were you I would put aside the question of quantity altogether. I would select a few of the ablest men you can find and train them how to proceed in the courts of law to secure civil and constitutional rights for your people," said Brandeis, noting that one of the biggest challenges facing African Americans was the fact that they had yet to secure basic civil and constitutional rights.[7] Brandeis went on to impart a highly confidential observation to Johnson, telling the college president that what he was about to say had to remain undisclosed until his death.

Brandeis confided that as a Supreme Court justice he had witnessed several cases where African Americans had sought to enforce their civil rights, but the cases had been lost due to a lack of mastery of constitutional law. "I have been made aware that the members of the Supreme Court desired greatly to decide these cases on their behalf. But in practically every instance, Dr. Johnson, these important cases have been so poorly prepared by both white and Negro lawyers that the Court was obliged to throw the cases out or to decide them apparently against you, because the . . . constitutional issue was not clear. . . .

"Dr. Johnson, your civil rights are in that constitution."[8]

Buoyed by the words of Brandeis, Johnson set about building a law school with a faculty and program focused on civil rights and constitutional law. His first step was to shift from a part-time night school curriculum to a full-time day school curriculum. Next, he focused on building a first-class faculty. In 1929 Johnson sent a telegram to deans at leading law schools asking them to forward the names of black graduates who had finished near the top of their classes and who "were men of integrity."[9] He received no less than ten replies.

Johnson appointed then-current law school professor Charles Hamilton Houston as vice dean of the School of Law and gave him the responsibility of revamping the curriculum into a full-time day school program. The Howard president was able to offer little in the way of financial compensation, considering the professional caliber of the attorneys whom he sought to secure as faculty. Still, his goal of creating an intense training ground for the mastery of constitutional law was an attractive incentive for the legal minds that joined the staff. Houston recruited future Circuit Court of Appeals judge William Hasties, Texas attorney James M. Nabrit, who later succeeded Johnson as president, Leon A. Ransom, George C. Jefferson, and D. C. Municipal Court judge James Adali Cobb to serve on the faculty.

One of the first tasks of the new faculty was creating a civil rights case review and analysis class, which became the core of the new curriculum. In this course, students dissected failed cases, analyzed why they had not been successful, then developed new grounds on which the cases could be argued. In what would become one of the most successful and important legal partnerships in American history, the students essentially became law clerks for the NAACP's legal counsel. In this capacity they were exposed to and helped develop arguments for precedent-setting civil rights cases. The new law school's first class entered in the fall of 1930 and graduated in the spring of 1933. Among the students were Thurgood Marshall and respected civil rights attorney Oliver W. Hill Sr.

THURGOOD MARSHALL

Thurgood Marshall received his higher education exclusively at HBCUs. When he arrived on the campus of Lincoln University in 1926 he was a huckster who rarely studied and was noted for pranks and boisterous stories around the bonfire before football games. Born July 2, 1908, the only indication that Marshall would one day play a pivotal role to end legal segregation and become the nation's first black Supreme Court justice was when he made the Lincoln debate team during his freshman year.

He pledged Alpha Phi Alpha and immediately became involved in fraternity pranks. This would prove costly his sophomore year when Marshall, along with a group of his classmates, was expelled for hazing. Among them was Langston Hughes who drafted a confession, presented it to the faculty, and got Thurgood and the other students readmitted.

At the time, Lincoln's faculty was all white. The school was founded by the Presbyterian Church, as was Princeton University. So Lincoln was called "the black Princeton," and Princeton graduates dominated the faculty.

While there, Hughes called for a campuswide vote to integrate the faculty. Amazingly, 68 percent of the students voted to keep the faculty exclusively white. Growing up in middle-class Baltimore and having white and Jewish friends, Marshall was shielded from the worst forms of southern race prejudice. After an altercation at a movie theater in Oxford, Pennsylvania, when Marshall was told to sit in the colored section, he began to critically examine racial discrimination. Hughes graduated the year the referendum to integrate the faculty was defeated, but Marshall took up the fight the following year, in 1930, and it passed. Marshall's career as a champion of integration had begun. Lincoln's first black faculty member was hired the next year. At the same time that Marshall acquired his new race consciousness, he started to apply himself in the classroom, graduating with honors in 1930.

Howard Law School was Thurgood Marshall's next stop. It wasn't his first choice, however. His desire was to attend the University of Maryland law school, but they did not admit blacks. This deeply affected Marshall, and he set about proving that he was as qualified as any Maryland law graduate. In 1935 Marshall would demonstrate his merit when he successfully argued a case against the University of Maryland law school that led to the desegregation of the entire university.

When Marshall came to Howard law school in 1931, the school was in transition. Charles Hamilton Houston had taken over as dean and was determined to turn the program into a top-notch institution that would graduate black lawyers who would change the course of legal history. He raised the standards so high that only 25 percent of the first-year class was invited back the second year. Marshall made up his mind that he was going to be one of them. He finished first in his class after the first year, which earned him a job in the law library as a student assistant. This gave him an opportunity to work closely with Houston and dig deeply into law books and cases while he was at work.

Sometimes Marshall would skip class and go to the Supreme Court to hear the best lawyers in the country argue cases. What Marshall learned through observing the law at work, along with his personal study in the law library, helped him when he was elected to the Court of Peers his second year, which judged cases presented by students. All of these experiences were laying the groundwork for him to argue some of the most significant legal cases in U.S. history.

Houston gave the best students from Marshall's class a chance to work on real cases during their senior year. Marshall and his classmates helped Houston defend a Virginia man accused of killing two white women. The man was found guilty and given life in prison, but for 1933 this was a victory because the man was not given the death penalty.

Thurgood Marshall graduated first in the Howard law school class of 1933. Only six out of the thirty-six students who entered completed the rigors of Charles Hamilton Houston's program. Marshall passed the Maryland bar on his first attempt, October 11, 1933. His work as a civil rights attorney and Supreme Court justice forever changed race relations in this country.

Marshall entered Howard's law school on the heels of a personal experience that would shape his legal future and the country's educational future.
In 1930 he was denied admission to the University of Maryland law school
because of his race. He attended Howard by default, but the laboratory
atmosphere of the new law school proved to be the perfect training ground
for Marshall's legal destiny. Immediately following his graduation from
Howard, Marshall successfully sued the University of Maryland for refusing
to admit Donald Gaines Murray, an African American graduate of Amherst
University. Five years later, as head legal council for the NAACP, Marshall
began the massive, organized legal assault against segregated education that
resulted in the landmark 1954 desegregation case, *Brown v. Board of Education*.

HBCU Students, Faculty, and Administrators Search
for Political Identity

Johnson's efforts to restructure Howard School of Law coincided with a growing
civil rights and protest movement germinating within African American communities. HBCU faculty, graduates, administration, and students were solidly
represented among the activist vanguard. Many began to explore political systems that offered alternatives to the United States' failing system of capitalism.
Sociologists such as Ira de Augustine Reid of Atlanta University and E. Franklin
Frasier of Howard promoted the thesis that racism was becoming more a construct of economic class than of skin color. They argued that black and white
laborers faced many of the same challenges and that unity between the two
groups of workers would produce greater equality and financial gains. HBCU
graduates such as George Streator, a student leader during the campus uprising
at Howard University in the mid-1920s, became active in the emerging workers'
rights movement of the 1930s. Streator served as an organizer for the Amal-
gamated Clothing Workers.

African Americans' growing political sophistication and anticapitalist ideology did not emerge without significant challenges. Mordecai Johnson was
accused of promoting communism and soundly criticized by federal politicians and blacks and whites alike following a 1931 gathering in Washington,
D.C., during which he stated, "It would be well to watch Russia or any agency

seeking to uplift humanity."[10] In response to the remark, several public officials called for Johnson's resignation.

Awakened by the depression, college students throughout the country became significantly more politically active during the 1930s than they had been in previous decades. Many joined the Socialist and Communist parties, or became labor organizers. Black college students were also among these ranks. But where white students were concerned primarily with remedying the depression's destruction of the working class, black students were also seeking the systematic destruction of the South's segregationist Jim Crow laws. On HBCU campuses across the country the social climbing and classism of the previous decade gave way to activism that was simultaneously race-conscious and Pan-African in scope.

In his book, *Confronting the Veil,* Jonathan Scott Holloway writes that the growing political movement profoundly affected Kenneth Clark, an under-graduate student at Howard University during the early 1930s. "The whole atmosphere of the place was heady, and every scholar was eager to relate classroom work to social action," said Clark.[11]

Students did not have to look far for the opportunity for social move-ment. As with other defining and stressful times in U.S. history, blacks became the public scapegoats of the era. They were the first to be dismissed from jobs when companies were forced to make layoffs and the last to receive assistance from the government. Lynchings were again on the rise, and a growing number of assault and legal cases reflected the hostilities that many whites felt for blacks, against whom they competed for jobs and government assistance.

One case that rallied the involvement of HBCU students across the country was that of the Scottsboro boys. On March 25, 1931, nine young black men between the ages of 13 and 25 were arrested for allegedly raping two white women on board a freight train near Paint Rock, Alabama. Even though a preponderance of evidence pointed to the young men's innocence and one of the women recanted her testimony a month before they were tried, an all-white jury convicted eight of the nine defendants to death. The verdict out-raged African Americans, as well as white activists, many of them involved in the Socialist and Communist parties. Legal support for the Scottsboro boys' appeals, though often competitive in nature, sprang up on a number of fronts. Members of Alpha Phi Alpha fraternity were among the black college groups to organize a legal defense fundraising campaign for the nine defendants. Additionally, Howard law students worked with the NAACP in developing an appeals strategy for the young men.

By 1933, the depression was at full tilt, and any confidence that college-educated African Americans had that their schooling elevated them above the economic concerns of those less educated was erased. African Americans as a whole suffered more than the general population of whites during the thirteen-year economic crisis. The price for a pound of cotton dropped from 33 cents in 1920 to just 6.4 cents by 1932. According to the *Journal of Negro Education,* this drop in income forced well over half a million agricultural workers into unemployment. With more than 40 percent of black workers employed as farm laborers, the African American community was particularly hard hit by the loss of such jobs.

On the urban front black industrial and unskilled laborers were also the first to be fired. In many cases blacks who had served long and well in their jobs were terminated so that unemployed whites could take their positions. That is precisely what happened in 1933, when the white owner of the Hamburger Grill, an eatery located in the Washington, D.C., black business community, fired three black employees (two were Howard University students) and hired three whites to replace them. Outraged Howard students and faculty quickly organized a boycott of the business, and within two days the owner rehired the black employees.

The protest group, which formalized itself as the New Negro Alliance, staged boycotts of other Washington, D.C.–based businesses that practiced similar discrimination. Their protests received the support of other HBCU students, faculty, and administrators. Mary McLeod Bethune was among the supporters who joined the picket lines.

HBCU sociology departments began to grow in prominence and effectiveness around this time. Sociology students and professors often debated and conferred about issues facing African Americans, and explored options and models for economic and social advancement.

In 1942, Dr. Charles S. Johnson, head of the sociology department at Fisk, established the Institute of Race Relations, a forum that convenes social scientists, educators, religious and community leaders, and government officials to address issues surrounding race and economic and educational equality. The ideas and work generated during these debates and conferences became particularly relevant following the 1933 election of Franklin Delano Roosevelt. The new president often relied on black sociologists when creating policy and programs to address the needs of the larger African American community.

A New Deal?

Roosevelt was elected president on the strength of a platform of economic reform, dubbed the "New Deal." Thirteen million Americans were unemployed when Roosevelt took leadership in March 1933. His plan promised to bring economic relief to the country by employing citizens in federally financed development projects. Agencies such as the Civilian Conservation Corps (CCC) paid men $30 a month to reforest parks and construct bridges, buildings, and roads. The Works Progress Administration (WPA) employed writers and artists in large-scale research projects like the oral history interviews with former slaves that were collected by black sociologists and public art projects such as murals and plays.

The Fifth Annual Institute of Race Relations

June 28th to July 16th 1948

Held under the auspices of the
RACE RELATIONS DEPARTMENT OF THE AMERICAN MISSIONARY ASSOCIATION
at the
SOCIAL SCIENCE INSTITUTE
FISK UNIVERSITY
NASHVILLE, TENNESSEE

Program for the fifth annual Institute of Race Relations conference at Fisk University in 1948.

The New Deal provided employment and other lifelines to desperate Americans across the country, and its policies were even successful in persuading African Americans—who traditionally had voted Republican in recognition of the party's role in ending slavery—to vote for Democrats. Bethune-Cookman College president Mary McLeod Bethune, an advisor to the National Youth Administration (NYA), and Howard University economics professor Abram Harris Jr., who served as an advisor to the National Recovery Administration (NRA), were among the forty-five African Americans that Roosevelt appointed to cabinet positions. Bethune became an advisor and close confidant of First Lady Eleanor Roosevelt, who worked tirelessly for civil rights causes.

But the New Deal was hardly equitable in the relief assistance it provided to black and white citizens. Administrators at the NRA gave preference to white workers when filling positions, and African Americans who were employed by

Mrs. Eleanor Roosevelt and Howard students in 1944.

the agency received lower salaries for the same work. In addition, the jobs typically filled by black workers were not covered by the Social Security Act of 1935, which guaranteed government-backed pensions for workers. And the Triple A acreage reduction contract, which paid farm owners to decrease their crop product in order to drive up product demand, forced hundreds of thousands of tenant farmers into joblessness and homelessness.

These inequities greatly concerned black sociologists, and in 1935, Ralph Bunche, chair of Howard's sociology department, organized a conference entitled "The Position of the Negro in Our National Economic Crisis."

The conference took place on the university's campus and drew notables such as W. E. B. DuBois, who had returned to his teaching post at Atlanta University; A. Philip Randolph, the president of the Brotherhood of Sleeping Car Porters; Fisk sociology department chair Charles Johnson; and the executive director of the Labor Advisory Board of the NRA, A. Howard Myers.

The conference attendees varied from political moderates who wholeheartedly backed the New Deal philosophy to radical activists who promoted workers' rights and embraced socialist or communist philosophies. The vast majority of the conference participants agreed, however, that blacks had received a raw deal under the New Deal. "The present burdens we bear in a period of national economic crisis might find some excuse if there emerged promises of a more equitable treatment of the Negro in the future. But when we view future plans of the New Deal, the plight of the Negro is as dismal as it has been in the past," wrote black lawyer and activist John P. Davis in a paper presented at the conference and later published in the *Journal of Negro Education*.[12]

"Capitalism is only a few hundred years old; as feudalism is dead so may it die," wrote Davis. "I believe the conclusion will be inescapable that there must be an immediate change in emphasis from protection of private property to protection of human beings from the misery of poverty."[13]

More radical participants advocated for organization of black and white workers into a unified workers movement that would ensure equal pay for equal work. They argued that the failure of the New Deal was in fact the failure of capitalism to address the needs of the total society.

Black college faculty members and administrators such as E. Franklin Frazier, Ralph Bunche, and to a great extent Mordecai Johnson, agreed with the more radical faction of the conference even if they did not embrace or promote socialist and communist manifestos. The ideological views expressed at the conference would bring Howard University under intense congressional scrutiny, however. Some members of Congress said Howard was "encouraging communism" and threatened to take away the school's appropriations.[14] An investigation was launched to flush out the Communists who had attended the conference, but it was soon dropped when special agents discovered that no transcripts of the conference existed.

As critical as some members of Congress were of the conference, many of the attendees would nevertheless go on to play central roles in shaping the Roosevelt administration's future response to economic problems within black communities.

Although the New Deal did much to mitigate the economic disaster of the nation, citizens would not feel full relief from the crisis until the country entered World War II.

War Wages

On December 7, 1941, the Japanese bombed Pearl Harbor. For nearly three years, the United States had avoided involvement in the raging world war, but with Hitler advancing his doctrine of world dominance, and the Axis (Germany, Italy, Japan, and their supporters) taking control of much of Europe, Asia, and Africa, the United States was under pressure to enter the war on the side of the Allies (Great Britain, France, the Soviet Union, and their supporters). Certain that Roosevelt would soon cave in to those pressures, Japan wanted to shake the U.S. military's confidence and weaken the country's stomach for war, so it attacked the naval base in Pearl Harbor, Hawaii.

The resource demands of the war kicked the U.S. economy into high gear. Machinery and weapons were produced by American manufacturers, and hundreds of thousands of men and women found work in the military. In addition, U.S. companies produced food, uniforms, and other goods to support troops overseas.

While World War II pulled the country out of its long-running depression, the war ushered in a new set of challenges for HBCUs. Across the nation colleges and universities played an important part in the war effort. Not only did they provide continuing moral support to many of their students and alumni who were sent into combat, but the schools also produced war-related materials and became training grounds for soldiers. Using the resources of colleges, the federal government established defense-related aeronautics, engineering, naval, and aviation training programs. They also engaged agricultural and technical schools to produce food and other supplies for military personnel.

The military programs provided a much-needed financial lifeline to colleges and universities that had barely managed to keep their doors open during the depression. But as a 1942 report from the *Journal of Negro Education* concluded, black colleges and universities did not benefit as extensively as their white counterparts from the war effort. Compared to white colleges, the resources at HBCUs were quite meager. Science and agricultural programs at black schools often used out-of-date and inferior equipment, and because of the depression, the schools were operating with skeleton teaching staffs by the start of the war. The lack of resources meant black colleges were often unable to attract military programs to the same degree as their white counterparts. Nevertheless, continued racial segregation of the troops demanded that HBCUs play a substantial role in training African American soldiers.

Prior to U.S. engagement in the war, African Americans, with a great deal of support from Senator Harry S. Truman of Missouri, began pressing for the admission of black pilots into the Civilian Pilot Training Program. In November 1940, the War Department initiated the creation of an Air Force training corps for black pilots. Tuskegee Institute was chosen by the military to provide primary training for prospective black airmen in early 1941. The Julius Rosenwald Fund of Chicago loaned Tuskegee $200,000 to build the necessary training facilities and dormitories for the military program, and the Ninety-ninth Squadron was established in March 1941. Twelve cadets began their training four months later. Benjamin O. Davis, who would later become the first black American general in the U.S. Army, was among the five cadets to complete the training.

Air Force Captain Daniel "Chappie" James was a graduate of Tuskegee Institute. During the Korean War he flew 101 missions in fighters. In 1975 he was promoted to four-star general, making him the first African American to hold the top USAF rank.

Tuskegee was a solid choice for training prospective black pilots because school administrators had established an aviation course in 1939. Although the school's acquisition of such a prestigious military program was a major coup, not everyone in the black community was happy about the cadet program. The NAACP was infuriated by the continued segregation of black soldiers. Nevertheless, Tuskegee pressed forward with the program, and by the end of the war the Tuskegee Airmen had flown over 15,000 sorties and destroyed 1,000 German bombers.

The new war eased the financial constraints of young blacks who had been unable to pay for college during the depression. But now that they could afford school, many found themselves drafted into the military and sent overseas to battle Hitler's cancerous doctrine of Aryan supremacy. For HBCUs, enrollment remained a problem. The draft was expected to reduce the enrollment of black college men by 80 to 90 percent by early February 1943. At schools

Class of '39 Prairie View graduate and Tuskegee airman Lowell H. Cleaver.

like Talladega College in Talladega, Alabama, and Atlanta University, enrollment remained constant, but only by virtue of a greater number of women attending college.

The war had called so many Morehouse College students into service that the all-male school faced an even worse fiscal crisis in 1943 than it had during the depression. With the college facing bankruptcy, the board recommended that Morehouse shut down until the end of the war. But Morehouse president Benjamin Mays devised a plan that increased the school's enrollment and allowed it to remain open. He received approval from the board to alter admission standards and to admit younger students into the freshman class. In the fall of 1943, 15-year-old Martin Luther King Jr. was among the freshman class of students entering Morehouse.

THE KING FAMILY HBCU LEGACY

Although King was only 15 when he arrived at Morehouse on September 20, 1944, he was no stranger to the Morehouse legacy. His father, the Reverend Martin Luther King Sr., was a Morehouse man, as was his maternal grandfather, the Reverend Adam Daniel Williams, who attended Morehouse for a year in the late 1800s. Williams received an honorary degree from John Hope, the first black president of Morehouse, in 1906. Reverend. A. D. Williams was the second pastor of Atlanta's Ebenezer Baptist Church. In his thirty-seven years as the leader of Ebenezer, Williams built the church from thirteen members with no church building into one of the most prominent congregations in Atlanta. He was responsible for building the present church edifice.

When Martin Luther King Sr. arrived in Atlanta from rural Stockbride, Georgia, at the age of 18 he was reading at a fifth-grade level. Determined to make up for the deficiencies in his education, he enrolled in preparatory school. By coincidence, his sister had migrated to Atlanta years earlier and was boarding at the home of A. D. Williams, who by this time had become one of Atlanta's most prominent ministers. Through this connection, King met his future wife, Alberta Williams, Rev. Williams's daughter. They were married in 1926. Encouraged by the elder Williams to continue his education, King decided on Morehouse. After taking the entrance exam he was rejected and told that he was not college material. He became so upset that he later stormed into the office of President John Hope to plead his case. Hope was swayed by King's persistence and wrote him a letter allowing him to enroll despite his shortcomings. King's years at Morehouse were extremely difficult as he struggled to pass his courses. Alberta, who had graduated from Hampton, encouraged him to continue his studies when he wanted to give up. King's classmates also encouraged him with entreaties like "Morehouse men don't quit." He assumed the leadership of Ebenezer Baptist Church after A. D. Williams died in 1931. King Sr. later became a trustee at Morehouse and was involved in guiding the development of the religious studies program.

Martin Luther King Jr. entered college after completing the eleventh grade. The Morehouse environment molded King into the man who would become the world's most famous civil rights activist. The teachers and guest speakers who regularly visited the campus spoke candidly about race issues. Because Morehouse was a private institution, the threat of losing state funding did not restrict intellectual freedom. King was exposed to nonviolent social change first through Henry David Thoreau's discourse on civil disobedience and through his relationship with Dr. Benjamin Mays, who had visited Mahatma Gandhi in India while he was still the dean of the Howard School of Divinity.

King became involved with campus groups that advocated justice and action immediately upon entering school. He wrote a letter calling for equal rights for blacks and the right to vote, which was published in the *Atlanta Journal and Constitution* in 1946.

King's vision to become an instrument for social and economic change was first born on an HBCU campus. He decided to enter the ministry during his senior year at Morehouse. Mays was responsible for King accepting his call into the ministry. King had begun to doubt many of the things that he had learned about religion and the Bible growing up in his father's church. But Mays's example demonstrated to King how ministry could be used as an effective tool for social action.

King graduated with a degree in sociology in 1948 at the age of 19. His older sister Christine received her degree in economics from Spelman College on the same day.

The King-Morehouse legacy entered a fourth generation when both of King's sons, Martin III and Dexter, attended Morehouse. King's daughter Bernice followed her Aunt Christine to Spelman.

MLK at Morehouse

While Dr. Mays's innovative plan to increase student enrollment at Morehouse called for lowering admission standards and age requirements, it did not dramatically affect the quality of applicants, and the arrival of the younger Martin Luther King to the institution is testament to that fact. King's junior high education at the experimental Atlanta University Laboratory School had put him significantly ahead of his public school peers. Because of this advantage, he was promoted to grade 10 when he returned to public school at age 13, following the closing of AU's financially troubled preparatory school.

But as King quickly learned, despite his brilliance, things were not easy for him. The future civil rights leader was among the top students in high school but was still only reading at an eighth-grade level when he arrived at Morehouse. "I went to college from the eleventh grade. I never went to the twelfth grade, and skipped another grade earlier, so I was a pretty young fellow at Morehouse," he recalled.[15]

The free atmosphere and wide-ranging discussions at Morehouse were to King's liking, and this helped kindle his emerging social and political consciousness. There "I had my first frank discussion on race," he said of the liberal arts school. "The professors were not caught up in the clutches of state funds and could teach what they wanted with academic freedom. They encouraged us in a positive quest for a solution to racial ills. I realized that nobody there was afraid."[16]

King, a third-generation Morehouse man and the son of a Spelmanite who had also attended Hampton Institute, was staying true to his family legacy when he walked through the gates of the HBCU in the fall of 1943. His Morehouse alumnus father, Martin Luther King Sr., had grand plans for him. Chief among them was passing on the lead ministry at Ebenezer Baptist Church in Atlanta. The older King most certainly believed that Morehouse, which has its roots as a seminary, was the perfect place for his son to cultivate the ideals and training needed for his preordained future. But Morehouse fulfilled its promise to turn its students into critical thinkers, and this would stir up years of struggle between father and son. What MLK Jr. encountered in the classrooms and on campus forced him to reconsider his life's calling. King felt spiritually and intellectually limited by the fundamen-

Before becoming an internationally renowned figure,
Martin Luther King Jr. was a Morehouse man.

talist tenets of his religious upbringing. His exposure to broad social and
philosophical debates while at Morehouse compelled him to question those
tenets, and the ministry itself as his personal calling.

"The shackles of fundamentalism were removed from my body,"[17] King
wrote of his early Morehouse days. The young college student thought he
might be better suited to serve his community as a doctor or lawyer.

King's decision to pursue a different career path caused conflict with his
father, but it also freed him to live life out from under the microscope reserved
for those bound for the ministry. As a Morehouse man, he took full advantage of that new freedom. Early on, King became fast friends with classmates
Walter McCall and Larry Williams. The three developed reputations for being
sophisticated, life-of-the-party types. According to historian Taylor Branch,
King adopted the metropolitan style of favored professor Gladestone Chandler,

who smoked a pipe, wore stylish clothes, and employed a broad vocabulary. King and classmate Williams also became known as "The Wreckers"[18] due to their popularity with the ladies.

By 1946, his junior year, ministry began to tug at King once again. The ministers and professors that he encountered at Morehouse were helping him to explore and conceive the possibility of spiritual leadership that went beyond fundamentalism. Dr. George D. Kelsey, head of the school's theological department, was among the faculty members who most influenced King in this regard. In her book, *My Life with Dr. Martin Luther King, Jr.,* Coretta Scott King writes that more than anyone, Dr. Kelsey showed her husband-to-be "that the ministry could be intellectually respectable as well as emotionally satisfying."[19]

By King's senior year, the exemplary scholarship of Morehouse's President Mays and Professor Kelsey was clearly a factor in guiding him back to ministry as a vocation.

King is the most notable example of how HBCUs not only survived the dual threat of the depression and World War II but produced graduates who became the generation of leaders who in the 1950s would forever change the social order of the United States and have a huge impact on race relations and justice globally.

A statue of Martin Luther King Jr. on the campus of Morehouse College.

7

MANIFEST DESTINY

When the American Missionary Association began establishing HBCUs after the Civil War, its goal was to train African American leaders who could help the masses of black people gain equality. By the 1950s, HBCU students and alumni have begun to realize their destiny.

I N June 1948, less than a decade after Martin Luther King Jr. graduated from Morehouse, the young minister would be squarely situated as one of the nation's foremost civil rights leaders. Long before he gained worldwide recognition, HBCU students, faculty, administrators, and on-campus branches of organizations such as the NAACP were pushing the racial parity agenda and developing and practicing the nonviolent protest tactics that, by the 1950s, would become the hallmark of the growing Civil Rights Movement. It would be through leaders like King, who along with his peers forced a dramatic change in the position of African Americans, that HBCUs would finally realize their goal of creating leaders who could help the masses of African Americans gain equality.

As reports of mistreatment and poorly maintained facilities for black soldiers serving in World War II reached the states, African Americans became

A family celebrating graduation at Spelman College, 1950.

determined that their sons, husbands, and fathers would not return to the same type of racism and violence that had greeted them after World War I. The movement to end Jim Crow took on even more urgency in light of the war, and black leaders and communities began to employ both political and economic pressure to dismantle systemic racism.

By the early 1940s the NAACP had established student chapters at a good number of HBCUs, including Morehouse, Hampton, Lincoln at Pennsylvania, and Howard. The civil rights organization began to train HBCU students in nonviolent protest tactics, and it launched a program of direct action against segregated restaurants, department stores, and other public facilities.

Law school student Pauli Marshall was a member of the Howard chapter of the NAACP. She took part in the nonviolent training curriculum, which among other things stressed sit-ins, picketing, and economic boycotts as tactics for change. Marshall helped organize a series of boycotts against Washington, D.C.–based businesses that practiced Jim Crow policies. The boycotts targeted a number of establishments, but one account in particular illustrates African Americans' growing frustration with a government that was eager to send them off to war but unwilling to count them as equal citizens.

On April 17, 1943, a group of Howard students decided to have lunch at the Little Palace Cafeteria at Fourteenth and U Streets. Though the restaurant was located in a largely black neighborhood, the owner refused to serve African Americans. When the group was turned away, the students filed out of the restaurant and started picketing the establishment. Among the signs that they carried, at least one spoke directly to African Americans' growing anger over their treatment as second-class citizens: "Our bonds, boys and brothers are fighting for you, why can't we eat here?" it demanded to know.

Morehouse student Samuel Cook helped organize the NAACP chapter on his campus. The organization sponsored debates that considered the question of whether African Americans should protest segregation by refusing to serve in the Armed Forces. The debate was particularly relevant to students at the all-male school, who had seen so many of their classmates drafted and sent to fight against Hitler's racist regime while suffering under the racist policies of their own nation.

War on Racism

By 1945 the Allies were victorious and American soldiers began to return home. With the postwar economy boom and the education benefits made available under the GI Bill of Rights, enacted by Congress on June 22, 1944, many black returning soldiers decided to go to college. In a newsletter dated March 20, 1945, Howard University secretary James M. Nabrit Jr. wrote, "One hundred and six veterans are now studying at the University under Public Laws Numbers 16 and 346 [the GI Bill of Rights]."[1] Though returning black soldiers were determined to assert their citizenship rights and take advantage of their veteran status, not all white Americans were prepared to honor these rights. The end of the war was marked by a wave of lynchings. Southern mobs lynched six black World War II veterans in a single three-week period, in the summer of 1946.

Many African Americans became convinced that the federal government would not adequately protect their rights without pressure from outside sources. The recent war had helped to globalize American politics and economic relationships. With that in mind, black leaders looked to the United Nations to support their cause.

The UN was established in April 1945, and a number of African Americans with current or previous ties to HBCUs figured prominently in the opening conference, which took place in San Francisco. Bethune-Cookman College president Mary McLeod Bethune came on behalf of the National Council of Negro Women. Dr. Mordecai W. Johnson of Howard University was present, and Fisk alumnus and former Atlanta University professor W. E. B. DuBois attended representing the NAACP. Ralph Bunche, a former chair of the political science department at Howard University, was at the conference as an official member of the UN staff, serving as acting chief of the Division of Dependent Territories of the Department of State.

No agency provided by the UN charter was of greater interest to African Americans than the UN Educational, Scientific, and Cultural Organization, UNESCO, which emerged from the Economic and Social Council and the Trusteeship Council. At the core of this initiative was the development of a worldwide program of basic education. "At the first meeting of UNESCO in Paris, late in 1946, an American black, Charles S. Johnson, was in attendance as a member of the United States National Commission," John Hope Franklin wrote in *From Slavery to Freedom*.[2] Many black Americans hoped that the Fisk sociologist's presence at the meeting would have an impact on the fundamental educational problems they faced, though few were naïve enough to imagine the UN would put an end to the country's widespread racial violence and discrimination.

Nevertheless, having Johnson and Bunche in key positions at the UN was the sort of leverage the NAACP sought in 1947 when it presented a 155-page petition to the UN Office of Social Affairs demanding a redress of human rights grievances. Although DuBois was the chief author of the document, which was entitled "An Appeal to the World," as head of the NAACP's legal defense and education fund, Thurgood Marshall conceivably had a hand in creating it as well.

The petition was given serious attention by the drafting committee of the UN Human Rights Commission and was debated for two days. Other similar petitions were also presented, including one by attorney William Patterson and members of the Civil Rights Congress, which made a specific charge against the "criminal, racist policies of the U.S. government and the destructive impact this had on national integrity as well as its effect on world peace."[3]

As many expected, the UN informed the petitioners that it had no right to intervene in domestic issues and thus was powerless to do anything about the treatment of African Americans in the United States. Renowned Howard law professor Charles H. Houston, mentor to hundreds of aspiring attorneys, agreed that it had no jurisdiction to investigate civil rights violations, but that it did have the right on matters of national policy and where a people's democratic rights were being denied.

The agenda made little headway on the international front, however, and civil rights groups and their leaders finally set aside the issue and shifted their attention more decisively to the struggle against the federal government's attitude toward segregation and discrimination. Impetus for this change came partly from a speech President Harry S. Truman delivered in June 1947 at the NAACP's Thirty-eighth Annual Conference in Washington, D.C., in which he declared: "We can no longer afford the luxury of a leisurely attack upon prejudice and discrimination. State and local governments can do much in providing positive safeguards for civil rights. But we cannot, any longer, await the growth of a will to action in the slowest state or the most backward community. Our national government must show the way."[4]

Global Vision

While the effort to draw world support for the domestic civil rights agenda met with little success, the attempt to do so was consistent with several HBCUs' forays into international affairs. Administrators and faculty members at a number of schools were working to develop international studies curriculums, particularly in the area of African affairs. As early as 1930, Fisk sociologist Charles S. Johnson served as the U.S. delegate on the League of Nations Commission that investigated allegations of slavery in Liberia. He penned a report that detailed labor abuses and helped end forced servitude in the country.

Central to Howard University's endeavors in the international arena was the pioneering research of Professor Dr. William Leo Hansberry, who since the 1920s had been teaching a series of courses entitled "Negro Civilizations of

Dr. Charles S. Johnson attended the first UNESCO meeting in Paris in 1946. He is shown here with Georgia O'Keefe and Alfred Stieglitz.

AFRICAN LEADERS AND HBCUs

The appeal of the quality education available at HBCUs extended beyond the borders of the United States and reached into the land from whence black Americans had come—Africa. Institutions of higher learning had once flourished in the great cities of sub-Saharan Africa, and now, centuries later, colleges created for the progeny of those stolen from this land would serve as a refuge for African students in search of greater educational opportunities.

The stream of African students who attended black colleges began in the 1930s. HBCUs were beginning to exercise independence from their founding patrons and seeking accreditation. The New Negro movement inspired voices of protest that cried loudly for freedom and pan-African unity. These voices impacted African students who were coming from the bondage of colonial rule, which was even more oppressive than the segregated and hostile conditions in the United States.

One of the first African students to come to the United States was Nnamdi Azikiwe. He enrolled at two predominantly white institutions before matriculating at Howard in 1926. His stay at Howard was cut short when his on-campus job ended. After financial struggles and displacement, "Zik" arrived at Lincoln University in Pennsylvania with the promise of an on-campus job that would allow him to pay his fees. He completed a bachelor's degree in political science in 1930. After attaining a master's degree in anthropology at the University of Pennsylvania in 1933, he returned to Lincoln to obtain a second master's in political science. Azikiwe taught the first African history course at Lincoln, and later returned to his homeland to become the first president of a liberated Nigeria.

A similar path was taken by Kwame Nkrumah, who liberated the Gold Coast from British rule and became Ghana's first president. Nkrumah, the first head of state to espouse pan-Africanism, did his graduate and undergraduate studies at Lincoln.

Both Nkrumah and Azikiwe were profoundly influenced by the

philosophies of African American leaders during their studies in the United States. Azikiwe was influenced by W. E. B. DuBois, and Nkrumah by Marcus Garvey. Azikiwe wrote his first book, *Liberia in World Politics*, as a graduate student at Lincoln. The university continued to churn out African students who would go on to serve in influential roles in their countries. These alumni include the Reverend James Robinson, founder of Crossroads Africa, the model for Peace Corps; C. Cecil Dennis, minister of foreign affairs for Liberia; Ambassador Willie Fitzjohn of Sierra Leone; and Dr. Sibusio Nkomo, chair of the National Policy Institute of South Africa.

Lincoln wasn't the only HBCU to educate future African leaders. Ellen Mills Scarborough, who was the first woman to serve in the Liberian national legislature, and Dr. Rocheforte L. Weeks, former minister of foreign affairs and the first Liberian-born president of the University of Liberia, graduated from Howard. Angie E. Brooks, who served on the supreme court of Liberia and as president of the United Nations General Assembly, graduated from Shaw University. E. Romeo Horton, the founder of the Bank of Liberia and secretary of commerce of Liberia, attended Morehouse.

The "historically black" distinction of HBCUs does not accurately describe the diverse student bodies that compose HBCU campuses. Black students attending HBCUs come from throughout the African diaspora.

Ancient Africa." When he sought to expand the series in 1935, his plan was met with resistance from the administration, including President Mordecai Johnson. "I feel very strongly that my efforts and the cause of Negro History as I have tried to promote it at Howard University deserve better from the university," wrote Hansberry in a letter to Johnson.[5] So vast was his knowledge of black antiquity that Hansberry's files and syllabi were indispensable to such fellow scholars as DuBois and Professor Edwin Smith of Fisk University, who organized an African studies program at his school. A decade later, in 1945, with international issues of increased significance, Howard administrators were more eager for an African studies program, and Hansberry was appointed faculty advisor to African students. In addition, Johnson began to actively build relationships with African nations and increase enrollment of international students.

In November 1950, Lincoln University at Pennsylvania held a two-day conference to inaugurate the school's Institute on African Affairs, which sought to forge relationships with African leaders and governments, and to gain a better understanding of the role of the continent in the world community. In a letter sent to potential participants, Lincoln president Horace M. Bond wrote:

> You are familiar, of course, with the almost miraculous recent emergence of Africa, and of Africans, into the forefront of the Modern World. The rapid assimilation of Western Civilization by Africans makes the people of that continent a resource as important as its economic riches. Africa, and Africans, stand as key counterweights in world dynamics today.
>
> This new facet in world history justifies, we think, the most serious consideration by Americans of African descent. We can help; we can be helped. We believe that the time has passed when African policies of this Nation, and of other world powers, should be made by people possessing neither the affinity of sympathy nor that of common destiny with the African people.[6]

Through their efforts HBCU administrators were undoubtedly working to build an international power base that could be leveraged to gain a voice in domestic affairs and level the economic and educational playing field for blacks at home.

Separate and Unequal

True to his 1947 speech before the NAACP, President Truman established a Committee on Civil Rights. The group submitted a momentous 178-page report entitled "To Secure These Rights," which made recommendations for strengthening and safeguarding the civil rights of all Americans. The recommendations were guided by a conviction that civil rights were guaranteed by the Constitution and essential to domestic tranquility, national security, and the general welfare and continued existence of America's free institutions. Among the members of the committee was Dr. Channing Tobias, a graduate of Paine College in Augusta, Georgia.

Within a year of the report, Truman had appointed another interracial committee to assess the problems in the realm of higher education. The group's report was stinging in its indictment of the educational inequities between blacks and whites. "In 1940 the schooling of the Negro was significantly below that of whites at every level from the first grade through college,"[7] the report stated. It noted that 11 percent of the white population 20 and over had completed at least a year of college, and nearly 5 percent had obtained degrees. In contrast, only 3 percent of African Americans 20 and older had gained at least a year of college, and just 1.5 percent had graduated.

The committee also reported that 85 percent of the 75,000 black students who were enrolled in college during 1947 were attending segregated institutions, and that educational facilities for African Americans on all levels were inferior to those provided to whites. "Whether one considers enrollment, overall costs per student, teachers' salaries, transportation facilities, availability of secondary schools, or opportunities for undergraduate and graduate study, the consequences of the segregation are always the same, and always adverse to the Negro citizen," observed the report. The committee made several recommendations for remedying the inequities. Prominent among them was that the federal government pass legislation outlawing state segregation statutes and that federal monies be made available to bolster black schools until such legislation was passed and enforced.

The report was a significant blow to Jim Crow policies and a sound endorsement of what black educators and students had long argued for—equal support and equal access. Many African American educators and civil rights activists

Thurgood Marshall, so influential during the Civil Rights Movement, receives an honorary degree from Virginia State University in this undated photo.

viewed the committee recommendations as a sign that the time was ripe for challenging state laws that allowed segregated schools.

In 1950, the NAACP began to deploy its full arsenal of lawyers in the fight against school desegregation. Howard University law school graduates played indispensable roles in the court proceedings, which culminated with the pivotal 1954 *Brown v. the Board of Education* school desegregation case. Nine of the ten NAACP Legal Defense Fund lawyers who worked on the landmark case were Howard Law School graduates, including Thurgood Marshall, who successfully argued the case before the Supreme Court.

Even before *Brown* was presented before the Supreme Court, Marshall, who was director-counsel for the Legal Defense Fund, and his cauldron of fellow HBCU law school graduates were winning school desegregation cases, particularly in the arena of higher education. Between 1938 and 1950, the Fund sued and won four cases involving African Americans who were refused admission to all-white public universities. The cases included plaintiff Lloyd Gaines, who sued the University of Missouri law school and Ada Lois Sipuel, who sued the University of Oklahoma law school because they were denied entry into their respective state universities based on race. Since neither state provided a law school for blacks, there were no "separate but equal" educational opportunities. The fund won both cases and the plaintiffs were admitted to the schools.

Determined to maintain segregation, several southern states rushed to set up law school programs for blacks. In Texas, state officials chartered the Texas Law School for Negroes, and when African American student Heman Marion Sweatt, an alumnus of HBCU Wiley College, was admitted to that school instead of the prestigious, all-white University of Texas law school, he sued for admission into UT.

The NAACP lawyers argued that because the new school was haphazardly organized and staffed, it did not offer the same quality of education provided by UT. The Legal Defense Fund won that case as well. In the fourth case, student G. W. McLaurin was admitted to the University of Oklahoma but separated from his fellow white students. University officials insisted that McLaurin eat his meals at a separate table and even sit apart from other students while in class. NAACP council sued on the grounds that the segregation policy was a violation of the Fourteenth Amendment of the Constitution, which promises equal protection of rights. It won the case.

With each decision, southern black college students gained educational opportunities. The court victories struck blows for desegregation, but since they were state supreme court decisions, each only had the ability to affect school admissions in its respective regions. In addition, state officials often found ways to get around the court mandates. In theory the decisions held the potential for siphoning off the brightest African American students from HBCUs. In practice, however, the decrees had little effect on where African Americans chose to attend college. All that would change with the *Brown* decision.

While *Brown* argued for the desegregation of public primary and secondary schools, its effects were far-reaching, and forced significant changes in the admissions policies of all publicly funded colleges and universities as well. It is unclear whether the NAACP lawyers who tried the case—which included Howard University law professors James M. Nabrit and George E. C. Hayes— understood that *Brown* had the potential to negatively affect enrollment at HBCUs, vastly change the schools' demographics, and challenge the relevance of their historical mission. But even if the lawyers possessed that type of forward vision, it is unlikely that they would have set aside their ideals of a racially just society in favor of protecting HBCU enrollment rosters and supreme status among black college students.

Nor would HBCU administrators and faculties have encouraged them to do so. The civil rights principles at hand were far too important to fall victim to such fears and concerns. HBCU presidents, boards of directors, and employees vigorously supported the NAACP's efforts. In all, five cases were argued in the class action *Brown* suit. They included desegregation battles in Kansas, Delaware, South Carolina, Virginia, and the District of Columbia. In each case black grade school children were denied admission to all-white schools.

The challenge civil rights activists and lawyers faced now was to overturn

Plessy v. Ferguson, the case that established the separate but equal doctrine in 1896, and to show that it could not be extended to public education. As NAACP attorney Constance Baker Motley wrote, "We needed a persuasive argument as to why, even when facilities provided Black children were equal, segregation violated [the Fourteenth] amendment."[8]

The NAACP counsel depended heavily on the talents of Howard law school students and faculty in preparing the case. In establishing the school in 1938, Nabrit designed what most consider the first systematic civil rights course offered at an American law school.[9] What students learned in this course proved invaluable during trial preparation. Eager young law students spent hours poring through constitutional text, reviewing pertinent precedent-setting cases, and preparing briefs. Behind the cloistered doors of the old law school building, they staged moot courts and dry runs that helped prepare Marshall and other NAACP lawyers for their day before the federal Supreme Court justices.

Getting the Supreme Court to reverse a decision that had stood for over half a century was no easy task, but the lawyers for the NAACP were undaunted. In all, four briefs were filed charging that segregation was harmful to black children in five jurisdictions. In the Topeka, Kansas, case, Howard University alumni and psychologists Kenneth and Mamie Clark introduced a study involving children playing with dolls where black children preferred white dolls, to show the psychological impact of segregation on black children, their self-image, and their ability to learn.

A three-judge panel in federal district court in Kansas had ruled that segregation had a detrimental effect on black children, but because black and white schools in the state were deemed substantially equal, it denied injunctive relief. The federal decision, however, allowed an appeal, and the case was consolidated with the cases in the other districts. On May 17, 1954, Chief Justice Earl Warren delivered the unanimous Supreme Court ruling in the landmark civil rights case *Brown v. Board of Education of Topeka, Kansas:* state-sanctioned segregation of public schools was a violation of the Fourteenth Amendment and was therefore unconstitutional. This historic decision marked the end of the "separate but equal" precedent set by the same court nearly sixty years earlier, and served as a catalyst for the expanding civil rights movement during the decade of the 1950s. "We come then to the question presented," the Court began on the ruling. "Does segregation of children in public schools solely on the basis of race, even though the physical facilities and other tangible factors may be equal, deprive the children of the minority group of equal education opportunities? We believe that it does."[10]

A battle had been won, but the war against school segregation was far from over. It would take the passing of the Civil Rights Act of 1964 (which threatened to withhold federal dollars from state schools that practiced segregation), the deployment of National Guard troops, and endless litigation to get black students inside the doors of the University of Mississippi, the University of Alabama, Clemson College in South Carolina, and many other previously all-white institutions of higher learning.

Out of the Courts and into the Fields and Streets

Education was not the only area where HBCU administrators, faculty, students, and graduates aided or took the lead toward parity for African Americans. By 1952 major-league baseball had been integrated for five years. Jackie Robinson, who had broken the race barrier when he signed with the Brooklyn Dodgers in 1947, was continuing his Hall of Fame career that was highlighted in May 1952 when he stole home at Ebbets Field. Robinson wasn't the only black Dodger, however. The team also included catcher Roy Campanella and pitcher Joe Black, the Rookie of the Year who once played at Morgan State College.

On the tennis courts, integration was still moving at a lob's pace but increasingly, there were stories about the sensational ascendancy of Althea Gibson and how she would compete against the best white players after winning the all-black American Tennis Association title ten years in a row. She was a student at Florida A&M University when she competed at Wimbledon for the first time in 1951.

While the achievements of black athletes served to break down racial barriers in sports, scores of African Americans took on the challenge of dismantling segregation in everyday life. On December 1, 1955, Rosa Parks refused to relinquish her seat on a segregated bus in Montgomery, Alabama. Her defiant stance led to a citywide bus boycott and intensified the burgeoning civil rights movement. It also provided the moment of entry into the civil rights movement for one soon-to-be-famous Morehouse graduate, Martin Luther King Jr.

In 1947 HBCU graduate Jackie Robinson made history when he signed with the Brooklyn Dodgers and became the first African American to join a major-league baseball team.

Tennis legend Althea Gibson was a Florida A & M student when she competed at Wimbledon for the first time in 1951.

The movement was bolstered by several other African Americans with ties to HBCUs, the first of whom was Alabama State English professor Jo Ann Robinson. Late on the evening of Parks's arrest, Robinson, a member of the Women's Political Council—a group affiliated with King's Dexter Avenue Baptist Church in Montgomery—received news of the situation.

The call spun Robinson into action and she phoned members of the council, organizing a spur-of-the-moment meeting. The women met around midnight at Robinson's office on Alabama State's campus. Outraged by Parks's arrest and invigorated by her conviction to take the case to court and challenge the city's segregation laws, the women decided to call an immediate boycott of Montgomery's bus system. In the middle of the night, the council members drafted a letter calling for the boycott, and they used the school's mimeograph machines to run copies. The women realized that the HBCU was at risk of losing its state funding if state officials discovered that school facilities had been used to promote a call for civil disobedience and defiance of segregation laws, but they recognized that the larger issue of the African American community's civil rights were more important than protecting a single institution.[11] The school, after all, existed to build individuals who were equipped enough and brave enough to take leadership roles in exactly such a battle.

The call went out and the boycott was an overwhelming success. Four days after Parks's arrest, on the evening of her indictment, a group of black civic leaders and ministers met to discuss the growing movement in support of a boycott to end segregation on public transportation. King, who arrived late to the meeting, was surprised to find himself drafted to head the swiftly organized Montgomery Improvement Association. Just 28 years old at the time, accounts vary as to why King was nominated to take on such a prestigious position of leadership. Some attributed it to the fact that he was relatively new to the Montgomery community and had had little time to attract enemies. Others credited his stature and oratory abilities. Finally, some speculated that no other leader was willing to take on the risks associated with leading the boycott. Whatever the reason, drafting the third-generation Morehouse alumnus into leadership was a manifestation of his alma mater's motto: "To provide a comprehensive academic, social and spiritual experience that prepares its students for leadership and success in the larger society."

The boycott continued for more than a year, despite harassment and intimidation from white racists, not to mention the massive arrests of boycotters and the bombing of King's home. On December 13, 1956, the U.S. Supreme Court ruled that segregation on public buses in the city was illegal.

"Integrating the Montgomery buses did not go smoothly,"[12] Parks reflects in her autobiography. But eventually the sniper fire died down and the curfews ended. "African Americans in other cities, like Birmingham, Alabama, and Tallahassee, Florida, started their own boycotts of the segregated buses."[13] The direct-action movement, a protest tactic that had been employed mainly by HBCU college students, moved into the mainstream.

Strengthened by a landmark Supreme Court decision and encouraged by the invigorating leadership of a young Baptist minister, the movement would continue to escalate for the remainder of the 1950s. As the next decade approached, HBCU students would figure prominently in the winds of change and justice for African Americans.

8

AN EDUCATION
IN PROTEST

During the 1960s HBCU students educated in the art of nonviolent protest take their tactics from the campuses to the streets and win civil rights battles along the way.

T HE SIXTIES OPENED with a wave of HBCU students invading lunch counters, defying the whites-only restrictions that denied them service.

Sit-ins began in earnest in February 1960, with students protesting segregated eating establishments in cities like Greensboro, North Carolina, Orangeburg, South Carolina, Nashville, Tennessee, and Montgomery, Alabama. By October of that year black college students had staged sit-ins at lunch counters in some 100 Southern cities and counties.

Ironically, HBCU students' groundswell of synergetic action was not the result of some precisely planned agenda of activism. The fast-growing movement was instead ignited by an impromptu sit-in initiated by four students—Joseph McNeil, Franklin McCain, David Richmond, and Ezell Blair Jr.—from North Carolina A & T College.[1] All were freshmen and former members of the NAACP Youth Council when on the evening of Monday, February 1, 1960,

Sisters in Blackness was a political-action
and social-activist student organization at Spelman.

they spontaneously decided it was time to challenge Greensboro's long enforced Jim Crow laws. Historian Taylor Branch writes that the definitive moment resulted from a "bull session" during which the students had dared one another to sit down at a Woolworth's lunch counter.[2] Unwilling to back down from the challenge, the four went downtown to the store, did a little shopping, then sat at the whites-only lunch counter and attempted to order food.

The foursome's actions would come to be viewed as a genesis moment in the Civil Rights Movement. But not all blacks were supportive of the movement during its early stages. A black waitress working behind the lunch counter during the time of the students' sit-in was perturbed that the young men had decided to stage their protest during her shift. She refused them service and remarked that, "Fellows like you make our race look bad."[3] The words did not sway the students. Woolworth's management resisted calling the police to remove the determined patrons, but they continued denying them service. The young men stayed glued to their seats until closing time and left promising to bring more protesters the following day.

By the time McNeil, McCain, Richmond, and Blair made it back to their dorms news of their protest had already passed through the campus grapevine. Elected student leaders anxious to follow through on the young men's momentum came calling on the group. More students were willing to join the sit-in, they said. Even white college students at nearby Greensboro College were pledging to join the protest. Working fast, the organizers arranged to have nineteen students stage a daylong protest at the Woolworth's lunch counter the following day. The students agreed to sit in shifts so that no one had to miss classes. On Wednesday, eighty-five students joined the sit-in movement, and by Saturday, the protesters were 400-strong and sit-ins were also being staged at other Greensboro department store lunch counters. Store managers held fast to their refusal to serve African American patrons. Still, it wasn't until Klansmen and other white supremacist groups began showing up and threatening violence that managers began calling in police to break up the protests.

Within days of the Greensboro event, other HBCU campuses began to mount sit-ins. Students in the North Carolina cities of Raleigh, Durham, and Winston-Salem staged protests, and students at Alabama State College and Philander Smith in Arkansas also launched sit-ins. In Tallahassee, Florida A & M

University students were joined by white residents who were dissatisfied with segregation and discrimination.[4]

On February 12, 500 black college students from Fisk, Tennessee State, Meharry Medical College, and the American Baptist Theological Seminary took shifts sitting down at lunch counters throughout Nashville, requesting service and refusing to abandon their seats when it was denied. Two weeks into their protests, police cracked down, arresting seventy-seven HBCU students and five others who had also joined the movement.

When the protesters were arraigned on Monday, February 29, Fisk student Diane Nash, who would come to be one of the Civil Rights Movement's most respected and effective leaders, stood up in court and informed the judge that she and fifteen other students had decided to refuse bail, because paying the fees would be tantamount to supporting the South's continued system of Jim Crow. The judge jailed all sixteen of them.

Emboldened by their classmates' sacrifice, day after day, students showed up at lunch counters, were arrested, and refused to post bail. Nashville mayor Ben West was anxious to defuse the situation and avoid negative press and criticism for the jailings. He agreed to release the protesters and appoint a biracial committee to consider desegregation if the lunch counter sit-ins would end. The students accepted the offer, but they were hardly ready to end their civil rights activities. Upon release, Nash quickly organized a sit-in at the city's Greyhound bus station lunch counter, which was not covered by the agreement. Management there became the first segregated establishment to honor the protesters' request to be served, giving the students their first decisive victory and opening up the way for desegregation of Nashville's eating establishments.

Years later, Nash's conversation with an interviewer gave insight into why and how she and other HBCU students, despite their youth

Article from the 1960 Nashville *Tennessean* newspaper: "63 New Arrests Mark Sit-in Drive."

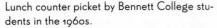
Lunch counter picket by Bennett College students in the 1960s.

Bennett students boycott a local movie theater.

and inexperience, found the courage to mount such direct action against segregation laws. "I remember realizing that with what we were doing, trying to abolish segregation, we were coming up against governors of seven states, judges, politicians, businessmen," Nash recalled in an interview. "And I remember thinking, 'I'm only 22 years old. What do I know? What am I doing?' I felt very vulnerable. So when we heard that other cities had demonstrations, it really helped, because there were more of us. And I think we started feeling the power of an idea whose time had come."[5]

In Orangeburg, South Carolina protesters met with less success. HBCU students at private Claflin College and at South Carolina State College also staged sit-ins. State officials immediately cracked down on the activity, however, threatening the publicly financed college with loss of funding if administrators didn't put a stop to the protests. Since state officials could do little to affect the financial well-being of Claflin, they erected a fence between South Carolina State and neighboring Claflin in an attempt to discourage interaction between the two campuses. When those actions didn't stop 400 HBCU students from staging a day of sit-ins at downtown lunch counters, state and local police used force to end the protest. They fired tear gas and water hoses on a crowd of HBCU students and arrested all but twelve of the marchers.

In other southern states, hundreds of HBCU students were tear-gassed, hosed, beaten, and arrested for protesting Jim Crow laws. A significant number were sentenced to time on chain gangs for their participation in the protests. Many parents were horrified by the thought of their children spending time in jail. They feared that an arrest record would negate the college educations that they'd worked so hard to provide their children, but more importantly, they feared that their children would be abused by racist jailers. Public HBCU administrators in other states were also being threatened with loss of funding, closure, and legal action if the protests continued.

On the other hand, civil rights organizations like the NAACP, Southern Christian Leadership Conference (SCLC) and Congress of Racial Equality (CORE) welcomed the student-initiated sit-ins to further their collective desegregation agenda and test the effectiveness of their doctrine of nonviolent protest on a large-scale level. Organizers within those groups supported the students' efforts.

That support was on display when Dr. King, head of the SCLC, addressed a crowd of more than a thousand students in Montgomery, Alabama, on February 29. Students there pledged to withdraw from Alabama State University if they were expelled for participating in sit-ins. Texas Southern University students conducted nonviolent protests in Houston, indicating that the movement was now making an impact in the Southwest.

In response to the widespread outbreak of sit-in protests, President Eisenhower called for biracial conferences throughout southern cities and communities to deal with the problem of segregation and the ever-expanding movement to bring it to an end.

Young Activists in Training

By April 1960, student-led civil rights activities had proliferated with such speed that the elder activists attached to CORE, SCLC, and the NAACP grew anxious to provide students with training in nonviolent protest tactics. They feared that the students, most of whom were unfamiliar with how to implement the tactics, were ill-prepared to deal with confrontational segregationists and abusive law officials who were not beneath beating, burning, and turning water hoses on black college students. Shaw University graduate Ella Baker, by then an SCLC executive officer, organized a nonviolent protest training event for HBCU student activists on the campus of her alma mater in Raleigh, North Carolina, the weekend of April 15–17. Approximately 150 students from nine states attended the session.[6]

Baker, whose political background and radical credentials included stints with Communists in the 1930s, the NAACP, and a number of militant organizations, was a student activist in the 1920s. The weekend was momentous—the Student Nonviolent Coordinating Committee (SNCC, pronounced "Snick") was forged. Baker's influence was pivotal, according to Barbara Ransby in her biography of the activist. "While Baker wanted to protect the students' autonomy, she was not the hands-off facilitator that some have made her out to be. She understood that the students needed guidance, direction, and resources from veterans like herself who shared their general political orientation."[7]

The landmark weekend found black college students immersed in the philosophy of nonviolent protest. They learned how to remain peaceable and stand their ground when confronted with violence. They were told what to do and who to contact if they were jailed, and they formed plans to support fellow HBCU students who were expelled for their civil rights activism. Voluntary withdrawal from school, hunger strikes, and a scholarship fund to assist expelled students with enrolling at other schools were all considered as a part of the plan.

Baker encouraged the students to exercise their idealism in defining SNCC's philosophy and goals. They agreed that their primary goal was "the acquisition of human rights and to remove stigmas attached to race."[8]

Fisk graduate student Marion Barry (who later became mayor of Washinton, D.C.) was elected president of SNCC, while Diane Nash chaired the Recommendations Committee. The group established headquarters at the SCLC office in Atlanta, and the executive committee agreed to reconvene on the campus of Morehouse in July.

CIVIL RIGHTS ACTIVISM

HBCUs have always been at the forefront of civil rights activism. From as far north as Pennsylvania to the deepest parts of the South, students and professors took up positions on the front lines of a movement that would result in one of the greatest social revolutions in U.S. history.

The first of these protests took place during the 1920s. African Americans were entering their fifth decade as freedmen and they were developing new attitudes. Veterans from World War I returned home with new hopes of freedom and the New Negro movement was flourishing through the arts and literature of the Harlem Renaissance. These attitudes spilled over onto the black college campuses. Between 1920 and 1930 black college enrollment skyrocketed from 600,000 to over 1 million. As HBCUs started to exert their independence from their white founding patrons, demands for greater black representation in the faculty, curriculum, student life, and administration began to surface.

In 1925 students at Fisk took over buildings and broke windows in opposition to the restrictive policies of its white president, Fayette McKenzie. In 1927 protests broke out at Hampton Institute. The 1930s saw demonstrations at Virginia Union College to protest the disparities in spending for white and black college students. In 1934 Ishmael Flory, a student at Fisk, organized a protest on the campus in response to a lynching that took place near the school. Students from Morgan College (now Morgan State University), Virginia Union, Virginia State, and Howard took part in an integrated antiwar protest staged by 150,000 college students in 1935. Lincoln University students took to the streets to desegregate the restaurants and movie theaters of Chester, Pennsylvania. Although the Lincoln protest was unsuccessful, the message resounded loud and clear that business as usual would no longer be acceptable to the emerging educated black class.

Although World War II tempered widespread protests during the 1940s, the 1950s saw a new wave of resistance spurred by the passage of *Brown v. Board of Education* and the independence movements of people of color in other countries. The country's black colleges and universities became incubators for political activists. Fisk's first black president, Charles S. Johnson, once stated that HBCUs were where the black students came to get the strength they needed "to confront the rest of the world." With this strength, student activists thrust themselves headlong into the fight for desegregation and equal justice. A number of individuals who established themselves as leaders in the civil rights movement first got involved while attending HBCUs.

Forging Cross-Cultural Partnerships

The Student Nonviolent Coordinating Committee was not the first civil rights group to organize black college students to help defeat segregation. The NAACP established a youth council division, and individual campuses also created student activist groups. But SNCC was the first national and most successful civil rights organization conceived and created by the students themselves. It was also the first through which black students forged bonds with their white counterparts to push the civil rights agenda.

While the vast majority of white southern colleges fought desegregation efforts tooth and nail, moved perhaps by media images of peaceful protesters being sprayed with water hoses and attacked by police, a growing number of white college students began supporting the movement to end Jim Crow. Initially, black and white students coordinated their civil right activities independent of one another, through their respective campus organizations. But many felt that if they were going to call for desegregation within the greater society there was a need for young people to break down the color barriers between their own organizations. The Student Nonviolent Coordinating Committee provided the first opportunity for black and white student activists to work through a single organization within a multiracial framework. By the time SNCC reconvened at Morehouse College for its third conference in October 1960, white students had joined the ranks of the organization. In his

Political activist Julian Bond talks with North Carolina A & T students prior to delivering the main address in observance of Men's Week.

conference address, Southern Regional Council Vice President Marion S. Wright told HBCU students that "Here and there in the South white college students and professors have marched with you on the picket line, sat with you on the lunch stools and gone with you to jail. If Leadership has been the Negroes,' [sic] loyal support has come from the whites. I think you may search Southern history without uncovering a precedent."

A Break in the Ranks

The Student Nonviolent Coordinating Committee was not a year old before two factions—one from Nashville and the other from Atlanta—began to vie for leadership and direction of the organization. The basic argument among the members of SNCC was whether the organization should continue to focus on direct action—confrontational but peaceful demonstrations against

STUDENT NONVIOLENT
COORDINATING COMMITTEE

The sit-in movement started by four North Carolina A & T students at a Woolworth lunch counter on February 1, 1960, inspired the formation of the Student Nonviolent Coordinating Committee, known as SNCC (pronounced "snick"). Two months after this seminal event, Ella Baker called a meeting of student activists on the campus of her alma mater, Shaw University, in Raleigh, North Carolina. This gathering drew students from HBCUs across the South. Baker, the director of Martin Luther King's Southern Christian Leadership Conference (SCLC), wanted to organize the protesters into an independent group that would have its own vision rather than serving as the student arm of an existing civil rights organization. The group was officially named the Student Non-Violent Coordinating Committee in October 1960. During the volatile 1960s, HBCU students from SNCC would be involved in every major civil rights struggle, and students from HBCUs were prominent in SNCC. Marion Barry, the group's first president, was a graduate student at Fisk; Chuck McDew, who would replace Barry, was a student at South Carolina State; Charles Jones attended Johnson C. Smith College; Charles Sherrod was enrolled at Virginia Union; Ruby Doris Smith was a Spelman student; Tim Jenkins was a graduate of Howard University; Ed King was a student at Kentucky State; and John Lewis began his junior year at Fisk with Diane Nash, after attending American Baptist Theological Seminary.

The names of some of the SNCC leadership would become synonymous with civil rights in the United States. Julian Bond was enrolled at Morehouse. Stokely Carmichael matriculated at Howard. The average age of SNCC workers was 23. What set SNCC apart from other organizations was that they concentrated their efforts in the rural South. SNCC focused on empowering blacks at the local level, and they drew the overwhelming majority of their members from HBCUs. The groundswell of student protest gripping the nation, coupled with the high concentration of black colleges below the Mason-Dixon line, resulted in SNCC having more workers in the South than any other organization just one year after their formation. From 1961 to 1964 SNCC registered black voters in areas known for violent opposition to black suffrage. The stakes were high for these young students who were willing to risk expulsion from school, jail, and even death to help bring economic and political power to poor blacks.

During the summer of 1964, SNCC became the driving force behind the Mississippi Project, which brought 1,000 volunteers to the state to register black voters. In August 1965, SNCC went into Lowndes County, Alabama, a hotbed of violent white oppression where not a single black person was registered to vote. A year after SNCC's visit there, 50 percent of eligible black voters were ready to cast ballots. But SNCC's successes did not come without a cost. In the space of five months two SNCC workers were murdered because of their efforts: Jonathan Daniels was shot in Hayneville, Alabama, in August 1965, and Sammy Younge Jr. was killed in Tuskegee in January 1966.

The threat of death was not a deterrent, however. The summer of 1966 brought about SNCC's first training institute in Atlanta. The summer schedule allowed the new recruits to become indoctrinated in the SNCC style of protest without missing classes. SNCC also maintained a scholarship program for staff members who wanted to take time off from school to work during the academic year. Stokely Carmichael considered dropping out of school after his junior year to work with SNCC, but his parents convinced him to complete his degree.

SNCC also created freedom schools and community centers, helped black farmers run for agricultural stabilization committees, and assisted blacks in running for the school board, sheriff, and other county elected offices. They even published a book, *Negroes in American History*, that was used in the freedom schools to educate black youth about African American history.

Over a quarter of a million people witnessed history in the making when they turned out for the March on Washington in 1963. It was here that Dr. King delivered his now famous "I Have a Dream" speech.

segregation—or concentrate on registering black voters in the Deep South. "We finally agreed that we would do both direct action and voter registration because we concluded that voter registration in Mississippi and Lowndes County, Alabama, was direct action," said Charles McDew, chairman of SNCC from 1960 to 1963. This issue was settled in 1961 at a meeting at the Highlander Folk School in Tennessee. Resolving this problem also put aside the split between the Atlanta faction (who favored voter registration) led by Morehouse man Julian Bond, and the Nashville faction (who espoused direct action) led by Fisk students John Lewis, Diane Nash, and James Bevel.

An even more divisive problem would occur in SNCC in 1962, when the issue surfaced concerning the role of whites in the organization. "We're all in this together," John Lewis told his comrades during an emergency meeting on the interracial question. "The Beloved Community isn't just an idea. It's real, and it begins with us. If you were committed to the idea of seeing the spark of the sacred in every human being, no matter how vile or violent, how could you hold yourself apart from someone else simply because he or she was white?" The mutual concern for the voter registration drive delayed further infighting among SNCC members.

As concerns for civil rights escalated, so did concerns about the war in Vietnam. Black students—activists or otherwise—were concerned about their draft status. By the end of December 1965, there were more than 20,000 African Americans in Vietnam, including 16,531 in the Army, 500 in the Navy, 3,580 in the Marines, and 908 in the Air Force. Black students who had been involved in fighting Jim Crow were now on the ramparts with thousands of white students protesting the Vietnam War. On January 4, 1966, SNCC formally announced its opposition to the war in Vietnam. It was the first civil rights organization to do so.

A Seismic Shift

Though SNCC was started by HBCU students, by 1965 the organization had little affiliation with its roots. Like Lewis, Nash, and Bevel, the majority of SNCC's original student leaders opted to leave school to become field workers in rural areas, where they launched voter registration and desegregation efforts. With energies focused on grassroots, community-based activities, the core leadership interacted less frequently with HBCU students and campus recruitment efforts all but ceased. That reality concerned some SNCC leaders, who recognized that the direction and tone of the organization was changing as a result of the disassociation. A more radical faction voiced their desire to exclude white students from participating in SNCC activities. Former Howard student Stokely Carmichael and H. Rap Brown, from Southern, were among SNCC members who called for whites to be ousted. In 1966 SNCC voted to remove whites from the organization, although by this time most of the whites had already left to participate in the antiwar and women's movements.

In an effort to move the organization back toward its ideological beginnings, SNCC launched an HBCU student recruitment effort. Student Nonviolent Coordinating Committee staff members were sent to black college campuses in Virginia, Texas, Alabama, Mississippi, Georgia, North Carolina, and South Carolina to encourage students to join the organization.

With SNCC leadership acknowledging that an important resource had been neglected, statewide conferences were held in an effort to recruit more southern black college students. With the civil rights struggle. . .

"The importance of encouraging Southern Negro college students to lend their talents to the movement cannot be overemphasized," writes an SNCC official in a report. "Too often the South's trained leadership goes North to seek better employment opportunities and very often the leadership that remains is . . . insensitive to the problems of (the) poor."[13]

The tethered relationship between SNCC and HBCU students was beyond repair, however. By 1966 the remaining SNCC members, led by new president Carmichael, aligned themselves with the newly formed Black Panther Party for Self-Defense. Huey Newton and Bobby Seale, the Party founders, invited the SNCC members to join them as they and other black militants began to make an even bolder stand against the war in Vietnam. It was a

potentially powerful formation that combined the philosophical thrust of Dr.
King's "I Have a Dream" speech of 1963 and the more radical demands from
the camp who revered the martyred Malcolm X. An aroused black youth
shouting anti-imperialist slogans and denouncing American aggression at
home and abroad were, for the powers that be, "a clear and present danger."
Alert to the growing dissent, J. Edgar Hoover and the FBI, through its counter-
intelligence program, and other law enforcement agencies, were successful in
a devastating campaign of dirty tricks to undermine and at last destroy the
merging elements of the civil rights and black liberation movements.

Black students at various HBCUs were emboldened by the antiwar positions taken by the Panthers and SNCC, however. Carmichael, addressing students at Morgan State in 1967, challenged them to break the tradition of
passivity at the college and assailed administrators for their conservative point
of view on political issues. He openly urged the students to resist the draft.

"Either you go to the Leavenworth Federal Penitentiary in Kansas, or you
become a killer," he boomed. "I will choose to suffer . . . I will go to jail. To hell
with this country."[9]

Carmichael's speeches, which urged young blacks to embrace more

Harlem rally, New York, 1963.

Activist Malcolm X photographed at a Black Muslim rally in
Chicago, 1963, by Gordon Parks.

aggressive tactics than nonviolent action in response to racial discrimination
and the Vietnam war, signaled a definitive shift in the mood of the Civil
Rights movement. Where young protesters, particularly black college students, once were willing to endure jailings and unprovoked physical attacks
from law enforcement officials in order to advance racial equality efforts, a
new generation of HBCU students met these provocations less passively.

On April 8, 1967, the day after Carmichael had given an address at Fisk University, unrest broke out on the campuses of Fisk and Tennessee State University. Nashville officials suggested that the confrontation between students

and the police was a result of Carmichael, who had already left town, agitating students and inciting them to riot. Students, however, insisted that the event was sparked when a male student was dragged out of a Fisk campus restaurant by a white police officer at the black restaurant owner's request. When other students began shouting protests in response to the removal, the riot squad, which had been on the ready since Carmichael's speech, was called in to disperse the crowd. Students responded to the billy club—wielding officers' blows by throwing rocks and bottles. Police then began firing shots in the air, a number of which ricocheted off buildings and into the girls' dormitories. Several dorm residents were wounded. When students at nearby Tennessee State got wind of the violence, they too began protesting the police action. Once again, riot squads moved in, shooting and injuring several students. By Sunday evening April 9, more than 100 HBCU students and Nashville residents had been arrested in conjunction with the unrest, and fifty people had been injured by stray bullets and billy clubs. Three SNCC workers were arrested for "inciting to riot."

"The black people and students of Nashville are angry," wrote an SNCC representative in the organization's Aframerican News Service. "They have seen what 'is going down' in their city and they now know that riot squads are not only ready to move into the poorest ghettoes of America's cities, but are now moving against black students and colleges."[10]

At Howard University during the same year, students protesting the war disrupted an on-campus speech given by General Lewis B. Hershey, director of the U.S. Selective Services. Further impetus against the war came from students at Tuskegee, many of whom were still mourning the death of SNCC member Sammy Younge in January 1966.

Thousands of black students demonstrated on campuses across the country. They embraced the words of Muhammad Ali: "I have no quarrel with the Vietnamese." Overall, the black student protest movement did persuade some universities to introduce black history, literature, and humanities courses, which were among the demands of black student protesters. In 1969 the Ford Foundation donated $1 million to Morgan State, Howard, and Yale Universities to prepare faculty members to teach courses in African American studies.

Julian Bond, state representative of Georgia, former SNCC organizer and Morehouse graduate, was staunchly opposed to the war, insisting that the Vietnamese had every right to govern themselves. These sentiments were echoed by Congressman Ron Dellums of Oakland, California. Dellums, whose uncle had helped A. Philip Randolph forge the Brotherhood of Sleeping Car Porters, said he considered the U.S. involvement in Indochina "illegal, immoral, and insane."[11]

But for every black student who opposed the war, there was at least one who supported it, and many of them went willingly to serve their country. These young men went into battle in a distant land to protect the freedom of others, despite not having those guarantees at home. Wallace Terry in his book *Bloods* said this of the black Vietnam veteran: "He fought at a time when his sisters and brothers were fighting and dying at home for equal rights and greater opportunities, for a color-blind nation promised to him in the Constitution he swore to defend. He fought at a time when some of his leaders chastised him for waging war against a people of color, and when his Communist foe appealed to him to take up arms instead against the forces of racism in America."[12]

It was in the context of this antiwar fervor that Dr. King began to publicly state his opposition to the war. Prodded by some of his chief lieutenants as well as his wife Coretta, King stepped up the crusade with a speech before a panel of antiwar senators, asserting that U.S. involvement in Vietnam had caused the public to forget about the civil rights movement. In March 1967, King participated in an antiwar demonstration in Chicago. A month later, at Riverside Church in Harlem, an interracial audience of 3,000 clung to each word of King's speech, "Beyond Vietnam." A blistering attack on the war, King referred to many HBCU recruits in his words: "the young black men who have been crippled by our society and sending them 3,000 miles away to guarantee liberties in Southeast Asia which they had not found in southwest Georgia and East Harlem."[18] Dr. James Cone, a graduate of Philander Smith College, has noted in his study of King and the politics of Malcolm X, a confluence of their ideas. The prophet of nonviolence was becoming more radical in his outlook, more internationalist, and more attuned to issues of class as well as race.

Unexpected Outcome

Inspired by other student demonstrations against segregated facilities, students at South Carolina State College, Orangeburg, protested against a local bowling

alley on February 6, 1968. On the second night of protesting, fifteen of the
students were arrested. When they returned on February 8, supporters started
a bonfire. As law enforcement tried to put it out, an officer was injured with
a piece of banister. In retaliation, the troopers began to shoot randomly into
the crowd. "Gunfire went off. I heard nothing that preceded it," said civil rights
activist Cleveland Sellers, who was among those wounded. "There were no warn-
ings, nothing." Three black students were killed and twenty-seven others were
wounded by South Carolina state troopers during the four-day disturbance. A
National Guard unit was dispatched to quell the turmoil, and the school was
closed for two weeks.[19] A number of students were jailed in the wake of the incident. Nine white officers were charged in the shooting, but all were acquitted.

What happened at Orangeburg was the most violent and bloody action by
local and state authorities to curb student militancy on black college campuses. "But the severe repressive measures, including the alleged framing of
militant student leaders on murder and rioting charges and police and
National Guard invasions of black campuses, were reportedly employed at a
host of schools," Robert Allen wrote in *Black Awakening in Capitalist America*.[20]
Allen noted that on "black campuses, students and militant teachers were
demanding not only curriculum changes, but a restructuring and reorientation of the colleges themselves."[21] There was widespread demand by pan-
Africanist and black nationalist advocates for students to resist integration and
assimilation to promote a curriculum that stressed Afrocentric courses.

The Orangeburg Massacre may have been on Dr. King's mind as his militancy became more pronounced. On April 4, 1968, when he was felled by an
assassin's bullet, more than 120 cities convulsed in rage and HBCUs were not
immune to riots and takeovers.

Across the south, black college campuses were rocked by another, more
violent wave of riots. Students burned on-campus armed forces training corps
facilities, and in response the National Guard, armed with tanks and artillery,
was called in by government officials to put down the uprising on several
HBCU campuses.

Robert Allen, in *Black Awakening in Capitalist America*, reported that the situation became so serious in 1968 that six presidents of black colleges called
on President Johnson and federal officials to "stop these invasions of college
and university campuses by the American version storm troopers."

The Arrival of Integration

Ultimately, HBCUs paid for the student unrest and violent response of government officials with the destruction of school property and the loss of lives in some cases. But the violence also yielded positive outcomes. Where previous generations of student activists had advocated for desegregated higher educational opportunities, a new generation began to view the efforts as potentially damaging to African American culture and the continued existence of HBCUs. Writer Robert Allen noted that on "black campuses, students and militant teachers were demanding not only curriculum changes, but a restructuring and reorientation of the colleges themselves."[22] There was widespread demand by pan-Africanist and black nationalist advocates for students to resist integration and assimilation and to instead promote a curriculum that stressed Afrocentric courses.

Beyond HBCU campuses, more than eighty black Americans had been elected to political office in the South by November 1968. Clearly, some of those communities were galvanized by the legacy of Dr. King as well as the impact of the Voting Rights Act of 1965. Black Southerners in particular were overjoyed to find representatives of their color for the first time in the legislatures in North Carolina, Florida, and Tennessee. Henry Frye, a graduate of North Carolina State A & T who later became an associate justice in the state's supreme court, won a seat in the North Carolina House.[23] Notable too was the ascendancy of Jesse Jackson, another North Carolina A & T graduate, who was among Dr. King's most promising and ambitious lieutenants, and Andrew Young, whose background at HBCUs included attendance at Dillard and Howard University.

Other Agendas

Not all the students at HBCUs were involved in the sit-ins. Some were busy perfecting their athletic skills in preparation for the 1960 summer Olympics in Rome. When the track-and-field events were over, the United States had won thirty-four gold medals, three of them belonging to Wilma Rudolph. With the memory of defeat still fresh from 1956, Rudolph, dubbed the "Black Gazelle" by Italian sportswriters, won the 100- and 200-meter dashes, and then led her Tigerbelles of Tennessee Agricultural & Industrial (now Tennessee State University) to victory in the 400-meter relay. Mae Faggs Starr, Isabelle Daniels, and Lucinda Williams were Rudolph's running mates on the relay team. Another fellow student at A & I, Ralph Boston, also won a gold medal in the broad jump, eclipsing Jesse Owens's world record.

By 1968, however, a sixteen-year-long court battle was beginning to unfold at Tennessee State University that would set the course for integration of publicly funded HBCUs, and in some cases tipped the racial makeup so that African Americans no longer represent the majority culture at the schools.

In 1947, the University of Tennessee at Nashville (UTN) opened as an extension of the predominately white University of Tennessee at Knoxville. For the first thirteen years, UTN offered its students only one year of extension courses, but by 1960 UTN board members were looking to expand the publicly funded extension into a four-year, degree-granting institution. Those plans greatly concerned a number of black and white educators alike. Many feared that an expansion of UTN, a land-grant institution, would deflect funding from the state's black land-grant college, TSU. That fear was not without validity, as southern state legislatures were notorious for providing less funding to HBCUs than to majority-white colleges. In 1890, the federal government was prompted to pass the second Morrill Act for the expressed purpose of forcing segregated states to provide funds for black colleges.

The 1954 *Brown v. Board of Education* case focused largely on public primary and secondary schools, but the desegregation decision ultimately required public colleges to integrate as well. Many civil rights advocates believed that UTN officials' move to establish four-year degree programs in engineering, business administration, education, and liberal arts—areas in which TSU already offered degrees—was a covert effort to keep Tennessee colleges segregated.

As early as 1966, a group of Nashville residents opposed to expansion met with the state's commissioner of education, J. Howard Warf, to express their concerns. Warf, who by law was a member of UTN's board of trustees, told the group that "a plan to establish a four-year degree program at the University of Tennessee branch here is not conceived as a means to keep Tenneesee A & I State University an institution for Negroes only. . . . A four-year program at the UT branch here is not supposed to affect A & I in any way."[24]

Not swayed by Warf's assertion, the group continued to question him, pointing out that the state had made no effort to desegregate TSU. The commissioner responded that he was in favor of efforts to integrate the school, but offered no plan for advancing that cause.

In September 1966, attorney Avon Williams wrote a letter to Tennessee governor Frank Clement on behalf of the Davidson County Independent Political Council, in which he reiterated the council's concern over UTN's proposed expansion. The letter also put forth a recommendation that the two universities be merged, with TSU becoming the state's official land-grant institution. Nearly two years later, however, state officials had made no efforts to respond to civil rights supporters' concerns, so on May 21, 1968, Rita Sanders, a black professor teaching at TSU, and Patrick Gilpin, a white professor teaching at UTN, filed a class action lawsuit against the governor of Tennessee, the commissioner of education, the State Board of Education, UTN, TSU, and other entities. The suit charged that the state's plans for UTN violated the Fourteenth Amendment of the Constitution by continuing to promote segregation in higher education. It also charged that state officials were not adequately funding TSU and noted that the financial allotment for faculty, administrators, the library, and other facilities at the black college weren't provided on a level equal to majority-white state colleges.

In his history of the *Sanders v. Ellington* case, author Christopher Cromwell wrote that as a consequence of the funding disparities, "Plaintiffs allege that at A & I, a specific school, namely the School of Engineering, is not and has never been, fully accredited. . . . Such failure of the State of Tennessee to provide the financial and other support necessary to secure accreditation for A & I while providing adequate financial and other support to the predominantly white schools in the state constitute [sic] a depreciation of Plaintiffs' rights under the Fourteenth Amendment to the Constitution of the United States."

The lawsuit asked the court to issue an injunction against further state or federal funding of the UTN expansion, and it also requested that the state be mandated to set out a plan for "meaningful desegregation of the public universities of Tennessee."[25]

In the summer of 1968, TSU and the federal government joined the plaintiffs in suing the State of Tennessee, and that August state officials issued their answers to the complaint. "It is admitted that segregation in public higher education has not been eliminated but it is insisted that rapid strides have been made in the direction," wrote the defendants. They noted that fifteen percent of college-age blacks and forty-four percent of college-age whites attended college, and opined that, "it appears that as a whole desegregation is approaching about the level that should be expected."[26]

State officials also denied TSU received less funding than its white counterparts.

On August 22, presiding Judge Frank Gray Jr. rendered a decision that denied the plaintiffs' request to halt the UTN expansion, but he did order state officials to develop and implement a plan for desegregating Tennessee's institutions of higher learning. State officials filed their plan with the U.S. District Court for Middle Tennessee on April 1, 1969. The strategy called for the state's education department to actively recruit college-bound students at predominantly black high schools into Tennessee's predominantly white state-supported universities. Financial support was to be made available to black students to encourage their enrollment at traditionally white schools. Tennessee State University's facilities were to be substantially upgraded to make the campus more appealing to all races, and active recruitment of white faculty and students was to occur. State officials also proposed a joint engineering degree program between TSU and UTN to heighten desegregation efforts.

Two years later, the state's plans had produced few tangible results, however. Black enrollment at UTN had increased 42.2 percent, from 2,720 students in 1968 to 3,869 in 1970, but TSU's white student enrollment actually decreased, from 45 to 44 students. Black students still represented 99.7 percent of the student population there. In response to the slow progress, Judge Gray issued a memorandum ordering the state to submit a specific plan for attracting white students and faculty to TSU.

"It is . . . clear that Tennessee State remains, in all practical respects, a black institution, while the institutions in close proximity to it, as well as some institutions in other parts of the state, remain largely white," wrote Gray in 1972. "The phenomenon of a black Tennessee State, so long as it exists, negates both the contention that defendants have dismantled the dual system of public higher education in Tennessee, as ordered by this court, and the contention that they are, in any realistic sense, on their way toward doing so."[27]

In his response to the court order, TSU President Andrew Torrence wrote that he accepted the judge's ruling because while the university's faculty, which was 13 percent white, was more integrated than other state university faculties, their white student enrollment, at 1.85 percent, was all but nonexistent. "It seems obvious, therefore, that a more substantial desegregation of the TSU student body is to be realized immediately."[28]

The battle to desegregate Tennessee's institutions of higher learning waged until 1984 and ultimately resulted in the court adopting an earlier recommendation from the Davidson County Independent Political Council to merge TSU and UTN, *with TSU becoming the state's official land-grant institution!* The agreement also stipulated that state officials would work to maintain a 50 percent full-time white undergraduate enrollment. Over the years, the case took on a variety of complexions and tones as both blacks and whites struggled to make peace with the unexpected results of desegregation and the sacrifices that each group would need to make to ensure equal access to higher education.

On a larger scale, the TSU case was indicative of the struggles that publicly sponsored HBCUs across the country would face when confronted with the realities of desegregation—a cause long championed by HBCU students, faculty, and administrators. While desegregation did provide better state funding of HBCUs, and greater access for students and professors wishing to attend or teach at historically white colleges, it also provided greater integration of black schools, and in many cases forced HBCU administrators and staff to refocus their colleges' long-held educational and cultural objectives.

Class Day, 1947: In this time-honored school tradition, Spelman alumnae lead senior class through Alumnae Arch signaling their transformation from students to alumnae. Meanwhile, battlelines were being drawn that would challenge the separate but equal law of the land.

In the coming decades HBCUs would struggle to redefine themselves and remain relevant in the midst of desegregation. Where the 1960s ushered in a freedom movement that provided black college students with greater educational opportunities, the '70s and '80s would witness HBCUs struggling with a loss of student enrollment and tuition funds as college-bound blacks exercised their options to attend predominantly white colleges and universities.

9

꘏ . ꘏

CALMING THE STORM, HEALING THE CUT

The 1970s found HBCU administrations searching for ways to heal the psychological and financial wounds caused by the radicalism and sweeping changes of the previous decade. Black college presidents also struggled to keep their school relevant and desirable places of learning for blacks while simultaneously diversifying their appeal to other racial groups during an age of integration.

THE 1970S ARE MOST often portrayed as the age of integration and affirmative action—a time when the African American community swiftly reaped the benefits of decades of civil rights struggle. But while traditionally white institutions of higher learning, large corporations, and federal and state government officials employed aggressive measures for mainstreaming blacks into the educational, employment, and legislative fabric of America, desegregation was not without its casualties. Ironically, HBCUs, among the most vociferous champions of desegregation, were among the institutions that stumbled in

Jackson State University students in 1970.

Adorned in African dress, these Jackson State women get in touch with
their heritage in 1971.

the wake of the massive changes brought on by integration efforts such as those
implemented at TSU.

The Ups and Downs of Desegregation

Almost overnight, public black colleges found themselves grappling with issues
of cultural identity as they struggled with federal and state mandates to diversify their student bodies and faculties. In some cases, public HBCUs were closed
or threatened with closure as Southern states dismantled their century-old systems of dual education that resulted from Jim Crow laws. Now that Southern states
were mandated to admit blacks into their historically white public colleges,
many state officials saw no reason to continue funding their black land-grant
universities.

There were, however, efforts to address the problems that HBCUs faced
in redefining their positions and missions in the midst of integration. The
Carnegie Commission of Higher Education released its report calling for federal aid to the nation's HBCUs. According to the report, black colleges were
"faced with special difficulties at a time of major transition." It was determined

that HBCUs were at a terrible disadvantage when competing against major white institutions to enroll black students. Moreover, black colleges "had to meet the special expenses of remedial training for poorly prepared students and financial aid for the 70 percent of their students who required some type of scholarly assistance."[1]

Although gains by blacks in other areas were applauded, by the summer of 1970, HBCUs were deemed in imminent danger of losing their identity "through integration, merger, reduced status, or outright abolition," according to a report released by the Race Relations Information Center (RRIC), based in Nashville. The report, entitled "The Black Public College—Integration and Disintegration," stated that, "The 1970–71 academic years marked the first time in their history that the nation's thirty-three black state-supported colleges enrolled more than 100,000 students."[2] This figure represented an increase of over 75 percent during the previous decade. However, the growth in enrollment masked a deeper quandary—the significant enrollment of white students at some HBCUs shifted the cultural balance so that some HBCUs became predominantly white institutions. This development posed a threat of countering the goal of greater minority access to and presence within institutions of higher learning.

Originally, thirty-five state-support colleges had been established for African Americans. But two of them—Maryland State College and Bluefield State College (West Virginia)—had become predominantly white as a result of desegregation efforts. Then, West Virginia State and Lincoln University (Missouri) met the same fate. According to the RRIC, three more colleges—Delaware State, Bowie State (Maryland), and Kentucky State—eventually would lose their original status. The report speculated that the majority of the remaining black state-supported colleges were in jeopardy of being abolished because they were in competition with major white institutions for funding, students, and top faculty.

In a related study, the Office of Civil Rights of the Department of Health, Education and Welfare (HEW) disclosed that black student enrollment in the nation's colleges and universities had increased at five times greater than white enrollment since 1968. Almost 50 percent of all black undergraduates, the report noted, were enrolled in colleges with black minorities, and not HBCUs. Most of the increase occurred in the eleven Southern states.

LEGAL CASES AND HBCUS

On May 8, 1896, the U.S. Supreme Court provided legal protection for Jim Crow laws by ruling that "separate but equal" accommodations did not violate the Thirteenth and Fourteenth Amendments. The *Plessy v. Ferguson* case provided legal justification for the de facto segregation that had been a way of life in many parts of the country since the demise of Reconstruction. This case made segregation legal for the next fifty-eight years. Although *Plessy v. Ferguson* came six years after the Morrill Act of 1890 during a boom for black college development, it would adversely effect the quality of instruction available at those institutions.

Texas in the 1940s was a microcosm of the debilitating effects that segregation had inflicted on African Americans across the country. The overwhelming majority of African Americans worked in unskilled labor and service positions. There were six times more white doctors than black doctors, four times more white dentists than black dentists, and 251 times as many white engineers as black engineers. These disparities were not due to lack of ability, but had more to do with economics and opportunity. White schools had two to three times more undergraduate majors from which students could choose. Not a single black college in Texas had a medical, dental, or law school. Doctoral work was available only at white institutions. In 1945 one white state-supported teacher's college had more books in its library than all of the black colleges in Texas combined. For every $6.40 the state allocated for a black school's physical plant and endowment, $28.66 was spent for white institutions.

These racist conditions faced Wiley College alumnus Hemann Sweatt when he applied to the University of Texas law school in 1946. Not surprisingly, Sweatt was denied admission solely based on his race. He promptly filed suit against the University of Texas in district court. W. J. Durham and Thurgood Marshall were his legal counsel. On June 26 the district court of Travis County, Texas, ruled that Sweatt's constitutional rights were violated and the school's decision to deny Sweatt admission was in violation of Texas state law. The ruling was held in abeyance for six months to allow the state to establish a law school for blacks.

The new law school that was developed was in rented quarters in Houston near a black law firm. The two lawyers from the firm were hired as faculty. Because of this move by the state, the district court ruled in favor of the university. Sweatt appealed and the lower court's decision was reversed and sent back for retrial.

By May 1947, when the case was revisited, Durham and Marshall had shifted their argument to contest the inherent inequality of the "separate but equal" doctrine. This was the first direct challenge to *Plessy v. Ferguson*, and the court ruled that "a segregated law school for Negroes could not provide them equal educational opportunities." A similar ruling was granted in 1950 in Oklahoma in the *McLaurin v. Oklahoma* case. The court, in that case, ruled that public graduate schools could not adhere to a policy of segregation. The outcome of these cases in district and state courts set the stage for a federal challenge of segregation.

Although the landmark *Brown* case mentions only the surname of Oliver Brown, the case had over 200 plaintiffs, and combined cases from Kansas, Virginia, Delaware, and South Carolina. Thurgood Marshall, arguing for the NAACP, presented a case that he had been preparing for nearly two decades, after winning thirteen of fifteen legal challenges argued before the Supreme Court. The magnitude of this victory can be understood better when considering that the decision overturned legal segregation laws in twenty-one states. The ramifications for HBCUs, however, would be felt from the athletic fields to the lecture halls. Although desegregation did not occur overnight, some of the brightest black scholars were finally able to enroll in white institutions.

Despite integration, HBCUs continue to educate a disproportionate number of black college students. Black public and private colleges comprise approximately 3 percent of the total number of institutions in the United States but graduate more than 25 percent of black college students nationwide. Although legal victories have made entry into white colleges available to black students, HBCUs continue to train leaders in business, science, industry, and the arts.

On September 4, 1970, representatives of nine black colleges charged the Nixon administration with failure to support black higher education. "The educators, meeting in Detroit, Michigan under the leadership of president Lucius H. Pitts of Miles College (Birmingham, Alabama), called for increased government and private funds to strengthen the more than 100 Black colleges and universities. The Nixon administration was assailed by Vivian Henderson, president of Clark College, charging the president with an "utter lack of sensitivity" to the needs of black colleges. Vernon Jordan, a Howard University graduate and head of the United Negro College Fund, insisted that at least $2 billion was needed to maintain the black colleges. A reply from Nixon's press secretary, Ronald Ziegler, indicated that something would be done about the request.

Hope in the Face of Disappointment

It wasn't long though before HBCUs received encouraging financial news. The Ford Foundation set forth a six-year, $100 million fund providing individual grants to a select number of minority students enrolled in black private colleges. Among the HBCUs chosen to receive the awards, averaging more than $300,000, were Benedict College, Hampton and Tuskegee Institute, Fisk University, and all the schools at the Atlanta University complex.

As if to counter the general disdain and flagrant disinterest of the Nixon administration's interest in the affairs of African Americans, Admiral Elmo R. Zumwalt Jr., Chief of Naval Operations, announced in March the creation of a six-man team to launch a five-year program to recruit more black officers and enlistees in the navy. This was a bold move given recent campus protests against the Vietnam War, during which armed forces property was deliberately damaged by students.

Blacks, at the time, represented 12 percent of the national population, but their total number in the navy was well below this figure. Zumwalt's purpose was to balance these numbers. His first initiatives occurred at HBCUs. At Savannah State College in Georgia, and at Southern University at Baton Rouge, Louisiana, the admiral ordered a Navy Reserve Officer Training Corps to be established, which would supplement the nation's only black navy ROTC unit at Prairie View A & M College in Texas. Later that spring, the army would begin similar plans to improve the presence of minorities, adding a number of blacks to its office personnel.

Private black colleges also struggled in the midst of integration efforts. Hugh Gloster, president of Morehouse College during the early seventies, observed that private HBCUs were particularly challenged to maintain enrollment numbers and diversify their student bodies because they received no funding support for the purpose of attracting white students. What's more, these schools were also losing potential black students as they could not compete with the scholarship and financial aid opportunities being offered by predominantly white shcools. Gloster characterized the challenge in this manner:

"In the South while students attend predominantly black colleges in significant numbers only if there are no predominantly white colleges in the community or if the predominantly black colleges are public institutions with low tuition rates, we try to recruit white students but are unsuccessful. In a country where foundations and corporations have provided millions of dollars to predominantly white colleges to recruit black students, we have sought funds to recruit white students but have been unsuccessful. As a matter of fact, I know of no predominantly black college that has received a large grant providing scholarship money to attract white students."[3]

Former Morehouse president Benjamin Mays asserted that the unbalanced approach to integration, which focused on supporting African Americans' access to traditionally white institutions and gave little support to whites accessing traditionally black institutions, ultimately dismissed the value of black institutions and relegated them to second-class status.

"Desegregation is not and certainly should not be designed to perpetuate or create an inferiority complex in Negroes or a superiority complex in whites to the end that we feel the desegregation can come about only one way—only if we abolish all banks and insurance companies, all churches and educational institutions, all newspapers and magazines, all businesses and professions built and established with Negro brain and sweat," offered Mays in a visionary speech given at Livingstone College shortly after the *Brown v. Board of Education* decision. "Rather, the aim should be to incorporate everything that is good and everything that is needed into the mainstream of American life."[4]

Most HBCU administrators were ill-prepared to counter the one-sided approach to integration efforts, but as early as 1952 at least one black college president saw clearly that though desegregation was a necessary, noble effort it could well effect the demise of HBCUs. Prior to the Supreme Court decision on *Brown v Board of Education*, then Morgan State College president Martin D. Jenkins offered that systematic integration would most likely find HBCUs participating in a public education system reorganized to offer services to the majority. The danger, he warned, was that services designated for African American students would be phased out and existing patterns of discrimination would continue under the guise of equality.[5]

Image v. Reality

Historically black colleges and universities were battling more than resource problems during the era of integration. Black colleges also found themselves saddled with labels of irrelevancy and ineffectiveness. In 1967, Harvard University sociologists David Riesman and Christopher Jencks published "The American Negro College" in the *Harvard Educational Review*. The article was critical of HBCUs, stating that "by almost any standard these 110 colleges are academic disaster areas."[6] The derisive assertions not only dismissed proof to the contrary—namely a century-long list of HBCU graduates who had made significant contributions to and helped guide the direction of the country—but they also completely trivialized the leadership role that Southern blacks played in establishing the country's public school system and launching the Civil Rights Movement by stating that "Southern Negroes never had a revolutionary tradition."[7]

The journal article also charged that black colleges were run "as if they were the personal property of their presidents,"[8] while Ann Jones, a white professor who taught at an HBCU for just two semesters, opined that the president at her school was a "paternalistic dictator."[9]

The Harvard journal article outraged HBCU presidents, administrators, and supporters, who now found themselves battling a misleading image. Benjamin Mays characterized the criticisms as being part of "a subtle move afloat to abolish black colleges."[10]

Those educators and government officials who supported, either covertly or overtly, the abolishment of HBCUs often cited the belief that black schools lacked the resources to prepare students for careers in an integrated world. But Howard Zinn, a white Spelman professor and former SNCC member, argued that HBCUs were actually better equipped to offer students of all colors experience in how the global world operated. "There is too much wistful talk in education circles about how far Negro colleges must go to 'catch up' with the rest," offered Zinn. "What is overlooked is that the Negro colleges have one supreme advantage over the others: they are the nearest this country has to a racial microcosm of the world outside the United States, a world largely non-white, developing, and filled with the tensions of bourgeois emulation and radical protest. And with more white students and foreign students entering, Negro universities might become our first massively integrated, truly international education centers."[11]

A Meeting of the Minds

Displeasure over the Riesman and Jencks article was not the first incident that fostered mistrust between black college officials and Ivy League college officials. Nor was it the first time that someone associated with an Ivy League was accused of promoting the demise of a black school. In 1829, a group of Yale alumni, faculty members, and administrators had blocked the development of Samuel Cornish's proposed Negro college in New Haven.

In an effort to defuse the most recent controversy, however, Harvard University administrators put together the Black College Conference, held during separate two-day sessions in March and April 1976. Conference organizer and Harvard professor Charles Willie said the event was an attempt to "eradicate racism in education"[12] and allow HBCU educators and administrators the opportunity to tell and analyze their own histories, present-day achievements, and challenges.

Securing the participation of HBCU faculty and administrators in the conference was no simple task, as the suspicion and anger in response to Riesman and Jencks's article was substantial. Several HBCU presidents declined to participate in a Harvard study that sought to verify or debunk statistical facts about HBCUs put forward by the two sociologists in their article. One administrator responded to the request by writing that "Those of us who work in the historically black colleges feel that we have been studied enough, too often by persons who know least about these institutions and their contributions to American Higher Education and to the American Society [sic]. The reports and writings flowing from these studies have been too often hyper and unfairly critical of our institutions, showing little sensitivity and even less understanding."

The completed study, though conducted nearly ten years after Riesman and Jencks's original study, did raise doubt about the duo's original statistics and subsequent criticisms of HBCUs. The authors characterized black colleges as typically enrolling no more than 500 students, employing a teaching staff of 20 or 30 professors, and managing on an operating budget of no more than a half million dollars. The follow-up Harvard study found, however, that only a handful of the schools they surveyed had student bodies of less than 1,000 and that the average size of the schools' faculties was 154. The average annual budget was $9.9 million.

Resistance and Backlash

Not all African Americans believed that educational integration was the answer to the racial ills plaguing America. By the early seventies, the Black Power agenda had taken hold, and instead of calling for desegregation of their schools, many HBCU students were advocating for greater focus on black studies and Afrocentric traditions on campus. In the spring of 1974, the black studies movement, launched six years earlier, was beginning to gain respectability. More than 1,200 institutions around the nation reported at least one course offering in the field. Still, there were academics—some of them African Americans such as Dr. Martin Kilson of Harvard University—who viewed the programs as essentially "anti-intellectual" and counterproductive. Kilson was a member of the black intelligentsia that included such prominent figures as Andrew Brimmer of the Federal Reserve Board; Kenneth Clarke, who had resigned from the board of trustees of Antioch College after they yielded to student demands for a black residence hall; Bayard Rustin, "and a number of old guard Negro administrators from Southern Negro Colleges [who seemed] to have become the cutting edge of the establishment backlash against the movement for Black Studies."[13]

Eldridge and Kathleen Cleaver, photographed by Gordon Parks in Altiers in 1970. A portrait of Huey Newton is in the background.

Just prior to a report from the *New York Times* on the subject of black studies and its relevance, three scholars—including Tobe Johnson, director of undergraduate African American studies programs for the Atlanta University Center, and Henry Cobb, dean of Southern University at Baton Rouge—completed an assessment of twenty-nine black studies programs for the U.S. Office of Education. They concluded that more study of black Americans was needed. But uppermost in their minds was how to structure good programs, particularly during a stressful period of economic downturn. With financial retrenchment being the order of the day, many black institutions realized the futility of seeking federal funds and began to look elsewhere for aid.

THE UNITED NEGRO COLLEGE FUND

In the early 1940s private HBCUs were suffering due to declining dona-tions from benefactors and charitable organizations. Even the most finan-cially sound institutions were experiencing the aftershocks of the Great Depression and the United States' entry into World War II. Unlike the black land-grant and state institutions, private HBCUs did not have the luxury of receiving funding from state governments. In response to these changes to the economic landscape, Dr. Frederick Patterson, presi-dent of Tuskegee Institute, published a letter in one of the country's most influential black newspapers, the *Pittsburgh Courier,* directed to other private HBCU presidents, appealing to them to collectively pool their resources to raise money. Twenty-seven schools joined forces, and the United Negro College Fund was born on April 25, 1944. Under the leadership of Patterson, UNCF established its annual fundraising drive, which in the first year alone raised $765,000. This tripled the amount the individual schools had raised in the previous year.

Since its founding, UNCF has raised more than $1.7 billion for African American college students attending the thirty-nine member institu-tions. The United Negro College Fund is one of the most recognizable names in black education and has been named the number one education nonprofit organization in the country by the *Chronicle of Philanthropy*. For more than two decades, the popular television special, *Lou Rawls' Parade of Stars,* has featured the nation's best recording artists and has raised more than $157 million for the fund. UNCF's popular slogan, "A mind is a terrible thing to waste," has become a permanent part of the American lexicon.

In the summer of 1974 the United Negro College Fund (UNCF) was the recipient of a windfall from Links, a national black women's social organization. Links gave the UNCF $132,000, which was the largest donation made by a black organization. The gift was largely the handi-work of Helen Edmonds, president of Links and a professor of history at North Carolina Central University.

The United Negro College Fund has taken on a new challenge with the establishment of the Technology Enhancement Capital Campaign. This initiative raises funds to upgrade the technology infrastructures of all member institutions. In addition to providing students and faculty with the latest technology, UNCF sponsors programs in scientific research, premedical studies, foreign language studies, and international affairs.

What started as an open letter in the black press has grown into the nation's most successful higher-education assistance organization for African American college students.

In February 1975 dissent rumbled from Fort Valley State College in Georgia after the U.S. District Court judge approved plans to desegregate the predominantly black institution. This action followed a suit filed by a group of white citizens who charged that they were being discriminated against. It was announced that black students and faculty were poised to appeal the decision. At this time, about a quarter of the faculty and student body were white. What happened at Fort Valley was part of a growing trend, and many of the HBCUs faced with this dilemma feared the worst since they were at the mercy of white-controlled state boards or regents or trustees who favored such a change. If the plans were affected, black students claimed, it would make it harder for them to attend the schools.

Smoothing the Stony Road

That historically black colleges were struggling to prove their relevancy in the wake of desegregation was ironic given the growing success of HBCU alumni on the political front and within mainstream corporate America. While the doors to the political and business worlds were finally swinging open, African Americans claiming positions within these arenas still had to sink or swim based on their abilities to do the job. In many cases, blacks were required to be more successful than their white counterparts if they wanted continued advancement.

When *Time* magazine issued a special supplement in July 1974, fifteen blacks were listed among two hundred people destined to be leaders in the new generation. More than half of them—Julian Bond, Marian Wright Edelman, Earl Graves, Maynard Jackson, Barbara Jordan, John Lewis, Vernon Jordan, and Andrew Young—were at one time or another affiliated with HBCUs.

In Atlanta, five blacks were elected or re-elected to the eighteen-member city council (Board of Aldermen), and three were elected to the board of education. Maynard Jackson, a Morehouse graduate and later the city's first black mayor, won a vice mayoral position and presided over the city council. Jackson received his law degree from North Carolina Central University Law School. Dr. Benjamin Mays was selected to head the school board.

Similar political developments were occurring in Texas. Barbara Jordan, a magna cum laude graduate of Texas Southern University, was in her fourth year as a state senator. In Tennessee, Benjamin Hooks, who attended LeMoyne-Owen and Howard University, had recently resigned from a judgeship in Shelby County and would soon be appointed the first black to serve on the U.S. Federal Communications Commission. Marian Wright Edelman, who had been active in the civil rights movement, was awaiting appointment to head the Harvard University Center for Law and Education. These were but a few significant gains made by notables who had attended HBCUs.

In 1977, the School of Medicine at Morehouse College, under the leadership of its dean, Dr. Louis Sullivan, received provisional accreditation. Meharry Medical College in Nashville and Howard University were the only other black medical schools.

During this period HBCUs were in heated competition with major white institutions that, since the urban upheavals, had begun to actively recruit African American students. But such competition was no indication of racial harmony in education.

Aside from the political and educational fronts, a less violent form of protest was taking place in corporate America. At a May 1970 General Motors stockholders meeting, a reform group had demanded that a black director be admitted to the company's board. On January 4, 1971, the group's demand was answered. The Reverend Leon H. Sullivan, a minister from Philadelphia, was elected to the board. Sullivan, who earned his bachelor's degree from West Virginia State University, one of three HBCUs with a predominantly

The Jackson State campus in the 1970s: New Horizons in Black Dimensions welcomes alumni and friends.

white student body, had acquired much of his political leverage through his organization Opportunities Industrialization Centers of America, a job-training program for African Americans and other minorities. A few years later Sullivan would use this position to apply additional pressure on the apartheid government of South Africa with the introduction of his Sullivan Principles, calling for dramatic reform of the repression and racial discrimination that had denied blacks access and opportunity.

Black History Month commenced with news that Howard Jordan Jr., president of Savannah State College in Georgia, had been promoted to vice chancellor of the Georgia State Board of Regents, the first black named to the position. Since 1963 Jordan had been the president of the college. Now he would oversee the administration for all the state-run colleges and universities. Reports of Jordan's promotion was followed by eruptions in Wilmington, North Carolina, where racial violence left one black youth and one white man dead.

CORPORATE LEADERS AND FINANCIERS

HBCU alumni have climbed the corporate ladder by creating successful businesses and by taking the reins as executives at some of the top American corporations. The nurturing and training they received at HBCUs have factored heavily in their many successes in business.

Reginald Lewis graduated with honors from Virginia State University in 1965. In 1987 he engineered the largest leveraged buyout of an international company when he acquired Beatrice Foods, a pan-European company based in France. Although his life was cut short by brain cancer at the age of 50, at the time of his death he had become one of the country's wealthiest African Americans. He lived his philosophy to "keep going, no matter what" while an undergraduate at Virginia State. Lewis's success didn't begin in the corporate boardroom, however; it started on the gridiron. He entered Virginia State College on a football scholarship in 1961. During his freshman year, Lewis struggled in the classroom because he devoted more time to learning the playbook than his textbooks. Only after suffering a career-ending shoulder injury did Lewis start to shine in the classroom. He graduated on the dean's list with a degree in political science and economics despite having become a working student after losing his scholarship.

His Virginia State education factored heavily in his entrance into Harvard. During a summer minority program at Harvard Law School, he so impressed professors that he was granted admission without taking the entrance exam. Lewis contributed freely and frequently to his alma mater, Virginia State. He also made an unsolicited donation of $1 million to Howard University in 1988. His presence on HBCU campuses continues to be felt through the NAACP Reginald F. Lewis Youth Entrepreneurial Institute, which is a program designed to provide youth with an opportunity to learn how to develop and run a successful business. The institute is hosted annually on several HBCU campuses.

A member of Kappa Alpha Psi fraternity, Lewis and fraternity brother Sam Chisholm often shared their dreams, but neither of them could have imagined just how successful they would become after college. Chisholm became the chairman and CEO of the Chisholm-Mingo Group, a black-owned advertising agency. Chisholm gives Virginia State a great deal of credit for where he is today. The teachers, the students, and the rigorous education he received at VSU strengthened his ability to compute, to write, and to comprehend—tools he uses every day to expand his business. Chisholm compares his experience at an HBCU to working at a black company. He clearly knew where the bar was set and he was reminded of it if he tried to pull the bar down. Chisholm recalls that his professors con-

Samuel J. Chisholm, formerly chairman and CEO of the Chisholm Mingo Group, graduated from Virginia State University in 1965.

gratulated him when he was right and constructively criticized him when he was wrong. After graduating, Chisholm felt that he could "walk through a wall."[14]

The Chisholm-Mingo Group provided a scholarship fund at VSU for marketing students and has done pro bono work for the Thurgood Marshall Scholarship Fund since its inception.

Dixie Garr arrived at Grambling with a National Merit Scholarship and graduated with honors in three years, with a double major in mathematics and computer science. She is now the vice president of Customer Success Engineering at Cisco Systems, one of the world's leading high-tech corporations. Before coming to Cisco, Garr worked at Texas Instruments for nineteen years, where she led a team of 800 software engineers in a division that developed software for communications and defense systems. In 1997 the Council of Engineering Deans of the Historically Black Colleges and Universities and *U.S. Black Engineer and Information Technology* magazine recognized her as Black Engineer of the Year in Industry. Garr found at Grambling a safe stage on which to practice her leadership skills. Grambling's environment made her strong enough and capable enough to compete in the real world by supporting and nurturing her. But while there she also was challenged and allowed to take the necessary risks that are a part of effective leadership. She maintains that many of her colleagues from large, majority-white schools didn't have the leadership experiences she had at Grambling. She sums up the value of an HBCU education by asserting that when she hires someone from an HBCU it's not just a social act of giving back, but rather a conscious act of self-interest to get the best graduates to work for her company. Garr asserts that "it's important that we not underestimate the power of our legacy [which is] the power of our overcoming and perseverance. We must [also] celebrate that it's not just a struggle anymore. We're celebrating our successes."[16]

Success is a word that would adequately describe Earl Graves, a 1958 graduate of Morgan State University. Graves has used his Morgan State degree in economics to become an authority on black business development, and one of the most successful businessmen in the United States. His diverse business interests include founding and publishing *Black Enterprise* magazine, which has a readership of more than 3 million and generates yearly sales in excess of $33 million. Graves also presided over the largest minority-controlled Pepsi franchise in the country when he was chairman and CEO of Pepsi-Cola of Washington, D.C. He bought the $60 million franchise in 1990 and sold it back to the parent company in 1998. He continues to be a significant stockholder in the company. His media empire earns an estimated $56 million per year. In addition to excelling academically, Graves was a member of ROTC and Omega Psi Phi fraternity when he was at Morgan State. In 1995 he donated $1 million to his alma mater, and in return the business school was renamed the Earl G. Graves School of Business and Management.

Dixie Garr correctly believes that the thing that all top black executives from HBCUs have in common is that they knew they were good when they graduated because they were constantly reminded of their value. The supportive environment for black students that can only be found at historically black colleges and universities has produced, and will continue to produce, the best and brightest black leaders in the country.

Good Reason to Be Proud

While every gain was at great cost, by the mid-seventies black Americans had achieved more than a modicum of political power, evident from the record number of elective offices blacks held throughout the land. Although there were still widespread complaints about the inability of blacks to obtain top governmental positions, practically every federal department had at least one or two blacks in or near the top ranks. Furthermore, black Americans could point with pride to the accomplishments in the area of education of the Legal Defense Fund, the National Urban League, the NAACP, and the Congressional Black Caucus.

Historically black colleges were also beginning to recover from the many unexpected outcomes of educational desegregation. Toward the end of 1977, the *Atlanta Constitution* reported that HBCUs were experiencing increased enrollments. "The ten black colleges with the largest enrollments in 1977 were: Howard University, Washington, D.C. (9,752); Texas Southern University, Houston (9,552); Southern University, Baton Rouge (9,002); Jackson State University, Mississippi (7,884); Norfolk State College, Virginia (7,263); Morgan State College, Baltimore (6,424); Florida A&M, Tallahassee (5,837); North Carolina A&T State University, Greensboro (5,515); Tennessee State University, Nashville (5,348); Prairie View A&M University, Texas (5,146)."[17] Also in that year, Professor Thomas Cripps, a film scholar, published *Slow Fade to Black: The Negro in American Film, 1900–1942*.

Students with attitude at Bennett College in the 1970s.

The forthcoming decades would find HBCUs striving to prove, as Howard Zinn suggested in 1966, that black colleges were well equipped to prepare students for success in a rapidly globalizing world.

POLITICAL LEADERS

Historically black colleges and universities have molded and shaped a number of men and women who have gone on to establish themselves in the political arena. From members of congress to governors to mayors and even a presidential candidate, HBCUs have produced dynamic and capable leaders who have governed at the highest levels in the United States.

When Lawrence Douglas Wilder enrolled at Virginia Union University in 1947 he had two goals—to play on the football team and to become a dentist. He failed to realize his first goal when he was cut from the team because of his small frame, but he still hoped to be a dentist and pursued a major in chemistry. In his third year in college he began to feel an inclination toward law since he had always been a gifted debater, but he dismissed these aspirations, and went on to graduate with a degree in chemistry in 1951.

After Wilder graduated, he was drafted and fought in the Korean War, earning a Bronze Star for valor in combat. When he returned to the United States, he was able to pursue his dream of becoming a lawyer through the GI Bill. But there was one small problem: in 1956 blacks were not allowed to enroll in Virginia law schools. Undeterred, he enrolled in Howard University School of Law, graduated in 1959, and started a law practice. While at VU, Wilder paid his tuition by waiting on the white guests of the Hotel John Marshall, a Richmond institution. Little did he know that more than thirty years later he would give his victory speech at the same hotel after being elected lieutenant governor—the first black man to hold statewide office in Virginia since Reconstruction. And in 1990, in the same state where his grandparents had toiled as slaves, Doug Wilder went on to become the first elected African American governor in U.S. history.

Tennessee native Marion Barry first became involved in politics while a student at Lemoyne College in Memphis. Growing up in the segregated South, Barry had accumulated years of frustration from being forced to adhere to the tenets of Jim Crow. As he studied U.S. history and the principles of freedom expressed in the ideals of American government, it became obvious that his experiences as a black man were a direct contradiction to all that the United States claimed to stand for. Barry became active in the campus branch of the NAACP as a sophomore. During his junior year he and a group of friends attempted to visit a science exhibit at the local fair on a day that was designated for whites only. They were turned away by the police. The experience left him feeling powerless and further fueled his feelings of resentment.

Barry became president of the NAACP youth chapter during his senior year and this mantle would catapult him into direct protest of segregation for the first time in his life. While Barry was president, the city of Memphis retained a white lawyer to argue a suit brought against them to force the desegregation of the city bus system. The lawyer was also a trustee at Lemoyne College. During his arguments the lawyer stated that blacks should be treated like a little brother. This statement offended many Lemoyne students, including Barry. The Lemoyne College chapter of the NAACP drafted a letter calling for the trustee's resignation. As president of the chapter, Barry signed the letter, which was published in the local papers along with Barry's picture. This experience, coupled with Barry's past skirmishes with racial discrimination, drove him headlong into the politics of race in America.

After graduating with a degree in chemistry in 1958, Barry accepted a teaching assistantship and began his graduate studies at Fisk. He organized the first campus chapter of the NAACP at Fisk and became active in the student movement. He was arrested several times during protests and once spent five days in jail. Eventually Barry joined the Student Nonviolent Coordinating Committee. After being sent to Washington, D.C., by SNCC leader James Farmer in 1965 to raise funds for the organization, Barry became involved in activism in the nation's capital. After leaving a more radicalized SNCC in 1967, Barry became involved in local politics and slowly rose through the ranks to become the first black activist ever elected mayor of a major city.

Julian Bond founded the Committee on Appeal for Human Rights (COAHR) while he was a junior at Morehouse College in 1960. His organization was directly responsible for integrating Atlanta's movie theaters, lunch counters, and parks. He became the communications director for the Student Nonviolent Coordinating Committee and edited its newsletter, *The Student Voice*. He was arrested once during a sit-in at a segregated lunch counter in Atlanta's city hall.

Jesse Jackson took up the mantle of civil disobedience in 1962 during his summer break from North Carolina A & T. He took center stage in the struggle when he led a demonstration of 500 students to the county courthouse in Greensboro. The students blocked off an intersection by lying in the street. A warrant was issued for his arrest, and he was taken into custody after giving a speech at a local church.

In 1961, as a freshman at Howard, Stokely Carmichael (later Kwame Touré) joined student protests against segregated facilities in Washington, D.C., Maryland, and Delaware. He took part in a freedom ride to Jackson, Mississippi, where he was arrested after entering a waiting room reserved for whites. He would later lead the Student Nonviolent Coordinating Committee as chairman. Touré is credited with coining the phrase "Black Power!"

HBCUs have produced their fair share of women political leaders. While volunteering at the Atlanta office of the NAACP as a Spelman student Marian Wright Edelman was motivated to go to law school to become a civil rights attorney because of the shortage of lawyers who represented poor blacks. Sharon Pratt Dixon was the first woman elected mayor of Washington, D.C., and Shirley Clarke Franklin was the first woman mayor of Atlanta. Both women are Howard graduates.

Other activists who attended HBCUs were Rosa Parks (Alabama State), Medgar Evers (Alcorn State University), and Andrew Young (Howard). Political leaders educated at HBCUs include Patricia Roberts Harris (Howard), Vernon Jordan (Howard Law School), Randall Robinson (Norfolk State and Virginia Union), Maynard Jackson (Morehouse), and David Dinkins (Howard).

FILMMAKERS

What do *Malcolm X, Once upon a Time When We Were Colored, Sister Act 2: Back in the Habit*, and *Sankofa* have in common? The tie that binds these four films is that an HBCU alumnus or professor directed each of them. Spike Lee, Tim Reid, Bill Duke, and Haile Gerima have successfully served in every aspect of filmmaking, from executive producing and directing to film distribution and studio ownership. They have worked both within the Hollywood system and independently. They are continuing the tradition begun in 1912 by William Foster who, through his Foster Photoplay Company, became the first African American to produce and control his own image on the screen.

Spike Lee's unique view of African American life has made him a cult figure in American cinema. His determination to make his vision reality was demonstrated during his senior year at Morehouse. As the producer, director, and writer of the homecoming queen coronation, Lee wanted to create something original. He envisioned a grand affair that would feature women donning elegant, floor-length gowns. This idea clashed with the flesh fest that men had come to expect during homecoming. An overzealous group of male students threatened to beat Lee up if he didn't change his mind and conform to tradition. Not easily swayed or intimidated, Lee's vision won in the end. This tenacity and unwillingness to compromise his artistic vision has made him one of the most prolific directors working today, churning out fifteen feature films in seventeen years. In 1979 Shelton Jackson "Spike" Lee graduated from Morehouse College with a major in mass communication. His tuition was provided by his grandmother, Zimmie Jackson Shelton, a class of 1929 alumna of Spelman College. Lee would later attend New York University and earn a master's degree in fine arts. Among his feature films is *School Daze,* a musical that captures some of the campus life he experienced while at Morehouse.

Actor-director Tim Reid attended Norfolk State University, majoring in business and marketing. He is best known for his roles as Venus Flytrap

Tim Reid

on the CBS sitcom *WKRP in Cincinnati* and Ray Campbell on the popular WB network series *Sister, Sister*. Reid had used the business and marketing training that he received at Norfolk State to found and preside over New Millennium Studios in Petersburg, Virginia. Reid's most recent film, *Asunder,* featured Blair Underwood, Debbi Morgan, and Michael Beach. Reid not only directed the film; he also produced and distributed it through New Millennium Releasing.

By the time Bill Duke arrived on Howard's campus to chair the Department of Radio, Television and Film, he had established himself as a solid Hollywood veteran—as an actor, director, and producer. In addition to *Sister Act 2,* Duke also directed *Deep Cover, Hoodlum,* and *Deacons of Defense.* His decision to take the Howard job came because of the large, untapped talent pool available at Howard. During Duke's time at Howard he brought "Hollywood to the Hill" and added name recognition to a department that already included teachers such as Haile Gerima.

Gerima has taught in Howard's film school since 1975. His unflinching look at American slavery made his film *Sankofa* an independent black film classic. Gerima's vision and dogged determination to have his voice heard is what has made him well known in independent film circles around the world. He takes this same approach into the classroom at Howard, encouraging students to take seriously their responsibility of cultivating truthful black images, free of the conventions that have resulted from years of white cinematic dominance. Gerima distributes his films through his company, Mypheduh Films, to ensure that the story on the screen is what he envisioned in the scriptwriting process.

Not since Oscar Micheaux have black directors like Tim Reid and Haile Gerima been able to showcase their work successfully to audiences without the help of the Hollywood juggernaut. This new birth of independent black cinema, coupled with Spike Lee and Bill Duke's efforts inside Tinseltown, give movie-goers a diverse palette of African American images from which to choose. Black filmmakers from HBCUs represent a living expression of the phrase, "I'll find a way or make one."

NEW DAY,
NEW CHALLENGES,
NEW HOPE

> *One hundred and seventy-two years after their inception, his-torically black colleges and universities stand at the crossroad ready to take on the future.*

WHAT HBCUs HAVE accomplished during their 172 years of existence is nothing short of miraculous in light of the challenges that they have faced. The 109 schools in existence today are part of a legacy that took an entire group of Americans from a state of illiteracy into advanced education. His-torically black colleges and universities are most responsible for that accomplishment.

From the beginning, HBCU alumni have had a revolutionary effect on the fabric of the United States. Booker T. Washington, a former illiterate slave, used his Hampton-gained knowledge to lift thousands of other blacks out of the darkness of ignorance. Howard-educated Zora Neale Hurston infused the literary world with never-before captured scenes of black life and culture.

King's progeny at Howard on their way to the March on Washington in 1983.
From left: Martin III, Bernice, Yolanda, and Dexter. Marching with them is
Ralph D. Abernathy III, son of King's companion in the civil rights movement.

Tennessee State University track star Wilma Rudolph won Olympic gold and the hearts of the world. Lincoln, Pennsylvania, graduate Kwame Nkrumah became president of his homeland, Ghana. Oprah Winfrey, another Tennessee State alumna, has built an unprecedented media empire and uses her wealth and influence to help perpetuate the cause of HBCUs.

OPRAH WINFREY

Oprah Winfrey has won the most distinguished awards in broadcasting. In 1994 the Tennessee State graduate was inducted into the Television Hall of Fame, and she received the George Foster Peabody Individual Achievement Award in 1996. The International Radio and Television Society granted her the Gold Medal Award in 1996, and she was awarded the National Academy of Television Arts and Sciences' Lifetime Achievement Award in 1998.

Born January 29, 1954, Winfrey was the first black woman to host a nationally syndicated talk show, which has received numerous Emmy Awards. The Oprah Winfrey Show has become one of the most popular programs in television history. Not limited to television, she has also made her mark in film, publishing, and philanthropy. She was nominated for an Academy Award and a Golden Globe for her role as Sophia in the film *The Color Purple* in 1986. She received the National Book Foundation's 50th Anniversary Gold Medal in 1999. Winfrey is the first black woman and only the third woman in history to own a television and film production studio.

She entered Tennessee State University on a full scholarship at the age of 16, studied in the speech communications and performing arts departments, and graduated in three years with a bachelor of arts degree. While still a student at Tennessee State she won the Miss Black Nashville and Miss Black Tennessee pageants and started her career in television at the CBS affiliate WTVF-TV as a reporter and anchor.

In recent years maverick talents such as Howard alumnus Sean "P Diddy" Combs and visionary entrepreneurs and magazine publishers Keith Clinkscales and Leonard Burnett, both graduates of FAMU, have continued to demonstrate the influence and educational power of HBCUs.

The power and influence of black institutions of higher learning move beyond the boundaries of individual accomplishment, however. Historically black colleges and universities have been the conscience of America, pushing the country to hold true to its founding principles of liberty and justice for all of its citizens. The brave teaching efforts of both black and white educators in the midst of the Civil War; the vibrant, unsuppressed artistic expression that began on black college campuses and flourished in the Harlem Renaissance; and the valiant fight waged by HBCU administrators, faculty, students, and alumni to end Jim Crow are examples of the determined, powerful spirit that was born in the hallowed halls of black academia.

Over the past two decades, however, educators, sociologists, and Americans in general have questioned the continued relevancy of HBCUs in this post–Civil Rights era. The debaters ask whether schools created in response to segregation laws are now obsolete. Some even suggest that their continued existence perpetuates the very type of racial separatism and exclusivity that HBCU students, faculty, and administrators have battled against for so many years. But a brief stroll through the American higher-education landscape will reveal the HBCUs are as relevant and needed today as they were in 1832 when the first black college, Cheyney University, opened its doors.

CHALLENGES TO AFFIRMATIVE ACTION IN HIGHER EDUCATION

In June 2003 the U.S. Supreme Court issued contentious decisions on two cases that challenged whether the majority-white University of Michigan has the constitutional right to consider race as a factor in its admissions criteria.

Barbara Grutter was 43 years old when she applied for admission into U of M's law school in December 1996. With a 3.8 undergraduate grade point average and law school board examination scores that placed her among the top 86 percent of test takers, she had little doubt that she'd be accepted into the prestigious school. Several months later, intead of an acceptance letter, Grutter, who is white, received notice that she had been placed on the school's wait list for fall 1997. When a space didn't become available, however, U of M denied Grutter admission.

Similarly, Jennifer Gratz and Patrick Hamacher applied for admission to U of M's College of Literature, Science and Arts for the fall 1995 and 1997, respectively. Gratz had a 3.8 GPA and Hamacher a 3.3 GPA. Both had solid ACT test scores. Nevertheless, they were wait-listed and finally denied entrance into the undergraduate program. In all three cases, students of color whose test scores and GPAs were slightly lower were accepted in keeping with U of M's efforts to achieve diversity among its student body. Filing two separate cases, Grutter sued the law school and Gratz and Hamacher sued the undergraduate school for violating their Fourteenth Amendment rights, which provide equal protection under the law. They asserted that the university's affirmative action policy discriminated against whites.

The two cases that came before the nine Supreme Court justices were the first in 25 years to revisit the question of whether institutions of higher learning can employ affirmative action policies when considering applicants for admission. Predominantly white colleges and universities first adopted the practice during the mid-1970s in an effort to correct years of educational discrimination and segregation, and they have continued to employ such policies through various means as counterbalances to minority students' significant lack of access to prestigious college preparatory schools and solid public school curriculums.

Recognizing that decades of civil rights advances stood to be unraveled if the plaintiffs won their cases, Howard University was one of the ninety-four parties that filed legal briefs in response to the lawsuits. Lawyers for the HBCU argued in support of U of M's admissions policies. Howard president H. Patrick Swygert said that U of M's approach helped disadvantaged groups "function fully, fairly, and effectively in a pluralistic society."

Determined to advance the cause of inclusion, Swygert opined, "There is a compelling national interest for institutions of higher education having student populations that show a historic under-representation of various ethnic groups to engage in sustained and substantial efforts to promote racial and ethnic diversity."

Ultimately, the justices upheld the law school's policy to consider race on an individual basis, ruling that the pursuit of diversity is an important goal for educational institutions. But the panel struck down the undergraduate level process, which gave additional points toward acceptance to minority applicants, ruling that race in and of itself should not add or subtract from an applicant's chances of acceptance.

Interestingly, the plaintiffs never contested other equally subjective conditions considered in U of M's undergraduate admissions process. For example, the admissions committee also gave points to applicants who had alumni family members, who lived in certain areas of the country, who attended prestigious private schools, or who possessed certain athletic or artistic talent. Apparently, the plaintiffs did not consider those criteria to be exclusive admissions factors.

The justices' ruling verified the validity of considering race as one among many factors in school admissions, but the assault against the effort to achieve racial parity in higher education continues. Conservative groups such as the Center for Equal Opportunity in Sterling, Washington, and the Center for Individual Rights in Washington, D.C., push to end precollege tutoring, scholarship, and mentoring programs that endeavor to place financially disadvantaged minorities on an even playing field.

The University of Michigan case, along with other activity, was compelling proof to a number of observers that nearly 140 years after the demise of slavery Americans are still grappling with the complex relationship between color and privilege. For many citizens race remains the lone or most significant point of contention when addressing educational parity issues.

Celebratory Fort Valley State University graduates.

Elusive Opportunities

Historically black colleges are as focused as ever on their mission to give young African American men and women, who otherwise might not have an opportunity, access to higher education and to instill in them leadership skills. But higher education often has been an elusive endeavor for African Americans, and on many levels it remains so.

Only 16.4 percent of black men and 17.5 percent of black women over the age of 25 are college graduates, compared to 33 percent of white men and 27.3 of white women within the same age group. Substandard public school educations (which leave economically strapped black students at a disadvantage when competing for admission into top schools and for scholarships), a lack of guidance toward higher education, and the inability to pay tuition are among the roadblocks that African Americans face in gaining advanced education.

Despite these and other challenges, HBCUs continue to find or make a way for greater numbers of African Americans to gain access to the hallways of academia.

On average, 45 percent of HBCU freshmen are the first in their families to attend college. The high percentage of first-generation college students at HBCUs proves that these institutions remain committed to a vision of the outstanding contributions that each generation of alumni can make to their communities, their nation, and the world at large.

HBCU PRESSES

Universities around the world recognize that one of the primary ways to bolster their reputation as research institutions is to create and distribute printed works under a university press imprint. By the late 1800s and early 1900s, both Howard and Atlanta University had issued titles under imprints bearing their institutions' names. But these works were in no way independent scholarly publishing entities with their own editorial, marketing, and production staffs. It wasn't until 1972 that the board of trustees at Howard, under the administration of President James Cheek, formally established the first academic press at an HBCU. Amistad Press founder Charles F. Harris was the first director, and he remained at the helm until 1987.

According to current director D. Kamili Anderson, the goal of the press was to publish books that served to "increase the knowledge, understanding, and appreciation of the contributions and interests of African Americans, other U.S. minorities, and black people throughout the world." A dual purpose was to get more African Americans and people of color into the scholarly and trade publication industries. In line with this commitment, the press conducted the annual Howard University Press Book Publishing Institute. The institute was one of only four in the United States. The five-week-long program acquainted students with every aspect of the publishing industry.

Over the years, the press has published more than 140 books, many of which are used as supplemental texts in college courses. The best-selling title from Howard is Walter Rodney's *How Europe Underdeveloped Africa*. In the late 1980s production at the press dropped dramatically, as the bottom line and the expectations of the school's administration were no longer aligned. Funding cuts followed, which led to the demise of the summer publishing institute and reductions in staffing.

Anderson asserts that even though mainstream and scholarly presses publish books about the "conditions, concerns, and contributions of African Americans," her goal is for Howard University Press to return to its legacy to "publish books . . . with depth that other presses are not prepared to do."

The Atlanta University Press formally began operation in 1998. The goal of the press is to publish books that address black subject matter as well as texts that focus on multicultural concerns. Of particular interest are works written by emerging scholars and professors from the university. The AU Press seeks to build on the foundation established by writers such as W. E. B. DuBois, who founded the journal *Phylon* while he was a professor at Atlanta University. Eventually, the press wants to publish ten titles each year.

HBCUs have demonstrated that they are viable research institutions capable of producing scholarship that majority institutions simply cannot. The academic presses at Howard and Atlanta University preserve that scholarship simultaneously as they meet the growing demand for black intellectualism in book form.

Prepared for Greatness

Historically black colleges and universities provide the necessary education and historical perspective that current and future graduates will need to succeed and continue pressing for an equal society.

For a large number of black college students, attending an HBCU is also a conscious choice to flourish under the spotlight of assumed ability rather than one of presumed inability based on skin color and early disadvantage. Historically black school administrators and faculty often see genius and potential greatness in the faces of students who, due to early educational disparities that hardly reflect their abilities, are often rejected by the country's elite, predominantly white, colleges and universities.

Growing up, Kalimah Priforce and his brother were shuffled between group homes, and at times lived on the streets. Priforce suffered educational challenges throughout his life, and in 2000 experienced significant tragedy when his brother was murdered. But instead of viewing the young man's problems as

African American college students like the sense of confidence that they get from attending an HBCU. These Howard students are chatting on the main yard in front of Founder's Library.

insurmountable, the administration and faculty at Medgar Evers College, where Priforce was enrolled, saw his circumstances as a call to help a young man turn tragedy into triumph. By his third year, Priforce was holding down a dual major in global executive leadership and educational development. He also had become a Thurgood Marshall Scholar and had been recruited by Scheiffelin & Somerset, the beverage company.

Priforce credited the personalized attention that he received at Medgar Evers for helping him turn his life around. He blossomed at a school where even the college president gets involved in students' lives. The young man described Medgar Evers president Dr. Edison O. Jackson as someone who is "like a dad," and remembered that when he told Jackson about his coveted internship with Scheiffilin & Somerset, the college leader said, "I'm proud of you, son, but if you mess up that internship, I'm going to wring your neck! You're representing Medgar Evers."

Attending an HBCU gave Priforce a sense of accountability and the family experience that he had never had. "I'm a greater man and a greater student because of my experience at an HBCU," he said. That experience significantly shaped Priforce's future and recruited him to advance the ideological mission of HBCUs. "When I graduate my plan is to build schools for developing countries, so that all children can have a place to learn."

For some students, attending an HBCU is more than a life-altering experience. In the case of Livingstone College alumna Kristine Mack it proved to be a life-giving decision.

Shortly before beginning her freshman year at the Salisbury, North Carolina, school Mack attempted suicide. She was suffering from depression, and in her confused, overwhelmed mental state the high school student swallowed a bottle of painkillers. Fortunately Mack's attempt to take her own life failed, and she managed to finish her senior year and get accepted into Livingstone.

It was there, said Mack, that her life began to change. "I fell in love with the campus, and the people were really nice."[1]

The attentive teachers and small classrooms meant that Mack was not just another face in the crowd. She joined the marching band and became involved in campus politics. But most important, when Mack suffered from a second bout of depression, her professors were attentive enough and concerned enough to call her family and get them involved.

Individual stories like those of Priforce and Mack are hardly isolated cases. Time and again HBCU students and alumni have related that the sense of family present on black college campuses, and the willingness of professors and administrators to provide a nurturing environment, made the difference between their ability to succeed or fail. Stories abound of educators who shepherded their uncertain charges through fellowship and internship applications or professors who cooked dinner and held discussion groups at their homes to ensure that their students had a firm grasp of classroom material.

Success in Numbers

It is the numbers that best speak to the continued success of HBCUs in realizing their mission. While black colleges and universities make up just 4 percent of U.S. institutions of higher learning, they graduate 28 percent of all students who earn their undergraduate degrees. Seventy-five percent of African Americans with Ph.D.s earn them from HBCUs, as do 46 percent of black business executives, 50 percent of black engineers, 80 percent of black federal judges, and 85 percent of black doctors. Historically black colleges and universities provide academically challenging atmospheres that equal their predominantly white counterparts. Florida A & M, for example, has consistently been among the top five recruiters of National Achievement scholars, keeping company with Harvard, Yale, Stanford, and the University of Florida. Both Howard and Morehouse have produced Rhodes scholars, including Marianna Ofosu in 2003 and Oluwbusayo Folarin in 2004.

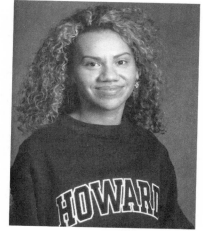

2003 Rhodes scholar Marianna Ofosu represents the high caliber of student for which Howard is known.

Surviving Uncertainty

Historically black colleges continue to build a strong and compelling legacy of educational achievement, but they often carry on in the midst of overwhelming financial challenges. Black college endowments, where they exist, are only a fraction of their predominantly white counterparts. That fact is no doubt a direct result of the wide income gap between African Americans and whites. The 2002 census listed the median income for black families at $29,026, compared to $46,900 for white families. Simply put, few African Americans are able to make the same type of sizable contributions to their institutions of higher learning as their white counterparts. And each year, HBCUs are challenged to meet the rising costs of education while offering unsurpassed career and life-training opportunities to students.

Organizations like the Thurgood Marshall Scholarship Fund and the United Negro College Fund provide tuition scholarships to students and offer programs that assist HBCUs with increasing their endowments, but the bulk of the fundraising falls squarely on the shoulders of college and university presidents.

As president of Spelman College during the 1990s, Dr. Johnetta B. Cole raised an unprecedented $114 million during a capital campaign for the school. She is now charged with accomplishing a similar task for Bennett College in Greensboro, North Carolina, which had a $2 million annual deficit when she assumed the helm. Cole has described herself, and other HBCU presidents, as "someone who lives in a big house and begs for money."[2]

Meeting fundraising goals has become even more of a challenge for HBCU presidents in recent years, as economic recession has eaten away at school endowments and reduced the funding abilities of foundations that traditionally support HBCUs. Alumni also have been less able to lend financial support as their incomes have been affected by corporate layoffs and stock market declines.

In recent years, HBCUs have found their tuition revenues declining as a result of growing recruitment competition from predominantly white colleges, which in an increasingly global world are eager to attract academically accomplished African American students.

In the past, the most academically competitive HBCUs have been able to cite affordable tuitions as a key attraction when recruiting potential students. Now, however, well-endowed schools like Princeton, which boasts an $8.4 billion endowment, and the University of North Carolina at Chapel Hill have begun awarding low-income students nonrepayable grants that allow them to graduate debt-free. Such incentives often prove irresistible to college-bound black students, 90 percent of whom require financial assistance. Spelman is among the best-endowed and most academically competitive HBCUs, yet it is able to offer full scholarships to only 100 or so of its 2,000 students.

Increased recruitment competition from largely white universities has affected HBCU enrollment rosters. Between 1976 and 1994 predominantly white colleges experienced a 40 percent increase in black enrollment; HBCU rosters increased by only half that amount.[3]

The struggle for revenue has been problematic to HBCUs on more than one front. Decreased and flat revenues have made it difficult for all but the wealthiest HBCUs to consistently develop new curriculums, upgrade their educational and administrative technology, and expand campus facilities. When Dr. Jackson wanted to establish a long-desired honors program at Medgar Evers four years ago, he and the faculty did so on a meager budget of $30,000. Officials were charged with stretching the funds, which were allocated for smaller classes, guest lectures, and other activities, to cover an entire year's worth of honors program activities. In addition, money for the program was only secured for the immediate year.

In October 2003, Clark Atlanta University trustees were forced to cut five academic programs, including engineering, allied health professions, library studies, and a Ph.D. program, in order to balance a $7.5 million deficit.

Howard University, one of the best-financed HBCUs, has expanded and renovated much of its student housing over the past fifteen years; however, the school faces annual housing shortages that require some students in the freshman women's dormitory to live three to a room.

Other schools work hard to finance major technological installations, such as wiring dorm rooms and building sophisticated campus intranets, only to discover that consistent upgrades to these systems are cost-prohibitive.

Stabilizing Leadership

Despite the challenges, historically black colleges and universities achieve a level of educational success that far surpasses their physical resources. That success is in large part due to the committed, visionary leadership of HBCU presidents. In recent years, however, decreased funding from state and federal sources for public HBCUs, a drop in alumni and foundation funding, and increased operating costs have made it difficult for even the most seasoned college presidents to keep their schools operating in the black. The demands of fundraising have taken their toll on a majority of black college presidents. Since 1990, eighty-five HBCU presidents have resigned or left their posts. Forty-four black colleges have installed new presidents in just the past four years.

After rescuing FAMU from financial demise in 1985, Frederick Humphries retired from his presidential post in 2001. A graduate of the school, Humphries doubled enrollment, raised $90 million for building renovations, and attracted significant corporate and individual donations. But in less than two years post Humphries's retirement, the institution faced an onslaught of concerns over financial mismanagement coupled with increasing pressure to raise more private funds.

In 2002, Morris Brown College in Atlanta lost its accreditation when federal government officials accused the school of claiming financial aid to which it was not entitled.

Devastating, albeit isolated troubles such as those faced by FAMU and Morris Brown have fueled rumors of the demise of HBCUs. While it is true that a number of HBCUs are experiencing financial challenges that range from tremendous to minor, the overwhelming majority of historically black colleges are meeting these challenges. In the process, HBCUs continue to produce some of the nation's best and brightest minds.

Though the oldest and most prestigious mainstream institutions of higher learning were in existence for nearly 150 years before the first HBCU opened its doors, every year thousands of students choose to attend historically black colleges and universities because they desire to be a part of an unmatched learning experience. What HBCUs lack in capital, cutting-edge technology, and campus opulence, they more than make up for in cultural wealth, committed educators, and a beautifully preserved sense of history. These less tangible qualities are the fiber of character building.

The accomplishments of black colleges have been essential to the social, moral, humanitarian, and economic development of our country. Traditionally, revered institutions of higher learning were created in the seat of wealth and literary enlightenment. HBCUs, however, built themselves up from the muck and mire of poverty, illiteracy, opposition, and the vestiges of war. It is perhaps the honorable spirit of that struggle that continues to guide HBCUs and keeps them on track toward their mission to give young African Americans access to higher education when they otherwise might not have an opportunity.

It is nearly impossible to overstate the educational, political, and social contributions of historically black colleges. With the continued and increased support of alumni, foundations, corporations, and individual donors it is equally impossible to overstate the possibilities for HBCUs and their students.

North Carolina A & T graduates in an undated photo.

PUBLISHERS

Historically black colleges and universities have produced publishers who have given black subject matter and black writers a voice in print media. As a result of the work of these pioneers, publications that speak to blacks in business, higher education, and the urban lifestyle have been established successfully.

Bill Cox

Dr. William E. Cox had never set foot on a college campus until he started at Alabama A & M College in 1960. He had no intention of continuing his education, but his high school required that every student write a letter to a college whether they planned to attend or not. A & M accepted Cox and thus began a journey that would culminate in three publications focused on issues relevant to African Americans.

Although Cox was an industrial arts education major and did not study journalism, Alabama A & M groomed him for success regardless of his career choice. His foray into publishing came after he ran higher-education programs in the U.S. Armed Forces. His first magazine, *Black Issues in Higher Education,* was born out of the lack of information on black students in mainstream trade publications on higher education. Begun in 1984, the magazine has a circulation of 40,000 and is now the second largest independent publication that reports on blacks and other minorities in American higher education. Cox also is responsible for the publication of *Community College Week,* which has a circulation of 18,000 and *Black Issues Book Review,* with a circulation of 75,000. This magazine, launched in 1999, is the only consumer publication that focuses on books by, for, and about African

Americans. It was named one of the ten best new magazines of the year in its first year of publication.

Another HBCU alumnus, Earl Graves, a 1958 graduate of Morgan State, influenced Cox, who received his degree in 1964. Graves started *Black Enterprise* in 1970, which has become the nation's premier black business magazine. Graves created his own niche with the founding of the publication and blazed trails for businessmen like Cox and the next generation of black magazine publishers like Keith Clinkscales and Leonard Burnett.

Keith Clinkscales, chairman and CEO of Vanguarde Media, graduated magna cum laude from Florida A & M University.

Clinkscales, called "the boy wonder of black magazine publishing" by the *Washington Post,* had his first publishing experience while a sophomore at Florida A & M. He and fellow classmate Leonard Burnett published the souvenir booklet for the Kappa Ball of Kappa Alpha Psi fraternity. Through this experience, they discovered that publishing could be a lucrative venture. Although Clinkscales credits Earl Graves and Bill Cox with creating a market for black publications at a time when the public wasn't as receptive to black print media, he was also inspired by filmmaker and Morehouse grad Spike Lee. Lee inspired Clinkscales through the book that he published for each of his early films. Clinkscales read all of his books and determined that just as Lee filled the void that existed in black cinema, he would fill the void for black magazines focused on the urban lifestyle. This led Clinkscales and Burnett to launch *Urban Profiles* while Clinkscales was enrolled at Harvard Business School. Four years later, the two of them then went on to *Vibe* magazine; Clinkscales served as president and CEO and developed the magazine into a music industry staple with a circulation of 700,000. Clinkscales and Burnett left *Vibe* in 1999 and successfully launched Vanguarde Media that same year. Clinkscales served as chairman and CEO, and Burnett functioned as the group publisher. Vanguarde was responsible for the publication of *Honey, Savoy,* and *Heart & Soul* magazines, which had a combined circulation of over 1 million.

Cox maintains that the one thing black publishers from HBCUs have in common is that they are entrepreneurs first. The training they received at black colleges instilled in them the belief that if they could imagine it, they could accomplish it.

Profiles of
Historically Black
Colleges and Universities

Alabama A & M University:
Huntsville, Alabama

CHARTERED: Founded in 1875.

FOUNDER: William Hooper Council.

MISSION: To provide a setting for the emergence of scholars, leaders, thinkers, and other contributors to society.

FIRST PRESIDENT/PRINCIPAL: William Hooper Council.

CURRENT PRESIDENT: John T. Gibson.

NOTABLE GRADUATES: Political leader James Turner; James Earl Robinson Sr., president of Carver Technical College, Alabama; James Jenning, NASA; Dr. Shelton Riggins, surgeon.

ENDOWMENT: $18.7 million.

ENROLLMENT: 5,475.

CURRICULAR STRENGTHS: Alabama A & M is the oldest university in Alabama offering a bachelor's degree in computer science and the only 1890 land-grant university with three doctoral degree programs.

KEY HISTORICAL EVENTS: Alabama Agricultural and Mechanical University was chartered in 1875 as a junior college, "to provide a setting for the emergence of scholars, leaders, thinkers, and other contributors to society." Then known as Huntsville Normal School, the institution was organized as a result of a bill passed by the Alabama State Legislature. An ex-slave, William Hooper Council served as the college's first president for almost thirty-five years.

In 1878, the school's name was changed to the State Normal and Industrial School, and in 1890, after an appropriation from the Morrill Act, Congress passed the second land-grant act, which granted the school the status of a land-grant institution. The next year, the school's name changed to the State Agricultural and Mechanical College for Negroes.

Over thirty years later, in 1922, Joseph Fanning Drake assumed the presidency and proceeded to upgrade the school from a junior college to a four-year institution. Finally, in 1969, the school was given its current name and classified as a full-fledged university.

In just over 125 years, the 200-acre campus has blossomed into a prosperous university covering over 2,000 acres with over 5,000 students. Today, Alabama A & M offers a combination of liberal arts, professional, and vocational programs, all designed to develop students into capable, competent producers in society.

Currently, the university hosts five accredited undergraduate schools with over seventy majors. Also, Alabama A & M has one of the largest graduate schools among all HBCUs where students can receive degrees in sixty-three areas. Alabama A & M is the oldest university in Alabama offering a bachelor's degree in computer science and the only 1890 land-grant university with three doctoral degree programs.

Often called "The Hill," Alabama A & M is proud of its proven success and reputation of offering something for everyone.

Alabama State University:
Montgomery, Alabama

CHARTERED: 1873.

FOUNDER: William Burns Paterson.

MISSION: To prepare students for an effective and productive role in American society as professionals and as citizens.

FIRST PRESIDENT/PRINCIPAL: George N. Card.

CURRENT PRESIDENT: Dr. Joe A. Lee.

NOTABLE GRADUATES: Civil rights activist Ralph Abernathy.

ENDOWMENT: $23 million.

ENROLLMENT: 5,216.

CURRICULAR STRENGTHS: Alabama State produces more teachers than any other institution in the state of Alabama.

KEY HISTORICAL EVENTS: Immediately following the end of the Civil War, Alabama's African American church leaders and northern white missionaries endeavored to create schools to educate the newly freed blacks in the state. In 1867, black leaders in Perry County, Alabama, founded Lincoln Normal School at Marion, one of the oldest institutions of higher learning founded by African Americans. The following year, in 1868, the American Missionary Association leased the building that the school operated and continued to assist in financing the school until the state of Alabama began its support in 1870. The school's mission was to prepare students for an effective and productive role in American society as professionals and as citizens.

In 1871, Peyton Finley, the first black person elected to the Alabama State Board of Education, petitioned the state legislature to financially support the establishment of a "university for colored people." Although his initial request was denied, Finley was undaunted and continued his petition until it was finally granted two years later, in 1873. Thus Lincoln Normal School at Marion was reorganized and changed to the State Normal School and University for the Education of Colored Teachers and Students. This became the first state-supported institution of higher learning for blacks in the United States.

The school continued at Marion for the next thirteen years, but blacks continued to press for an institution with better financial support. In response to their appeals the state legislature authorized the creation of the Alabama Colored People's University in 1887. The legislature provided money for the purchase of land, building construction, and annual operating expenses.

Despite opposition from white citizens, Alabama Colored People's University moved to Montgomery in 1886 and held its first classes in Beulah Baptist Church in October 1887. The move was made possible after black citizens who wanted the school in Montgomery pledged to provide $3,000 in cash, as well as land and buildings for classrooms. The school's president, William Burns Paterson, who was white, was in leadership when these changes were orchestrated.

Even after the school found a home, the challenges that faced Alabama Colored

People's University were far from over. Angered by state support of a black institution of higher learning, whites filed suit in state court and won a ruling in 1887 from the Alabama Supreme Court that declared the establishment of a university for blacks unconstitutional. The university continued its mission even without state support, relying on donations from the community and student tuition to keep the school open. The legislature passed an act to resume its support in 1889. The name was changed from "university" to Normal School for Colored Students to comply with the supreme court's decision.

The next two decades brought the school's first black teacher and president, John William Beverly, and saw its development from a normal school to a four-year teacher training high school. Under the leadership of George William Trenholm, the training high school became a junior college.

The school experienced tremendous growth over the next thirty-seven years during the tenure of Trenholm's son, Harper Councill Trenholm. He assumed the presidency at age 25 after the death of his father in 1925. In three short years, he oversaw the change from junior college to four-year institution, and in 1929 the school changed its name to State Teachers College to reflect its focus. The first bachelor's degree was granted in 1931 in teacher education. Trenholm also initiated a graduate degree program in 1940. Three years later, in 1943, the first master's degree was conferred and the school received class A recognition from the Southern Association of Colleges and Schools. In 1954 the institution became Alabama State College.

Housed at the epicenter of the civil rights movement, Alabama State was profoundly affected by the turbulence of the struggle. Students, faculty, and staff were active participants in the Montgomery bus boycott and other direct-action campaigns, but their involvement brought harsh consequences from state officials. Much of the state's financial support was withdrawn, which resulted in the loss of accreditation in 1961. The school functioned without accreditation for five years, until 1966. Alma mater to the Reverend Ralph D. Abernathy, Alabama State College attained university status in 1969 and today produces more teachers than any other institution in the state of Alabama.

Despite its humble beginnings in Perry County over a century ago, Alabama State University has endured and developed into one of the premier HBCUs in the country.

Albany State University:
Albany, Georgia

CHARTERED: 1903.

FOUNDER: Dr. Joseph Winthrop Holley.

MISSION: To foster growth and development of the region, state, and nation through teaching, research, creative expression, and public service.

FIRST PRESIDENT/PRINCIPAL: Dr. Joseph Winthrop Holley.

CURRENT PRESIDENT: Portia Holmes Shields.

NOTABLE GRADUATES: James Blaylock, member of the Georgia Department of Veterans Service; Dan Land, retired NFL player for the Oakland Raiders; Dr. Phelan Thomas, only African American cosmetic dentist with national board certification.

ENDOWMENT: $23 million.

ENROLLMENT: 2,771.

CURRICULAR STRENGTHS: Albany State offers a Board of Regent's engineering transfer program as well as a dual degree program in engineering with Georgia Tech.

KEY HISTORICAL EVENTS: Founded in 1903 as the Albany Bible and Manual Training Institute, Albany State University was established for the purpose of equipping black teachers with the fundamentals to train black youth in the area of trades and industries, domestic science, and art. The institution was founded with the support of religious and private organizations.

In 1917 the state took over the school, renamed it the Georgia Normal and Agricultural College, and transformed it into an agricultural, industrial, and normal school. However, the school still focused primarily on training elementary school teachers and offered very little instruction in agriculture.

In 1932 the school was incorporated into the recently established University of Georgia system. Over a decade later, the college was granted four-year status, and the name was changed to Albany State College. Albany State continued to grow and the college's mission expanded as new programs and courses developed. Less than a decade ago, the school acquired its present name, Albany State University, granted by the Board of Regents.

The present campus of Albany State encompasses 128 acres and is a flourishing school that has taken its place as a highly respected university. Albany State offers instructional and professional degrees in over forty graduate and undergraduate programs. The university continues its original purpose of educating African American students, and students from all backgrounds.

Alcorn State University:
Alcorn State, Mississippi

CHARTERED: Founded in 1871.

FOUNDERS: Founded in 1871 as an act of the Mississippi Legislature.

MISSION: To provide well-rounded quality educational programs to meet the needs of all students; being sensitive to and active in educating those students who suffer under the handicaps of socioeconomic and cultural deprivation, while remaining committed to the further development of educational programs to serve the best interests, needs, and aspirations of talented students.

FIRST PRESIDENT/PRINCIPAL: Hiram R. Revels.

CURRENT PRESIDENT: Clinton Bristow Jr.

NOTABLE GRADUATES: Civil rights activist Medgar Evers; Tennessee Titans quarterback Steve McNair; Olympic Gold Medalist Mildrette Netter.

ENDOWMENT: $11,329,935.

ENROLLMENT: 3,100.

CURRICULAR STRENGTHS: Alcorn regularly exceeds the national average graduation rate, the national average graduate school attendance rate, and the national average passage rates on national licensure exams.

KEY HISTORICAL EVENTS: Alcorn State University was founded in 1871 on the former site of Oakland College, a white Presbyterian school that shut down during the Civil War so that its students could answer the Confederate call to arms. When Oakland College remained closed at the end of the war, the state bought the land and designated it as a site to educate black youth. John R. Lynch, a leading black politician in the Mississippi House of Representatives, signed the bill, creating the oldest historically black land-grant institution in the United States. The name was chosen to honor Mississippi's white governor, James Alcorn.

The school's first president, Hiram R. Revels, was also the first black U.S. senator in the nation's history. He resigned his senate seat to assume the presidency, where he remained until his retirement in 1882.

In 1871 Alcorn consisted of three areas of study: the college course of four years; the preparatory course of two years; and the graded course of three years. The departments were English, Latin, mathematics, and industrial education. In 1878 the Mississippi State Legislature changed the name to Alcorn Agricultural and Mechanical College to better align the school with the legislature's goals, which were to train rather than to educate.

During the first twenty-four years of its existence, Alcorn trained mostly local black men. Women were not admitted until 1895, and they now outnumber male students by almost two to one.

Today all of the more than fifty degree programs in Alcorn's seven schools are fully accredited, and its curriculum prepares students for professions in agriculture, the arts, business, human services, education, law, politics, medicine, and nursing. The school has grown to include two campuses covering 1,700 acres.

Allen University:
Columbia, South Carolina

CHARTERED: Founded in 1870.

FOUNDERS: The African Methodist Episcopal Church.

MISSION: To provide baccalaureate education with a strong commitment to teaching and community service.

FIRST PRESIDENT/PRINCIPAL: The Reverend W. C. Waters.

CURRENT PRESIDENT: Dr. Charles Young.

NOTABLE GRADUATES: LeMoyne-Owen College president Dr. James Wingate; former college president Dr. William C. Brown; former college professor and president Dr. Sylvia P. Swinton; Richand, South Carolina, school superintendent Dr. John R. Stevenson.

ENDOWMENT: Approximately $2 million.

ENROLLMENT: 500.

CURRICULAR STRENGTHS: The Housing Office and Student Life are placing learning resource centers in each residence hall in order to provide every possible avenue to achieve higher learning.

KEY HISTORICAL EVENTS: Allen University was first established as Payne Institute in 1870. The African Methodist Episcopal (AME) Church set out to develop an institution of higher learning in South Carolina for the betterment of African Americans. The church wanted to develop an institution that would teach Christian values as well as educational principles.

After several rocky years the school was reorganized in 1880 as Allen University in honor of the founder of the AME Church, Richard Allen. The school began to blossom and develop a varied curriculum for its students.

Today Allen University offers open admissions to all students who desire an education. The Christian liberal arts institution offers students nine majors from which to choose. Allen is continuously striving to provide students with an education that will benefit not only the recipient but also society as a whole.

Arkansas Baptist College:
Little Rock, Arkansas

CHARTERED: Founded in 1884.

FOUNDERS: The Colored Baptists of the State of Arkansas.

MISSION: Arkansas Baptist College is committed to producing self-actualized graduates who are competent researchers, effective communicators, and culturally competent planners, prepared for succesful careers in an ever-changing global society. The College seeks to develop in its students an understanding of high morals and Christian ethics.

FIRST PRESIDENT/PRINCIPAL: Dr. Joseph A. Booker.

CURRENT PRESIDENT: Dr. William Thomas Keaton.

NOTABLE GRADUATES: The Reverend Jerry Black, dubbed one of Atlanta's "Best Loved Preachers" by the State of Georgia; former president of the North Central Association College Accrediting Association Dr. Emeral Crosby; Glenda Black, founder, publisher, and editor of *Good News* magazine.

ENDOWMENT: The new administration is reestablishing the college's endowment.

ENROLLMENT: 355.

CURRICULAR STRENGTHS: Outstanding instruction in the social and behavioral sciences, social sciences, business administration, theology, and activities on campus for worship, Bible study, the acquisition of appropriate social habits, and the application of the Gospel."

KEY HISTORICAL EVENTS: After slavery was abolished African Americans still had tremendous obstacles to overcome, one of the biggest being their lack of formal education. In 1884 the Colored Baptists of the State of Arkansas fellowshipped at their annual convention. Out of that meeting came the inspiration for the establishment of a "minister's institute." This dream came to fruition later that year when Arkansas Baptist College, formerly the Baptist Institute, began training African American students in facilities at the Mount Zion Baptist Church.

Reverend J. P. Lawson was appointed as the "principal teacher" and the school sought to train ministers and provide the foundations of education for African American youth. A year after the school's inception, the demand from potential students was so great that land was purchased to expand the school's campus. In the spring of 1885 the institute was renamed Arkansas Baptist College.

Dr. Joseph A. Booker was the school's first president, a position he honorably held for nearly four decades. Under Dr. Booker's leadership, Arkansas Baptist College experienced considerable expansion in its curriculum and in the development of its campus. In 1947 the State Department of Education granted the school two-year accreditation because of the college's proven success. Four decades later, Arkansas Baptist College was accredited by the North Central Association of Colleges and Schools.

Arkansas Baptist College is growing continuously; today students can earn bachelor's degrees in liberal arts, education, and computer science. As this historic institution continues to flourish in the twenty-first century, it continues to produce competent, capable leaders for the future.

Barber-Scotia College:
Concord, North Carolina

CHARTERED: Founded in 1867.

FOUNDER: The Reverend Luke Dorland.

MISSION: To provide a cadre of educated black leaders.

FIRST PRESIDENT/PRINCIPAL: The Reverend Luke Dorland.

CURRENT PRESIDENT: Sammie Potts.

NOTABLE GRADUATES: National Council of Negro Women founder Mary McLeod Bethune; Vivian Ayers-Allen, founder of the Adept New American Museum, New York; Mable Phiefer, Ph.D., founder of the Black College Network.

ENDOWMENT: $3.4 million.

ENROLLMENT: 480.

CURRICULAR STRENGTHS: Fully 65 percent of business administration majors obtain an M.B.A.; 10 percent of the male student body majors in elementary education; between 15 and 20 percent of the student body are international students.

KEY HISTORICAL EVENTS: In 1867 the Reverend Luke Dorland, under the instruction of the Presbyterian Church, founded Barber-Scotia College, then called Scotia Seminary. The school's original focus was on the preparation of black women for careers in education and social work. During that time, the South felt that it needed an institution to develop leaders in the growing free black community. The name of the school was first changed to Scotia Women's College in 1916. Fourteen years later, it merged with Barber Memorial College of Anniston, Alabama, prompting the institution to adopt its current name in 1932.

By the 1930s there was great concern about the institute gaining accreditation, and because of the school's long-standing service, Barber-Scotia was awarded a class A junior college ranking in 1934. Later, in the 1940s, owing to the support of the Board of National Missions, the school was able to grant bachelor's degrees to the worthy class of 1945.

Another notable change occurred in 1954, when Barber-Scotia began to allow men to enroll. Today Barber-Scotia has grown into a twenty-five-building campus, which includes a hall named after one of its honorable alumni, Mary McLeod Bethune, class of 1894. Bethune later founded Bethune-Cookman College in 1904.

Today the college offers bachelor of arts and science degrees in a wide range of concentrations, from accounting to straight chiropractic. Barber-Scotia College is still affiliated with the Presbyterian Church, and the college continues to strive to produce diligent black leaders in today's society.

Benedict College:
Columbia, South Carolina

CHARTERED: 1870.

FOUNDERS: Bathsheba A. Benedict and the American Baptist Home Mission Society.

MISSION: To prepare men and women to be "powers for good in society."

FIRST PRESIDENT/PRINCIPAL: Timothy L. Dodge, D. D.

CURRENT PRESIDENT: David H. Swinton, Ph.D.

NOTABLE GRADUATES: Dr. Luns C. Richardson, president, Morris College; Leroy T. Walker, twenty-second president of the U.S. Olympic Committee.

ENDOWMENT: $17 million.

ENROLLMENT: 1,469.

CURRICULAR STRENGTHS: Physics, social work.

KEY HISTORICAL EVENTS: Established in 1870 as Benedict Institute, the school was founded by the American Baptist Home Mission Society for the purpose of giving an excellent education while combining the principles of black heritage and Christian faith. The school was first developed on an 80-acre former slave plantation that was purchased by Mrs. Bathsheba A. Benedict for approximately $13,000. The school's original mission was to develop blacks recently freed from the bondage and oppression of slavery into "powers of good for society."

Benedict initially offered postsecondary instruction to establish teachers and preachers in the black community since both professions were valued and respected in society. Blacks of that time needed teachers whom they could look to and model themselves after and preachers from whom to seek counsel and knowledge.

In 1894, after the South Carolina legislature chartered the institution as a liberal arts college, the name was changed to Benedict College. Until 1930 in spite of the school's commitment to the advancement of African Americans, the college was managed by white Baptist ministers. John J. Starks changed this trend when he became the first African American president of the institution in 1930.

Currently, Benedict College offers bachelor's degrees in the arts and sciences and in social work. The college is embarking upon a $42 million expansion that will add to the high quality of education that has been provided to students for over 131 years.

Bennett College:
Greensboro, North Carolina

CHARTERED: Founded in 1873.

FOUNDERS: Freedmen's Aid and Southern Education Society of the Methodist and Episcopal Church.

MISSION: To maintain distinction as an institution of higher learning while offering women an
education conducive to excellence in scholarly pursuits, preparation for leadership roles,
and lifelong learning in a contemporary society.

FIRST PRESIDENT/PRINCIPAL: W. Parker.

CURRENT PRESIDENT: Dr. Johnetta B. Cole.

NOTABLE GRADUATES: Dorothy Lavinia Brown, first African American female surgeon in the
South; the Reverend Jacquelyn Grant, Professor at Interdenominational Theological Center.

ENDOWMENT: $10 million.

ENROLLMENT: 517.

CURRICULAR STRENGTHS: Over 80 percent of the faculty have doctoral degrees from a wide
range of highly esteemed universities across the country.

KEY HISTORICAL EVENTS: In 1873, inspired by the vision of emancipated slaves, the
Freedman's Aid and Southern Education Society of the Methodist Episcopal Church
gave birth to a co-ed institution of learning, Bennett Seminary. Mr. W. Parker served as
the school's first principal.

In 1877 the Reverend Edward Thayer assumed the position of president, and although the
school grew, the Methodist Church still attempted to raise funds in order to foster improve-
ments. Lyman Bennett, a kind-hearted entrepreneur from New York for whom the institution
was named, donated $10,000 for building and land needs. After only six years, it blossomed
from a meager room in a church basement into a small campus with dormitories and classrooms.

In 1889, under the leadership of the Reverend Charles N. Grandison, the first African
American president ever elected by the Freedman's Aid Society, the school was chartered
and renamed Bennett College.

By 1926 American society was in the midst of several changes, mostly due to World War
I, and the country was embarking upon the age of industrialization. These changes led to
opportunities for women to become more involved in tasks outside of their common domes-
ticity; therefore, Bennett College was reorganized as a college for women. The school is one
of only two historically black women's colleges, and one of the few remaining liberal arts
colleges for women.

Under the leadership of its first female president, Dr. Willa B. Player (1956–1966), the
college experienced significant growth and became one of the first HBCUs to be inducted
into the Southern Association of Colleges and Secondary Schools.

Today Bennett consists of four major departments: education, natural science, social science, and humanities, which together provide twenty-seven majors. The New York Times has
called the 55-acre campus "one of the most beautiful in America." Bennett College continues
to instill a standard of lifelong learning and the pursuit of moral justice in all of its students.

Bethune-Cookman College:
Daytona Beach, Florida

CHARTERED: 1904.

FOUNDER: Mary McLeod Bethune.

MISSION: To serve in the Christian tradition the educational, social, and cultural needs of its students—traditional and nontraditional—and to develop in them the desire and capacity for continuous intellectual and professional growth, leadership, and service.

FIRST PRESIDENT/PRINCIPAL: Dr. Mary McLeod Bethune.

CURRENT PRESIDENT: Dr. Oswald Perry Bronson Sr.

NOTABLE GRADUATES: William Turner, Florida state senator; James Bush, Florida state legislator; Sadye Martin, mayor, Plant City, Florida; Daytona Beach commissioner Rufus Young Jr.

ENDOWMENT: $27 million.

ENROLLMENT: 1,772.

CURRICULAR STRENGTHS: The fourth largest of the thirty-nine-member UNCF colleges.

KEY HISTORICAL EVENTS: The union of two establishments of education for black men and black women, Cookman Institute and Daytona Educational and Industrial Training School brought to life the thriving Bethune-Cookman College. In 1872 the Reverend D. S. S. Darnell founded Cookman Collegiate Institute in Jacksonville, Florida, for the purpose of educating black men as leaders in society. Thirty-two years later in Daytona, Florida, Dr. Mary McLeod Bethune had a similar vision and founded the Daytona Normal and Industrial Institute for girls. In 1923 there was a historic merger between these two institutes and a charter was issued establishing the school as the Daytona-Cookman Collegiate Institute. A year later the school gained the support of the United Methodist Church and evolved into a high school as well as a junior college.

In 1931 the school's name was changed to Bethune-Cookman College to include the name of its determined founder and first president, Mary McLeod Bethune. Over a decade later, the institution evolved into a four-year college when the Florida State Department of Education approved the bachelor's program, which consisted of liberal arts and teacher education. The school awarded its first bachelor of science degree in 1943.

During the leadership of Richard V. Moore Sr. the school experienced significant growth in several areas, including enrollment and construction. In 1970, during Moore's tenure, the Southern Association of Colleges and Schools accredited the school. Dr. Oswald P. Bronson, an alumnus of Bethune-Cookman College, took over the presidency in 1975, and he stresses that "excellence in academic study as a religious endeavor is given top priority."

Today Bethune-Cookman functions as a coeducational, residential college offering bachelor's degrees in thirty-nine major fields, including education and social sciences. The college maintains its level of excellence and its close affiliation with the United Methodist Church and still rests on the power of Christian and intellectual principles. Bethune-Cookman College welcomes all prospective students to partake of their "opportunities for a trained mind, skilled hands, determined will and warm heart."

Bishop State Community College:
Mobile, Alabama

CHARTERED: 1936.

FOUNDER: Sandford D. Bishop.

MISSION: To provide supportive services such as personal and academic counseling, tutorial laboratories, and cultural enrichment.

FIRST PRESIDENT/PRINCIPAL: Sandford D. Bishop.

CURRENT PRESIDENT: Dr. Yvonne Kennedy.

NOTABLE GRADUATES: Dr. Yvonne Kennedy, Alabama state legislator and the first black woman to head a black college east of the Mississippi River.

ENDOWMENT: $250,000.

ENROLLMENT: 5,312.

CURRICULAR STRENGTHS: Bishop State provides high-quality educational and support services in each of the institution's six academic divisions: education, humanities, natural science and mathematics, business and economics, social sciences, and the health-related professions.

KEY HISTORICAL EVENTS: Bishop State Community College's foundation is rooted in Alabama State University. During the summer of 1927 Alabama State developed a summer extension program to train teachers. Nine years later, the course evolved into a two-year program, and the Mobile Branch of Alabama State Teachers College of Montgomery was established in the fall of 1936.

The two-year program was successful, and almost three decades after its inception, the legislature finally granted the program junior college status; the school was renamed Mobile State Junior College. The state legislature changed the school's name again in 1971 to S. D. Bishop State Junior College in appreciation of the school's then president.

In the 1980s the school experienced continued progress and began to strive to reach more students in other areas. This expansion resulted in the addition of three branch campuses: Southwest State Technical College, Carver State Technical College, and Baker-Gaines Central Campus. In 1989 the school adopted its present name, Bishop State Community College, to represent its development of new programs and rapid expansion.

Bishop State Community College is fully accredited by the Southern Association of Colleges and Schools to grant associate degrees in the arts and sciences as well as an applied science degree. The school is still implementing new programs to serve its students and offers stimulating challenges and quality education.

Bluefield State College:
Bluefield, West Virginia

CHARTERED: Founded in 1895.

FOUNDERS: The school was developed by an act of the West Virginia Legislature.

MISSION: To provide students an affordable, geographically accessible opportunity for public higher education and to promote the students' intellectual, personal, ethical, and cultural development.

FIRST PRESIDENT/PRINCIPAL: Hamilton Hatter.

CURRENT PRESIDENT: Dr. Albert L. Walker.

NOTABLE GRADUATES: Maceo Pinkard, the musician and songwriter who wrote "Them There Eyes," performed by Billie Holiday; William Gray, president of Florida A & M University; Elizabeth Drewry, first African American female elected to the West Virginia legislature; Cecil B. Moore, Philadelphia lawyer and city councilman who served as president of Philadelphia branch of the NAACP.

ENDOWMENT: $7.5 million.

ENROLLMENT: 2,405.

CURRICULAR STRENGTHS: Engineering technology, allied health sciences, business, teacher education, and criminal justice and law enforcement.

KEY HISTORICAL EVENTS: In 1895 the West Virginia legislature passed an act that resulted in the birth of Bluefield State College. The school, first named Bluefield Colored Institute, was established to prepare African Americans for leadership roles in the field of education. In 1931 the school expanded its curriculum to include postsecondary education, and one year later the school conferred its first bachelor's degrees. Over a decade later the school was chartered as Bluefield State College.

The college was integrated in 1954, and over the next few years Bluefield broadened its programs and developed a comprehensive four-year teacher education program. New departments in arts and sciences, as well as engineering technology, also emerged. The college adopted new programs based on local needs, including various two-year technical courses. The college's focus became two- and four-year career and technical programs designed to enhance students' cultural and intellectual development.

Today Bluefield State College is one of only two historically black colleges in the state of West Virginia. Surprisingly, Bluefield's African American student population accounts for only 6 percent of the total student body. Bluefield is a state-supported school that offers an affordable education to a diverse group of students. The school currently offers instruction in engineering technologies, business, teacher education, arts and sciences, nursing, and health science professions. The school has designed a "two-plus-two" program where students can earn most associate's degrees and apply those credits toward a bachelor's degree. Bluefield will continue to proudly serve its community and outlying areas by developing leaders for the future.

Bowie State University:
Bowie, Maryland

CHARTERED: 1865.

FOUNDERS: Baltimore Association for the Moral and Educational Improvement of Colored People.

MISSION: Through effective and efficient management of its resources, to provide high-quality and affordable educational opportunities at the baccalaureate, master's, and doctoral levels for a diverse student population of Maryland citizens and the global community.

FIRST PRESIDENT/PRINCIPAL: Don Speed Goodlow.

CURRENT PRESIDENT: Calvin W. Lowe.

NOTABLE GRADUATES: Sharon Christa McAulifffe, teacher selected for the space shuttle *Challenger* flight; William Missouri, judge, Prince George's County, Maryland.

ENDOWMENT: $2.4 million.

ENROLLMENT: 4,770.

CURRICULAR STRENGTHS: Maryland's oldest historically black college/university. Ranks first nationally in graduating African Americans with master's degrees in computer science and information sciences.

KEY HISTORICAL EVENTS: Started in a basement of an African Baptist church, Bowie State University began as the Industrial School for Colored Youth. In 1865, the Baltimore Association for the Moral and Educational Improvement of Colored People sponsored the very first classes offered to students. Soon afterward, the Baltimore Association received a grant from the Freedmen's Bureau, which enabled it to purchase a building for classes in 1868.

In 1871 the school received additional funding from a trust established by Nelson Wells for the purpose of educating emancipated black children in the state of Maryland. The school was reorganized in 1883 with the sole purpose of training black teachers. For the next century, the school established itself as an institution for training black teachers. After receiving funding from the state, the school was moved from a three-story building to a 187-acre tract in Prince George's County. Six years later, in 1914, the name was changed to the Maryland Normal and Industrial School at Bowie.

In 1935 the two-year education curriculum that had been active for ten years was revamped into a four-year program designed to train teachers in elementary education, and the name changed again to Maryland State Teachers College at Bowie. Over the next fifty-three years the name changed twice after an expansion of the school's curriculum and the development of a graduate studies program in 1970. The final name change, to Bowie State University in 1988, clearly signified the advancement of the institution and reflected the many milestones the university has conquered.

Today Bowie State offers competitive academic programs where students can earn bachelor's, master's, and doctoral degrees in a variety of areas, including education and information technology. Bowie State University takes pride in being a student-centered institution for higher learning.

Central State University: Wilberforce, Ohio

CHARTERED: 1887.

FOUNDERS: Ohio State Legislature.

MISSION: To foster academic excellence through teaching, research, and service.

FIRST PRESIDENT/PRINCIPAL: Charles H. Wesley.

CURRENT PRESIDENT: John W. Garland.

NOTABLE GRADUATES: Vince Buck, NFL; actor Tyreese Burnett; Kedar Massenburg, CEO of Motown; Eddie Milner, MLB; Leontyne Price, opera star.

ENDOWMENT: $3,733,283.

ENROLLMENT: 1,130.

CURRICULAR STRENGTHS: Signature programs include computer information systems, communications, early childhood education, education, engineering, manufacturing engineering, military science, and water resources.

KEY HISTORICAL EVENTS: The history of Central State University is rooted in its mother institution, Wilberforce University. Wilberforce was established in 1856 and was so named as a tribute to the great abolitionist William Wilberforce. The parent school was located in Tawana Springs, Ohio, and affiliated with the African Methodist Episcopal Church. Remarkably, Wilberforce is the oldest private black institution of higher learning in the nation.

Thirty-one years after the school's founding, the Ohio General Assembly passed legislation that brought about the development of a dual normal and industrial department at the university. Wilberforce established a standard for the department that called for teacher training, the launch of technical training programs, and the stabilization of these programs for black students. The university sought to maintain a financial base commensurate with that of other state-supported schools.

In 1890 the expansion of the school's educational facilities was marked by the completion of O'Neill Hall, named after the senator. The normal and industrial department functioned in conjunction with Wilberforce; however, the department had its own board of trustees.

The department converted to a four-year education and industrial arts program in 1941, and the Ohio General Assembly changed the name from the Normal and Industrial Department to the College of Education and Industrial Arts.

Six years passed and the college was functioning more independently, yet it still operated under the name of Wilberforce until 1951, when the Ohio General Assembly granted the school authority to award degrees in the arts and sciences. The extension was renamed Central State College. In 1965, after more development, the college was granted university status by the Ohio General Assembly and given its current name, Central State University.

Today Central State is the only predominantly black state university in Ohio; the school is also one of the few black institutions of higher learning located in the North. Students can receive bachelor of arts and science degrees in several areas, including English literature, anthropology, theater, accounting, and special education. The university also offers students the opportunity to earn a master's degree in several disciplines. Today Central State University thrives as a prominent institution of higher learning.

Cheyney University:
Cheyney, Pennsylvania

CHARTERED: February 25, 1837. Classes were first held on a farm seven miles outside of
    Philadelphia.
FOUNDERS: Quaker philanthropist Richard Humphreys endowed through his will a school for
    descendants of the African race.
MISSION: To educate leaders.
FIRST PRESIDENT/PRINCIPAL: Isaac and Ann Jones served as the school's first superinten-
    dent and matron from 1840 to 1842.
CURRENT PRESIDENT: W. Clinton Pettus has served as university president since 1996.
NOTABLE GRADUATES: Journalist Ed Bradley of 60 *Minutes*; Philadelphia *Tribune* publisher
    and CEO Robert W. Bogle; Chancellor Gladys Styles Johnson, University of Nebraska at
    Kearney; Congressman Curt Weldon.
ENDOWMENT: $4 million.
ENROLLMENT: 2,000.
CURRICULAR STRENGTHS: Cheyney has a strong educational department and a long history
    of training teachers. Its sole master's degree program is in the field of education.
KEY HISTORICAL EVENTS: The first and oldest American institution of higher learning
    founded for blacks, Cheyney's roots were planted in 1829 when Richard Humphries, a
    Pennsylvania Quaker and member of the Friends Religious Society, established a $10,000
    trust for the creation of a school for "the descendants of the African Race." Shortly after
    his death, nine trustees appointed by his will began work on the school's charter. In early
    1837 the group founded the African Institute, but soon changed the school's name to the
    Institute for Coloured Youth and established as its goal the education of African Amer-
    ican boys and girls "in the various branches of the mechanik [sic] arts and trades and in
    Agriculture: in order to prepare and fit and qualify them to act as teachers."

During its first fifty years, the school's curriculum was focused primarily on agricultural studies,
but it was expanded in 1883 to include industrial arts and home economics. Initially, in 1837,
the founders purchased a 133-acre farm for the school. In 1902 the trustees relocated the
school after purchasing a 275-acre farm outside of Philadelphia, from Quaker George Cheyney.
In 1914 the Institute for Coloured Youth became Cheyney Training School for Teachers. The
name change reflected the school's movement toward a normal school curriculum. Eight
years later the state of Pennsylvania took over Cheyney and it became a public institution of
higher learning. In 1930 the curriculum again expanded, offering a four-year curriculum in
elementary education. The college awarded its first bachelor of science degree in May 1932.
    Cheyney State earned full accreditation from the Middle States Association of Colleges
and Secondary Schools in March 1951, and in 1968 the school established an educational
graduate program. The college experienced several other name modifications before joining
Pennsylvania's state university system in 1983 and becoming Cheyney University of Pennsylvania. Cheyney is located 24 miles from Philadelphia and 15 miles from Delaware; three-
quarters of the student population hail from these areas.

Chicago State University:
Chicago, Illinois

CHARTERED: 1867.

FOUNDER: John F. Eberhart founded Cook County Normal School.

MISSION: To provide access to higher education for residents of the region, the state, and beyond, with an emphasis on meeting the educational needs of promising graduates from outstanding secondary schools as well as educating students where academic and personal growth potential and promise may have been inhibited by lack of economic, social, or educational opportunity.

FIRST PRESIDENT/PRINCIPAL: John F. Eberhart, first superintendant of schools for Cook County, Illinois.

CURRENT PRESIDENT: Dr. Elnora Daniel.

NOTABLE GRADUATES: U.S. Representative Danny K. Davis; Chicago police superintendent Terry Hillard; Washington, D.C., police chief Charles Ramsey; U.S. federal district judge Blanche Manning; Dr. Margaret Burroughs, Chicago parks district commissioner and founder of Chicago's DuSable Museum of African American History.

ENDOWMENT: $2 million.

ENROLLMENT: 9,462.

CURRICULAR STRENGTHS: More teachers and principals in the Chicago public schools graduated from Chicago State than any other college or university. Chicago State University participates in a consortium, along with eight other universities, that promotes general interinstitutional sharing of resources among private and public colleges and universities.

KEY HISTORICAL EVENTS: Not long after the signing of the Emancipation Proclamation, Cook County Normal School was established on an experimental basis to train white teachers. After numerous name changes and a shift in the demographics of the student population, the school would eventually become the only HBCU in the nation's third largest city.

For nearly the first century of its existence, Chicago State University was largely a white institution. The school did not become predominantly black until the 1960s, and achieved university status shortly thereafter in 1971. A major milestone took place in 1974, when Dr. Benjamin Alexander became the university's first black president. Today the Chicago State student population is 90 percent African American, and the university continues striving to fulfill its mission of providing students with an education that will ensure their future success in society. Chicago State University prides itself on "fostering a collaborative and intellectually stimulating community that promotes academic freedom, mutual respect and integrity for its graduate and undergraduate students, faculty and staff."

Claflin University:
Orangeburg, South Carolina

CHARTERED: 1869.

FOUNDERS: Massachusetts Governor William Claflin and his father Lee Claflin, along with leaders of the South Carolina Mission Conference.

MISSION: To provide each student with a professional liberal arts education designed to produce graduates who understand themselves, as well as the historical and social forces that impact their world.

FIRST PRESIDENT/PRINCIPAL: Dr. Alonzo Webster.

CURRENT PRESIDENT: Dr. Henry N. Tisdale.

NOTABLE GRADUATES: The Honorable Ernest A. Finney Jr. (retired), the first African Americans to serve on the South Carolina Supreme Court; Dr. Leo Twiggs, artist; Dorothy Elmore, philanthropist.

ENDOWMENT: $12.3 million.

ENROLLMENT: 1,600.

CURRICULAR STRENGTHS: Over 70 percent of the award-winning faculty hold doctoral degrees.

KEY HISTORICAL EVENTS: Claflin University was founded in 1869; however, its seeds were planted in 1866 with the emergence of the Baker Biblical Institute in Charleston, South Carolina. Leaders of the Methodist Church used the institute's facilities to operate the South Carolina Mission Conference, which was organized on April 2, 1866. Notable churchmen sought to establish an institution where emancipated slaves could receive an education.

Prominent white philanthropist Lee Claflin of Boston, along with his son, Massachusetts governor William Claflin, provided funds to purchase the property where Claflin was initiated. The land was formerly the site of the Orangeburg Female Academy. Two other key figures, Dr. Alonzo Webster and the Reverend T. Williard Lewis, also contributed to the founding of the school. In 1871 Dr. Webster was appointed as the first president of Claflin, and under his leadership the Baker Biblical Institute relocated to Orangeburg to partner with Claflin.

Another expansion occurred in 1875 when the South Carolina State Agricultural and Mechanical Institute became a coordinate department of the college. As a result of an act of legislation passed by the South Carolina General Assembly in 1872; however, in 1896 this department branched out to become what is today South Carolina State University.

Since Claflin's inception, a key element of instruction has been teacher training, and in 1879 the university's first class of teachers graduated. Three years later, in 1882, the College Department of Claflin granted its first degree.

Today Claflin University still strives to provide educational opportunities for students seeking a liberal arts education within the warmth and goodness of a Christian environment. The 29-acre campus is proud to be the oldest historically black insitution of higher learning in the state. Students can receive a bachelor of arts or bachelor of science degree from a variety of majors and participate in one of the thirty clubs or organizations that the school offers. Claflin University still pays homage to its founders by reinforcing the ideal that "nowhere in South Carolina was there another institution with Claflin's forward-looking scope and purpose, and there still isn't."

Clark Atlanta University:
Atlanta, Georgia

CHARTERED: 1988.

FOUNDERS: Board of Trustees of Clark University and of Atlanta University.

MISSION: To provide the highest quality of education and training for students [while maintaining] a commitment to the shaping of graduates who are productive, creative, socially and economically responsible citizens in a dynamic global society.

FIRST PRESIDENT/PRINCIPAL: Dr. Thomas W. Cole Jr.

CURRENT PRESIDENT: Dr. Walter D. Broadnax.

NOTABLE GRADUATES: Marva Collins, educator.

ENDOWMENT: $30 million.

ENROLLMENT: 4,200.

CURRICULAR STRENGTHS: Voted by *Essence* and *Money* magazines as "Best Educational Buy" among the top five historically black institutions, based on class size and graduation rate.

KEY HISTORICAL EVENTS: Clark Atlanta University was established after two historic institutions, Atlanta University and Clark College, merged in 1988. Atlanta University was founded in 1865 by the American Missionary Association with the assistance of the Freedmen's Bureau. Atlanta University began awarding bachelor's degrees and producing educators for southern public schools in the late 1870s.

Founded in 1869 as Clark University, the school was developed by the Freedmen's Aid Society of the Methodist Episcopal Church (later known as the United Methodist Church). The school was named in honor of the first president of the Freedmen's Aid Society, Bishop David W. Clark. The university's purpose was to provide a formal education for blacks in the South, and the first class convened in meager accommodations in a Methodist church. Property was later purchased for the expansion of the university in 1871 and the school relocated. Six years later, in 1877, the institution was chartered by the state of Georgia as Clark College.

Bishop Gilbert Haven viewed Clark as a model school representing all educational institutions that were sponsored by the Methodist Episcopal Church to formally train black youth. Bishop Haven succeeded Bishop Clark as president and began to make his vision for the university come to life. Under the leadership of Bishop Haven, the school acquired 450 acres for the school's new location. More expansion occurred in 1883 when the Gammon School for Theology, named in honor of Dr. Elijah H. Gammon, was established. This new department became an independent theological seminary in 1888 and has evolved into a branch of the Interdenominational Theological Center that exists today.

During the 20th century, the university continued to expand, and in the 1930s the institution added graduate programs to its curriculum, making it the nation's oldest graduate institution for African Americans. As Atlanta University adopted new programs, the school partnered with other black colleges to devise the plan called the Atlanta University system, which included Morehouse, Morris Brown, and Spelman College.

Clinton Junior College:
Rock Hill, South Carolina

CHARTERED: Founded in 1894.

FOUNDERS: Isom Caleb Clinton, W. M. Robinson, and N. L. Crockett.

MISSION: To prepare students to successfully complete a college major at a four-year institution.

FIRST PRESIDENT/PRINCIPAL: Professor Robert J. Crockette.

CURRENT PRESIDENT: Dr. Elaine J. Copeland.

NOTABLE GRADUATES: Jonathon Blount, one of the founders of *Essence* magazine; Bishop George E. Battle Jr., eastern North Carolina Episcopal district; Bishop S. Chuka Ekemam of Nigeria.

ENDOWMENT: $100,000.

ENROLLMENT: 100.

CURRICULAR STRENGTHS: Business administration.

KEY HISTORICAL EVENTS: Clinton Junior College was established in 1894 by determined, God-inspired men who wanted to ensure that illiteracy did not continue to stifle the quality of life for African Americans. The Reverend Nero Crockett, presiding elder of a branch of the African Methodist Episcopal Church, along with the Reverend W. M. Robinson, raised funds and, with assistance from the church and community, successfully developed a boarding school, the Christian Institute. With a mission to provide a quality education to recently emancipated slaves, the school immediately began to meet its goals by training numerous African Americans in South Carolina.

In 1909 because of the school's curriculum expansion, the name was changed to the Clinton Normal and Industrial College; it adopted its present name, Clinton Junior College, in 1956. Today Clinton Junior College is a successful liberal arts junior college still striving to maintain the standards of its founders. Clinton is faithful to its affiliation with the AME Church, and students who attend gain both spiritual and intellectual growth.

Coahoma Community College: Clarksdale, Mississippi

CHARTERED: Founded in 1949.

FOUNDERS: B. F. McLaurin, Lillian Rogers-Johnson, Wallace Higgins, Mamie Higgins, F. O. Alexander, L. L. Bryson, Ethel Dickerson, and Cleo Daughtery.

MISSION: To provide the best possible learning environment for students and to provide them with the knowledge and skills to take positions of leadership in our society.

FIRST PRESIDENT/PRINCIPAL: B. F. McLaurin.

CURRENT PRESIDENT: Dr. Vivian Presley.

NOTABLE GRADUATES: Dr. Lonnie Edwards, assistant superintendent of education for Dekalb County (Georgia) Schools; Dr. Tommy Robinson, speech pathologist in Washington, D.C.; Dr. Charles Barron Jr., Chicago physician; Dr. Marcus Reeves, Huntsville, Alabama, physician; Pauline Rhodes, superintendent of Coahoma County Schools.

ENDOWMENT: $3 million.

ENROLLMENT: 1,148.

CURRICULAR STRENGTHS: Early childhood and elementary education, practical nursing program, respiratory care program, social work, and criminal justice.

KEY HISTORICAL EVENTS: Coahoma Community College was founded in 1949, but its roots can be traced to 1924 when the Coahoma County Agricultural High School was established for African Americans. The high school was the first institution of its kind in Mississippi. Once the junior college department was added in 1949, the school was renamed Coahoma Junior College and Agricultural High School.

Two years after the establishment of the junior college, the state of Mississippi began to allot funds to support Coahoma, another first for the state of Mississippi. The school began to expand its curriculum, adopting new vocational programs to benefit its students. The school adopted the name Coahoma Community College in 1989.

Coahoma Community College continues to serve surrounding areas and offers numerous outreach programs. Students who attend the school as well as area residents can take advantage of Coahoma's Career Development Center, which offers various resources including career reference books, job search and résumé information, and materials on colleges and universities.

Coahoma will continue its mission by offering "a broad array of programs in the academic, vocational, and technical areas, as well as many other opportunities to serve its students' educational and training needs."

Concordia College:
Selma, Alabama

CHARTERED: 1922.

FOUNDERS: The Lutheran Church.

MISSION: To educate its students in accord with the teachings of the Christian faith for lives of responsible leadership and service in the church and community.

FIRST PRESIDENT/PRINCIPAL: Rev. R. O. Lynn.

CURRENT PRESIDENT: Dr. Julius Jenkins.

NOTABLE GRADUATES: Dr. Julius Jenkins, current Concordia president; Hon. Jo Celeste Pettway, Wilcox County, Alabama, judge; Rev. Dr. Robert King, fourth vice president of the Lutheran Church Missouri Senate.

ENDOWMENT: $4.1 million.

ENROLLMENT: 476.

CURRICULAR STRENGTHS: All of Concordia's graduates find employment in the surrounding school systems. *U.S. News and World Report* listed Concordia College Selma as one of the 300 best college tiers for their regions in the categories of "best university masters or best comprehensive bachelor's program."

KEY HISTORICAL EVENTS: During the fall of 1922 in rented accommodations, the first class was taught at Concordia College, formerly the Alabama Lutheran Academy and Junior College. Six years earlier, in 1916, an Alabama native, Miss Rosa Young, petitioned for help to begin an institution that would educate the black people of her community spiritually as well as intellectually. The Lutheran Synodical Conference of North America was favorable to her mission, and in response to her petition, this group sent the Reverend Nils Jules Bakke to help spread the gospel in Alabama. The Reverend Bakke saved souls and recruited several followers, which led to over twenty congregations being established in just a few years. Three years after the Reverend Bakke's arrival, the Lutheran missionaries decided to raise funds in order to establish a school to produce professional church workers, and in 1922 their hard work came to fruition.

In 1926 the first class, comprised of four females, graduated from the academy. In 1962, Alabama Lutheran Academy and College was completely adopted by the Lutheran Church Missouri Synod, and in 1981, under the leadership of Dr. Julius Jenkins, who was also an alumnus of the school, Alabama Lutheran Academy and College was renamed Concordia College. Two years later the school was granted accreditation as a junior college by the Commission on Colleges of the Southern Association of Colleges and Schools. In 1994 the college was fully accredited as a four-year institute of higher learning.

Concordia College is deeply committed to upholding and teaching Christian standards while offering academic training. Students can earn a bachelor's degree in early childhood and elementary education or an associate of arts degree in general studies. The 22-acre campus consists of nine buildings, including the first building ever constructed on Concordia's campus.

Coppin State College: Baltimore, Maryland

CHARTERED: Founded in 1900.

FOUNDERS: The school was founded by the Baltimore City School Board.

MISSION: To provide high-quality, innovative, career-oriented undergraduate and graduate education in the arts and sciences and in preprofessional and professional areas, including teacher education and nursing.

FIRST PRESIDENT/PRINCIPAL: Dr. Miles Connor.

CURRENT PRESIDENT: Dr. Stanley Battle.

NOTABLE GRADUATES: Bishop Robinson, Baltimore Police commissioner; Milton Allen, state supreme court justice; Vondalu Clark, assistant superintendent Baltimore Public Schools.

ENDOWMENT: $4.5 million.

ENROLLMENT: 4,200.

CURRICULAR STRENGTHS: Coppin State offers its students an academic resource center, and a free academic support service available to all students. The center consists of four labs—in mathematics, reading, study skills/CAI, and writing—which provide basic, intermediate, and advanced levels of instruction and tutoring.

KEY HISTORICAL EVENTS: In 1900, at Frederick Douglass High School in Baltimore, Maryland, the Baltimore City School Board launched a one-year teacher preparatory course to train African American elementary school teachers. Two years later, the course developed into a normal department that assembled inside the high school. In 1909 the program was separated from the high school and appointed its own principal.

The school adopted the name Coppin Teachers College in honor of the remarkable pioneer of education and former slave Fanny Jackson Coppin Normal School, and in the 1930s the school became a four-year institution with the authority to award the bachelor of science degree. Coppin struggled to continue its mission for over a decade until 1950, when the school was adopted as part of the Maryland higher education system under the State Department of Education and was renamed Coppin State Teachers College.

In 1963 the board of trustees passed a ruling that enabled Coppin to broaden its curriculum to include disciplines other than education, at which time the school became known as Coppin State College. In 1967 the first bachelor of arts degrees were conferred. The University of Maryland system inducted Coppin State into its newly formed organization in 1988, an addition that allows its students to access libraries and other facilities from fourteen other schools.

Today Coppin State College continues to prosper and is accredited by the Middle States Association of Colleges and Secondary Schools to award bachelor of arts degrees, bachelor of science degrees, and various master's degrees. Coppin is committed to producing leaders who are dedicated to their professions and concerned with creating solutions to help fellow citizens.

Delaware State University:
Dover, Delaware

CHARTERED: 1891.

FOUNDERS: Delaware General Assembly based on the Morrill Act of 1890.

MISSION: To provide the people of Delaware, and others who are admitted, education that emphasizes both the liberal and professional aspects of higher education.

FIRST PRESIDENT/PRINCIPAL: Wesley P. Webb.

CURRENT PRESIDENT: Dr. Allen L. Sessoms.

NOTABLE GRADUATES: Wayne Gilcrest, Maryland congressional representative; Kent Amos, former vice president, Xerox; William Granville, Vice President, Mobil Oil.

ENDOWMENT: $13 million.

ENROLLMENT: 3,328.

CURRICULAR STRENGTHS: Delaware State has accredited programs in social work, nursing, education, chemistry, and biology.

KEY HISTORICAL EVENTS: Under the provisions of the Morrill Act of 1890, the Fifty-eighth General Assembly of the state of Delaware enabled the establishment of a college to educate blacks. The focus was agriculture and the mechanical arts. As a result of this legislation, the State College for Colored Students was established in 1891.

Under the guidance of Governor Robert J. Reynolds, the board of trustees launched the school. Not long after the school's inception, a preparatory division was started for the purpose of grooming prospective students who were deemed as not advanced enough for the college curriculum. In 1897, the college adopted a three-year normal course to train teachers. In 1898, the first class received degrees.

Over the next forty-six years the courses of study advanced and the school went through different phases, including the rearranging of the preparatory department into a model grade school granting high school diplomas. The school also became certified to award four-year bachelor's degrees in elementary education and arts and sciences. In 1944, after the Middle States Association of Colleges and Schools granted the school provisional accreditation, the stage was set for the legislative action that passed three years later, changing the name to Delaware State College.

In spite of the school's commitment to provide higher education for both the academically advanced and the educationally challenged, the Middle States Association revoked the school's accreditation in 1949. This setback did not stop Delaware State; instead it sparked a new drive and momentum to excel that resulted in accreditation being reaffirmed in 1957. Finally, in 1993, Governor Thomas Carper signed the legislation that renamed the college Delaware State University.

Today, Delaware State offers numerous bachelor's and master's degrees in a wide array of subject areas from science to social work. The campus has grown into 400 acres of modern facilities designed to provide a well-rounded experience for students. The university still strives to be acquainted with its historical heritage while broadening its instruction and service to ensure that its "graduates become competent, productive, and contributing citizens."

Denmark Technical College:
Denmark, South Carolina

CHARTERED: Founded in 1947.

FOUNDERS: The school was developed as a result of legislation passed by the South Carolina Legislature.

MISSION: To provide affordable, postsecondary education culminating in associate's degrees, diplomas, or certificates, to citizens from diverse educational and socioeconomic backgrounds.

FIRST PRESIDENT/PRINCIPAL: L. H. Dawkins.

CURRENT PRESIDENT: Dr. Joann R. G. Boyd-Scotland.

NOTABLE GRADUATES: J. Anthony Brown, comedian and cohost of the nationally syndicated *Tom Joyner Morning Show*; John S. Goodwin, president and CEO of Good Food Service, Inc.; James E. Byrd, owner and manager of Byrd's TV, Furniture, Appliance, Sales, Service & Rental Stores.

ENDOWMENT: NA.

ENROLLMENT: 1,200.

CURRICULAR STRENGTHS: Denmark Technical College is the recipient of a grant through NASA's Curriculum Improvement Partnership program to establish a Robotic Center on campus. The college is testing a pilot program funded by the U.S. Department of Labor to train multiskilled maintenance technicians through an apprenticeship program. The prototype will be shared through a collaborative arrangement for other HBCUs.

KEY HISTORICAL EVENTS: After the South Carolina Legislature passed legislation sanctioning the establishment of an educational institution for African Americans, Denmark Technical College, formerly South Carolina Area Trade School, was organized in 1947. Classes began in 1948 with a focus on training black youth in various trade skills.

The school maintained continuous growth throughout its early years, and in 1969 it was adopted by the State Board of South Carolina Technical and Comprehensive Education. Ten years later Denmark was granted full accreditation by the Southern Association of Colleges and Schools and was renamed Denmark Technical College.

Today Denmark Technical College continues to focus on vocational training, continuing education programs, and its senior college/university transfer program. The school is also very involved in a host of regional and community service activities designed to meet the cultural and educational needs of local residents in surrounding areas.

Denmark Technical College is committed to ensuring that students partake of "well-balanced cultural and social experiences in an atmosphere of mutual respect."

Dillard University:
New Orleans, Louisiana

CHARTERED: 1869.

FOUNDERS: Formed by the merger of Straight College and New Orleans College.

MISSION: To develop graduates who are broadly educated, culturally aware, concerned with improving the human condition, and able to meet the competitive demands of a global and technologically advanced society.

FIRST PRESIDENT/PRINCIPAL: Rev. Will W. Alexander.

CURRENT PRESIDENT: Dr. Michael L. Lomax.

NOTABLE GRADUATES: Dr. Ruth Simmons, president of Brown University; jazz musician Dr. Ellis Marsalis Jr.; former Harlem Globetrotter Billy Ray Hobley.

ENDOWMENT: $49 million.

ENROLLMENT: 1,953.

CURRICULAR STRENGTHS: Cited in *U.S. News and World Report* as a top southern liberal arts college.

KEY HISTORICAL EVENTS: The origin of Dillard University dates back to the summer of 1869 with the founding of two separate institutions: Straight University, established by the Congregationalist Church, and Union Normal School, founded by the Freedmen's Aid Society of the Methodist Episcopal Church. Both schools were developed with the intention of offering teacher training in elementary education and later grew to include instruction on the secondary, collegiate, and professional levels.

Both institutions flourished, and, with expansion, each was renamed: Straight University became Straight College, and Union Normal School became New Orleans University. In 1874, Straight expanded its curriculum to include a law department that functioned for twelve years. New Orleans University also branched out and developed a medical department in 1889. This new branch of the university, named Flint Medical College, consisted of two schools—pharmacy and nursing. Some years after the turn of the century the medical college closed; however, the hospital and the nursing school, renamed Flint-Goodridge Hospital, continued to prosper.

Sixty-one years after the inception of New Orleans University and Straight College, the two institutions merged to become Dillard University in 1930. The new name honored the work of James Hardy Dillard, a renowned educator of African Americans in the South. The combined institutions continued to adhere to the principles of their parent schools by not allowing race, religion, or gender to influence the selection of faculty or the admission of students. Flint-Goodridge Hospital remained in operation for more than fifty years after the merger. It closed in 1983.

Today Dillard University continues to follow the example of its namesake, James Hardy Dillard. The university maintains an affiliation with the United Church of Christ and the United Methodist Church. Students have the opportunity to earn a bachelor of arts or science degree from thirty-eight academic majors. Dillard University is committed to "preparing students to demonstrate interest in and commitment to improving the human condition."

Edward Waters College:
Jacksonville, Florida

CHARTERED: 1866.

FOUNDERS: The Reverend Charles H. Pearce and the African Methodist Episcopal Church.

MISSION: To promote a positive and highly disciplined learning environment that provides a holistic approach to the education and development of its students.

FIRST PRESIDENT/PRINCIPAL: The Reverend William P. Ross.

CURRENT PRESIDENT: Dr. Jimmy R. Jenkins Sr.

NOTABLE GRADUATES: Major Keith P. George, United States Navy jet pilot; Nat Glover, former sheriff of Jacksonville, Florida, Betty Holzendorf, former Florida state senator.

ENDOWMENT: $1.2 million.

ENROLLMENT: 800.

CURRICULAR STRENGTHS: Edward Waters College promotes excellence in teaching, research, and community outreach. Emphasis is placed on small class sizes, broad-based offerings, state-of-the-art technology, and dynamic instruction.

KEY HISTORICAL EVENTS: Following the Civil War, the presiding elder of the AME Church, the Reverend Charles H. Pearce, was summoned to Florida by Bishop Daniel Alexander Payne to establish an African Methodist Episcopal church. With the help of the Reverend William G. Steward, the two pastors sought to raise enough funds to start a school to educate the newly freed slaves. In 1866 their vision became a reality when Brown Theological Institution for the Training of African American Clergy in the AME Church opened its doors. It holds the dual distinction of being Florida's oldest independent institution of higher learning and the first school established for the purpose of educating African American youth of the state.

The Florida state legislature chartered the school in 1872. From 1874 to 1883 the school suffered financial difficulty and survived an embezzlement scheme and a series of name changes. Later, in 1892, the school was renamed Edward Waters College to honor the third bishop of the AME Church, a change that reflected the abundant support provided by the denomination.

In 1904 tragedy again struck when the school was consumed by a horrific fire that destroyed most of Jacksonville. After functioning in rented quarters for several months, the college was able to purchase land and begin to develop its present site. In 1955, the school was accredited as a junior college by the Southern Association of Colleges and Schools. Five years later the college developed another four-year curriculum and began to award the bachelor's degree.

After more than a century of hardship and progress, Edward Waters was accredited by the Southern Association of Colleges and Schools as a four-year college in 1979. Today the 21-acre campus provides a "total learning environment" for all of its students.

The college is experiencing phenomenal growth, and students can receive a bachelor of arts or science degree from a wide range of majors. The college maintains its affiliation with the African Methodist Episcopal Church and continues to place high value on "developing morally and well accepted citizens among its students."

Elizabeth City State University:
Elizabeth City, North Carolina

CHARTERED: 1891.

FOUNDER: The Honorable Hugh Cale, North Carolina House of Representatives.

MISSION: To provide a challenging and supportive environment that prepares its students for knowledgeable, responsible participation and leadership in an ever-changing, technologically advanced society.

FIRST PRESIDENT/PRINCIPAL: Dr. Peter Wedderick Moore.

CURRENT PRESIDENT: Dr. Mickey L. Burnim.

NOTABLE GRADUATES: Dr. Jimmy R. Jenkins, president, Edward Waters College; Mary E. Sharpe, president, ECSU General Alumni Association; former Dallas Cowboy Jethro Pugh; Anthony Swain, commander of the USS *Carr* during the 1991 Gulf War; Annie Wiggins Everett, deputy regional administrator of the GSA's National Capital Region, honored by President George W. Bush as Presidential Rank Award winner in 2002; NASA scientist Sam James.

ENDOWMENT: $2 million.

ENROLLMENT: 1,932.

CURRICULAR STRENGTHS: The school yielded $46.3 million for capital improvements by assisting in maintaining the passage of a statewide higher education bond referendum.

KEY HISTORICAL EVENTS: Established in 1891 as Elizabeth City State Colored School, the university was created after House Bill 303 was passed by the North Carolina General Assembly, making provisions for the development of an educational institution designed to train teachers who would educate black youth in the state. Hugh Cale, a black representative from Pasquotank County, was very instrumental in the promotion of this bill.

Dr. Peter Wedderick Moore was the university's first president, and under his leadership, the school grew from twenty-three students and two faculty members to an enrollment of 355 and a faculty of fifteen. John Henry Bias succeeded Dr. Moore in the summer of 1928; he helped the institution evolve into a four-year teacher's college in 1937. Two years later, the school was renamed Elizabeth City State Teachers College and expanded its curriculum to accept the challenge of training principals in addition to teachers for elementary schools.

Two decades later, the school developed a vocational-technical program, and between 1959 and 1963, the school added twelve new academic majors. In 1961 the Southern Association of Colleges and Schools granted the school accreditation, which was reaffirmed in 1969 after the general assembly renamed the school Elizabeth City State University. In 1972 the general assembly included the school as one of the sixteen institutions of higher education that comprise the University of North Carolina system.

Over a century after its inception, Elizabeth City State University has grown into an economically sound institution with a student body of nearly 2,000. Currently the university offers thirty-four bachelor's degree programs and master's degrees through four schools of education. Elizabeth City State University has a rich heritage and continues to fulfill the promise of its motto: "Preparing Leaders for the 21st Century!"

Fayetteville State University:
Fayetteville, North Carolina

CHARTERED: 1867.

FOUNDERS: David Bryant, Nelson Carter, Andrew Chesnutt, George Grainger, Matthew Leary, Thomas Lonay, and Robert Simmons.

MISSION: To assist all students in their transition to the university and ensure that students develop the fundamental skills and knowledge necessary for success in all academic majors. It is one of the most affordable four-year public institutions in the country.

FIRST PRESIDENT/PRINCIPAL: Robert Harris.

CURRENT PRESIDENT: Dr. Willis B. McLeod.

NOTABLE GRADUATES: The Honorable Maggie Wallace Glover, the first African American woman elected to the South Carolina State Senate; the Honorable Ola M. Lewis Daley, the first African American woman judge in the state supreme court and the youngest judge appointed in North Carolina's history; Charles Chesnutt; the Honorable Mary McAllister, North Carolina state representative.

ENDOWMENT: $1.7 million.

ENROLLMENT: 4,300.

CURRICULAR STRENGTHS: Provides effective mentoring and advisement to students; offers strong programs of academic support in reading, writing, mathematics, critical thinking, and the natural sciences.

KEY HISTORICAL EVENTS: In 1867, the founders purchased two lots in Fayetteville for $140. This self-appointed board of trustees envisioned an educational institution for black youth; hence the Howard School, the forebear of Fayetteville State University, was born.

These seven black founders appointed Robert Harris as the school's first principal. Because of the school's success, ten years after its inception the state legislature provided funding that led to the school being chosen as the site for the State Colored Normal School. Charles W. Chesnutt succeeded Robert Harris as principal, and after Harris's death in 1880, three other principals followed before Dr. E. E. Smith took the reigns in 1898 and ushered the school into the next century.

In 1907, during Dr. Smith's tenure, the school was moved to its current site. Later, he and his wife enabled the institute to grow to 92 acres by deeding over land for the school's occupancy. After Dr. Smith's retirement in 1933, Dr. J. Ward Seabrook was elected president and in that same year, the school became a four-year college. Thirty-six years later, in 1969, under the leadership of Dr. Charles Lyons, the state legislature appointed the school as a regional university and the name was changed to Fayetteville State University.

Fayetteville State is the first and oldest state-supported school in North Carolina, and today the vision of seven honorable men and their $140 investment has grown into a 156-acre campus with a beautiful mix of modern and traditional buildings. The school offers thirty-nine undergraduate and twenty master's programs in the arts and sciences, business, economics, and education.

Fayetteville State University provides a nurturing environment and a closely knit campus community.

Fisk University:
Nashville, Tennessee

CHARTERED: 1866.

FOUNDERS: John Ogden, Rev. Erastus Milo Craveth, and Rev. Edward P. Smith.

MISSION: To prepare students for intellectual and social leadership in a technological society, a pluralistic nation, and a multicultural world.

FIRST PRESIDENT/PRINCIPAL: Rev. Erastus Milo Cravath.

CURRENT PRESIDENT: Interim President Dr. Charles R. Fuget (since 12/9/03)

NOTABLE GRADUATES: Nikki Giovanni, poet, writer, lecturer; W. E. B. DuBois, social critic, historian, scholar, educator; Constance Blake Motley, first African American female federal judge.

ENDOWMENT: $29 million.

ENROLLMENT: 752.

CURRICULAR STRENGTHS: A greater percentage of Fisk graduates achieve doctorates than minority graduates from any other U.S. college or university.

KEY HISTORICAL EVENTS: Fisk University was conceived in the months immediately following the abolition of slavery. The founders named Fisk in honor of General Clinton B. Fisk of the Tennessee Freedmen's Bureau. The first classes convened in 1866 in former Union Army barracks, which were provided by General Fisk. The Fisk commitment was to educate the newly emancipated slaves, who ranged in age from 7 to 70.

The American Missionary Association, which later become the United Church of Christ, sponsored the hard work of Fisk's founders, and the school maintains close affiliation with the UCC. Like other HBCUs, Fisk University endured struggles to keep the institution alive. In 1871, Fisk organized the Jubilee Singers, who began performing nationally and later internationally to bring much-needed funds to the school. Their success also funded the construction of Jubilee Hall, which was the South's first permanent structure developed with the purpose of educating black students. Today Jubilee Hall is a National Historic Landmark.

A dance performance at Fisk.

Fisk became the first African American school to receive accreditation by the Southern Association of Colleges and Schools, in 1930. Fisk was also the first black institution ever to be awarded university status. The university has always strived to produce educated leaders in the American community and they have managed to meet that goal through its alumni and faculty. One of the cofounders of the NAACP, the great thinker W. E. B. DuBois, graduated from Fisk in 1888; his "philosophical adversary," the exceptional educator Booker T. Washington, served on Fisk's board of trustees.

Fisk has received millions of dollars in donations from well-known African Americans, including Michael Jackson and Bill and Camille Cosby. Today the university continues to thrive and provide undergraduate and graduate programs of study. The oldest university in Nashville continues to grow and attract new students from around the world.

Florida A & M University:
Tallahassee, Florida

CHARTERED: October 3, 1887.

FOUNDERS: Thomas DeSaille Tucker and Thomas Van Gibbs.

MISSION: Excellence with caring.

FIRST PRESIDENT/PRINCIPAL: Thomas DeSaille Tucker.

CURRENT PRESIDENT: Dr. Fred Gainous.

NOTABLE GRADUATES: Tennis great Althea Gibson; NFL player and 1964 Olympic gold
    medalist Bob Hayes; opera singer Ron Spearman; musicians Julian "Cannonball" and
    Nat Adderly; Dr. LaSalle Leffall Jr., the first African American to serve as president of the
    American College of Surgeons and the American Cancer Society; former Congress-
    woman Carrie P. Meek.

ENDOWMENT: $65 million.

ENROLLMENT: 12,819.

CURRICULAR STRENGTHS: Over 35 percent of the college's graduates choose careers in
    business and industry.

KEY HISTORICAL EVENTS: Fifteen students and two instructors were in attendance at the
    State Normal College for Colored Students when it opened its doors in 1887. At its
    founding the college was housed at the present site of Florida State University but relo-
    cated when it became Florida's first land-grant institu-
    tion for African Americans with the passage of the
    second Morrill Act in 1890. The $7,500 the college
    received from the federal government brought about a
    name change to the State Normal and Industrial Col-
    lege for Colored Students and a move to its current
    location atop the tallest hill in Tallahassee.

Vespers at Florida A & M.

By 1910 the school had been renamed Florida Agricultural and Mechanical College for Negroes and had
grown from a normal school into an officially recognized
institution of higher learning. That same year a devastating fire swept through the campus, destroying the
school's main building, DuVall Hall. Despite the destruction of the cafeteria, the library, and
administration offices, the school still awarded its first degrees to a class of graduates.

Between 1944 and 1949 the school experienced a 146 percent spike in student enrollment, growing from 812 students to more than 2,000. University status was attained in 1953,
creating the popular acronym FAMU, which has come to identify the school around the
world. With university status in hand, the president, George W. Gore Jr., focused on developing graduate and professional schools to continue the quest for academic excellence. The
next fifteen years would be a time of exponential growth for FAMU as four graduate and
professional schools were created. The school became the first HBCU to become a member
of the Southern Association of Colleges and Schools in 1935.

In 1971, under the leadership of President Benjamin L. Perry, FAMU acquired full membership in the nine-member Florida state university system. During Dr. Perry's administration, the Black Archives Research Center and Museum, a state repository for black history and culture, was established; a joint medical studies program with Florida State University and the University of Florida and a degree-granting program in Afro-American studies were also created. The first doctorate was granted in 1984.

In 1992, FAMU enrolled more National Achievement finalists than any school in the nation, bypassing Harvard, Yale, and Stanford to achieve a national first-place ranking. *Sports Illustrated* named the Marching 100 the best marching band in the country, completing a banner year of achievement at FAMU.

Not only has Florida Agricultural and Mechanical University established itself as one of the greatest historically black colleges and universities; it has consistently demonstrated the excellence that makes it one of the best institutions of higher learning in the nation.

Florida Memorial College:
Miami, Florida

CHARTERED: Founded in 1872.

FOUNDERS: Founded as Live Oak Institute by the Baptist Church.

MISSION: To inculcate in students the importance of lifelong learning, character, and a commitment to leadership through service.

FIRST PRESIDENT/PRINCIPAL: The Reverend J. L. A. Fish.

CURRENT PRESIDENT: Dr. Albert E. Smith.

NOTABLE GRADUATES: The Reverend Howard Thurman, theologian, author-poet, human rights activist, professor; Harry T. Moore, educator, human rights activist, who served as the head of the Florida NAACP and became one of the early martyrs of the civil rights movement on Christmas Day, 1951; Arthur J. Hill, banker and financier, community activist, federal housing commissioner, former president of the Government National Mortgage Association (GNMA).

ENDOWMENT: $6.3 million.

ENROLLMENT: 2,260.

CURRICULAR STRENGTHS: Ranked ninth in the nation in producing African American graduates who earn bachelor's degrees in education.

KEY HISTORICAL EVENTS: The origin of Florida Memorial College can be traced back to the founding of two institutions, Florida Baptist Institute, established in Live Oak in 1879, and Florida Baptist Academy, established in Jacksonville in 1892. Both private institutions prospered independently for several decades, abiding by Christian doctrine and accomplishing their mission of educating African Americans and producing leaders to have a positive influence on society. It was at Florida Baptist Academy where faculty member Rosamond Johnson, along with his brother James Weldon Johnson, composed the famous song dubbed the Negro National Anthem: "Lift Ev'ry Voice and Sing."

In 1941 it was decided that Florida Baptist Institute and Florida Baptist Academy would merge to form Florida Normal and Industrial Memorial Institute, located in St. Augustine. Four years after this union the school upgraded to a four-year institution and awarded its first bachelor's degrees to the class of 1949. The next year the school was renamed Florida Normal and Industrial College.

In 1963, after much growth, the school's charter was amended again and its current name, Florida Memorial College, was acquired. Five years later the school relocated to its present location in Miami to become the only historically black college or university in Florida's southern region.

Today Florida Memorial College maintains its commitment to excellence, and students can receive a bachelor of arts degree in disciplines ranging from communications to religion and philosophy or a bachelor of science in such areas as accounting or urban studies. The college also offers various master's degrees and preprofessional degrees in forensic science, hospitality management, and law. Florida Memorial College invites prospective students to join their winning team, "a team that makes your success their goal."

Fort Valley State University:
Fort Valley, Georgia

CHARTERED: Founded in 1895.

FOUNDERS: Fort Valley State was founded as a high school by fifteen black and three white citizens of Fort Valley led by John W. Davison.

MISSION: To provide a learning and living environment for critical thinkers, problem solvers, and responsible citizens.

FIRST PRESIDENT/PRINCIPAL: John W. Davison.

CURRENT PRESIDENT: Dr. Oscar L. Prater.

NOTABLE GRADUATES: Calvin Smyre, Georgia state representative; Thomas Dortch, president of 100 Black Men of America Foundation; NFL player, former "All Pro" Greg Lloyd.

ENDOWMENT: $6.5 million.

ENROLLMENT: 2,100.

CURRICULAR STRENGTHS: Biology, science, preengineering, and agriculture.

KEY HISTORICAL EVENTS: Fort Valley State University is the product of a union between Fort Valley High and Industrial School, which was established in 1895, and the State Teachers and Agricultural College of Forsyth, founded in 1902.

In 1895 prominent white and black citizens formed an alliance to create an institution of learning for blacks in the South. Through their labor and determination, Fort Valley High and Industrial School was created. The school continued to grow through donations, and students contributed to the construction of new buildings. Fort Valley became affiliated with the American Church Institute of the Protestant Episcopal Church in 1919, a union that lasted for twenty years, until the state assumed management of the school in 1939.

Mr. William Merida Hubbard founded the State Teachers and Agricultural College of Forsythe in May 1902, and classes began with seven pupils. The school evolved into a high school, and in 1922, the school was renamed the Agriculture and Mechanical School as a result of Georgia legislation.

In 1939 both institutions had experienced remarkable growth, and the two schools merged to become Fort Valley State College. Two years after this merger, the college awarded its first bachelor's degree. In 1949 the Georgia legislature adopted Fort Valley as a land-grant college, making it one of only two land-grant schools in the state of Georgia. Fort Valley State College also became one of the thirty-four public colleges that comprise the university system of Georgia.

In 1996 the college was granted university status and became Fort Valley State University. The school is situated on a 650-acre campus and is still striving to prepare students for innovative careers in a variety of disciplines. The university offers undergraduate degrees in more than fifty majors, ranging from agriculture to education. Students also can earn master's or specialist's degrees at the off-campus sites in Macon, Warner Robins, Cochrin, and Dublin, Georgia. Fort Valley State University will continue to produce critical thinkers, problem solvers, and responsible citizens.

Gadsden State Community College:
Gadsden, Alabama

CHARTERED: Founded in 1985.

FOUNDERS: The Alabama Board of Education initiated a merger of three institutions, which resulted in the establishment of Gadsden State Community College.

MISSION: To provide general education that includes basic knowledge of communications, humanities, social sciences, mathematics and natural sciences, and computer skills as required for certificate and degree programs.

FIRST PRESIDENT/PRINCIPAL: Eugene Prater.

CURRENT PRESIDENT: Dr. Renee D. Culverhouse.

NOTABLE GRADUATES: John G. "Jack" Page, former Gadsden city councilman and Alabama state representative; Jennifer Jordan Sims, principal of Anniston Middle School; Willie F. Brown, Etowah County Commissioner.

ENDOWMENT: NA.

ENROLLMENT: 5,816.

CURRICULAR STRENGTHS: The carpentry program at Gadsden State was solicited to assist in writing the initial competency examination for the Home Builder Licensure Board. The Valley Street Campus is the only practical testing site in Alabama for heating and air conditioning certification and was selected by Auburn University as a testing site for the National Occupational Competency Testing Institute. The Valley Street Campus is also the location of the Gadsden Job Corps Center, the first job corps center to be located on a two-year college campus.

KEY HISTORICAL EVENTS: Gadsden State Community College is the product of a merger between three institutions: Gadsden State Technical Institute, Gadsden State Junior College, and Alabama Technical College. In 1985 the Alabama State Board of Education completed the merger; however, the three institutions all have rich histories dating back to 1925, when Alabama Technical College was established.

Alabama Technical College, formerly Alabama Trade School, was the first state-operated trade school in the southern United States. The school provided excellent vocational training for the communities it served in Alabama. In 1960 the Gadsden Vocational Trade School was established and functioned privately for its first two years of existence until the state of Alabama assumed control of the institution, renaming it Gadsden State Technical Institute in 1972.

Twelve years after the union that formed Gadsden State Community College, the U.S. Department of Education assigned the college HBCU status. Gadsden State Community College strives to educate its students in a variety of fields that will successfully prepare them for further education and the job market. The college also seeks opportunities to actively contribute to its surrounding community. Students have the opportunity to achieve their fullest potential when becoming a member of the Gadsden State Community College family.

Grambling State University: Grambling, Louisana

CHARTERED: Founded in 1901.

FOUNDER: Charles Phillip Adams.

MISSION: To achieve excellence in higher education through teaching, research, and service governed by the principles of academic freedom.

FIRST PRESIDENT/PRINCIPAL: Charles P. Adams.

CURRENT PRESIDENT: Dr. Neari Francois Warner, the first woman to ever serve as acting president of Grambling State University.

NOTABLE GRADUATES: Robert Hopkins, former Seattle Sonics coach; playwright Judy Mason; Doug Williams, NFL quarterback and current Grambling football coach; Tank Younger, first Grambling player drafted into the NFL; the Reverend Edward Jones, former president of the National Baptist Convention of America.

ENDOWMENT: $1.7 million.

ENROLLMENT: 4,650.

CURRICULAR STRENGTHS: For five consecutive years, Grambling ranked first among the nation's colleges and universities in awarding four-year degrees in computer science to African American students.

KEY HISTORICAL EVENTS: Although founded in 1901 Grambling State University was born in the hearts and minds of Louisiana's African American farmers five years prior. In 1896, a farm organization made up of African Americans was formed in northeastern Louisiana, with Lafayette Richmond presiding. One of the goals of the group was to develop an institution of higher learning for their children. In 1898, an African American named John Monk sold the organization 23 acres of land at the price of $5 per acre and the construction of Grambling began.

During the erection of the schoolhouse, two local white store owners, Allen and Charlie Greene, leased their property for classroom space. Henry Wynder and Alice Wilson served as Grambling's first teachers. After only two sessions, both three months each, the Farmer's Relief Association realized they needed guidance and requested assistance from Dr. Booker T. Washington. Their request for aid was granted when Charles P. Adams arrived from Tuskegee Institute.

Adams endeavored to establish a successful institution by raising funds and forming alliances with people in the community. He also donated his own funds for the development of the school after selling a farm he coowned. In the fall of 1901 Grambling, then known as the Colored Industrial and Agricultural School, began classes with three teachers and 125 students.

Four years later, in 1905, the school experienced some significant changes. It relocated to its present location with the help of funds donated by Fredelia Jewett, and it was renamed the North Louisiana Agricultural and Industrial School. Almost a decade later, the Lincoln Parish School Board acknowledged the school's progress and outstanding service by declaring the institution semipublic; in 1919 the name was changed to the Lincoln Parish Training

School. In 1928 Adams petitioned Governor Huey Long for state support, and the school then became a junior college, offering two-year professional certificates and diplomas.

After thirty-five years of dedicated service to Grambling, Charles P. Adams retired in 1936 and R. W. E. Jones became the school's second president. During Jones's presidency, a four-year program was initiated and the worthy class of 1944 was awarded bachelor of science degrees in elementary education. Three years later, President Jones requested the school's name be changed to Grambling College and the legislature accepted his appeal. In 1948 the school's curriculum adopted secondary education, and in 1954 programs in preliminary training for medicine and dentistry were developed. By 1958 Grambling had evolved into a full liberal arts college, and in 1974 it was granted university status and renamed Grambling State University.

Today Grambling is situated on a beautiful 360-acre campus and accredited to award a variety of associate's, bachelor's and master's degrees. Grambling is still committed to its motto, "GSU is the place where everybody is somebody."

Hampton University:
Hampton, Virginia

CHARTERED: Founded in 1868.

FOUNDERS: Brigadier General Samuel Chapman Armstrong established the university along with aid from the American Missionary Association.

MISSION: Hampton University is "dedicated to the promotion of learning, building of character and preparation of promising students for positions of leadership and service."

FIRST PRESIDENT/PRINCIPAL: General Samuel Chapman Armstrong.

CURRENT PRESIDENT: Dr. William R. Harvey.

NOTABLE GRADUATES: Booker T. Washington, national leader and founder of Tuskegee Institute; Susan La Flesche, first Native American woman to receive an M.D.

ENDOWMENT: $163 million.

ENROLLMENT: 5,700.

CURRICULAR STRENGTHS: Hampton is the first historically black college or university to offer a doctorate degree in nursing.

KEY HISTORICAL EVENTS: In American history, the days of Reconstruction were a very promising time for African Americans and it was during this period that Brigadier General Samuel Chapman Armstrong, with the help of the American Missionary Association, founded Hampton University. In 1868 the school was chartered as Hampton Normal and Agricultural Institute and was located on the banks of the Virginia peninsula. General Armstrong was a determined 29-year-old son of missionaries who sought to develop a learning institution where the multitudes of recently emancipated blacks could receive an education and function as productive leaders in their communities and society as a whole.

When classes began at the institution, the first classroom or dormitory had not yet been erected, so housing was a problem for the masses of free African Americans desiring an education. Male students lived in army tents, while female students were situated in army barracks until Virginia Hall was erected. Ten years after Hampton opened its doors, the school explored the idea of educating various cultures and developed a training program for Native Americans. This historic program was extremely successful and continued through the 1920s, when the last student graduated in 1923.

Initially Hampton's funding was from various sources, including the Freedmen's Bureau and donations from philanthropists and religious groups. The school prospered and grew rapidly, and after gaining postsecondary status, it awarded the first bachelor's degrees in 1922. In 1924 the school was renamed Hampton Institute to reflect its four-year college status.

After over 100 years of service, the college's board of trustees officially developed a university structure and the school was renamed Hampton University. Today Hampton still maintains its high standard of quality education for students from various cultures from all over the world. The university has been called one of the nation's most beautiful campuses.

Harris-Stowe State College:
St. Louis, Missouri

CHARTERED: Founded in 1857.

FOUNDERS: The public school system of St. Louis, Missouri.

MISSION: To serve populations that would otherwise not have the opportunity to take advantage of institutions of higher learning.

FIRST PRESIDENT/PRINCIPAL: Oscar M. Waring (first principal of Sumner High School).

CURRENT PRESIDENT: Dr. Henry Givens Jr.

NOTABLE GRADUATES: The Honorable Maxine Waters, U.S. House of Representatives (D-Calif.); Julius Hunter, former St. Louis news reporter; the Honorable Charles Shaw, federal judge; Charles Hessel, director of the St. Louis Zoo.

ENDOWMENT: $800,000.

ENROLLMENT: 1,316.

CURRICULAR STRENGTHS: Harris-Stowe State College is known for its excellence in teacher education programs.

KEY HISTORICAL EVENTS: Harris-Stowe State College's roots were planted in St. Louis, Missouri, over 145 years ago. In 1857 a normal school designed to train teachers was developed by the St. Louis public school system. Not long after its establishment, the institution was named Harris Teachers College in honor of educational pioneer William Torrey Harris, who not only served as the superintendent of instruction in St. Louis but was also a U.S. commissioner of education.

Harris Teachers College was established for the purpose of training white students, and in 1920 the school was upgraded to a four-year degree-granting institution. In 1924 the North Central Association of Schools and Colleges awarded the school full accreditation.

Over thirty years after the birth of Harris Teachers College, the St. Louis public school system developed a normal school to train African American teachers in 1890. This school began as an extension at Sumner High School. By 1924 this extension had evolved into a four-year degree-granting program, and the school was renamed Sumner Normal School. Five years later the school's name was changed to Stowe Teachers College in memory and honor of the prominent author and abolitionist Harriet Beecher Stowe.

During the tumultuous decades of the civil rights struggle, the St. Louis Board of Education tackled integration by merging Harris Teachers College and Stowe Teachers College to form one institution. After the merger the school maintained the name Harris Teachers College until the Missouri General Assembly passed legislation in 1979 adopting the school into the state system of public higher education; at that time the name was changed to Harris-Stowe State College.

The college's education program was broadened to include early childhood, elementary, and middle/high school education departments. Harris-Stowe State College continues to expand its curriculum and currently offers urban education programs that are designed for the development of professional educators of the future.

Hinds Community College:
Utica, Mississippi

CHARTERED: Founded in 1917.

FOUNDER: Established as Utica Institute by William Holtzclaw in 1903.

MISSION: To offer pertinent and diverse educational programs and services for persons with various interests and abilities.

FIRST PRESIDENT/PRINCIPAL: W. M. Taylor.

CURRENT PRESIDENT: Dr. Clyde Muse; Dr. George E. Barnes, vice president, Utica campus (the Utica campus is the historically black campus of Hinds Community College).

NOTABLE GRADUATES: Congressman Bennie Thompson; Beverly Hogan, Tougaloo College president; Robert Smith, M.D.; Johnny Simmons, state senator.

ENDOWMENT: $1 million.

ENROLLMENT: 1,800.

CURRICULAR STRENGTHS: Student Learning Assistance Program, music department, math and science, radio and TV broadcasting technology.

KEY HISTORICAL EVENTS: Hinds Community College can trace its origins to an agricultural high school established in 1917 as Hinds County Agricultural High School. Classes began with 117 students instructed by eight teachers. In 1922 the school expanded to include a junior college that had an initial enrollment of thirty students.

During World War II, Acting President George M. McLendon began to develop a wide range of courses in vocational education because of society's booming demands in business and industry. Today the vocational division is a flourishing part of the school's curriculum.

During the 1980s Hinds was ordered by the federal court to merge with Utica Junior College, and this union became official in 1982. Utica was established in 1903 when Dr. William Holtzclaw founded the school as Utica Normal School and Industrial Institute with the purpose of training African American students in the fundamentals of reading and writing. The addition of this historic institution brought considerable wealth to Hinds Community College. One year after this merger, Hinds established another branch campus known as Pearl-Rankin Vocational/Technical Center. This campus provides college courses for high school students and adult commuter students.

In 1984 the Jackson branch, which is the Academic/Technical Center, was opened to offer programs including nursing and allied health. The college continues to expand and develop branch campuses; today the school consists of seven locations, including the Vicksburg-Warren County branch, two Jackson campuses, the Rankin branch, the Raymond campus, and the Utica campus.

The school became Hinds Community College in 1987 in order to "reflect its commitment to meet the educational needs of everyone in the district." Today Hinds Community College is consistent with providing a quality education for all students who attend the school and has several plans for expansion. Hinds Community College remembers its rich past and looks forward to its bright future.

Howard University:
Washington, D.C

CHARTERED: Founded in 1867.

FOUNDERS: The U.S. Congress.

MISSION: To provide an educational experience of exceptional quality to students of high academic potential with particular emphasis upon the provision of educational opportunities to promising Black students.

FIRST PRESIDENT/PRINCIPAL: Dr. Charles Boynton.

CURRENT PRESIDENT: H. Patrick Swygert.

NOTABLE GRADUATES: Patricia Robert Harris, first African American woman to hold two U.S. cabinet positions; Edward W. Brooke, first African American senator in the twentieth century; David Dinkins, first African American mayor of New York City.

ENDOWMENT: $328 million.

ENROLLMENT: 12,000.

CURRICULAR STRENGTHS: Howard University has produced "more than ten percent of the nation's black doctors, lawyers, business leaders, politicians, social workers, engineers, artists, musicians, and other professionals."[7]

KEY HISTORICAL EVENTS: A little over three years after the signing of the Emancipation Proclamation, the First Congressional Society, a group of individuals dedicated to the well-being of newly freed slaves and the thousands of free-born blacks, met to devise a plan that would begin to further the education and better the lifestyle of these Americans. Led by Dr. Charles Boynton, the Society established Howard Theological Society, initially designed to train preachers. General Oliver Otis Howard, for whom the school was named, was a decorated soldier who dedicated his life to the advancement of African Americans.

The newly established institution changed its name to Howard Normal and Theological Institute for the Education of Teachers and Preachers just two months after being founded. The school was eventually named Howard University because the founders wanted the school to advance a wide range of educational goals in order to fully educate African Americans during this crucial time in history.

Classes began in the spring of 1867 with only four students, but enrollment quickly grew to nearly one hundred. The University also began to broaden its curriculum to include a variety of courses in the liberal arts. Because of General Howard's connections, which included appointments by presidents Abraham Lincoln and Andrew Johnson, lack of finances did not hinder the growth of the university. The university was well on its way to becoming a prominent institution that would educate hundreds of thousands of African Americans in the decades to come.

At the turn of the century, Howard continued to expand its campus and initiate new programs of learning. In 1926 the university elected its first black president, Dr. Mordecai Johnson, and he immediately began employing black faculty and staff.

Today Howard University is highly regarded as an institution of higher learning because of its rich history, prominent alumni, and the continued commitment to promoting "truth and service."

Huston-Tillotson College:
Austin, Texas

CHARTERED: Founded in 1875.

FOUNDERS: Tillotson College was founded by the American Missionary Association of the Congregationalist Church; Samuel Huston College was founded by the Reverend George Warren Richardson, a Methodist minister.

MISSION: To provide a diverse student body with an exemplary education that is grounded in the liberal arts and sciences, balanced with professional development, and directed to public service and leadership.

FIRST PRESIDENT/PRINCIPAL: Dr. John Jarvis Seabrook was the first permanent president after the merger.

CURRENT PRESIDENT: Dr. Larry L. Earvin.

NOTABLE GRADUATES: The Honorable Azie Taylor Morton, thirty-sixth treasurer of the United States; Bert Collins, CEO of North Carolina Mutual Life Insurance Company, the nation's largest black insurance company; Robert Stanton, the first African American director of the National Park Service.

ENDOWMENT: $6,464,719.

ENROLLMENT: 618.

CURRICULAR STRENGTHS: Huston-Tillotson maintains a biological field station south of the city of Austin that is used by faculty and students for environmental research.

KEY HISTORICAL EVENTS: Huston-Tilloston College has a rich history dating back to 1875.

The seeds for Tillotson College were sown in 1875 when the Reverend George Jeffrey Tillotson raised $16,000 for the establishment of an institution to educate African Americans in Texas. Although chartered in 1877, Tillotson Collegiate and Normal Institute did not begin classes until the winter of 1881. At the school's inception, the state of Texas lacked an educational program for African Americans so the school's determined students possessed no prior education. Before the first year of classes was complete, enrollment reached 100.

As a result of its rapid growth, the school adopted the name Tillotson College. The college originally was developed to train teachers. In 1925 Tillotson converted to a junior college, and a year later it changed to a woman's college. Finally, in 1931, the school reverted to its coeducational, four-year status, and in 1943 it was granted accreditation by the Southern Association of Colleges and Schools.

Samuel Huston College can trace its roots to 1876 when the Reverend George Warren Richardson established a school to educate African American youth. His school began with only six students, but enrollment dramatically increased to sixty before the end of the first year. Over the next few decades the institution experienced numerous name and location changes, but in 1887 a farmer from Iowa, Samuel Huston, donated a large amount of valuable land in exchange for the school carrying his name. In 1910, the school was chartered by the state of Texas as Samuel Huston College. The college experienced consistent growth, and in 1934 was accredited by the Southern Association of Colleges and Schools.

Interdenominational Theological Center:
Atlanta, Georgia

CHARTERED: 1958.

FOUNDERS: Morehouse School of Religion, Gammon Theological Seminary, Turner Theological Seminary, and Phillips School of Theology.

MISSION: To eradicate societal ills via a theological education of high quality allowing students to serve varying denominations of the black religious community.

FIRST PRESIDENT/PRINCIPAL: Dr. Harry V. Richardson.

CURRENT PRESIDENT: Dr. Michael A. Battle.

NOTABLE GRADUATES: Diana James, the highest-ranking female Army chaplain; Allen J. Sloan II, twelfth president of Miles College; Dr. Katie Cannon, professor at New York Theological Seminary.

ENDOWMENT: $11 million.

ENROLLMENT: 300.

CURRICULAR STRENGTHS: Of the trained black ministers worldwide, the Interdenominational Theology Center has educated more than 35 percent of them. ITC has also educated 50 percent of the U.S. military's black chaplains.

KEY HISTORICAL EVENTS: The Interdenominational Theological Center, chartered in 1958, was designed to train individuals who wished to deepen their understanding of the power of the Spirit and further their knowledge of how to live in obedience to God through Jesus Christ.

The ITC consists of six theological institutions whose collective tenure spans over 130 years. Morehouse School of Religion was the first, founded in 1867, by the American Baptist Home Mission Society to train men who could lead African Americans to Christ. The institution experienced various changes in its leadership and curriculum through the years; all of these changes proved beneficial because the school still exists today as a charter member of the ITC and continues to train leaders who lovingly spread the Gospel of Jesus Christ.

In 1872, five years after the Morehouse School of Religion opened its doors, the school was blessed with a kindred institution just a few miles away. Gammon Theological Seminary branced off from Clark University, where it originally served as a department of religion and philosophy. Gammon achieved its independence in 1972. The institution began to diligently train its student body, which consisted of twenty-six Christian students dedicated to learning God's word and spreading it as far as their faith and God's grace could carry them. In 1883 the Methodist Episcopal Church adopted the school of its own, and today the seminary continues to carry out the calling that it received wll over one hundred years ago.

Almost nineteen centuries after the death and resurrection of Jesus Christ, twelve students occupied the newly developed halls of Turner Theological Seminary. The institution was recognized by a board of trustees in Georgia in 1885 but did not begin to fulfill the doctrines of the African Methodist Episcopal Church until 1894, with Reverend T. G. Steward acting as Dean of Theology. The seminary, which originated at Morris Brown College, did not relocate to facilities separate from Morris until 1957. It received its charter in

1975. Turner received its own board of trustees the same year and rapidly multiplied its enrollment. Turner Theological Seminary still prospers today, holding fast to its original principles of truth.

Since the emancipation of the enslaved Africans in America, the Presbyterian Church has been active in the development of theological institutions for African Americans. In the spring of 1867 the church founded Johnson C. Smith to train leaders in religion. The first class of moral scholars graduated in 1872. Nearly a century later, after much growth and success, Smith's "religion department" relocated to Atlanta, Georgia, and became the independent Johnson C. Smith Theological Seminary, which still thrives today as a major limb of the ITC.

The fifth addition to the ITC is the Phillips School of Theology. This institution, named in honr of the twentieth bishop of the Christian Methodist Episcopal Church (CME), serves as a capstone in the demonination's ability to train leaders to carry on the CME's traditions and beliefs. The institution prides itself on representing its namesake, Bishop Charles Henry Phillips, who was considered one of the best-trained ministers in his day. Phillips School of Theology produces capable servants who williingly fulfill the privileged responsibility of carrying out the tenets of the Christian faith.

Plans for the Charles H. Mason Theological Seminary began developing in the mid-1960s. These plans were completed in the spring of 1970, when the school was sanctioned by the General Assembly of the Church of God in Christ and became an official member of the ITC. This addition was successful in adding another sweet-smelling savor to the abundance of truth already present at the ITC.

Today the ITC continues to produce leaders in Christian education, pastoral counseling, church musicians, and community facilitators. "The ITC specializes in the education of women and men who serve the African American Church and the world community. There is a special recognition of the role of denominations, not as the basis of division but as the foundation of ecumenism."

J. F. Drake State Technical College:
Huntsville, Alabama

CHARTERED: Founded in 1961.

FOUNDERS: Department of Postsecondary Education in Alabama.

MISSION: To provide excellence in vocational and technical training while showing concern for a diverse population by respecting students' values, traditions, and aspirations.

FIRST PRESIDENT/PRINCIPAL: S. C. O'Neal.

CURRENT PRESIDENT: Dr. Helen T. McAlpine.

NOTABLE GRADUATES: Graduates consist primarily of local business owners.

ENDOWMENT: NA.

ENROLLMENT: 700.

CURRICULAR STRENGTHS: Drake was the first Alabama technical college to receive a charter from the National Vocational-Technical Honor Society. Drake was also the first two-year college in Alabama to be approved as a Microsoft-authorized academic program institution.

KEY HISTORICAL EVENTS: Over the last century society has become increasingly reliant on technology, and as technology grew, educational institutions sprang up to train individuals to service and increasingly sophisticated technical infrastructure. J. F. Drake State Technical College is one such institution.

Forty-three years ago, the school began instruction as The Huntsville State Vocational Technical School. S. C. O'Neal was the first president of the fledgling institution. In 1966, five years after its founding, the school adopted the name of J. F. Drake State Technical Training School, in memory of the deceased and honored educator Dr. Joseph Fanning Drake, former president of Alabama A&M University. A year later the institution desegregated and opened its doors to all races. The school experienced rapid expansion and was recognized in 1973 by the State Board of Education, thus accepting its present name of J. F. Drake State Technical College.

Today Drake offers technical and vocational classes ranging from nursing and cosmetology to electronics, computer information systems, and automotive technology. The college boasts on-campus training sites for Chrysler and Toyota. As technology evolves, J. F. Drake State Technical College will continue to participate in that evolution by advancing its curriculum and producing leaders who are equipped to bridge the gap in the technological divide.

Jackson State University: Jackson, Mississippi

CHARTERED: Founded in 1877.

FOUNDERS: The American Baptist Home Mission Society.

MISSION: To develop responsible leaders who are capable and willing to seek solutions to human, social, and technological problems with special emphasis on those relevant to the metropolitan and urban areas of the state, the nation, and the world.

FIRST PRESIDENT/PRINCIPAL: Dr. Charles Ayer.

CURRENT PRESIDENT: Dr. Ronald Mason Jr.

NOTABLE GRADUATES: The late Walter Payton, former Chicago Bears team member; the Honorable Robert G. Clark, representative for the state of Mississippi.

ENROLLMENT: 5,100.

CURRICULAR STRENGTHS: Jackson State is the only HBCU offering doctoral degrees in environmental science and childhood education. The school is also the first HBCU to offer an undergraduate meteorology program.

KEY HISTORICAL EVENTS: In 1877, the American Baptist Home Mission Society sought to develop an educational facility "for the moral, religious, and intellectual improvement of Christian leaders of the colored people of Mississippi and the neighboring states." Out of their vision came the birth of Jackson State University, originally Natchez Seminary. In 1882, after it was concluded that a central location in the state was beneficial, the school was moved from Natchez to Jackson, Mississippi. Seven years later, after considerable growth, the school was renamed Jackson College.

Students at a dance at Jackson State in 1971.

For over sixty years, Jackson functioned privately under the authority of the church. In 1940 the state adopted the institution for the purpose of training teachers. Four years later, the school awarded its first bachelor's degrees. Between 1953 and 1956 Jackson developed a graduate program as well as bachelor's programs in the arts and sciences. Also in 1956 the school added "State" to its title to become Jackson State College.

Throughout the next two decades, Jackson State experienced continued expansion and carried out its mission to educate leaders; in 1974 the college was granted university status and renamed Jackson State University. Five years later, Jackson State was deemed the Urban University of Mississippi, a highly regarded title that the school is honored to hold. As a result of this honor, Jackson State has established programs and activities designed to address and correct urban problems.

In 1983 the university began immense renovations after completing an $11.2 million campaign. Jackson State has a rich history and this four-year state-supported liberal arts university still rests on its core values: tradition, accountability, learning, nurturing, service, and responsibility.

Jarvis Christian College:
Hawkins, Texas

CHARTERED: Founded in 1912.

FOUNDERS: The school was established by the efforts of the Negro Disciples of Christ and the Christian Woman's Board of Missions.

MISSION: To prepare students intellectually, socially, and personally to function effectively in a global and technological society.

FIRST PRESIDENT/PRINCIPAL: James Nelson Ervin.

CURRENT PRESIDENT: Dr. Sebetha Jenkins.

NOTABLE GRADUATES: Dr. C. A. Berry, former president of Jarvis Christian; Rev. T. J. Bottoms, youngest minister to head All Souls Church in Los Angeles, California.

ENDOWMENT: $12 million.

ENROLLMENT: 600.

CURRICULAR STRENGTHS: The school offers cooperative premedical programs with Fisk University and Meharry Medical College.

KEY HISTORICAL EVENTS: Four years after the turn of the twentieth century the seeds of Jarvis Christian College were sown in rich Texas soil. The Negro Disciples of Christ in Texas and the Christian Woman's Board of Missions were inspired to establish an educational facility to train African Americans. They began raising funds and gathering support to make their vision a reality, and finally, in 1912, their efforts were rewarded with the establishment of Jarvis Christian Institute.

Two years after classes began, the school added a high school curriculum and later expanded to offer junior college courses. In 1937 the school was elevated to senior college status and the name was changed to Jarvis Christian College. Today Jarvis maintains a close relationship with the Christian Church (Disciples of Christ) and strives to instill Christian values in all of its students. Jarvis will continue to "provide an education on the precepts of Christianity, service, knowledge, and industry."

Johnson C. Smith University: Charlotte, North Carolina

CHARTERED: 1867.

FOUNDERS: The Reverend S. C. Alexander and the Reverend W. L. Miller.

MISSION: To provide an outstanding education for a diverse group of talented and highly motivated students from various ethnic, socioeconomic, and geographical backgrounds.

FIRST PRESIDENT/PRINCIPAL: The Reverend Stephen Mattoon.

CURRENT PRESIDENT: Dr. Dorothy Cowser Yancy.

NOTABLE GRADUATES: The Honorable Richard C. Erwin, U.S. district judge; Mildred Mitchell Bateman, West Virginia's first African American department head.

ENDOWMENT: $31 million.

ENROLLMENT: 1,200.

CURRICULAR STRENGTHS: The first HBCU to create a Centers of Excellence program. Johnson C. Smith is the only HBCU where every student receives an IBM laptop computer.

KEY HISTORICAL EVENTS: In 1867 two men of God were inspired to establish an institution to educate African Americans in North Carolina. The Reverend S. C. Alexander and the Reverend W. L. Miller succeeded in their goals and opened the doors to Biddle Memorial Institute in the spring of 1867. The school was named after the deceased Major Henry Biddle at the request of his widow, Mary Biddle, who raised $1,400 to contribute to the development of the school. Another generous citizen, the wealthy Colonel W. R. Myers, donated 8 acres of land, which housed the original facilities.

The university prospered through the next century, and in the 1920s Mrs. Jane Berry Smith made numerous contributions to the school, resulting in several new facilities being constructed on the campus. Smith also gave the school a sizable endowment in honor of her late husband, Johnson C. Smith, which led the trustees to acknowledge her generosity by renaming the institution Johnson C. Smith University.

In 1923 the legislature of the state of North Carolina amended the school's charter to reflect the new name. Another generous businessman, James B. Duke, made a considerable difference in the growth of the university with the establishment of the Duke Endowment in 1924, which allotted funds to the university throughout the years. In that same year, the North Carolina State Board of Education also recognized the school as a four-year college.

Originally functioning as an educational institute for men, the university's charter was amended in 1932, allowing for the admission of women. Today Johnson C. Smith functions as a coeducational, private liberal arts institution affiliated with the Presbyterian Church, USA. One of the oldest historically black institutions in the United States, Johnson C. Smith upholds its Christian roots and instills the importance of moral and ethical values in its students. The school offers bachelor of arts and science degrees on its 100-acre campus in a wide range of majors.

Kentucky State University:
Frankfort, Kentucky

CHARTERED: 1886.

FOUNDERS: Edgar Enoch Hume, John H. Jackson.

MISSION: KSU's educational mission, though centered on programs that emphasize liberal studies, also places considerable importance on the university's public service commitments.

FIRST PRESIDENT/PRINCIPAL: John Henry Jackson.

CURRENT PRESIDENT: Mary Evans Sias.

NOTABLE GRADUATES: Whitney M. Young Jr., civil rights leader and executive director of the National Urban League.

ENDOWMENT: $8 million.

ENROLLMENT: 2,204.

CURRICULAR STRENGTHS: Kentucky State University's aquaculture program has been designated as a Program of Distinction by the state of Kentucky. The university's land-grant cooperative extension program received national recognition at the Association of Extension Administrators National Conference in 2003. In addition, KSU has a rich legacy as a teacher's college, matched by a focus on graduate studies and public policy.

KEY HISTORICAL EVENTS: In 1886 Kentucky State University, known at its founding as the State Normal School for Colored Persons, was started with a mission to prepare black teachers to train black students. Frankfort city residents raised $1,500 and also donated land for the humble beginnings of the institution. The first building, Recitation Hall, was constructed one year later, and classes began with three teachers offering instruction to fifty-five students. In 1890 the Morrill Land-Grant Act enabled the institution to add three new departments: home economics, agriculture, and mechanics. That same year the college graduated its first class.

After the turn of the century the school was renamed Kentucky Normal and Industrial Institute for Colored Persons; the school's name would change four more times over the next seven decades before becoming Kentucky State University in 1972, having gained full accreditation. The following year the National Register of Historic Places inducted Jackson Hall, formerly Recitation Hall, into the annals of U.S. landmark structures.

Today Kentucky State University continues to grow: the school's enrollment and faculty have doubled in the last twenty-five years. The school, although originally developed for black students, has branched out culturally, and presently the student population is almost 50 percent white. Kentucky State University is one of only seventeen land-grant institutions of 1890 still thriving and conducting valuable research, extension, and teaching in the food and agricultural sciences. Funded by the U.S. Department of Agriculture, this aspect of the university offers students an opportunity to gain extensive knowledge about food and agricultural sciences. Kentucky State University houses the 203-acre, highly recognized Aquaculture Research Center and farm that is active in agricultural research and assistance. The school offers bachelor's and graduate degrees in the arts and sciences. Kentucky State is continually growing and successfully producing leaders for the future.

Knoxville College:
Knoxville, Tennessee

CHARTERED: Founded in 1875.

FOUNDERS: Missionaries of the United Presbyterian Church of North America.

MISSION: To provide students, regardless of their backgrounds, a distinctive opportunity for educational achievement and professional careers.

FIRST PRESIDENT/PRINCIPAL: Dr. John Schouller McCulloch.

CURRENT PRESIDENT: Dr. Barbara R. Hatton.

NOTABLE GRADUATES: William Blaky, attorney; George Curry, journalist; Dr. Edith Irby Jones, physician.

ENDOWMENT: NA (Confidential).

ENROLLMENT: 300.

CURRICULAR STRENGTHS: Knoxville College is dedicated to providing programs that develop relationships with the local community, industry, and commerce in order to enhance the educational and entrepreneurial experience of its students.

KEY HISTORICAL EVENTS: In 1875 missionaries of the United Presbyterian Church of North America founded Knoxville College to fulfill the need to educate emancipated slaves. These missionaries also sought to impart religious and moral values to their students. A year later, McKee Hall, the college's first building, was constructed, and in 1877 the first postsecondary-level instruction was offered and the school was officially recognized as a college.

Dr. John Schouller McCulloch, a former Civil War chaplain, acted as the school's first president and led the mission of training students for ministry and education as well as craftsmanship and homemaking. Because there were not many African Americans prepared to receive training on the college level, Knoxville offered instruction from grade 1 to the college level up until the 1920s.

Knoxville College was resourceful in using its students to construct buildings to expand the campus; Wallace Hall and McMillan Chapel were built with student labor and McMillan Chapel was designed by former student William Thomas Jones. The students not only constructed the buildings, they also manufactured the bricks!

In 1890, after witnessing the school's progress, the state of Tennessee used funds provided by the Morrill Act to expand the school's curriculum to include training in agriculture and the industrial arts. With the addition of a college of arts and sciences in 1931 and the expansion of the liberal arts department, Knoxville College completed its evolution into a liberal arts institution. Over twenty-five years later, in 1958, the Southern Association of Colleges and Schools granted Knoxville College full accreditation. In 1980 the state of Tennessee honored the college's history by designating its buildings as the Knoxville College Historic District and added the school to its National Register of Historic Places.

Today the school is known as the "new" Knoxville College and holds fast to its "renewed commitment" of "providing challenging and stimulating educational experiences for talented students demonstrating leadership in their fields but afforded little opportunity within society."

Lane College:
Jackson, Tennessee

CHARTERED: Founded in 1882.

FOUNDER: Bishop Isaac Lane.

MISSION: To develop the whole student. In addition to its priority of academic excellence, the college is also concerned about the student's spiritual, social, and ethical development.

FIRST PRESIDENT/PRINCIPAL: Bishop Isaac Lane.

CURRENT PRESIDENT: Dr. Wesley Cornelious McClure.

NOTABLE GRADUATES: Nathan Mitchell, attorney; Yvonne Griggs Allen, educator.

ENDOWMENT: $2.2 million.

ENROLLMENT: 635.

CURRICULAR STRENGTHS: Lane College has substantially reduced the rate of illiteracy among Negroes in the South in fewer than fifty years.

KEY HISTORICAL EVENTS: In 1882 the Colored Methodist Episcopal High School was founded to ensure that recently emancipated slaves would have the opportunity to learn to "read, write, and speak correctly." Four years earlier, the Reverend J. K. Daniels had presented the idea of developing a school to train teachers and preachers to the 1878 Tennessee Annual Conference. That same year there was a severe outbreak of yellow fever and Daniels's idea was put aside until Bishop Isaac Lane, a former slave fathered by his owner, took over as the presiding bishop of the conference. Bishop Lane immediately began plans to organize the school, and after much persistence and hard work, 4 acres of land were purchased in 1880 for the site of the school.

When classes convened in 1882, Bishop Lane's daughter Jennie functioned as the school's first teacher. Two years later, in 1884, the school was chartered by the state of Tennessee as Lane Institute. Over a decade later, in 1896, the board of trustees renamed the school Lane College. Lane carried out its mission of educating African Americans when there were no other opportunities for them to receive an education. In 1936 Lane was accepted by the Southern Association of Colleges and Secondary Schools, and in 1961, after thirty-five more years of service and commitment to excellence, Lane was granted full accreditation.

Today Lane is flourishing and holds the honor of being the first four-year institution established by the Christian Methodist Episcopal Church. The college upholds its commitment to spiritual development and students are required to attend a minimum of twelve chapel services per semester as part of their graduation requirements. Lane continues to grow and will continue to rely on support from a committed faculty and staff, alumni, and friends.

Langston University:
Langston, Oklahoma

CHARTERED: Founded in 1897.

FOUNDERS: Former slaves in the all-black city of Langston petitioned the territorial government to set up a separate school for blacks.

MISSION: As a land-grant institution with an urban mission, to provide excellence in instruction leading to associate, baccalaureate, and master's degrees, thus placing its graduates in a highly favorable position to enter graduate and professional schools and meet the changing demands, both domestic and international, of rural and urban society.

FIRST PRESIDENT/PRINCIPAL: Dr. Inman Page.

CURRENT PRESIDENT: Dr. Ernest L. Holloway.

NOTABLE GRADUATES: Ada Louis Fisher, the first black woman to attend the University of Oklahoma Law School; the Honorable Opio Toure, Oklahoma state representative.

ENDOWMENT: $12 million.

ENROLLMENT: 861.

CURRICULAR STRENGTHS: Langston sponsors a technical assistance project, whereby students and members aim to provide outreach services that equip underserved farmers, ranchers, and rural communities with necessary resources to improve their quality of life.

KEY HISTORICAL EVENTS: Langston University, founded as the Colored Agricultural and Normal University in 1897, dates back to 1892, before Oklahoma had achieved statehood.

African American citizens, fed up with their children's inability to receive an education in any of the institutions of higher learning in the territory, petitioned the Oklahoma Industrial School and College commission for the establishment of a black college in Langston. Territorial governor William Gary Renfrow eventually responded to the community's pleas by initiating a reform bill to establish the university; in 1897, the Colored Agricultural and Normal University was founded as a land-grant school in compliance with House Bill 151. The African American settlers were determined to help the school succeed, and they raised funds through auctions, picnics, bake sales, and donations to purchase land on which the school would be constructed. A year after the legislation was passed, the school began classes in a Presbyterian church with a $5,000 budget. Dr. Inman Page, the son of a former slave who bought his family's freedom, served as the school's first president. The university instructed African American men and women in education, agriculture, and industrial arts. During Dr. Page's tenure the school experienced substantial growth in enrollment and development. The college continued to expand, and in 1941 the school was renamed Langston University in honor of John Mercer Langston, a black educator who served in the Virginia House of Representatives from 1890 to 1891.

In the 1970s Langston instituted two urban centers, in Tulsa and Oklahoma City. These two extensions offer junior- and senior-level courses and provide a wide range of community services, including career counseling, adult education, and direct contact with local, state, and federal agencies. The school is currently situated on 440 acres of land and has full accreditation from the North Central Association of Colleges and Schools to award associate degrees in science, bachelor's degrees in arts and science, and master's degrees.

Lawson State Community College:
Birmingham, Alabama

CHARTERED: Founded in 1963.

FOUNDERS: Lawson State Community College was established as a result of an act of the Alabama Legislature.

MISSION: To provide educational programs and services that are comprehensive, flexible, accessible, community-related, and available at affordable prices.

FIRST PRESIDENT/PRINCIPAL: Dr. T. A. Lawson.

CURRENT PRESIDENT: Dr. Perry W. Ward.

NOTABLE GRADUATES: Larry Langford, president of the Jefferson County, Alabama, Commission and former mayor of Fairfield, Alabama; Denise Seltzer, director of nursing at HealthSouth Hospital in Fairfield; independent owner of All-State Insurance Company Terry Jackson, 2002 Alabama Small Businessman of the Year.

ENDOWMENT: $100,000.

ENROLLMENT: 1,500.

CURRICULAR STRENGTHS: The college provides higher educational opportunities and supports the economic growth of the community by sponsoring numerous programs and services for student participation.

KEY HISTORICAL EVENTS: In 1963 Alabama established two-year college programs, and as a result of that legislation, Lawson State Community College, named after its first president, Dr. T. A. Lawson, was developed in 1965.

Over a decade earlier the Wallace Patterson Trade School Act of 1947 was passed, resulting in the establishment of the Wenonah State Technical Institute. In the fall of 1963 Wenonah State merged with Lawson College to become the Lawson-Wenonah State Junior College and Technical Institution. Not long after this union, the school adopted its present name, Lawson State Community College. The school was the only two-year public community college in central Alabama designed to serve the needs of African American students. Dr. T. A. Lawson honorably served the college until 1971.

Lawson State has experienced considerable growth in its forty years of existence. The school currently consists of fourteen buildings that are full of modern technology, which enhances the students' learning experiences. Under the leadership of current president Dr. Perry Ward, enrollment has increased more than 60 percent. Lawson State has created new outreach programs and partnerships that provide numerous opportunities for students to get hands-on training and secure future employment.

Lawson State Community College is fairly new when measured against other HBCUs in the country; however, the college is constantly expanding its curriculum as well as developing the campus. Lawson State has a bright future and will continue to provide a quality education for all students who enter its halls.

LeMoyne-Owen College:
Memphis, Tennessee

CHARTERED: 1968.

FOUNDERS: American Missionary Association and the Tennessee Baptist Missionary and Education Convention.

MISSION: To prepare men and women for lives of success, service, and leadership in a nurturing, student-centered community.

FIRST PRESIDENT/PRINCIPAL: Lucinda Humphrey (principal).

CURRENT PRESIDENT: Dr. James G. Wingate.

NOTABLE GRADUATES: Marion Barry, former mayor of Washington, D.C.; the Honorable Willie W. Herenton, mayor of Memphis.

ENDOWMENT: $11 million.

ENROLLMENT: 850.

CURRICULAR STRENGTHS: LeMoyne-Owen has strong academic programs in business, education, and biology, an active service learning program where students can earn credit through community service, and an ambitious adult degree completion program.

KEY HISTORICAL EVENTS: In 1862 a dedicated hospital nurse, Lucinda Humphrey, was determined to contribute to the improvement and much-needed education of African Americans, having worked at Camp Shiloh, a Union camp where escaped slaves sought refuge. She taught groups of five students the basic fundamentals of reading and writing.

In 1863, a school formally opened in Memphis and classes were held in the Lincoln Chapel. Tragically, in 1866 the chapel was destroyed in a fire during race riots that began after the departure of federal troops. Miraculously, the school was rebuilt and reopened only one year later, with six instructors and 150 students. Even after this dramatic recovery, Lincoln endured financial crisis. Dr. Francis Julian LeMoyne, a physician and member of the American Missionary Association, donated $20,000 to the school. The school adopted the name LeMoyne Normal and Commercial School in 1871.

In 1914 LeMoyne College moved to its current site and was classified as a junior college ten years later. After another decade of considerable growth, the school was chartered by the state of Tennessee as a degree-granting institution in 1934.

The seeds for Owen College were planted in 1946 when the Tennessee Baptist Missionary and Educational Convention began making arrangements to purchase property to be used as the site of a Baptist junior college. Seven years into the planning of the school, a board of trustees was appointed, and the school opened a year later in 1954. Owen Junior College was named after the honorable religious and civic leader the Reverend S. A. Owen. The school soon dropped "Junior" from its name. Owen College gained accreditation in 1958.

In 1967 plans to merge Owen and LeMoyne Colleges were brewing, and a year later the schools were formally joined to become LeMoyne-Owen College.

Today LeMoyne-Owen College is a thriving institution of higher learning with a strong foundation in the United Church of Christ and the Baptist Church. The school is accredited by the Southern Association of Colleges and Schools.

Lewis College of Business:
Detroit, Michigan

CHARTERED: Founded in 1928.

FOUNDER: Dr. Violet T. Lewis.

MISSION: To enhance and enrich the total education experience of its constituents, while maintaining our unique historical responsibility of providing training for minority students.

FIRST PRESIDENT/PRINCIPAL: Dr. Violet T. Lewis.

CURRENT PRESIDENT: Dr. Marjorie Harris.

NOTABLE GRADUATES: Marcus Stepp, international vice president of UAW-CIO Union; Dr. Castell Vaughn-Bryant, president of Miami Dade Community College North Campus; Rose Hubbard, director, Detroit Federal Executive Board.

ENDOWMENT: Lewis College of Business is establishing a foundation for an endowment.

ENROLLMENT: 200.

CURRICULAR STRENGTHS: Lewis is known for its business school. The college sponsors the Brother-to-Brother program in order to afford young men an opportunity to bond and create a supportive and trusting environment for high academic performance. Lewis also has a Sister-to-Sister support system designed to train and encourage women to become entrepreneurs.

KEY HISTORICAL EVENTS: In 1928 Dr. Violet T. Lewis fulfilled her dream of establishing an institution where African Americans could receive an education that would enable them to make a smooth transition into successful careers. Dr. Lewis's determination and a $50 loan resulted in the establishment of Lewis Business College, an institution that is still successful today. Dr. Lewis originally began classes in Indianapolis, Indiana, at a time when African Americans did not have easy access to higher education.

The Indiana school was successful, and in 1938 the Detroit Chamber of Commerce persuaded Dr. Lewis to open an extension campus in its city. Once Dr. Lewis researched and found that vocational schools in Detroit were not open to African Americans, she obliged and opened the second branch there a year later.

In 1978 a merger between the Indianapolis and the Detroit branches was completed, and this union caused the school's stature to increase. The Michigan Historical Commission recognized Lewis College of Business as a historical institution in 1987. Later that year Lewis College of Business was granted HBCU status by the U.S. Secretary of Education, making the school the only institution holding that title in the state of Michigan.

Lewis College of Business is committed to preparing its students for their future careers and for future education. The school is constantly growing and seeking new programs to benefit students by staying abreast of society's ever-changing business demands. Its curriculum of computer information, business administration, and office information systems will continue to expand and produce competent, prepared leaders for tomorrow.

Lincoln University:
Chester, Pennsylvania

CHARTERED: Founded in 1854.

FOUNDERS: John Miller Dickey and his wife Sarah Emlen Cresson.

MISSION: To provide the best elements of a liberal arts and sciences-based undergraduate core curriculum and selected graduate programs to meet the needs of students living in a highly technological and global society.

FIRST PRESIDENT/PRINCIPAL: John M. Dickey.

CURRENT PRESIDENT: Ivory V. Nelson, Ph.D.

NOTABLE GRADUATES: The Honorable Thurgood Marshall, first African American Supreme Court justice; Langston Hughes, poet; Hildrus A. Poindexter, internationally known authority on tropical diseases; the Reverend James Robinson, Crossroads Africa founder.

ENDOWMENT: $16 million.

ENROLLMENT: 3,500.

Dr. Horace Mann Bond, Lincoln class of 1923, and the first black president of Lincoln. He is also the father of Julian Bond.

CURRICULAR STRENGTHS: Lincoln is ranked second in the nation in graduating African Americans with bachelor's degrees in the physical sciences. Between 1989 and 2000, eighteen chemistry graduates earned Ph.D. degrees in chemistry and related fields. Seventeen percent of graduating seniors were admitted to graduate school in 2000. Lincoln enrolled 7 percent of African American physics majors in the United States in 1999. Seventy-seven percent of Lincoln's faculty have doctorates or terminal degrees. Lincoln is currently developing four centers of excellence: in natural and environment science, teacher education, business and technology, and communications.

KEY HISTORICAL EVENTS: In the spring of 1854 Lincoln University was founded as Ashmun Institute in Pennsylvania. The school was established for the purpose of educating African American men in the arts and sciences. In 1866, Ashmun Institute was renamed Lincoln University in honor of President Abraham Lincoln.

Almost a century after the university opened its doors, Lincoln became coeducational, admitting women in 1952. During the school's first century of operation, Lincoln University was responsible for training 20 percent of black physicians and more than 10 percent of black attorneys in the United States.

Lincoln boasts of its abundance of international and interracial students. The school is especially proud of its alumni, including poet Langston Hughes and the first African American Supreme Court justice, Thurgood Marshall. The university is also responsible for training several international students who became notable leaders, including Nnamdi Azikiwe, who later became Nigeria's first president, and Kwame Nkrumah, the first president of Ghana. Remarkably, Lincoln's alumni have presided over thirty-five colleges and universities and several prominent churches. The university has produced ten U. S. ambassadors and a host of federal, state, and municipal judges, as well as mayors and city managers. Lincoln will continue to provide outstanding programs and success for all people and hold fast to its traditions, rich legacy, and mission to produce African American leaders.

Lincoln University:
Jefferson City, Missouri

CHARTERED: Founded in 1866 as Lincoln Institute.

FOUNDERS: The school was established through the contributions of the Sixty-second United States Colored Infantry.

MISSION: To provide excellent educational opportunities for a diverse student population in the context of an open enrollment institution.

FIRST PRESIDENT/PRINCIPAL: Richard Baxter Foster.

CURRENT PRESIDENT: Dr. David B. Henson.

NOTABLE GRADUATES: Joe Torry, comedian and actor; Jesse Hill, former president of Atlanta Life Insurance Company; Lorraine (Graham) Fenton, silver medalist in the 2000 Olympics.

ENDOWMENT: $3 million.

ENROLLMENT: 3,500.

CURRICULAR STRENGTHS: Lincoln's strongest departments are education, business, nursing, agriculture, criminal justice, computer science, and music. Lincoln provides an Ethnic Studies Center for its students and the community, which serves as the official repository for the historical records and documents of the university.

KEY HISTORICAL EVENTS: Lincoln University has a remarkable history that dates back to the close of the Civil War. African American soldiers who served in the Sixty-second and Sixty-fifth Infantry were determined to establish an educational facility for blacks in their native state of Missouri. Together the visionary soldiers raised $5,000, and Lincoln Institute began classes in the fall of 1866.

Three years after the school's inception Lincoln relocated to its present site and initiated a teacher training program after the state of Missouri began offering financial support to the institution. Lincoln continued to expand its curriculum and added college-level courses in 1877. The same year a law was passed authorizing graduates from Lincoln's normal department the ability to "teach for life without further examination." Two years later the school was officially adopted by the state of Missouri.

In 1890 another significant change occurred when Lincoln became a land-grant institution under the provisions of the second Morrill Act and broadened its curriculum to include industrial and agricultural programs. The first bachelor's degrees were awarded to the proud class of 1891. The school continued to experience much progress, and by 1936, several of Lincoln's programs were accredited by the North Central Association of Colleges and Secondary Schools. In 1940 Lincoln established its graduate department, which included courses in education, history, and English.

Lincoln University continues to be a flourishing institution in the state of Missouri. Today Lincoln is committed to serving a diverse student population, and through its open admissions policy the university is able to provide education for students who otherwise may not have had access to higher education.

Livingstone College: Salisbury, North Carolina

CHARTERED: 1882.

FOUNDERS: Dr. Joseph Charles Price and the African Methodist Episcopal Zion Church.

MISSION: To provide an environment in which students from all ethnic backgrounds can develop their potential for leadership and service to society.

FIRST PRESIDENT/PRINCIPAL: Dr. Joseph Charles Price.

CURRENT PRESIDENT: Dr. Algenia Warren Freeman.

NOTABLE GRADUATES: Solomon Carter Fuller, first black neurosurgeon in the United States; Elizabeth Duncan Koontz, first African American president of the National Education Association; Brigadeer General Velma Richardson, superintendent of schools for the state of Mississippi; Henry Johnson, current president of Morehouse School of Medicine; Dr. James R. Gavin, past president of the American Diabetes Association.

ENDOWMENT: $2.5 million.

ENROLLMENT: 1,000.

CURRICULAR STRENGTHS: Liberal arts, teacher education, and the sciences.

Livingstone College cheering squad, 1965.

KEY HISTORICAL EVENTS: Livingstone College, formerly Zion Wesley Institute, was founded by the African Methodist Episcopal Zion Church with the goal of training ministers. After only three sessions under the leadership of Bishop C. R. Harris and Professor A. S. Richardson, the school discontinued instruction. In 1881 Dr. Joseph Price and Bishop J. W. Hood began raising funds in order to reopen their school. Zion originally was located in Concord, North Carolina; however, the people of Salisbury enticed the ministers to relocate to their town with a $1,000 pledge. Dr. Price and Bishop Hood obliged the town, and in 1882 Zion Wesley Institute opened its doors in Salisbury with Dr. Joseph Price residing as president.

Dr. Price was a noble man of God and served Livingstone College faithfully until his death in 1893. He contributed a great deal to the growth and development of the college with his Christian compassion and abundance of knowledge. He often expressed his genuine faith with these words: "I do not care how dark the night; I believe in the coming morning."[5] Dr. Price proposed Zion's name be changed to Livingstone College to honor the British Christian missionary, philanthropist, and African explorer David Livingstone; in 1887, an act of the North Carolina legislature granted his request.

Livingstone College remains connected to the AME Zion Church and still strives to provide a quality education to its students and produce capable leaders. Students can earn a bachelor of arts, bachelor of science, or master of theology degree from this historical institution.

Mary Holmes College:
West Point, Mississippi

CHARTERED: Founded in 1892.

FOUNDERS: The Board of Freedmen of the Presbyterian Church.

MISSION: To serve a student population from the southeast region of the United States, which is largely underserved and economically disadvantaged.

FIRST PRESIDENT/PRINCIPAL: The Reverend Mead Holmes.

CURRENT PRESIDENT: Dr. Nathaniel Jackson.

NOTABLE GRADUATES: The Honorable Bennie L. Turner, Mississippi state senator; Lester Coffey, president of Coffey Communications; Dr. Evelyn Bonner, director of the Learning Resource Center, Barber-Scotia College.

ENDOWMENT: NA.

ENROLLMENT: 350.

CURRICULAR STRENGTHS: The college offers special courses and programs to assist educationally disadvantaged students as well as accelerated courses and enrichment activities for academically talented students.

KEY HISTORICAL EVENTS: In 1892 the Board of Freedmen of the Presbyterian Church established the Mary Holmes Seminary in Jackson, Mississippi. It offered a Christian education to African American girls, with instruction in the domestic sciences. The school was named in honor of Mary Holmes, a selfless woman who dedicated her life to improving the quality of life of former slaves. Five years after the school began classes, a tragic fire mercilessly devoured the original building, and the school was reconstructed in West Point, Mississippi.

Mary Holmes underwent major changes in 1932, when the institution began admitting men and broadened its curriculum to include a college department designed to provide teacher training. During this period there was a great need for African American teachers in the South, and Mary Holmes was a success in filling that societal demand.

In the late 1950s Mary Holmes discontinued its elementary and secondary education departments and expanded into a two-year college. The school was accordingly renamed Mary Holmes Junior College. After the state of Mississippi granted a charter in 1969 the school became Mary Holmes College and established its own board of trustees.

Today Mary Holmes College is committed to "providing quality liberal arts and vocational/technical programs in a caring Christian environment." The school maintains its affiliation with the Presbyterian Church. Mary Holmes has a wide variety of courses designed to enlighten students in liberal arts; they also offer unique courses and programs that appeal to disadvantaged students. The college is fully accredited by the Southern Association of Colleges and Schools to award associate degrees in the arts, sciences, and applied sciences.

Medgar Evers College:
Brooklyn, New York

CHARTERED: September 1970.

FOUNDERS: The Board of Higher Education of the City of New York and the Bedford-Stuyvesant Coalition on Educational Needs and Services.

MISSION: Creating success one student at a time.

FIRST PRESIDENT/PRINCIPAL: Dr. Richard Trent.

CURRENT PRESIDENT: Dr. Edison O. Jackson.

NOTABLE GRADUATES: Leroy Richardson and Alford Smith, physicians; Winston Dove, senior accountant, Rockefeller Foundation.

ENDOWMENT: $60,000.

ENROLLMENT: 5,300.

CURRICULAR STRENGTHS: Since 1986 Medgar Evers College has directed and hosted the renowned National Black Writers' Conference. The biennial conference is open to new and established writers and has featured such bards as Maya Angelou, Walter Mosley, and Terry McMillan. The highly successful event led to the establishment of the Center for Black Literature, which promotes the creation, study, and preservation of black literature. Medgar Evers scored among the top 15 percent in the Level of Academic Challenge category of the National Benchmarks of Effective Educational Practices' 2000 assessment of more than 276 colleges. It was among the best-scoring colleges within the CUNY system.

KEY HISTORICAL EVENTS: A public college under the City University of New York (CUNY) system, Medgar Evers College was named in honor of murdered civil rights activist Medgar Wiley Evers. The school admitted its first students in the fall of 1971 and conferred its first bachelor degree in 1975.

Medgar Evers is the youngest of the HBCUs, but like its predecessors the college owes its birth to civil rights activists, particularly African Americans. Founded during the height of the Black Power movement, Medgar Evers was created in response to grassroots activism initiated by neighborhood organizations in Brooklyn's Bedford-Stuyvesant community. Residents of this central Brooklyn area had long recognized the need for an institution of higher learning that would serve their culturally diverse community. Through such organizations as the NAACP and the Bedford-Stuyvesant Restoration Corporation, they successfully lobbied the state for a public four-year college.

Medgar Evers's campus culture is nontraditional when compared to other predominantly black colleges. The city-based school serves a commuter population and offers no on-campus housing. A large percentage of the students are of West Indian descent, reflecting the demographics of the central Brooklyn community it serves.

Meharry Medical College:
Nashville, Tennessee

CHARTERED: Founded in 1876.

FOUNDERS: Samuel Meharry, the Methodist Church of America, Dr. W. J. Sneed, and Dr. George Whipple Hubbard.

MISSION: To provide superior health sciences education primarily to African Americans and other students of color by providing a specialized, uniquely supportive learning environment for students.

FIRST PRESIDENT/PRINCIPAL: Dr. George Whipple Hubbard.

CURRENT PRESIDENT: Dr. John Maupin.

NOTABLE GRADUATES: Dr. Dorothy Brown, the first board-certified African American female surgeon; Dr. Maurice Clifford, former president of the Medical College of Pennsylvania; Agnes Donahue, D.D.S., director of the Office of Women's Health, U.S. Public Health Service; Dr. Edward S. Cooper, past president of the American Heart Association; Dr. Clive Callender, chairman of the Howard University School of Medicine Department of Surgery.

ENDOWMENT: $32 million.

ENROLLMENT: 837.

CURRICULAR STRENGTHS: Seventy-six percent of Meharry's medical graduates and 64 percent of dental graduates practice in areas that are socioeconomically deprived. Meharry is number one in producing African American doctors, dentists, and graduates with doctorates in the biological sciences. Meharry is the primary producer of doctoral graduates who go on to work in NIH agencies and institutes. Nearly 60 percent of medical school graduates practice in the primary care specialties of internal medicine, family medicine, obstetrics and gynecology, and pediatrics.

KEY HISTORICAL EVENTS: Meharry Medical College is a premier institution of higher learning in the United States. The school was developed in 1876 after the Meharry family donated a generous amount of funds to ensure that the school was established successfully. Meharry was originally developed as a medical department at Central Tennessee College, which later became Walden University.

The medical department soon expanded and developed a dental branch, and later a pharmacy extension. At the turn of the twentieth century, Walden's medical department adopted the name Meharry College of Walden University. Fifteen years later, in 1915, Meharry was granted a charter by the state of Tennessee and the school was reorganized independently as Meharry Medical College.

In 1931 the school relocated to its present site where it currently occupies 26 acres of land. Students who attend this prestigious, highly acclaimed institution have the opportunity to earn numerous doctoral degrees ranging from medicine to dental surgery and pharmacology. Meharry Medical College continues its traditions of excellence and growth and abides by its motto: "Keeping the Promise . . . Delivering the Dream."

Miles College:
Fairfield, Alabama

CHARTERED: Founded in 1905.

FOUNDERS: Colored Methodist Episcopal Church.

MISSION: To ensure the personal development of all individuals, regardless of race, who upon graduation, will possess an understanding of their own mission in a global society.

FIRST PRESIDENT/PRINCIPAL: Bishop William Henry.

CURRENT PRESIDENT: Dr. Albert J. H. Sloan II.

NOTABLE GRADUATES: Dr. Richard Arington, first black mayor of Birmingham, Alabama.

ENDOWMENT: $10 million.

ENROLLMENT: 1,400.

CURRICULAR STRENGTHS: Liberal arts, business administration, communication, education, social and behavioral sciences, humanities, natural science, and mathematics.

KEY HISTORICAL EVENTS: In 1905 the Colored Methodist Episcopal Church established Miles College out of its desire to train African Americans in ministry. The school was designed to enlighten students both spiritually and intellectually, and the curriculum reflected these ideals. The school originally was named Miles Memorial College in honor of the presiding bishop of the Colored Methodist Church, William Henry Miles.

Once Miles Memorial began classes, the institution was a powerful force in the state of Alabama, producing African American leaders in a time when they were desperately needed. The school awarded its first bachelor's degree in 1911 and continued to expand its curriculum and physical plant. Three decades later, the name was changed to Miles College as a result of its extensive growth. Miles College has experienced continuous growth since its inception and its curriculum has expanded to become a fully accredited liberal arts college.

Today Miles College maintains its affiliation with the Christian Methodist Episcopal Church, formerly the Colored Methodist Episcopal Church, and strives to instill Christian values in its students. Students may study a wide variety of majors, including Asian studies, biology, communications, elementary education, political science, social work, and several others. Miles is approaching its century mark with determination and a pledge to continue serving its community and producing competent leaders for the future.

Mississippi Valley State University:
Itta Bena, Mississippi

CHARTERED: Founded in 1950.

FOUNDERS: The Mississippi Legislature authorized the establishment of a vocational school in 1946.

MISSION: To provide educational programs and services designed to serve students who can move at an accelerated pace, students who have adequate prior preparation, and students who are educationally deficient in their prior preparation.

FIRST PRESIDENT/PRINCIPAL: Dr. J. H. White.

CURRENT PRESIDENT: Dr. Lester C. Newman.

NOTABLE GRADUATES: Dr. Samuel McGee and Dr. Carolyn Smith, educators; Jerry Rice, professional football player.

ENDOWMENT: $2 million.

ENROLLMENT: 2,283.

CURRICULAR STRENGTHS: MVSU has a Talent Search program that assists at-risk students to prepare them for entry into college.

KEY HISTORICAL EVENTS: In 1946 the state of Mississippi passed legislation endorsing the establishment of a vocational school offering teacher training in elementary education. After four years of planning, Mississippi Valley State University opened in 1950 with seven faculty members and fourteen students. The school, formerly known as Mississippi Vocational College, offered bachelor of science degrees in fourteen major departments. Students could also study through its extension programs.

Fourteen years after the school's beginning, the curriculum expanded to include degrees in liberal arts and education. The name was changed to Mississippi Valley State College to reflect these additions, and preprofessional, technical, and specialized areas were given more attention. Dr. J. H. White, the institution's first president, loyally served the university for over two decades and was succeeded by Dr. E. A. Boykins in 1971. Under the leadership of Dr. Boykins the school experienced significant growth, including a bill passed in 1974 by Governor William Waller granting university status and the present name, Mississippi Valley State University. Two years later, Mississippi Valley initiated a graduate program where students could study environmental health, elementary education, criminal justice, and special education.

Today Mississippi Valley State continues to grow and the school has two flourishing satellite sites, the Greenwood Center and the Greenville Center, making the school easily accessible to a larger pool of students. The 450-acre campus provides a close-knit atmosphere where the current president and several faculty members and their families reside. The university is a public institution that has various funding resources, including the Mississippi legislature, private gifts, and grants.

Morehouse College:
Atlanta, Georgia

CHARTERED: Founded in 1867.

FOUNDERS: The Reverend William Jefferson White, with support from Richard C. Coulter and the Reverend Edmund Turney.

MISSION: To provide a comprehensive academic, social, and spiritual experience that prepares its students for leadership and success in the larger society.

FIRST PRESIDENT/PRINCIPAL: The Reverend Dr. Joseph T. Robert.

CURRENT PRESIDENT: Dr. Walter E. Massey.

NOTABLE GRADUATES: Nobel Peace Prize laureate and civil rights martyr Dr. Martin Luther King Jr.; Shelton "Spike" Lee, filmmaker and president of 40 Acres and a Mule; former U.S. ambassador to Botswana Howard E. Jeter; Oscar-nominated actor Samuel L. Jackson.

ENDOWMENT: $98.9 million.

ENROLLMENT: 3,000.

CURRICULAR STRENGTHS: The college sponsors a program entitled the Morehouse College Institutional Values Project, which is a multiyear project designed to develop a sense of community where ethical behavior is exhibited and the individual is treated fairly.

KEY HISTORICAL EVENTS: Not long after the Civil War, the Reverend William Jefferson White, a Baptist minister who made cabinets to support his family, developed a school to teach newly emanicpated slaves the fundamentals of reading and writing. The school was founded in Augusta, Georgia, and was known as the Augusta Institute; it was from this institution that Morehouse College emerged.

The Reverend White founded Augusta Institute with assistance from a former Augusta slave, Richard C. Coulter, and the Reverend Edmund Turney, who organized the National Theological Institute for educating freedmen in Washington, D.C. The first classes were held in the basement of Springfield Baptist Church, the oldest independent African American church, still on its original site.

Twelve years after its inception, Augusta Institute relocated to Atlanta, set up facilities in Friendship Baptist Church, and was renamed Atlanta Baptist Seminary. Soon thereafter, the school moved to its own 4-acre lot and continued its new mission of training African American men for ministry. In 1885, during the presidency of Dr. Samuel T. Graves, the school moved to its current location. Later, in 1897, the school granted its first degree and was renamed Atlanta Baptist College.

In 1906 the college appointed its first African American president, Dr. John Hope, who began to expand the school's mission and purpose. In 1913, during Dr. Hope's tenure, the school was renamed Morehouse College in honor of the corresponding secretary of the Atlanta Baptist Home Mission Society, Henry L. Morehouse.

Morehouse has experienced continuous growth under the direction of its eight former presidents; most notable among them is the Reverend Dr. Benjamin E. Mays, who mentored many great Morehouse men, including Dr. Martin Luther King Jr. For twenty-seven years, Dr.

Mays planted seeds of revolution in the minds of Morehouse men in the Sale Hall Chapel at Morehouse.

Current president Dr. Walter E. Massey has successfully steered Morehouse into the twenty-first century. Morehouse is the nation's only private liberal arts HBCU for men. The college is also a member of the Atlanta University Center, which is the largest private African American educational system in the world. Dr. Massey has developed the campus as well as new programs for students. Morehouse is committed to "developing men with disciplined minds, emphasizing the continuing search for truth as a liberating force."

Morehouse School of Medicine:
Atlanta, Georgia

CHARTERED: Founded in 1975.

FOUNDERS: The citizens of Georgia and those who reside in medically underserved areas of the nation, the National Medical Association, and a host of other organizations, including the Georgia State Medical Association, the Georgia General Assembly, and the Carnegie Council supported the development of a medical school at Morehouse College.

MISSION: Recruiting, educating, and graduating more students from minority and socioeconomically disadvantaged backgrounds for service as primary-care physicians in our nation's medically underserved communities.

FIRST PRESIDENT/PRINCIPAL: Dr. Louis Sullivan.

CURRENT PRESIDENT: James R. Gavin III, M.D., Ph.D.

NOTABLE GRADUATES: Regina Benjamin, president of the Alabama Medical Association, Dr. Rhonda Meadows, secretary of the Agency for Health Care Administration for the state of Florida.

ENDOWMENT: $25.6 million.

ENROLLMENT: 2,500.

CURRICULAR STRENGTHS: Ninety-seven percent of fourth-year medical students passed the USMLE Step II exam during the 1999–2000 academic year.

KEY HISTORICAL EVENTS: The history of Morehouse School of Medicine begins in 1973, when a study conducted by Morehouse College found an extreme shortage of African American health-care providers in rural and inner-city areas. After this disturbing discovery, the National Medical Association authorized the establishment of a medical school at Morehouse College.

The all-male Morehouse College was founded in 1867 to "prepare its students for leadership and success in the larger society." Here, an undated photograph of Morehouse's Graves Hall.

In 1975 the school was organized as a two-year program in basic medical sciences and named the School of Medicine at Morehouse College. Three years later the "charter class," consisting of twenty-four students, was under way. In 1981 the Morehouse School of Medicine became an independent institution and began plans to develop a four-year program. The next year the Liaison Committee on Medical Education granted the institution the authority to develop a program that would award doctor of medicine degrees in the spring of 1985.

In 1985 the first class of fully trained doctors graduated from Morehouse School of Medicine; every year since, the school has produced doctors dedicated to the "reformation of our nation's health care system." The Morehouse School of Medicine is committed to research and has a "strong focus on developing cures for those diseases that disproportionately affect the African-American community." The Morehouse School of Medicine will continue to educate health-care leaders for the future and develop partnerships with organizations with common goals to ensure the success of medicine in the future.

Morgan State University:
Baltimore, Maryland

CHARTERED: Founded in 1867.

FOUNDERS: Baltimore Conference of the Methodist Episcopal Church.

MISSION: To serve a multiethnic and multiracial student body and to help ensure that the benefits of higher education are enjoyed by a broad segment of the population.

FIRST PRESIDENT/PRINCIPAL: J. Emory Round.

CURRENT PRESIDENT: Dr. Earl S. Richardson.

NOTABLE GRADUATES: Parren J. Mitchell, former U.S. congressman; Kweisi Mfume, president and CEO of the NAACP; Earl Graves, publisher, *Black Enterprise* magazine.

ENDOWMENT: $5 million.

ENROLLMENT: 6,000.

CURRICULAR STRENGTHS: The university awards more bachelor's degrees to African American students than any campus in Maryland.

KEY HISTORICAL EVENTS: Morgan State University, formerly Centenary Biblical Institute, was founded by the Baltimore Conference of the Methodist Episcopal Church in 1867. The church's original mission was to establish an institution to train men for the ministry, but the school soon adopted teacher education training into its curriculum and permitted women to attend classes. The first chairman of the board of trustees, the Reverend Lyttleton Morgan, donated land for development of the school, and in 1890 the school was renamed Morgan College.

Almost thirty years after its inception, Morgan awarded its first bachelor's degree to George McMechen, who later became a prominent civic leader in Baltimore.

In 1939, after conducting a study, the state of Maryland realized that its black citizens were not receiving enough opportunities for advancement. As a result of these findings Morgan, which had always been a private institution, was taken over by the state and became a public campus; Morgan was then open to students of all races.

Morgan's curriculum remained comprehensive throughout the 1960s, but gradually evolved into a liberal arts college. By 1975 the Maryland state legislature had granted Morgan university status, and the college was renamed Morgan State University. That same year the university began a doctorate program. In 1988 the university received an invitation to become part of the University of Maryland system; the state also declared the campus Maryland's public urban university.

Today Morgan State is one of the ten universities most sought by African American students. Students who are accepted have the opportunity to receive a wide range of undergraduate degrees and graduate degrees at the master's and doctoral level. Over the last fifteen years Morgan State has experienced considerable growth, including a dramatic increase in enrollment. Morgan State University is striving for excellence and "will continue to play a prominent role in Maryland's educational future."

Morris Brown College:
Atlanta, Georgia

CHARTERED: Founded in 1881.

FOUNDERS: Reverend Wesley John Gaines aided by the African Methodist Episcopal Church.

MISSION: To provide educational opportunities in a Christian environment that will enable its students to become fully functional persons in society.

FIRST PRESIDENT/PRINCIPAL: Mary McCree.

CURRENT PRESIDENT: Dr. Leroy Frazier.

NOTABLE GRADUATES: James McPherson, Pulitzer Prize winner; Beverly Harvard, first female police chief of Atlanta; Rev. Dr. Hosea Williams, civil rights leader; Dr. Gloria Campbell D'Hue, president of the Atlanta Medical Association.

ENDOWMENT: $13 million.

ENROLLMENT: 2,400.

CURRICULAR STRENGTHS: Morris Brown has graduated thousands of men and women who are leaders in government, education, business, technical fields, and the professions.

KEY HISTORICAL EVENTS: In 1881 at the North Georgia Annual Conference at Big Bethel AME Church, the Reverend Wesley John Gaines petitioned for the establishment of a school that would educate African American youth.

Four years later Morris Brown, named in honor of the second consecrated bishop of the African Methodist Episcopal Church, began instruction in meager accommodations with nine teachers instructing 107 students.

Morris Brown became the first institution in Georgia developed by African Americans for the education of African Americans. The school initially consisted of training in home economics, nursing education, tailoring, printing, and a few other courses on a primary, secondary, and normal level.

In 1894 the school developed a theological department designed to produce ministers; later that year it expanded to include a college department as well.

In 1913 the college was granted university status and began to establish extension branches; however, because of the school's budgetary instability, the branch institutions were forced to close in 1929. These financial setbacks did not stop the school from carrying out its purpose. After regrouping as a four-year senior college, Morris Brown has successfully expanded its curriculum and its campus.

Morris Brown College has evolved from a cramped wooden structure with just over 100 students and a handful of teachers to a prominent institution of higher learning with over 400 faculty members and 2,400 students. The fourth member of the Atlanta University Center, the private liberal arts college offers students undergraduate training in teaching, research, public service in the arts, humanities, education, professional programs, social sciences, and natural sciences.

Morris Brown College was created with the purpose of providing an education for all African Americans who otherwise might not have had an opportunity to learn.

Morris College:
Sumter, South Carolina

CHARTERED: Founded in 1908.

FOUNDERS: Baptist Educational and Missionary Convention of South Carolina.

MISSION: To provide sound liberal arts and career-based programs with a particular
emphasis on teacher education.

FIRST PRESIDENT/PRINCIPAL: Dr. Edward M. Brawley.

CURRENT PRESIDENT: Dr. Lums C. Richardson.

NOTABLE GRADUATES: Dr. James Solomon, commissioner of the South Carolina Department
of Social Services; the Honorable James D. Weeks, South Carolina House of Representatives; the Reverend Dr. C. Mackey Daniels, former president of the Progressive
National Baptist Convention.

ENDOWMENT: $4.2 million.

ENROLLMENT: 844.

CURRICULAR STRENGTHS: Teacher education and business education.

KEY HISTORICAL EVENTS: Morris College was founded in 1908 by hardworking African Americans without material wealth but with steadfast determination to provide their children
with the tools necessary to succeed. Two years before the school's establishment, in
1906, the Baptist Educational and Missionary Convention in South Carolina authorized
the development of Morris College "for the Christian and intellectual training of Negro
youth." Once the conception of the school was approved, these loyal, God-fearing
Christians began working toward completing their mission of founding an educational
institution for their children.

Morris College originally offered a curriculum that consisted of elementary, high school, and
college-level courses. The college department provided training in teaching and ministry.
Three years after classes began in the spring of 1911, Morris College was formally recognized by the state of South Carolina upon receiving a certificate of incorporation.

In 1915 Morris College was proud to grant bachelor of arts degrees to its first two graduates. Over the next three decades the institution phased out several parts of its initial curriculum, including the elementary school in 1930 and the high school in 1946.

In 1961 Morris College integrated its campus after removing the word "Negro" from its
certificate of incorporation and allowing all ethnic groups to attend the college.

Seventy years after its humble beginning Morris College was granted full accreditation
by the commission on colleges of the Southern Association of Colleges and Schools. Today
Morris College strives to accomplish the goals set by its founders. The school has remained
a private institution from its initial establishment, and it is one of very few colleges that has
been fully operated by African Americans throughout its history.

Morris College prides itself with continuous growth and improvement, which enables the
college to render even better service to its students, and to the community.

Norfolk State University: Norfolk, Virginia

CHARTERED: Founded in 1935.

FOUNDERS: The school began as an extension campus of Virginia Union University.

MISSION: To provide an affordable high-quality education for an ethnically and culturally diverse student population, equipping them with the ability to become productive citizens who continuously contribute to a global and rapidly changing society.

FIRST PRESIDENT/PRINCIPAL: Lyman Beecher Brooks.

CURRENT PRESIDENT: Dr. Marie V. McDemmond.

NOTABLE GRADUATES: Tim Reid, filmmaker and actor; Carl McCall, author; Randall Robinson, TransAfrica founder; Julian Patterson, CEO and founder of Omniplex; Judge Susan Wiggington, first African American female to sit on the U.S. Magistrate Court; Tom Morris, senior corresponding writer for *America's Most Wanted* television series; Derrick Dingle, vice president of *Black Enterprise* magazine.

ENDOWMENT: $4.8 million.

ENROLLMENT: 8,000.

CURRICULAR STRENGTHS: Norfolk State University ranks sixth in granting bachelor's degrees to African Americans.

KEY HISTORICAL EVENTS: Norfolk State University began as a branch of Virginia Union University in 1935; seven years later the school was granted an independent charter, becoming Norfolk Polytechnic College. The school functioned independently for only two years when the Virginia legislature passed an act requiring the school to become a branch of Virginia State College.

Even in an ever-growing climate of protests and boycotts, black students were still able to share some happy times and light moments. Here Norfolk students chat on the Wood Street campus in the 1950s.

Norfolk State baseball team, 1964.

The institution served a large student population, and in 1956 the school granted its first bachelor's degree. As the school continued to expand and attract more students, the Virginia legislature finally granted the school independence in 1969. Ten years later, the school was granted university status, thus becoming Norfolk State University.

Today Norfolk State is one of the largest HBCUs in the nation. The school maintains a student body of about 8,000 and the campus is situated on 123 acres in the Hampton Roads area. Students have the opportunity to earn bachelor's degrees from a wide range of majors, as well as master's degrees and doctrates. Norfolk State University will continue to fulfill its purpose of educating prominent leaders who will have a concern for all humankind.

North Carolina A & T State University:
Greensboro, North Carolina

CHARTERED: Founded in 1891.

FOUNDERS: The general assembly of North Carolina.

MISSION: To fulfill its fundamental purposes through exemplary undergraduate and graduate instruction, scholarly and creative research, and effective public service.

FIRST PRESIDENT/PRINCIPAL: Dr. J. O. Crosby.

CURRENT PRESIDENT: Dr. James Carmichael Renick.

NOTABLE GRADUATES: The late astronaut Dr. Ronald McNair; the Reverend Jesse Jackson Sr., civil rights activist; U.S. Congressman Edolphus Towns (D-N.Y.); Brigadier General Clara Adams-Ender; Elvin Bethea, NFL Hall of Famer.

ENDOWMENT: $10 million.

ENROLLMENT: 7,500.

Jesse Jackson, a graduate of North Carolina A & T, talks to his teammates during his student days.

CURRICULAR STRENGTHS: North Carolina A & T is the number one producer of African American engineers and technologists. In addition, the university is one of the largest producers of certified public accountants among HBCUs.

North Carolina A & T shutterbugs on campus.

KEY HISTORICAL EVENTS: North Carolina Agricultural and Technical State University was established as an extension of Shaw University in 1891. The school originally was entitled A & M College for the Colored Race, and the school immediately began to serve the African American community of North Carolina by providing a much coveted education.

The college provided training that was essential for a land-grant institution and awarded its first bachelor's degrees to the proud class of 1896. The school continued to expand its physical plant and curriculum. In 1915 it was renamed Agricultural and Technical College of North Carolina; the school adopted its present name, North Carolina Agricultural and Technical State University, in 1967. Five years later the school became a member of the North Carolina university system.

Students from North Carolina A & T visit a farm to see the turkey flock.

Today North Carolina A & T State University serves a large, multicultural student body and is committed to providing a quality education for its students so that they may become productive members of society.

North Carolina Central University: Durham, North Carolina

CHARTERED: Founded in 1909.

FOUNDERS: Dr. James E. Shepard.

MISSION: To prepare students academically and professionally and to promote conscious-ness of social responsibility and dedication to the advancement of the general welfare of the people of North Carolina, the United States, and the world.

FIRST PRESIDENT/PRINCIPAL: Dr. James E. Shepard.

CURRENT PRESIDENT: Dr. James H. Ammons.

NOTABLE GRADUATES: Mike Easley, governor of North Carolina; Willie Gary, listed as one of the nation's top 50 attorneys by *Forbes* magazine; Senator Jeanne Lucas, first African American female to serve in the North Carolina General Assembly.

ENDOWMENT: $18.2 million.

ENROLLMENT: 4,100.

CURRICULAR STRENGTHS: NCCU is the nation's first state-supported black liberal arts col-lege and one of only two public institutions in North Carolina offering law degrees. NCCU provides undergraduate research opportunities to graduates through its Biomedical-Biotechnology Research Institute and has received $19.1 million to establish the Biomanufacturing Research Institute and Technology Enterprise (BRITE), which would offer undergraduate and graduate degrees in related fields for the biomanufacturing industry in North Carolina. NCCU is also the only HBCU accredited by American Library Association to offer a master's degree in library and information studies.

KEY HISTORICAL EVENTS: Chartered in 1909 as The National Religious Training School at Chautauqua, North Carolina Central University has flourished for nearly a century. Dr. James E. Shepard founded the university and acted as the school's chief fundraiser for its first forty years. Despite financial challenges, NCCU remained open, but in 1915 the school was forced to regroup and was consequently renamed the National Training School.

In 1923, the North Carolina General Assembly took action and began to provide funding for the institution as well as to play a role in the organization of the curriculum. These vital modifi-cations resulted in several name changes, the most significant being in 1925, when the school was organized as a liberal arts institution and renamed North Carolina College for Negroes.

Nearly two decades after its inception, NCCU experienced a wave of expansion due to the receipt of various grants and contributions by agencies and wealthy individuals, including B. N. Duke of Durham, North Carolina. The institution went on to initiate a grad-uate program in 1939, followed by a law program just one year later. Sadly, in the midst of growth, Dr. Shepard, the school's founder, who played a vital role in the development of this rapidly expanding institution, passed away in the fall of 1947.

In 1969 the school adopted its present name, North Carolina Central University. Today, almost a century after the opening of its doors, NCCU is situated on over 100 acres of land, offering a wide range of courses to students who are eager to learn and carry on the legacy of the many successful North Carolina Central University alumni.

Oakwood College:
Huntsville, Alabama

CHARTERED: Founded in 1896.

FOUNDERS: Ellen White, together with the Seventh-Day Adventists.

MISSION: Oakwood College, a coeducational Seventh-Day Adventist institution, has as its fundamental purpose quality Christian education. Its mission embodies access to educational opportunity, academic excellence, and spiritual development for its students, who come from diverse geographical, cultural, educational, and socioeconomic backgrounds. Its programs and activities are designed to integrate faith and learning, encourage a vibrant spiritual experience, prepare individuals for service to God and humanity, and provide an atmosphere for appreciation for oneself and affirmation of cultural diversity.

FIRST PRESIDENT/PRINCIPAL: James I. Beardsley.

CURRENT PRESIDENT: Dr. Delbert W. Baker.

NOTABLE GRADUATES: Barry C. Black, chaplain of the U.S. Senate; the Reverend Clifton Davis, minister and actor; the Reverend Wintley Phipps, minister and educator; the Honorable John Street, mayor of Philadelphia.

ENDOWMENT: $6 million.

ENROLLMENT: 1,736.

CURRICULAR STRENGTHS: Theology, nursing, education, and music.

KEY HISTORICAL FACTS: Oakwood Industrial School was founded in 1896 when the Seventh-Day Adventists put their faith and efforts into creating an institution to educate African Americans. Classes began in the old mansion of a slave plantation. The school's focus was training students for ministry, education, and nursing.

Ellen White was very involved in the establishment and growth of the institution for its first twenty-one years and she was revered as God's spokesperson, a title earned due to her determination and perseverance and the positive results she always managed to extract. During Oakwood's early existence the general conference provided funds for teachers' salaries only; the school was financially independent and recognized God as the source of its ability to survive. In spite of the school's goals, the students who attended Oakwood typically ended up working in industrial capacities, often on the campus.

In 1904 the school's name changed to Oakwood Manual Training School because of its focus on manual labor. In 1909 Oakwood granted nursing degrees to five students, and in 1912 the first ministry degree was awarded. In 1917, the general conference approved advancement to a postsecondary curriculum and the school was renamed Oakwood Junior College.

After fifty years of progress, there was another issue to be resolved: the lack of African Americans in leadership roles at the school. In 1932, after a student strike the year before, the first black president, James L. Moran, was appointed, as well as several black faculty and staff members. In 1944 Oakwood was upgraded to four-year status and the school's present name was adopted. The first bachelor's degrees were awarded the following year.

Today Oakwood flourishes on a beautiful 1,185-acre campus and offers students a curriculum of over fifty majors.

Paine College: Augusta, Georgia

CHARTERED: Founded in 1882.

FOUNDERS: Members of the Methodist Episcopal Church.

MISSION: To provide a liberal arts education of the highest quality that emphasizes academic excellence, ethical and spiritual values, social responsibility, and personal development; to prepare men and women for positions of leadership and encourage them to serve the African American community, the nation, and the world.

FIRST PRESIDENT/PRINCIPAL: Morgan Callaway.

CURRENT PRESIDENT: Dr. Shirley A. R. Lewis.

NOTABLE GRADUATES: Dr. Mack Gibson, NASA consultant and the first African American Ph.D. in geology; Dr. Shirley McBay, former dean of student affairs at Massachusetts Institute of Technology; Dr. Charles Gomillion, plaintiff in *Gomillion v. Lightfoot*, the Supreme Court case that outlawed gerrymandering in the United States; Dr. Erskie Peters, professor of literature, Notre Dame University; Dr. Charles Larke, first African American superintendent of the Richmond County (Georgia) public school system; Ruth Crawford, executive administrator of the Shiloh Comprehensive Community Center and designer of the Paine College flag.

ENDOWMENT: $10.5 million.

ENROLLMENT: 800.

CURRICULAR STRENGTHS: The Division of Business Administration has been inducted into the Delta Mu Delta Business Honor Society. All of the students who graduate with a degree in education are offered teaching jobs across the state of Georgia. The Division of Biology and Pre-Professional Sciences has received a number of grants and awards in the areas of environmental sciences and student development.

KEY HISTORICAL EVENTS: In 1882 members of the Colored Methodist Episcopal Church established Paine Institute so that recently emancipated slaves could receive an education. The school was designed to train African American men and women in teaching and ministry.

The school included both postsecondary and college departments, and the first bachelor's degrees were awarded in 1885. The school adopted its present name, Paine College, in 1903 to more accurately reflect its course offerings and degree programs.

Paine College is located in Augusta, Georgia, and maintains its affiliation with the Methodist Church. The college will continue to fulfill its mission throughout the twenty-first century.

Paul Quinn College:
Dallas, Texas

CHARTERED: Founded in 1872.

FOUNDERS: A group of "circuit-riding preachers" affiliated with the African Methodist Episcopal Church.

MISSION: To provide a quality education that addresses the academic, social, and Christian development of students.

FIRST PRESIDENT/PRINCIPAL: Bishop J. M. Brown.

CURRENT PRESIDENT: Dwight J. Fennell (interim president).

NOTABLE GRADUATES: Hiawatha Williams, CEO of Williams Chicken; Charmion Polk, founder of the Original Kings Kids of America; Rudy Eastman, founder of Jubilee Arts Theater; Bernard Durant, CEO of Durant Enterprises Consulting Engineers; Harold Stanley, CEO of Total Home Health Care.

ENDOWMENT: $5 million.

ENROLLMENT: 750.

CURRICULAR STRENGTHS: Paul Quinn College has recently begun a marching band and men's and women's golf teams.

KEY HISTORICAL EVENTS: Paul Quinn College is the oldest liberal arts college for African Americans in the state of Texas. Today, it is a school dedicated to imparting to its students a well-rounded education consisting of liberal arts, science, and technology.

The college was founded in Austin, Texas, by a group of African Methodist Episcopal preachers in 1872. Its purpose was to teach a variety of skills, including blacksmithing, carpentry, and tanning, to recently emancipated slaves. In accord with its original name, Waco College, the school was moved to Waco, Texas, in 1881. The college was chartered by the state of Texas in 1882.

Upon its relocation to Waco and subsequent chartering by the state, the school changed its name to Paul Quinn College in 1882 in honor of William Paul Quinn, AME bishop of the western states for thirty years.

The expansion of the African Methodist Episcopal Church throughout the southern states facilitated the college's expansion through increased funding. This enabled the purchase of 2 acres of East Waco's Garrison Plantation, which allowed for expansion beyond the college's original one-building trade school. Eventually, an additional 20 acres were added.

Despite the AME's increased southern presence, there was insufficient funding for the college's further development. This would lead to the "Ten Cents a Brick" campaign in 1881, which prompted the construction of the first new building. Some of the main contributors were poor blacks who desired a better life for themselves and for future generations.

In 1990 Paul Quinn College relocated to its present site in Dallas, Texas—the former location of Bishop College (now closed)—where it maintains its affiliation with the African Methodist Episcopal Church. Paul Quinn will continue the tradition of its founders by educating productive leaders to serve humankind.

Philander Smith College:
Little Rock, Arkansas

CHARTERED: Founded in 1877.

FOUNDERS: The General Conference of the Methodist Episcopal Church.

MISSION: To provide higher education to individuals who are, or have the potential to be, academically talented, regardless of their social, economic, or educational background.

FIRST PRESIDENT/PRINCIPAL: The Reverend Thomas Mason.

CURRENT PRESIDENT: Dr. Trudie Kibbe Reed.

NOTABLE GRADUATES: Dr. M. Jocelyn Elders, former surgeon general of the United States; the Reverend Dr. James H. Cone, author and professor at Union Theological Seminary; Lottie Shackelford, Little Rock's first female and first African American mayor; Elijah Pitts, former NFL player and assistant head coach of the Buffalo Bills; Hubert "Geese" Ausbie, a manager-coach and former player for the Harlem Globetrotters.

ENDOWMENT: $9.5 million.

ENROLLMENT: 1,000.

CURRICULAR STRENGTHS: Ninety percent of its students who apply to medical school are accepted. The school was also the only college in Arkansas to be included in the 2000 publication *The 201 Best Colleges for the Real World*, where it received praise for quality, convenience, and cost.

KEY HISTORICAL EVENTS: Philander Smith College began its mission of educating African Americans in 1877 as the Walden Seminary. The school was developed after the General Conference of the Methodist Episcopal Church initiated an annual conference where African American preachers in Arkansas could promote educational facilities for former slaves. This conference became known as the Little Rock Annual Conference, and in 1877 it chose Walden Seminary as its official educational institution.

During the leadership of the first president, the Reverend Thomas Mason, the school experienced a mixture of growth and instability. In 1882 the wealthy widow of Philander Smith, Mrs. Adeline Smith, donated $10,500 to the seminary, which allowed the school to begin expanding the campus and offering more programs for students. In honor of Mrs. Smith's generosity the trustees of the school renamed the school Philander Smith College. The next year the state of Arkansas chartered the institution as a four-year college. The school awarded its first bachelor's degrees in 1888.

Philander was growing rapidly before the turn of the twentieth century, and the curriculum broadened to include a grammar and preparatory school along with a teacher-training normal department. The college also offered a variety of bachelor's degrees through its well-developed college department. Philander Smith also maintained departments of carpentry and printing, but all that remains of these departments today is the college department.

In 1925 another black college, George R. Smith College, was destroyed by fire. Rather than rebuilding, the school officially merged with Philander Smith College in 1933.

Today Philander Smith maintains its ties with the Methodist Church and receives funds from the General Board of Higher Education and Campus Ministry of the United Methodist Church.

Prairie View A & M University:
Prairie View, Texas

CHARTERED: Founded in 1876.

FOUNDERS: The institution was developed under the Morrill Act of 1890.

MISSION: To provide access to quality college education for the historically underserved and bypassed; to provide excellence in teaching, research, and service.

FIRST PRESIDENT/PRINCIPAL: L. W. Minor.

CURRENT PRESIDENT: Dr. C. A. Hines.

NOTABLE GRADUATES: Lieutenant General J. W. Beckton, an alumnus who also became the fifth president of the university.

ENDOWMENT: $27 million.

ENROLLMENT: 6,200.

CURRICULAR STRENGTHS: One of the nation's top producers of African American engineers.

KEY HISTORICAL EVENTS: The year 1876 is important in Texas history because it not only marks the beginning of the Texas constitution and the "common free school system," it is also the year that the legislature approved the opening of an institution for the purpose of educating African American men and women. Under the provisions of the Morrill Land Grant College Act, $20,000 was allotted to secure a site for a school. In 1878 the Agricultural and Mechanical College of Texas for Colored Youth, presently known as Prairie View A & M University, opened. The school was only the second institution of higher learning in Texas, and when classes began the eight students in attendance became the first African Americans in Texas to attend a state-supported institution.

After the first year of operation the college's enrollment increased with the addition of fifty-two new students; the school taught thirteen subjects on the elementary and secondary levels. The school began developing the campus with new buildings and a broadened curriculum. By 1889 the school was renamed Prairie View State Normal and Industrial College to reflect its extensive growth.

After the turn of the century, Prairie View began offering four-year programs in education, agriculture, home economics, and mechanical arts, giving students the opportunity to earn a bachelor of science degree. In 1918 a nursing program was added, and a year later a four-year senior college program was enacted, which offered liberal arts training, vocational agriculture training, and other divisions as well. The graduate program was developed in 1937 and afforded students the opportunity to earn master's degrees from various disciplines, including school administration and rural sociology. During the term of Prairie View's eighth principal, Dr. E. B. Evans, the board of directors changed the position title to dean in 1947; a year later the title was changed to president.

Fifteen years after gaining accreditation by the Southern Association of Colleges and Schools, the school adopted its present name. The university continues to grow and serve the educational needs of African Americans.

Rust College:
Holly Springs, Mississippi

CHARTERED: Founded in 1866.

FOUNDERS: Freedmen's Aid Society.

MISSION: To educate individuals who are, or have the potential to be, academically talented, regardless of their social, economic, or educational background.

FIRST PRESIDENT/PRINCIPAL: Reverend A. C. McDonald.

CURRENT PRESIDENT: Dr. David L. Beckley.

NOTABLE GRADUATES: Carolyn McKinney, corporate attorney with Amoco Oil; Dr. Anthony Falandy, AIDS project director for the U.S. Department of Health and Human Services; Lonear Heard Davis, cofounder of the Heard Management Corporation; Ida B. Wells Barnett, award-winning journalist and social activist; Hiram Revels, first black U.S. congressman from Mississippi; Eddie L. Smith, first black mayor of Holly Springs, Mississippi.

ENDOWMENT: $11 million.

ENROLLMENT: 900.

CURRICULAR STRENGTHS: Science and mathematics majors comprise 33 percent of the total enrollment; business is the second most popular major, with 26 percent, followed by social science, at 21 percent.

KEY HISTORICAL EVENTS: The Freedmen's Aid Society of the Methodist Episcopal Church was a pioneer in developing educational institutions for African Americans after emancipation. In 1866 the society established Rust College, the first school in Mississippi developed for African Americans.

Originally the school was located in the Asbury Methodist Episcopal Church and was named Shaw School in honor of S. O. Shaw, who made generous contributions to help fund the institution. The school offered basic elementary education to adults as well as children of all ages. A year after classes began, the school relocated to its present site and the curriculum broadened to include high school level classes and later, college courses.

In 1870 the state of Mississippi chartered the school as Shaw University, and in 1878 the first class, consisting of two graduates, received degrees. The school consistently made progress, and in 1892 it was renamed Rust University in honor of Richard S. Rust, secretary of the Freedmen's Aid Society, Ohio branch. In 1915 the name Rust College was adopted to accurately reflect the school's status and course offerings.

As Rust began to adopt more college departments, the school gradually phased out the elementary and secondary programs, which had both been discontinued by the 1950s. Today Rust College is steadily expanding, and the school continues to instill in all of its students the idea that education is made up of teaching, research, and community service. The school continues to train students that adhere to the motto of their first president, the Reverend A. C. McDonald: "By their fruits ye shall know them."

Saint Augustine's College:
Raleigh, North Carolina

CHARTERED: 1867.

FOUNDERS: The clergy of the Episcopal Church.

MISSION: To sustain a learning community in which students can prepare academically, socially, and spiritually for leadership in a complex, diverse, and rapidly changing world.

FIRST PRESIDENT/PRINCIPAL: The Reverend J. Brinton Smith.

CURRENT PRESIDENT: Dr. Diane Boardley-Suber.

NOTABLE GRADUATES: The first African American state auditor of North Carolina, the Honorable Ralph Campbell Jr.; George Williams, internationally acclaimed track-and-field coach; Hannah Diggs Atkins, the first African American woman elected to the Oklahoma House of Representatives; Bessie and Sadie Delany, renowned centenarians who published their best-selling memoirs at the ages of 102 and 104.

ENDOWMENT: $17.2 million.

ENROLLMENT: 1,400.

CURRICULAR STRENGTHS: St. Augustine's was the nation's first HBCU to have its own on-campus commercial radio and television stations. St. Augustine's is also the only institution in the Raleigh-Durham area offering a degree in film production.

KEY HISTORICAL EVENTS: Two years after the signing of the Emancipation Proclamation the Protestant Episcopal Church and the Episcopal Diocese of North Carolina established Saint Augustine's Normal School and Collegiate Institute to educate freed slaves. Originally designed to train African Americans in the rudiments of education, the school expanded to include postsecondary instruction in 1919, after which the name was changed to Saint Augustine's Junior College.

In 1927 "St. Aug," as it is affectionately called, changed its curriculum to a four-year program. A year later the school adopted its present name. The college awarded its first bachelor's degrees to the class of 1931. Saint Augustine's has consistently focused on expansion of its curriculum as well as its campus. The main campus is situated on 55 acres of land with thirty-seven facilities, including its registered historic landmarks—St. Agnes Hall, Taylor Hall, and the chapel.

Saint Augustine's boasts of its 13-to-1 student-faculty ratio, which creates an intimate learning environment where students can receive the individualized attention they need. The college is accredited by the Southern Association of Colleges and Schools to award a wide range of bachelor's degrees in the arts and sciences. Students can choose from majors including communications, exceptional children's education, theater and film production, African American studies, computer science, and premedical sciences. Saint Augustine's College is proud to be recognized as one of the country's most highly respected private HBCUs. The college will continue its emphases on "scholarship, research, and community service."

Saint Paul's College:
Lawrenceville, Virginia

CHARTERED: Founded in 1888.

FOUNDER: Dr. James Solomon Russell.

MISSION: A private, church-related, coeducational institution with a Christian heritage, Saint Paul's has created an environment in which the attributes of integrity, objectivity, resourcefulness, scholarship, and responsible citizenship are emphasized. Its liberal arts, career-oriented, and teacher-education programs prepare graduates for effective participation in various aspects of human endeavor.

FIRST PRESIDENT/PRINCIPAL: James Solomon Russell.

CURRENT PRESIDENT: Dr. John Kenneth Waddell.

NOTABLE GRADUATES: Shirlene W. Baskerville, past eastern regional director of the Inter-Alumni Council of UNCF and the recipient of the National Council of Negro Women Mary McLeod Bethune Award; Erma L. Freeman, first black woman to graduate from Medical College of Virginia School of Dentistry and be appointed to the Virginia Board of Dentistry, and the first woman elected president of the Old Dominion Dental Society; Darrell Green, seven-time all-pro defensive back for the Washington Redskins.

ENDOWMENT: $5 million.

ENROLLMENT: 600.

CURRICULAR STRENGTHS: Business and humanities.

KEY HISTORICAL EVENTS: In 1888 Dr. James Solomon Russell founded Saint Paul's College, formerly known as Saint Paul's Normal and Industrial School. The school has a Christian background and today rests on its original principles and values. Saint Paul's focus was more than just educating the mind but also nourishing the spirit. The school developed an atmosphere where integrity and responsible citizenship are the basic goals for every student to achieve.

The college's curriculum was developed to prepare African Americans to be successful teachers and career-oriented leaders in society. In 1941 the school was authorized to upgrade its curriculum to a four-year program and the name was changed to Saint Paul's Polytechnic Institute. Three years later the college awarded its first bachelor's degree.

Saint Paul's has continued to grow and develop its teaching and liberal arts programs. In 1957 the school adopted its present name. The college is affiliated with the Episcopal Church and as a private institution has intentionally remained small in enrollment. Its 600 students represent a diverse group, with faith being a common strand among the student body. This intimacy has created a close-knit, family-oriented campus.

Saint Paul's College offers students a wide variety of majors, including business, education, humanities, mathematics, natural sciences, and social sciences. The college is nestled on 185 acres of beautiful greenery and is thriving and growing every day.

St. Philip's College:
San Antonio, Texas

CHARTERED: Founded in 1898.

FOUNDER: Bishop James Steptoe Johnston of St. Philip's Episcopal Church, West Texas Diocese.

MISSION: To provide a quality educational environment that stimulates leadership, personal growth, and a lifelong appreciation for learning.

FIRST PRESIDENT/PRINCIPAL: Miss Bowden.

CURRENT PRESIDENT: Dr. Angie S. Runnels.

NOTABLE GRADUATES: Dr. Frank Bryant, San Antonio physician; Dr. Lanier Byrd, vice president for academic affairs; Tommy Atkinson, former county commissioner; Frank Wing, former San Antonio city councilman.

ENDOWMENT: NA.

ENROLLMENT: 8,000.

CURRICULAR STRENGTHS: Tourism, hospitality, and culinary arts; respiratory therapy; radiography technology; and the developmental education program (reading, writing, etc.).

KEY HISTORICAL EVENTS: St. Philip's College was born in 1898 as a result of the pioneering efforts of Bishop James Steptoe Johnston to establish an educational institution for African Americans and Hispanics. When classes convened there were fewer than twenty students cramped into a house, with the primary lesson being sewing. Miss Bowden, a teacher one generation removed from slavery, took the reigns and began to establish a curriculum of variety. The school underwent numerous changes in its early years. The focus shifted from the parochial level to an industrial curriculum, and eventually to junior college status.

Miss Bowden also was instrumental in the school relocating to a new site in 1917. In 1942 the school partnered with San Antonio College and the San Antonio Independent School District. Over four decades later, in 1987, the college expanded by opening up an extension campus. St. Philip's is growing continuously and the school has numerous expansion projects on the horizon.

St. Philip's College offers service to over 8,000 students per semester and pledges to continue its efforts to educate its students and serve its community.

Savannah State University:
Savannah, Georgia

CHARTERED: Founded in 1890 in Athens, Georgia.

FOUNDERS: An act passed by the Georgia General Assembly required the opening of an institution for the purpose of educating African Americans.

MISSION: To graduate students prepared to perform at higher levels of economic productivity, social responsibility, and excellence in their chosen fields of endeavor in a changing global community.

FIRST PRESIDENT/PRINCIPAL: Richard R. Wright.

CURRENT PRESIDENT: Carlton E. Brown.

NOTABLE GRADUATES: Shannon Sharpe, player for Denver Broncos; Brigadier General Walter Gaskin, Naval Corp.

ENDOWMENT: $1.2 million.

ENROLLMENT: 2,000.

CURRICULAR STRENGTHS: Marine sciences, mass communication, social work, and information technology

KEY HISTORICAL EVENTS: In 1890 Savannah State University, originally known as Georgia State Industrial College for Colored Youth, was established under the Morrill Land Grant Act of 1890, which required states to provide educational training for African Americans. The school first opened in Athens, Georgia, but moved to its location in 1891. The first president, Major Richard Wright, dedicated thirty years of service to the institution.

In 1921 the institution opened its doors to women, who were admitted as boarders. Seven years later, during the presidency of Benjamin F. Hubert, the college advanced into a full-time degree-granting institution. In 1932 the school was renamed Georgia State College. The college continued to experience significant growth and embarked upon another name change in 1950, becoming Savannah State College.

In 1979 desegregation mandates caused a merger between the education department at Savannah State and the business department at Armstrong State College, which evolved into a new School of Business at Savannah State College. Almost two decades later the college was granted university status by the board of regents of the university system of Georgia, thus becoming Savannah Sate University in 1996.

Savannah State still strives to set a precedent as Georgia's oldest public historically black college. The university offers twenty-five undergraduate programs and graduate degree programs in business administration, liberal arts, social sciences, and sciences and technology.

The university is proud to be one of the only campuses in the Georgia university system that is connected wirelessly, allowing students Internet access to registration, the library, and financial aid from any location on campus. Savannah State boasts of a "progressive, closely knit, and inspirational learning community where your life will be changed forever."[7]

Selma University:
Selma, Alabama

CHARTERED: Founded in 1878.

FOUNDERS: The school was established with help from the Alabama State Missionary Baptist Convention.

MISSION: To prepare men and women for Christian ministry and Christian living in the modern world based on the example of Jesus Christ.

FIRST PRESIDENT/PRINCIPAL: The Reverend H. Woodsmall.

CURRENT PRESIDENT: Dr. Alvin Cleveland.

NOTABLE GRADUATES: The Reverend Dr. Theodore Jemison, former president of the National Baptist Convention, USA, Inc.; the Reverend Nelson Smith, civil rights leader; the Reverend Fred Shuttlesworth, civil rights leader and founder of the Alabama Christian Movement for Human Rights.

ENDOWMENT: $500,000.

ENROLLMENT: 287.

CURRICULAR STRENGTHS: One of the more popular bachelor's degrees offered at Selma is in Bible and pastoral ministry. Students can choose from a variety of general studies disciplines with concentrations in either biology and physical education, business, or Bible and Christian education.

KEY HISTORICAL EVENTS: Selma University opened its doors in 1878 in order for African American men and women to have a brighter future by gaining a much-sought-after education. The Alabama State Missionary Baptist Convention played an important role in the founding of the school, formerly known as Alabama Baptist Normal and Theological School, which was developed to train African Americans for positions in teaching and ministry.

From the school's humble beginnings, courses were offered in the basic rudiments as well as specialized teacher and ministerial training. In 1908 the school was chartered as Selma University after being granted the authority to award degrees. The curriculum included courses on the elementary and high school level in addition to its college courses.

In the 1950s after extensive development in the college curriculum, Selma discontinued its elementary and high school departments. The school continued to expand not only its course offerings but also its physical plant, which occupies over 30 acres today. Selma University still serves as a leading educational force in the state of Alabama.

Shaw University:
Raleigh, North Carolina

CHARTERED: Founded in 1865.

FOUNDERS: Henry Martin Tupper, with aid from the Baptist Church.

MISSION: Teaching with the commitment to maintain excellence in research and academic programs that foster intellectual enhancement and technological skills. Additionally, the university stresses character development, which includes religious, cultural, social, and ethical values. Ultimately, Shaw University endeavors to graduate students with demonstrated competencies in their chosen fields of study.

FIRST PRESIDENT/PRINCIPAL: Henry Martin Tupper.

CURRENT PRESIDENT: Dr. Clarence G. Newsome.

NOTABLE GRADUATES: Willie Gary, nationally known attorney.

ENDOWMENT: $12.3 million.

ENROLLMENT: 2,700.

CURRICULAR STRENGTHS: After only one year, students in the Shaw University honors program won the National Quiz Bowl championship. The university also offers students certification in nonprofit management through its American Humanics Program. This "degree enhancement and service" program is flexible in its ability to embrace diverse academic disciplines of students and multiple needs of nonprofit communities.

KEY HISTORICAL EVENTS: In 1865 the first historically black university in the South opened its doors and accepted the responsibility and the privilege of educating newly emancipated African Americans: this institution was Shaw University. A New England missionary named Henry Martin Tupper founded the school, with help from Baptist organizations, in order to train African Americans in theology and biblical interpretation.

A year after the school's inception it was named Raleigh Institute; in 1870 the charter was changed to Shaw Collegiate Institute to honor Elijah Shaw's generosity toward the institution. In 1874 Shaw expanded its curriculum to include postsecondary education, and a year later, by an act of the North Carolina general assembly, the school adopted its present name. The university first awarded bachelor's degrees to the worthy class of 1878.

Shaw University is proud to be called "the Mother of African-American colleges in North Carolina."[3] Interestingly, graduates of the university have gone on to found other HBCUs in North Carolina, including North Carolina Central and Fayetteville State University. Additionally, the founder of Livingstone College received his first two years of college-level instruction at Shaw. Another HBCU, North Carolina A & T State University, began as an extension on Shaw's campus. Because of one school's pioneering service and dedication to educating African American leaders, several other institutions of higher learning sharing those goals have come into existence.

Shaw University is proud of its ongoing affiliation with the Baptist Church. The student body is a diverse cultural mix, as the college hosts international students from the Caribbean, Africa, and the Middle East.

Shelton State Community College, C.A. Fredd Campus: Tuscaloosa, Alabama

CHARTERED: Founded in 1952.

FOUNDER: Dr. Chester A. Fredd Sr.

MISSION: To provide the highest-quality service to our primary "customer," the student.

FIRST PRESIDENT/PRINCIPAL: Dr. Chester A. Fredd Sr.

CURRENT PRESIDENT: Rick Rogers.

NOTABLE GRADUATES: Harrison Taylor, Tuscaloosa (Alabama) City Council; Annie Mary Gray, administrative assistant at Stillman College; Eliza Smith, secretary to Title III Programs at Shelton State–Fredd State Campus.

ENDOWMENT: NA

ENROLLMENT: 826.

CURRICULAR STRENGTHS: Auto mechanics, auto body repair, computer education, carpentry and buildings, commercial art and printing.

KEY HISTORICAL EVENTS: Shelton State Community College was established after the merger of several institutions over a number of years in order to create the best possible learning institution for the citizens of Alabama.

In 1952 Shelton State Technical College was established to provide technical training for area students. In the spring of 1963 the Alabama state legislature passed the Alabama Trade School and Junior College Authority Act, which resulted in the development of a state system of public colleges. More than fifteen years after the passage of this legislation, Shelton State merged with Brewer State Junior College to become Shelton State Community College.

Shelton State continued to grow over the next two decades, enhancing its various programs and expanding the campus to include facilities that would create a better learning environment for its growing student population. In 1994 Shelton State Community College completed a merger with Fredd State Technical College, a union that continues to be a successful combination today.

Fredd State Technical College was founded as the Tuscaloosa State Trade School in 1963. The school immediately began to grow and serve a diverse student population. In 1974 the school was granted the authority to award associate's degrees by the Alabama State Board of Education and the name was changed to Tuscaloosa State Technical College. Two years later the name changed to C. A. Fredd State Technical College in honor of the school's first president, and was soon adopted as an HBCU.

Since the merger in 1994 Fredd State Technical College maintains its goals and visions under the name of Shelton State Community College, C. A. Fredd Campus.

Shelton State Community College will continue to develop new programs to prepare its students for careers and further education. The school is a positive force in its community and the entire state of Alabama.

Shorter College:
North Little Rock, Arkansas

CHARTERED: Founded in 1886.

FOUNDERS: African Methodist Episcopal Church.

MISSION: To provide quality higher education, enabling and encouraging student commitment to active lifelong learning, personal spiritual values, responsible citizenship, and community and societal leadership in a global context.

FIRST PRESIDENT/PRINCIPAL: Julius Talbot Bailey.

CURRENT PRESIDENT: Dr. Ed L. Schrader.

NOTABLE GRADUATES: Daisy G. Bates, businesswoman, author, publisher, and civil rights activist; Dr. James Cone, author and distinguished professor at Union Theological Seminary; Corliss Williamson, NBA player; the Honorable Dr. Irma Hunter Brown, state senator.

ENDOWMENT: $175,000.

ENROLLMENT: 200.

CURRICULAR STRENGTHS: Business management, medical assistant certificate program, and education.

KEY HISTORICAL EVENTS: Shorter College was originally established as Bethel University in 1886 through the efforts of the African Methodist Episcopal Church in South Carolina. Its mission was to develop an educational institution for African Americans in the state. The school adopted its present name in 1903.

Shorter experienced success and eventually formed a union with Philander Smith College and Arkansas Baptist College, which provides a college system with greater resources for students. Shorter is centered on Christian principles, which the school strives to instill in every student who enters into its warm learning community. The college offers quality undergraduate liberal arts programs, professional programs and, specialized graduate programs. "The College affirms a commitment to the Christian faith and strives to integrate Christian values within a nurturing community in its whole process of education."[20]

South Carolina State University:
Orangeburg, South Carolina

CHARTERED: Founded in 1896.

FOUNDERS: The South Carolina Legislature enacted legislation for the establishment of South Carolina State College. The college began as a land-grant institution.

MISSION: The university is fully committed to providing lifelong learning opportunities for the citizens of the state and qualified students of varied talents and backgrounds in a caring and nurturing learning environment.

FIRST PRESIDENT/PRINCIPAL: Thomas E. Miller.

CURRENT PRESIDENT: Chief Judge (Retired) Ernest A. Finney Jr.

NOTABLE GRADUATES: The Honorable Ernest A. Finney Jr.; the Honorable Matthew J. Perry Jr.; Congressman James E. Clyburn.

ENDOWMENT: $3.2 million.

ENROLLMENT: 4,693.

CURRICULAR STRENGTHS: South Carolina State has the only nuclear engineering program and the only doctor of education degree in South Carolina. It has the only undergraduate environmental sciences field station and the nation's only master of science degree in transportation. The university developed the model and is the resource center for the National Summer Transportation Institute. South Carolina State also has produced the highest number of minority officers in the country. In 2002–2003 South Carolina State had the highest graduation rate among student athletes in NCAA Division I athletics.

KEY HISTORICAL EVENTS: In 1872 the school, then known as South Carolina Agricultural and Mechanical Institute, was an extension of Claflin College. In 1895 legislation was passed by the South Carolina general assembly that resulted in the school becoming an independent college. A year later, in 1896, the school opened its doors as the Normal Industrial Agricultural and Mechanical College of South Carolina.

South Carolina State University developed an extension program designed to go into communities and provide informative lessons to underprivileged African American families. The school sponsored and trained farm and home demonstration agents who traveled to different rural areas and offered their expertise to farm families. Dedicated to providing teacher education training, South Carolina State University has produced thousands of successful teachers for over 100 years.

After World War II, the state legislature authorized the development of a graduate program and a school of law; around the same time the school's funding received a substantial increase. However, these perks were merely a ploy to ensure that African American students did not attempt to enroll in the graduate or law programs at the University of South Carolina; the legislature was attempting to appease the supporters of "separate but equal" education.

The 1950s and 1960s students from the college were jailed for protesting, but in 1968 the consequences became deadly when three students were murdered and twenty-seven wounded by the state police in what has come to be known as the Orangeburg Massacre.

In spite of tragedy and struggle, South Carolina State University has prospered over the years to become a top producer of African Americans leaders.

Southern University A & M College: Baton Rouge, Louisiana

CHARTERED: Founded in 1880.

FOUNDERS: The school was established as a result of the efforts of African American politicians in the state of Louisiana.

MISSION: To offer a wide range of opportunities that allow students of different abilities to obtain an education that will withstand rigorous scrutiny. Through urban-rural programs, Southern makes available educational, cultural, and developmental resources to enhance the quality of life of its students.

FIRST PRESIDENT/PRINCIPAL: Dr. Joseph S. Clark.

CURRENT PRESIDENT: Dr. Leon Tarver.

NOTABLE GRADUATES: Dr. Delores Spikes, first female college president in the state of Louisiana; Branford Marsalis, jazz musician; Mel Blount, NFL Hall of Famer; Lou Brock, Baseball Hall of Famer; William Jefferson, first African American elected to Congress from the state of Louisiana since Reconstruction; Judge Janice Clark, plantiff responsible for desegregating the Louisiana judiciary.

ENDOWMENT: $5 million.

ENROLLMENT: 9,000.

CURRICULAR STRENGTHS: Law, engineering, nursing, business, social work, and public policy. Southern has several exchange programs throughout Africa and the Caribbean.

KEY HISTORICAL EVENTS: During the 1879 Louisiana State Constitutional Convention, four African American delegates promoted the establishment of educational institutions for blacks in the state. One year later Southern University at Baton Rouge was founded.

The college was first located in New Orleans, and classes began in 1881 with only twelve students enrolled. In 1886 the rapidly growing institution required larger facilities, so the state of Louisiana funded the school's relocation to a new site. In 1890 the curriculum broadened to include an agricultural and mechanical department, and a year later the school was adopted as a land-grant college under the provisions of the second Morrill Act. Southern continued to expand its course offerings, and in 1912 the first class was awarded bachelor's degrees. Two years later the school relocated to its present site in Baton Rouge, known then as Scotlandville, Louisiana.

In the late 1950s the school began to expand and established two branch locations. Southern University at New Orleans was reopened as an extension campus in 1959; five years later the Shreveport branch was created.

Today Southern University A & M at Baton Rouge is situated on 512 acres of beautiful landscape. Students can earn various associate's, bachelor's, master's, and doctoral degrees from a wide variety of majors. Southern University will continue its commitment to excellence and continue to produce dedicated leaders for the future.

Southern University at New Orleans:
New Orleans, Louisiana

CHARTERED: Established as an extension of Southern University and Agricultural and Mechanical College in 1956.

FOUNDERS: The school was founded by an act of the Louisiana State Legislature.

MISSION: To create and maintain an environment conducive to learning and growth, to promote upward mobility of all people by preparing them to enter into new as well as traditional careers, and to equip them to function optimally in the mainstream of the American society.

FIRST PRESIDENT/PRINCIPAL: Dr. Emmett W. Bashful.

CURRENT PRESIDENT: Dr. Press L. Robinson.

NOTABLE GRADUATES: Michael Bruno, owner of the largest black-owned CPA firm in the South; Dr. Elton Lawson, obstetrician and gynecologist.

ENDOWMENT: $2 million.

ENROLLMENT: 4,000.

CURRICULAR STRENGTHS: Southern University at New Orleans (SUNO) has an on-campus DNA laboratory, and a grant from the National Science Foundation for its Program for Excellence in Science, Mathematics, and Computer Technology (PESMACT). Graduates from the School of Social Work are presently employed in countries around the globe, and the program is one of the most racially diverse in the state of Louisiana.

KEY HISTORICAL EVENTS: In the fall of 1956 the Louisiana legislature passed Act 28, which mandated the establishment of an extension branch of Southern University and A & M University. This new division was called Southern University at New Orleans, and classes commenced in 1959 with 158 students. The first graduating class of fifteen students received bachelor's degrees in 1963.

At the time of Southern's inception, segregation was still lawful in several parts of the country, so the student population at the university consisted solely of African Americans. In 1964, Virginia Cox Welch, a white high school teacher, filed a lawsuit against the Louisiana State Board of Education denouncing segregation in Louisiana schools. A federal court ruled in her favor. After this monumental decision, Southern University at New Orleans was open to admission for students of all races.

The school provides numerous programs that have been designed with its land-grant status in mind, and the curriculum continues to grow to provide education of the highest quality. Southern maintains its open admissions policy so that all students, regardless of prior circumstances, have an opportunity to receive higher education. The Southern University at New Orleans offers over 375 courses, and the school pledges to "continue to make a meaningful contribution to the upward mobility of the people of the community which it serves."[15]

Southern University at Shreveport:
Shreveport, Louisiana

CHARTERED: Founded in 1964.

FOUNDERS: An act passed by the Louisiana legislature.

MISSION: To provide excellence in instruction and community service, promote cultural diversity, provide developmental and continuing education, and seek partnerships with business and industry.

FIRST PRESIDENT/PRINCIPAL: Dr. Walter M. Austin.

CURRENT PRESIDENT: Dr. Ray L. Belton.

NOTABLE GRADUATES: Judge Vernon Claville; Nicky Jefferson, Ph.D; Frank Norris, Shreveport city councilman; Judge Michael Walker; Chancellor Dr. Ray Belton.

ENDOWMENT: Currently under development.

ENROLLMENT: 1,700.

CURRICULAR STRENGTHS: Southern University at Shreveport is the only HBCU offering an associate's degree in dental hygiene. The program has been in existence since 1999, and for the past two years 100 percent of graduates have passed the certification exam administered by the American Dental Association. Approximately one-third of Southern University at Shreveport's certificate and associate degree programs are in allied health, making them second in the state of Louisiana for the number of allied health programs. For the past four years, 100 percent of radiologic technology graduates have passed the state registry examination.

KEY HISTORICAL EVENTS: Southern University at Shreveport was established in 1964 as an extension campus of Southern University A & M College after the Louisiana state legislature passed an act mandating the establishment of a two-year commuter college. Although the act was passed in 1964, the school did not begin classes until the fall of 1967. The school began with a curriculum ranging from office administration to humanities.

Throughout the school's early years, new vocational programs were added to serve the demands of potential area students. In the spring of 1978 the board of regents granted the school approval to award associate's degrees in medical laboratory technology. This addition caused Southern to reevaluate its current offerings and focus on paraprofessional and occupational education courses, thus becoming a comprehensive community college.

The school has increased enrollment consistently, and by 2000 the school had reached its peak enrollment of 1,700. Southern University at Shreveport has acquired significant resources that enhance students' educational experience, including allied health labs, a media production studio, a compressed video distance-learning classroom, and an art museum. Southern University at Shreveport has achieved much in a short amount of time. The school continues to grow in order to effectively serve its students and community.

Southwestern Christian College:
Terrell, Texas

CHARTERED: Founded in 1949.

FOUNDERS: The school was founded and sponsored by the Churches of Christ.

MISSION: To offer a holistic educational program that will motivate the student to value and achieve academic excellence within the context of commitment to moral and spiritual values; to assist students in making their transitions from high school to higher education on various levels; to assist students in preparing for varied vocations in life; to prepare future leaders for their distinct communities and the world at large.

FIRST PRESIDENT/PRINCIPAL: E. W. McMillan.

CURRENT PRESIDENT: Dr. Jack Evans.

NOTABLE GRADUATES: Michael Wilburn, founder of a patented treatment of sickle-cell anemia; Veronica Williams, Broadway actress; Silvia Rose Cobb, lyricist and songwriter.

ENDOWMENT: $1.1 million.

ENROLLMENT: 215.

CURRICULAR STRENGTHS: Religious education and training ministers for Church of Christ.

KEY HISTORICAL EVENTS: Southwestern Christian College was established in 1949 as the Southern Bible Institute in Fort Worth, Texas. The school was founded on the basis of Christian doctrine, which still stands as their basic philosophy. When classes first convened in the fall of 1948, forty-five students eagerly embarked on an educational experience that would benefit them for a lifetime.

The board of trustees immediately started to search for property to develop the school's campus, and eventually they purchased land in Terrell, Texas. The site they purchased was the former location of the Texas Military College; this property houses the first building ever erected in the city of Terrell.

Southwestern Christian College is committed to offering more than scholarly training; its primary goal is to train its students in the principles of Christian living.

Spelman College:
Atlanta, Georgia

CHARTERED: 1881.

FOUNDERS: Sophia B. Packard and Harriet E. Giles, with the support of the Woman's American Baptist Home Mission Society.

MISSION: The educational program at the college is designed to give students a comprehensive liberal arts background through study in the fine arts, humanities, social sciences, and natural sciences. The college provides an environment that enables self-confidence, cultural enrichment, and spiritual well-being. Spelman offers an educational experience characterized by excellence. Spelman has been and expects to continue to be a major resource for educating black women leaders.

FIRST PRESIDENT/PRINCIPAL: Sophia Packard.

CURRENT PRESIDENT: Dr. Beverly Daniel Tatum.

NOTABLE GRADUATES: Janet Harmon Bragg, first black female student to enroll at the Aeronautical School of Engineering and one of a group of black aviators who started their own airport in Robbins, Illinois, in the 1930s; Marian Wright Edelman, founder and president of the Children's Defense Fund; Ruth A. Davis, first African American director of the Foreign Service Institute in Washington, D.C.; Marcelite J. Harris, first African American woman general in the history of the U.S. Air Force; Varnette Honeywood, artist and creator of the Little Bill character image for the award-winning children's book series and television show.

ENDOWMENT: $215 million.

ENROLLMENT: 1,900.

CURRICULAR STRENGTHS: In 2004 Spelman was the only HBCU to be listed in *U.S. News & World Report*'s top 100 liberal arts colleges. One-third of Spelman students major in the sciences. The college is also home to the Women's Research and Resource Center, the first of its kind on a black college campus devoted to curriculum in women's studies.

KEY HISTORICAL EVENTS: Spelman College was founded in 1881 after Sophia Packard and Harriet Giles spent two years examining the condition of recently emancipated slaves in the South. The two missionaries were sponsored by the Woman's American Baptist Home Mission Society. After they reported their findings, plans were implemented to develop a facility to teach African Americans how to read and write. In the spring of 1881 classes began in the basement of a Baptist church in Atlanta with a budget of $100. The first eleven students consisted of ex-slaves thirsting for an education.

Packard and Giles poured all their energies into raising funds for the school, and in 1883 they acquired 9 acres for the campus. The school prospered with the help of the black community and the church; even teachers volunteered their time and service. John D. Rockefeller was a major contributor to the school in the 1880s and his generosity resulted in support from other sources as well. In 1884 the Spelman *Messenger* was developed as an outreach to communities as well as a great tool for informing African Americans about issues that otherwise would not have reached them.

In 1888 Sophia Packard's persistence resulted in the school being granted a charter by the state of Georgia, and at the turn of the twentieth century Spelman awarded its first degrees. The school originally offered training for African American women ranging from the elementary to the college level; however, by 1927 the elementary program was discontinued because legislation passed that allowed the development of public educational facilities for black children. In 1930 Spelman was proud to be one of only six African American schools to hold membership in the American Association of Colleges. Two years later the college received an A rating from the Southern Association of Colleges and Schools. In 1946 the presidency was assumed by Dr. Albert E. Manley, the first African American and the first man in the position.

As the decades passed, the school's curriculum advanced and new opportunities for students were constantly being devised. Spelman College has remained focused on its mission to produce positive leaders who truly have a positive impact on society. Today the four-year liberal arts college for African American women is one of the premier colleges in the nation. Spelman will continue to produce graduates and maintain leaders who are "outstanding in many fields and their achievements [will continue to] attest to the quality of the institution."[21]

Stillman College:
Tuscaloosa, Alabama

CHARTERED: Founded in 1876.

FOUNDERS: Presbyterian missionaries, led by the Reverend Dr. Charles Stillman.

MISSION: Stillman College is a liberal arts institution, committed to fostering academic excellence and providing high-quality opportunities for students with diverse levels of academic preparation.

FIRST PRESIDENT/PRINCIPAL: Professor W. F. Osburn.

CURRENT PRESIDENT: Dr. Ernest NcNealey.

NOTABLE GRADUATES: Dr. Harris-Lopez, widely published in the area of African literature.

ENDOWMENT: $22 million.

ENROLLMENT: 1,017.

CURRICULAR STRENGTHS: Premedicine and prelaw programs.

KEY HISTORICAL EVENTS: In 1874 the Reverend Dr. Charles Allen Stillman was compelled to begin petitioning for the development of an educational facility designed to prepare African American men for ministry. Stillman and his followers presented this idea to the general assembly of the Presbyterian Church, and in 1875 the assembly granted Stillman's request, which resulted in the establishment of Stillman College, formerly known as Tuscaloosa Institute. A year later, in 1876, instruction commenced.

In 1895, almost two decades after its inception, Stillman was officially chartered by the state of Alabama. Three years later Dr. Stillman passed away; later that year the school was renamed Stillman Institute in memory of its late founder.

In 1899 the general assembly authorized the admission of women to the school. At the turn of the century Stillman entered a period of curricular expansion that would last for almost fifty years and included the development of a junior high school, a high school, and a fully accredited junior college started in 1937. In 1948, under the leadership of Dr. Samuel Burney Hay, the school was renamed Stillman College; it became a four-year liberal arts institution in 1949. The first bachelor's degrees were awarded to the class of 1951. The Southern Association of Colleges and Schools granted Stillman full accreditation in 1953.

Stillman has always been committed to educating African Americans but up until 1967 only white Americans had presided over the college. That year, Dr. Harold N. Stinson became the third president of the college and the first president of African American descent. Dr. Stinson served the college for thirteen years, and during his tenure the school experienced several additions and renovations to the campus.

Today Dr. Ernest McNealey serves as Stillman's fifth president and has successfully steered the college into the twenty-first century. The administration is committed to ensuring continued growth for Stillman by staying focused on the road ahead and keeping imagination, intuition, and planning on the horizon.

Talladega College:
Talladega, Alabama

CHARTERED: Founded in 1867.

FOUNDERS: William Savery and Thomas Tarrant, with assistance from General Wager
Swayne and the Freedmen's Bureau.

MISSION: Talladega seeks to instill in its graduates the values of morality, intellectual excellence, and hard work. The college seeks to nurture the whole person through close personal relations between faculty and students and by providing experiences that develop
a strong personal value system and sense of responsibility.

FIRST PRESIDENT/PRINCIPAL: The Reverend Henry Brown.

CURRENT PRESIDENT: Dr. Henry Ponder.

NOTABLE GRADUATES: Eunice Johnson, founder and director of the Ebony Fashion Fair and
secretary-treasurer for Johnson Publishing Company; Odessa Woolfolk, president
emerita of the Birmingham Civil Rights Institute.

ENDOWMENT: $5 million.

ENROLLMENT: 642.

CURRICULAR STRENGTHS: Fully 80 percent of Talladega's graduates pursue advanced
degrees. The college boasts a student-faculty ratio of 13 to 1.

KEY HISTORICAL EVENTS: Visionaries William Savery and Thomas Tarrant became acquainted
at a Freedmen's convention in the fall of 1865. The two recently emancipated slaves
made a pact to develop an institution where African American youth could receive a
much-cherished education. From this meeting came the birth of Talladega College.

A one-room schoolhouse was erected with lumber found at an abandoned carpentry shop.
Under the direction of Savery, Tarrant, and General Wager Swayne of the Freedmen's
Bureau, Talladega began classes in 1867.

The school's attendance was so great that larger facilities were needed immediately.
Savery and Tarrant persuaded General Swayne to petition the American Missionary Association for funds to help this needed expansion. The American Missionary Association purchased the Talladega Baptist School, which had been built by slaves for white students but
had come under mortgage default. The AMA invested $23,000; they also purchased the 20
acres surrounding the former Baptist academy. In 1867, when classes convened in the new
building, which was renamed Swayne School, there were 140 students in attendance.

The school was chartered as Talladega College in 1869, and the first postsecondary-
level classes were offered over twenty years later in 1890. Talladega was the only school in
Alabama that conferred college degrees regardless of race throughout the early 1900s, the
first being awarded in 1895.

An edifice originally constructed by slaves for white students, it has now become one of
the finest liberal arts colleges in the country. The converted Baptist church that became the
school's original structure is still in use and has been designated a historic landmark.

Tennessee State University:
Nashville, Tennessee

CHARTERED: Founded in 1912.

FOUNDERS: An act of the Tennessee General Assembly.

MISSION: To promote and nurture students' growth and development as persons who are liberally educated, appreciate cultural diversity, and embody a sense of civic and social responsibility.

FIRST PRESIDENT/PRINCIPAL: W. J. Hale.

CURRENT PRESIDENT: Dr. James A. Hefner.

NOTABLE GRADUATES: Oprah Winfrey, television talk show host, producer, and media mogul; Wilma Rudolph, first woman to win three gold medals in a single Olympiad; General Lloyd "Fig" Newton, first African American to achieve four-star rank in the U.S. Air Force; Dr. Levi Watkins, first to perform heart surgery using an automatic defibrillator; Jesse Russell, developer of the cell phone micro chip.

ENDOWMENT: $1.6 million.

ENROLLMENT: 8,500.

CURRICULAR STRENGTHS: Consistently rated one of the nation's best in *U.S. News and World Report*'s "Guide to America's Best Colleges."

KEY HISTORICAL EVENTS: In 1909 an act of the Tennessee General Assembly authorized the development of a normal school for African Americans. Three years after the passage of this legislation, Tennessee State University, formerly known as the Agricultural and Industrial State Normal School, opened its doors with the purpose of improving the condition of African Americans. A decade after the school's inception, its curriculum was upgraded to a four-year teacher's college. In the summer of 1924 the college awarded its first bachelor's degrees. That same year the school's name changed to the Agricultural and Industrial State Normal College to reflect its new status.

In 1941 the Tennessee General Assembly granted the college the authority to establish a graduate studies program that focused on teacher education. Three years after this expansion, the school awarded its first master's degree. The institution received accreditation by the Southern Association of Colleges and Schools in 1946, and five years later, the State Board of Education granted the school university status. These two events led to several additions to the educational program, including the development of the School of Arts and Sciences and the School of Engineering.

Finally, in 1958, the state board of education awarded Tennessee State full land-grant status, which resulted in the establishment of the School of Agriculture and Home Economics, the Department of Aerospace Studies, and several other programs. In 1979 Tennessee State University experienced another major addition when the University of Tennessee at Nashville joined the university.

The University of Tennessee at Nashville was founded as an extension campus of the University of Tennessee in 1947. In the 1960s this extension center grew from offering one year of credits to three years of credits; however, degrees were only granted from its parent institution, located in Knoxville. In 1971 the university was granted full accreditation by the Southern Association of Colleges and Schools and was sanctioned as a full-fledged campus (versus an extension center) by the general assembly. The building where this new campus was located started a "decade long litigation to 'dismantle the dual system' of higher education in Tennessee." In 1981, a court order was issued and the merger of Tennessee State University and the University of Tennessee at Nashville was completed.

Tennessee State University still serves as a land-grant institution, offering various undergraduate and graduate degrees. The university pledges to "continue to cultivate diversity, honesty, integrity, hard-work, sensitivity and compassion" because those are the characteristics that TSU has long represented.

Texas College:
Tyler, Texas

CHARTERED: Founded in 1894.

FOUNDERS: A group of Colored (now Christian) Methodist Episcopal ministers.

MISSION: To provide educational opportunities, academic services, and career choices for thousands of African American youth from throughout Texas, the nation, and internationally.

FIRST PRESIDENT/PRINCIPAL: The Reverend O. T. Womack.

CURRENT PRESIDENT: Dr. Billy C. Hawkins.

NOTABLE GRADUATES: Dr. Mildred Fay Jefferson, surgeon and professor at Boston University Medical Center, and the first African American woman to graduate from Harvard Medical School; Gladys M. Square, the first woman and the first black mayor pro tem for Tyler, Texas; Billy S. Aaron, wife of baseball Hall of Famer Hank Aaron and retired vice president of the United Negro College Fund; the Honorable James W. Faison III, chief justice of Camden, Texas, municipal court; Sharnia "Tab" Buford, president and CEO of Freedom Card, Inc., who designed and implemented a plan to rehabilitate South Africa's only black-owned bank, Africa Bank Limited.

ENDOWMENT: $1.4 million.

ENROLLMENT: 400.

CURRICULAR STRENGTHS: Business administration and organizational management.

KEY HISTORICAL EVENTS: At the end of the nineteenth century a determined group of Colored Methodist Episcopal ministers felt driven to provide an educational institution for African Americans, and their efforts were rewarded in 1894, when Texas College was established. Texas College experienced struggles but managed to stay open in spite of a shortage of resources.

In the 1940s the school developed a junior college department that flourished for twenty years. Today Texas College provides thirteen bachelor's degree programs that include art, computer science, English, history, and social work. The school has maintained its affiliation with the Christian Methodist Episcopal Church, and all prospective students are invited to become part of the "Texas College family."

Texas Southern University:
Houston, Texas

CHARTERED: Founded in 1947.

FOUNDERS: An act of the Texas legislature.

MISSION: To establish a creditable college for African American students as a special-purpose institution with a distinct mission to the urban community.

FIRST PRESIDENT/PRINCIPAL: J. T. Fox.

CURRENT PRESIDENT: Dr. Priscilla D. Slade.

NOTABLE GRADUATES: Barbara Jordan and George Leland, members of the U.S. Congress; Yolanda Adams, gospel recording artist; Kirk Whalum, jazz artist.

ENDOWMENT: $14 million.

ENROLLMENT: 10,000.

CURRICULAR STRENGTHS: The College of Pharmacy and Health Sciences at Texas Southern University is a leading producer of African American pharmacists and other minority health professionals.

KEY HISTORICAL EVENTS: Texas Southern University, founded in 1947 as Texas State University for Negroes, has a history dating back to the 1930s. The Houston College for Negroes was an institution that provided an education for African Americans beginning in 1935. The Houston Independent School District owned this college, but the Texas legislature purchased the campus for $2 million. From this investment came the establishment of Texas Southern University in 1947. In that same year, after a court battle fueled by the bitter segregation laws of the times, Texas Southern also began a state-supported law school. Three years later Texas Southern granted its first doctor of jurisprudence degree. In 1951 the school adopted its present designation, Texas Southern University. Twenty-five years later the university law school was named the Thurgood Marshall School of Law.

Texas Southern University has developed into a prominent institution of higher learning, and in 1973 the Texas legislature recognized the school as a "special-purpose institution for urban programming." This title was awarded because of the university's metropolitan location, its performance in academics, and its inventive programs.

The university has many notable alumni, with local, regional, and national achievements in a wide range of professions, from politics to medicine. The university also houses a national resource center where major issues affecting society are researched, including various urban problems.

Despite its high standards, Texas Southern University maintains an open admissions policy for its undergraduate programs so that no student will be left behind because of circumstances or past mistakes. The beautiful 145-acre campus is expanding through new construction and constant curriculum development. The school boasts of its global student body and it is dedicated to "excellence in achievement."

Tougaloo College: Tougaloo, Mississippi

CHARTERED: Founded in 1869.

FOUNDERS: The American Missionary Association of New York.

MISSION: To ensure students become self-directed learners and self-reliant persons capable of dealing effectively with people, challenges, and issues both now and in the future.

FIRST PRESIDENT/PRINCIPAL: The Reverend Ebenezer Tucker.

CURRENT PRESIDENT: Edgar E. Smith, Ph.D.

NOTABLE GRADUATES: Rueben Anderson, the first black man to serve as a judge in the state of Mississippi and the first black man to graduate from the University of Mississippi School of Law; Alyce G. Clarke, the first black female legislator in the state of Mississippi; Robert G. Clark, the first black man to serve as legislator in the state of Mississippi.

ENDOWMENT: $12 million.

ENROLLMENT: 900.

CURRICULAR STRENGTHS: Thirty-eight percent of all African American physicians and 23 percent of all African American dentists in the state of Mississippi are Tougaloo graduates.

KEY HISTORICAL EVENTS: Tougaloo was established in 1869 after the New York chapter of the American Missionary Society bought 500 acres of land to develop an educational institution to train African American youth. Two years after the school began, the Mississippi state legislature formally recognized the institution and chartered it as Tougaloo University.

The university's teacher education program functioned as a normal department until 1882, when the state withdrew its funding. Five years later Tougaloo expanded its curriculum to include a college department; in 1901 the school awarded its first bachelor's degree. The school was renamed Tougaloo College in 1916.

During Tougaloo's early stages of development another group with Christian ideals, the Home Missionary Society of the Disciples of Christ, was in the process of establishing an educational institution in Edwards, Mississippi. In 1875 the Mississippi state legislature granted this group of missionaries a charter, and the Southern Christian Institute was founded.

Both institutions experienced significant growth through the 1950s, and because the schools had a common foundation and common goals, a merger of the two was proposed. In 1954 the schools combined to become Tougaloo Southern Christian College. Eight years after the union of these two historic institutions, their board of trustees renamed the institution Tougaloo College.

During the presidency of George A. Owens, the first African American to hold that title, Tougaloo experienced several additions, including several faculty changes that upgraded the quality of students' learning experiences. Several new programs were added to broaden the curriculum. The school continuously seeks advancement in all areas in order to provide students with the best possible education and training. Tougaloo College is proud of the acclaim it has received in several publications, including *U.S. News and World Report*, *Money* magazine, and the *Chronicle of Higher Learning*.

Trenholm State Technical College:
Montgomery, Alabama

CHARTERED: Founded in 1966.

FOUNDERS: Alabama Legislature.

MISSION: To provide accessible educational opportunities for career preparation, advancement, and lifelong learning; to promote economic growth, and to enhance the quality of life for people in central Alabama.

FIRST PRESIDENT/PRINCIPAL: Lucious W. Smiley.

CURRENT PRESIDENT: Dr. Anthony L. Molina.

NOTABLE GRADUATES: Gregory Calhoun, president of Calhoun Enterprises; Alfred Lawson, owner of Lawson Construction; Ann Flowers, broker at Alpha Realty.

ENDOWMENT: Trenholm State has recently created a foundation to fund an endowment.

ENROLLMENT: 1,200.

CURRICULAR STRENGTHS: The dental lab technology program at Trenholm is the only one of its kind to offer evening classes. The culinary arts programs at Trenholm has a 96 percent placement rate. The machine tool technology program has a placement rate of over 70 percent.

KEY HISTORICAL EVENTS: In 1963 the Alabama Legislature authorized the development of multiple public postsecondary occupational institutions in Alabama. Two years after the passing of this legislation, construction of H. Councill Trenholm State Technical College began. The college was named in honor of former Alabama State University president Dr. Harper Councill Trenholm. The facilities were completed a year later, and classes convened in 1966 with an enrollment of 275 students.

The technical college grew rapidly and several additions were made, including the Allied Health Occupations Building and the Joseph Dickerson Culinary Arts and Conference Center. The curriculum also broadened to offer students thirteen different programs from which to choose. In the spring of 2000 the technical college underwent a promising merger with Patterson State Technical College.

Patterson State Technical College came into being under a provision of the Alabama State Legislature Trade School Act 673 of 1947. Classes at Patterson State began in 1962 with an enrollment of 162 students under the direction of J. O. McCullough, who served the school for over a decade. The school was named after John M. Patterson, Alabama's acting governor during the school's inception. Patterson State expanded to include more than twenty academic programs. By 1974 the state board of education had accredited the school to award associate's degrees in applied technology and other programs.

Since the merger of H. Councill Trenholm State Technical College and John M. Patterson Technical School, the two campuses have continued to provide over thirty technical certificate and degree programs, adult learning opportunities, and civic, social, cultural, and personal development opportunities. The school operates under an open admissions program in order to provide educational opportunities for all students who want to succeed in gaining the skills necessary to become productive members of society.

Tuskegee University:
Tuskegee, Alabama

CHARTERED: Founded in 1881.

FOUNDERS: Lewis Adams, George W. Campbell, and Dr. Booker T. Washington.

MISSION: To educate the whole student, developing in them a lifelong process in education, superior scientific and technical skills for new knowledge, and continuous growth.

FIRST PRESIDENT/PRINCIPAL: Dr. Booker T. Washington.

CURRENT PRESIDENT: Dr. Benjamin Franklin Payton.

NOTABLE GRADUATES: George Washington Carver; the first African American four-star general, Daniel "Chappie" James; Lionel Richie; nationally syndicated radio show host and staunch HBCU supporter Tom Joyner.

ENDOWMENT: $60 million.

ENROLLMENT: 3,598.

CURRICULAR STRENGTHS: The university produces the greatest number of African Americans with bachelor's degrees in math, science, and engineering in the state of Alabama.

KEY HISTORICAL EVENTS: Former slaves Lewis Adams and George W. Campbell promoted the initiation of legislation that appropriated $2,000 annually for the purpose of educating African American youth in Alabama. With the passing of this legislation, the founders sought an individual who could train the youth; they contacted Hampton Institute, which had been successfully educating African Americans since 1868. Hampton's General Samuel Chapman Armstrong recommended 26-year-old Booker T. Washington, who became the first principal of the Normal School for Colored Teachers, now Tuskegee University.

Renowned botanist, agricultural chemist, and educator, George Washington Carver.

The first classes were held in Butler Chapel, an African Methodist Episcopal church with meager facilities. Dr. Washington soon acquired 100 acres of land for the campus facilities. Washington was the driving force of the institution, and under his leadership Tuskegee experienced extreme growth, becoming one of the most prominent institutions for higher learning in the nation. Dr. Washington served the school faithfully until his death in 1915.

In 1923, during the presidency of Dr. Robert R. Moton, the school established a Veterans Administration hospital, which set a precedent as the first VA hospital fully staffed by African Americans. In 1935 Dr. Frederick Patterson succeeded Dr. Moton. During his tenure, the legendary Tuskegee airman flight-training program was developed at the institution. The black squadrons earned honors and valor during World War II and remain highly revered.

Tuskegee has broadened its curriculum to include a National Center for Bioethic Research and Health Care, business, informational sciences, and several other disciplines. Tuskegee was granted university status in 1985 and remains committed to producing African American leaders to influence future generations.

University of Arkansas at Pine Bluff:
Pine Bluff, Arkansas

CHARTERED: Founded in 1873.

FOUNDERS: Arkansas State Legislature.

MISSION: To assist the United States in building a new social organism that will accommodate racial, ethnic, and cultural pluralism in a manner that will enhance the quality of lives and patterns of living and weld the nation into one people.

FIRST PRESIDENT/PRINCIPAL: Professor J. C. Corbin.

CURRENT PRESIDENT: Dr. Lawrence A. Davis.

NOTABLE GRADUATES: Dr. Samuel Kountz, world-renowned pioneer of kidney transplant technology; Harding B. Young, the first African American to earn a doctorate from and hold faculty rank at the Harvard Business School.

ENDOWMENT: $3.4 million.

ENROLLMENT: 3,000.

CURRICULAR STRENGTHS: The university offers premier programs in aquaculture and regulatory science. It provides technical and outreach services related to minority business development, agriculture, human sciences, and education.

KEY HISTORICAL EVENTS: In 1873 the Arkansas legislature passed an act that called for the establishment of an educational institution for the well-being of the "poorer classes." That institution became the University of Arkansas at Pine Bluff. The school opened its doors in the fall of 1875 as the Branch Normal College for Colored People. The school began in a small rented building with Professor J. C. Corbin instructing eleven students. In 1882 the two-story brick building that would house the school was constructed with the use of state funds.

In 1881 the school awarded its first bachelor's degrees; three years later the school reorganized to junior college status and operated on the two-year level until 1929. In 1927 the school experienced a boost in funds when the Arkansas State Legislature allotted $270,000 for the construction of a new campus. In addition, the Arkansas General Education Board contributed $183,000, and another $33,000 from the Rosenwald Fund was attributed to this expansion project. Two years after these plans were enacted, the university reverted to a four-year college and the school experienced a period of extreme growth. That same year, 1929, the school was renamed Arkansas Agricultural, Mechanical and Normal College.

In the summer of 1972, after extensive renovation and development of the college's curriculum and campus facilities, the school was adopted into the University of Arkansas system and renamed the University of Arkansas at Pine Bluff.

The university is committed to maintaining quality programs in the agricultural sciences because of its land-grant status. The school is fully accredited by the North Central Association of Colleges and Schools, and students can receive undergraduate and graduate degrees from a wide range of disciplines. The University of Arkansas at Pine Bluff has grown to a 220-acre campus serving a diverse student body.

University of the District of Columbia: Washington, D.C.

CHARTERED: Founded in 1974 after a merger between District of Columbia Teachers College, Federal City College, and Washington Technical Institute.

FOUNDERS: The school was founded with the D.C. City Council under Law 1-36.

MISSION: To provide programs that will prepare students for immediate entry into the workforce, for the next level of education, for specialized employment opportunities, and for lifelong learning.

FIRST PRESIDENT/PRINCIPAL: Lisle Carleton Carter Jr.

CURRENT PRESIDENT: Dr. William Lawrence Pollard.

NOTABLE GRADUATES: Dr. Denis G. Antoine, U.S. ambassador to Grenada; Clarence Holbert, artist (his design for the currency of Eritrea was part of the African Voices exhibit at the Smithsonian Institution Museum of American History).

ENDOWMENT: $12.7 million.

ENROLLMENT: 20,000.

CURRICULAR STRENGTHS: According to National Research Council, UDC ranks fifth in producing doctoral recipients in the physical sciences, tenth in professional fields, twelfth in both life and humanities, and sixteenth in the social sciences.

KEY HISTORICAL EVENTS: The University of the District of Columbia (UDC) was chartered as a land-grant institution in 1974, but the school's origins can be traced back to 1955 when the District of Columbia Teachers College was established. The D.C. Teachers College resulted from a merger between the Minor Normal School for black women and the Washington Normal School for white women. Not long after this union, President John F. Kennedy established the Chase Commission in response to the lack of teaching and liberal arts schools in the capital city. This commission began to fulfill its mission, and in 1966 two new institutions emerged—Federal City College and the Washington Technical Institute. That same year both institutions received land-grant status.

In 1974 the three institutions—District of Columbia Teachers College, Federal City College, and Washington Technical Institute—merged to form the only public university in the nation's capital city, the University of the District of Columbia. UDC fulfills its mission as a land-grant institution through teaching, research, and public service, which is used to "solve urban community problems and to improve the overall quality of urban living in the District of Columbia."

The university offers an open admissions policy and its three campuses serve a multicultural student body. Students can choose majors ranging from the physical sciences and engineering to public management and ecology. The University of the District of Columbia will continue to develop programs that benefit not just its students but communities throughout our nation's capital.

University of Maryland Eastern Shore:
Princess Anne, Maryland

CHARTERED: Founded in 1886.

FOUNDERS: The Methodist Episcopal Church, Delaware Conference.

MISSION: To provide quality education to persons who demonstrate the potential to become quality students, especially among minority communities, while fostering multicultural diversity.

FIRST PRESIDENT/PRINCIPAL: Benjamin O. Bird, chief administrator of the Delaware Conference Academy.

CURRENT PRESIDENT: Dr. Thelma B. Thompson.

NOTABLE GRADUATES: Art Shell, first African American NFL head coach; C. Payne Lucas, first president of Africare; Starletta DuPois, actress; Dr. Earl Richardson, president of Morgan State University; Jesse T. Williams, former vice president of human resources for the Goodyear Tire and Rubber Company.

ENDOWMENT: $7.8 million.

ENROLLMENT: 3,300.

CURRICULAR STRENGTHS: The university prides itself on its strengths in agriculture and marine, and environmental science training.

KEY HISTORICAL EVENTS: After successfully founding the Centenary Biblical Institute (presently known as Morgan State University) almost twenty years earlier, the Methodist Episcopal Church expanded its mission with the development of another institution. In the fall of 1886 the Delaware Conference of the Methodist Episcopal Church established an educational institution for African Americans that was initially named the Delaware Conference Academy and thrives today as the University of Maryland Eastern Shore. The school began instruction with one teacher training nine students, but by the end of the first year enrollment had quadrupled to thirty-seven pupils. In 1890, the Morrill Act dictated that southern states with separate schools for African Americans had to provide training in the fields of agriculture and technology, so the school became a land-grant institution.

In 1919 the state of Maryland took over control of the school and changed its name to the Eastern Shore Branch of the Maryland Agricultural College. Finally, in 1948, this branch was officially adopted as a division of University of Maryland and renamed Maryland State College. In 1970 the school assumed its present name.

Throughout numerous changes in the school's administrative control, one constant has been the level of academic excellence. UMES has grown and broadened its curriculum to include over twenty-five disciplines in the arts and sciences and professional and agricultural sciences. The university also offers a wide variety of teaching degree and preprofessional programs. The University of Maryland Eastern Shore "aspires to become an educational model of a teaching/research institution that nurtures and launches leaders."

University of the Virgin Islands:
St. Thomas, U.S. Virgin Islands

CHARTERED: Founded in 1962.

FOUNDER: Governor Ralph Paiewonsky.

MISSION: The university is committed to advancing knowledge through research and public service, particularly in areas that contribute to understanding and resolving issues and problems unique to the Virgin Islands and the Caribbean.

FIRST PRESIDENT/PRINCIPAL: Lawrence C. Wanlass.

CURRENT PRESIDENT: Dr. Laverne E. Ragster.

NOTABLE GRADUATES: Richard Skerritt, the first Rhodes scholar from an HBCU; Vance Amory, the premier of the island nation of Nevis.

ENDOWMENT: $24.3 million.

ENROLLMENT: 3,000.

CURRICULAR STRENGTHS: Biomedical science, mathematics, and tropical marine science.

KEY HISTORICAL EVENTS: The University of the Virgin Islands was established in 1962 to fulfill the educational needs of citizens of the Virgin Islands and surrounding areas in the Caribbean. In 1972 the institution was awarded land-grant status, which it maintains today. The school was chartered as the College of the Virgin Islands but was granted university status in 1980 and given its present name.

The university offers students the opportunity to study various programs and provides numerous research and instructional activities to maintain its land-grant status. Although the University of the Virgin Islands is a "new" historically black institution, it is dedicated to serving its community and outlying areas for decades to come.

Virginia State University:
Petersburg, Virginia

CHARTERED: Founded in 1882.

FOUNDERS: The Virginia General Assembly.

MISSION: Virginia State University is dedicated to the promotion of knowledgeable, percep-
tive, and humane citizens—secure in their self-awareness, equipped for personal fulfill-
ment, sensitive to the needs and aspirations of others, and committed to assuming
productive roles in a challenging and ever-changing global society.

FIRST PRESIDENT/PRINCIPAL: John Mercer Langston.

CURRENT PRESIDENT: Dr. Eddie N. Moore Jr.

NOTABLE GRADUATES: Vernard W. Henley, retired chairman of the board and
CEO of Consolidated Bank and Trust Company, the nation's oldest African
American bank; Dr. Rovenia Brock ("Dr. Ro"), one of the best known nutri-
tionists in the country; the Honorable James Coleman, first African American
to serve on the New Jersey Supreme Court; Hulon L. Willis, the first African
American graduate from the College of William and Mary.

ENDOWMENT: $11 million.

ENROLLMENT: 3,568.

CURRICULAR STRENGTHS: Virginia State's ROTC program has produced eight
generals. The most popular majors at the university are business management, health, physical education and recreation, mass communications, information systems and decision science, and psychology.

KEY HISTORICAL EVENTS: In 1882 the Virginia legislature authorized the initiation of an educational institution designed to train African Americans. Delegate Alfred W. Harris, an African American attorney, was the primary
supporter of the act. A bitter
lawsuit caused a nineteen-month delay
in the start of classes, but by the fall of
1883 the Virginia Normal and Collegiate Institute had opened its doors
with seven faculty members and 126
students. The school's first president,
John Mercer Langston, was a prominent African American leader. Until
1992 Langston had been the first and
only African American elected to the
U.S. Congress from the state of Virginia.

Alfred W. Harris, founder of
Virginia State University,
established in 1882.

The 1953 Virginia State wrestling champions.

Initially, the institution was located in one building that was situated on 33 acres of land, which
included a 200-book library. Six years after the school opened, the first bachelor's degrees
were awarded to the class of 1889. Not long after the turn of the century, the legislature
called for reorganization of the curriculum, which involved retracting the college program and

changing the school's title to the Virginia Normal and Industrial Institute. The school also gained land-grant status after the program was transferred from Hampton Institute in 1920.

The college continued to broaden its curriculum, and in 1923 the college program was reenacted; in 1930 the school was renamed Virginia State College for Negroes. In 1944 Virginia State expanded its service area by opening a two-year extension program in Norfolk, Virginia. This new branch was operating so well that it was upgraded to a four-year program in 1956. In 1969 this flourishing extension departed from the nest of its parent institution to become what is known today as Norfolk State University.

Almost a century after its inception, the Virginia legislature granted Virginia State university status. In 1979 the Virginia State University name was adopted. Virginia State is proud to set a standard as the first state-supported, four-year HBCU in Virginia. The university offers students a variety of undergraduate and graduate degree programs. VSU is one of only two land-grant institutions in the state and is dedicated to using all of its resources to promote the advancement of its students.

Virginia Union University:
Richmond, Virginia

CHARTERED: Founded in 1865.

FOUNDERS: Dr. Nathaniel Colver, Dr. Charles H. Corey, and Dr. Malcolm MacVicar.

MISSION: Virginia Union University seeks to maximize the potential of individuals from varied academic backgrounds within the context of a challenging and nurturing academic environment, offering students the opportunity to excel as scholars and leaders.

FIRST PRESIDENT/PRINCIPAL: Dr. George Mellen Prentiss King.

CURRENT PRESIDENT: Dr. Bernard Wayne Franklin.

NOTABLE GRADUATES: The Honorable Leonidas B. Young II, mayor of Richmond; L. Douglas Wilder, former governor of Virginia; Jean L. Harris, the first African American graduate of the Medical College of Virginia, the first woman to serve in the Virginia governor's cabinet, and the first woman mayor of Eden Prairie, Minnesota; Randall Robinson, founder of TransAfrica; Charles Oakley, NBA player and Olympic gold medalist.

ENDOWMENT: $12.5 million.

ENROLLMENT: 1,500.

CURRICULAR STRENGTHS: Virginia Union is the only HBCU that houses a police training facility on its campus.

KEY HISTORICAL EVENTS: After slaves were granted their freedom in 1865, the National Theological Institute branches in Washington, D.C., and Richmond, Virginia, separated to form independent institutions. These branches would eventually reunite to form Virginia Union University. The Washington branch became Wayland Seminary and was successfully guided by Dr. George Mellen Prentiss King for thirty years.

Meanwhile, in Richmond, determined educator Dr. J. G. Binney, started training African Americans during the evening hours; his efforts were eventually taken over by abolitionist Dr. Nathaniel Colver. The school originally held classes at rented facilities on the former site of Lumpkin's Jail. Under the leadership of Dr. Colver, along with the support of the community and the Baptist Church, the school changed locations in 1870.

Dr. Colver also developed the school's curriculum to include grammar, arithmetic, spelling, reading, and Bible study for the newly freed African Americans attending the institution. Because of Dr. Colver's great strides and commitment to the success of the educational facility, the American Baptist Home Mission Society named the school Colver Insititute in 1869.

In 1876, after much progress, the Virginia General Assembly chartered the school as Richmond Institute. The curriculum was broadened to include elementary and precollege courses, as well as a theological department. The first degree was conferred in 1879.

In 1883 another school was developed in Richmond for the education of African American women; Dr. Lyman Beecher Tefft became the institution's first president. Classes began in a church basement but the institute soon moved to its own facilities. The development of this school changed the student population at Richmond Institute; when women students ceased to attend, Richmond Institute became the Richmond Theological Seminary, focusing on training African American men for ministry.

In 1899 the historical merger between Wayland Seminary and Richmond Theological Institute was confirmed, and a ceremony was held on the school's present site. Later that year the new institution was renamed Virginia Union University. The university was advancing rapidly; soon the school developed a law school and a complete education department. VUU also implemented a graduate school of theology.

Today Virginia Union University is a light that represents the struggle of African Americans in this country. The school maintains its affiliation with the Baptist Church and is fully accredited by the Southern Association of Colleges and Schools to award bachelor's degrees in the arts and sciences and the master of divinity degree. Virginia Union is committed to excellence and will continue to produce African American leaders who have a positive, powerful impact on society.

Voorhees College:
Denmark, South Carolina

CHARTERED: Founded in 1897.
FOUNDERS: Elizabeth Evelyn Wright, with the aid of the Protestant Episcopal Church.
MISSION: To produce highly qualified graduates who combine intellect and faith in their preparation for strong professional performance, pursuit of lifelong learning, betterment of society, and an abiding faith in God.

A portrait of Elizabeth Evelyn Wright who, with the assistance of the Protestant Episcopal Church, founded Voorhees College in 1897.

FIRST PRESIDENT/PRINCIPAL: Gabriel Miller.
CURRENT PRESIDENT: Dr. Lee E. Monroe Jr.
NOTABLE GRADUATES: Rita Robinson, M.D.; Deborah Squirewell, IBM corporate executive; Prezell Robinson, former college president and U.S. ambassador; Jerome Gaethers, entrepreneur; Nathaniel Robinson, M.D.
ENDOWMENT: $6 million.
ENROLLMENT: 700.
CURRICULAR STRENGTHS: Biology and organizational management.
KEY HISTORICAL EVENTS: Voorhees College dates back to 1897 when Denmark Industrial School began classes with one teacher offering instruction to fourteen students. A pioneer in the education of African Americans in this country, Elizabeth Evelyn Wright founded the school with endless dedication to its success. The school's initial curriculum consisted of vocational instruction, so in 1902 the school was renamed Voorhees Industrial College. Like so many educational institutions of that time, Voorhees began to experience financial difficulties and struggled to raise funds in order to continue serving students. Borrowing an idea from Fisk University, the school developed a singing group in the 1920s that could perform to raise funds.

After the curriculum expanded in 1929 to include postsecondary education the name was changed to Voorhees Normal and Industrial School. The school continuously developed ideas to expand its curriculum and the physical plant. In 1947 the school added junior college courses and adopted the name Voorhees School and Junior College.

In 1962 Voorhees gained four-year accreditation and the name changed once more, to its present designation. Today the liberal arts college offers students the opportunity to choose from eleven majors within five different programs. Voorhees is still striving to be the best institution possible and will continue to produce students who are of great value to society.

West Virginia State College:
Charleston, West Virginia

CHARTERED: 1891.

FOUNDERS: West Virginia State College was founded under the provisions of the Morrill Act of 1890.

MISSION: To prepare students for future generations to teach strong fundamentals in English, science, math, and the liberal arts.

FIRST PRESIDENT/PRINCIPAL: John J. Hill.

CURRENT PRESIDENT: Dr. Hazo W. Carter Jr.

NOTABLE GRADUATES: Leon H. Sullivan; Vincent E. Reed, retired vice president for communications for the *Washington Post* and former assistant secretary of the U.S. Department of Education; Major General Charles C. Rogers, congressional Medal of Honor recipient; Earl Lloyd, Hall of Famer and the first African American to play in the NBA.

ENDOWMENT: $2.1 million.

ENROLLMENT: 4,700.

CURRICULAR STRENGTHS: West Virginia State College was recently accredited to offer two master's degrees—in media studies and biotechnology. West Virginia State College has also produced fourteen generals, more than any other public four-year college of its size.

KEY HISTORICAL EVENTS: After the second Morrill Act was passed in 1890, the state of West Virginia initiated plans for an institution to educate black youth in order to prevent the loss of federal funding for its institutions. One year later West Virginia Colored Institute was established, offering African Americans vocational and teacher training on the high school level. In 1915 the school broadened its curriculum and initiated college degree programs, and the name was changed to West Virginia Collegiate Institute.

In 1927, the North Central Association granted the school accreditation; two years later the school adopted its present name.

The 1950s began with change hovering over the nation. After the U.S. Supreme Court declared segregation in schools illegal in 1954, enrollment increased and West Virginia State College immediately began to serve a predominantly white student population. Unfortunately, soon after this wave of change the West Virginia Board of Education retracted the school's land-grant status.

After its shift in student demographics, the college began to grow tremendously in size. In the 1970s a community college extension was added to West Virginia State, which continues to successfully educate nontraditional students. In 2001 current college president Dr. Carter was successful in restoring the college's land-grant status. At present, the college is striving to achieve university status.

West Virginia State College is not a typical HBCU in that its student body, faculty, and staff are racially diverse and it does not serve a predominantly black population. The college is still expanding, however, and continues to generate successful results. Called a "laboratory of human relations," West Virginia State upholds that tradition by creating opportunities for women and minorities, as well as handicapped individuals.

Wilberforce University:
Wilberforce, Ohio

CHARTERED: Founded in 1856.

FOUNDERS: Methodist Episcopal Church.

MISSION: The mission of Wilberforce University is the development of the total person. Central to this mission is the preparation of students for leadership in today's complex job market and society at large.

FIRST PRESIDENT/PRINCIPAL: Bishop Daniel A. Payne, the first black college president in the United States.

CURRENT PRESIDENT: The Reverend Dr. Floyd H. Flake.

NOTABLE GRADUATES: William Julius Wilson, Charity Adams Early, the first black woman commissioned as an officer in the Women's Army Corps during World War II.

ENDOWMENT: $9.3 million.

ENROLLMENT: 800.

CURRICULAR STRENGTHS: Mass media communication, business, computer and information services.

KEY HISTORICAL EVENTS: The school was established in 1856 by the Methodist Episcopal Church, which envisioned a school to train African Americans.

Wilberforce originally offered instruction in the education fundamentals as well as teacher training on the elementary level. The school was named after William Wilberforce, a pioneer abolitionist and English statesman. The university was instrumental in the fight for outlawing slavery and played a vital role in assisting blacks seeking freedom as well as those recently emancipated.

Despite the successes at Wilberforce, like many others the school experienced financial difficulty and closed its doors in 1862. Remarkably, the school reopened one year later after being purchased by the African Methodist Episcopal Church and continued to fulfill its mission of providing an education to African Americans. Wilberforce was the first educational institution that was solely owned and operated by African Americans. The school awarded its first bachelor's degrees in 1867.

Wilberforce continued to expand its curriculum, seeking new programs and departments to provide greater opportunities for its students. The school became the first African American institution designated as a center for military training. Eventually, the school opened an extension campus.

Wilberforce University is still serving students today and is viewed by most as a guiding light and inspiration for the black colleges and universities that followed. The university's place in history has been widely recognized. The Ohio General Assembly has adopted Wilberforce as the location for the National Museum of Afro-American History and Culture Center. The university maintains its affiliation with the AME Church and students can earn bachelor's degrees in a wide range of arts and science disciplines.

Wiley College:
Marshall, Texas

CHARTERED: Founded in 1873.

FOUNDERS: Bishop Isaac Wiley and the Freedmen's Aid Society of the Methodist Episcopal Church.

MISSION: The college affirms the ideal of social responsibility and seeks to contribute to the welfare and revitalization of the community in which it is located.

FIRST PRESIDENT/PRINCIPAL: The Reverend F. G. Moore.

CURRENT PRESIDENT: Dr. Haywood Strickland.

NOTABLE GRADUATES: Dwayne Ashley, president of the Thurgood Marshall Scholarship Fund; Dr. Thomas W. Cole Jr., president of Clark Atlanta University; Dr. Johnnie Colemon, president and founder of Christ Universal Temple in Chicago; Warren Scott, president of Avecia Chemicals, one of the largest chemical companies in the state of Delaware; Dr. Julius Scott Jr., former president of Paine College, Albany State University, and Wiley College.

ENDOWMENT: $5.6 million.

ENROLLMENT: 550.

CURRICULAR STRENGTHS: Wiley College was the first school in east Texas to issue laptop computers to its faculty and students.

KEY HISTORICAL EVENTS: In 1873 a godly man of vision was inclined to open an institution for the purpose of educating the newly emancipated slaves. Bishop Isaac Wiley, with the aid of the Methodist Episcopal Church, sought to prepare African Americans for the new life they had acquired through freedom and provide them with teacher training on the elementary and secondary levels.

Since its inception, the school has adopted a variety of disciplines into its curriculum, including English, biology, and computer science. Wiley also developed the Wiley Management Institute Program, a two-fold program designed to help nontraditional students achieve their goals of higher learning and ensure that all who desire an education have both the opportunity and the necessary resources to pursue that goal. The college also boasts of its 12-to-1 student faculty ratio, which enables each student to receive the personalized attention needed to get the most out of the college experience.

Wiley College maintains and cherishes its affiliation with the United Methodist Church. The campus is centered on a 63-acre campus with a beautiful sunken garden and rose arbor that delight the eye.

Wiley is accredited to award bachelor's of arts and science, and offers over twenty majors. Wiley produces able, visionary leaders who value education and are dedicated to raising the standard of living, and aiding the disadvantaged of society. Wiley views education as an important expression of Christian faith, which elevates the spirit of humankind.

Winston-Salem State University:
Winston-Salem, North Carolina

CHARTERED: Founded in 1892.

FOUNDER: Dr. Simon Green Atkins.

MISSION: Winston-Salem State University's primary mission is to offer high-quality educational programs at the baccalaureate level for a diverse student population.

FIRST PRESIDENT/PRINCIPAL: Dr. Simon Green Atkins.

CURRENT PRESIDENT: Dr. Harold L. Martin.

NOTABLE GRADUATES: Selma Burke, world-renowned artist who sculpted the bust of Franklin D. Roosevelt that appears on the U.S. dime; Louis Farrakhan, leader of the Nation of Islam and organizer of the Million Man March; Earl "The Pearl" Monroe, NBA Hall of Famer and one of the "50 Greatest Players in League History"; the Honorable Jim Garner, president of the U.S. Conference of Mayors and mayor of Hempstead, New York; Louise Smith, credited with helping to establish the kindergarten program for the public schools of North Carolina; Joseph Johnson, listed as one of the top African American attorneys by *Black Enterprise* magazine.

ENDOWMENT: $14.5 million.

ENROLLMENT: 2,679.

CURRICULAR STRENGTHS: In May 2003, WSSU received a five-year, $350,000 U.S. Department of Education grant to provide scholarships for students in its undergraduate program in rehabilitation studies.

KEY HISTORICAL EVENTS: In the fall of 1892 twenty-five students sat in a tiny classroom anxious to partake of their teacher's lesson; the school was known as Slater Industrial Academy. Slater Academy's focus was on training African American teachers in elementary education. Three years after its inception the school was recognized by the state of North Carolina, and in 1897 the school was chartered.

Until 1925 Slater offered outstanding instruction on the high school level; that same year the general assembly acknowledged the school's achievements by granting it the authority to confer degrees. The school was appropriately renamed Winston-Salem Teachers College; it was the nation's first historically black college to grant degrees in elementary education.

In 1953 the college expanded its curriculum with the development of a nursing school that was authorized to grant bachelor of science degrees to its successful participants. Four years later, Winston-Salem's charter changed to include secondary education. In 1963 the North Carolina General Assembly approved the new title, Winston-Salem State College.

After seventy-seven years of quality service and training, the North Carolina legislature granted the school university status, and in 1969 the present name was adopted.

After the reorganization of colleges and universities in North Carolina, in 1972 WSSU became one of sixteen members of the University of North Carolina System.

Today, Winston-Salem State University is a vibrant 94-acre campus in a rapidly growing metropolitan area. The university is accredited by the Southern Association of Colleges and Schools and also offers some graduate programs through interinstitutional agreements.

Xavier University of Louisiana:
New Orleans, Louisiana

CHARTERED: Founded in 1915.

FOUNDERS: Katherine Drexel and the Sisters of the Blessed Sacrament.

MISSION: To prepare students to assume roles of leadership and service in society. This preparation takes place in a pluralistic teaching and learning environment that incorporates all relevant educational means, including research and community service.

FIRST PRESIDENT/PRINCIPAL: The Reverend Edward Brunner, S.S.J.

CURRENT PRESIDENT: Dr. Norman C. Francis.

NOTABLE GRADUATES: Bernard Randolph (retired, USAF), four-star general; Alexis Herman, first African American U.S. secretary of labor; Regina Benjamin, first African American woman named to the American Medical Association's board of trustees.

ENDOWMENT: $27 million.

ENROLLMENT: 3,994.

CURRICULAR STRENGTHS: The College of Pharmacy is ranked first in the nation in awarding doctors of pharmacy to African Americans. Since 1927 Xavier has graduated nearly 25 percent of the 6,500 black pharmacists practicing in the United States. Xavier is also first in the nation in placing African American students into medical school.

KEY HISTORICAL EVENTS: Saint Katherine Drexel and the Sisters of the Blessed Sacrament established Xavier as a high school in 1915.

Saint Katherine founded Xavier, along with several educational institutions in this country, with an inheritance from her father, former banker Francis Drexel. Two years after the founding of Xavier, the school developed a teacher education program. In 1925 a liberal arts and sciences college was added to the curriculum. Xavier was experiencing rapid growth and the seeds that the institution had sown were being reaped, producing a successful harvest.

In 1927 the school began a pharmacy program and five years later the graduate school was developed. In 1928 Xavier awarded its first degrees. In 1933 Saint Katherine's investment for campus expansion was completed with the opening of the administration building, now a New Orleans landmark.

In the 1960s desegregation and antidiscrimination laws were on the rise and as a result of these changes Xavier's enrollment underwent a dramatic increase. Over the last two decades, Xavier's undergraduate enrollment has doubled.

Xavier strives to promote a just and humane society and is a wonderful representation of Saint Katherine's goal to establish institutions to educate African Americans and Native Americans. Students may earn undergraduate degrees, various master's degrees, or a doctorate in pharmacy.

The university boasts of being the only "black Catholic" college in this country. Pope John Paul II honored the university in 1987 by selecting Xavier to deliver his address to the presidents of all the nation's Catholic colleges. The Sisters of the Blessed Sacrament still provide services to the campus, and deservedly, Katherine Drexel was canonized a saint in the Roman Catholic Church in 2000.

Defunct HBCUs

There are currently more than 100 historically black colleges and universities in the nation, fulfilling the educational needs of hundreds of thousands of students. They have overcome challenges and struggled to endure. Ten percent of HBCUs were unable to survive. The twenty defunct historically black colleges are

Avery College

Bishop College

Butler Junior College

Daniel Payne College

Durham College

Friendship College

J. P. Campbell College

Kittrell College

Mary Allen Junior College

Mississippi Industrial College

Morristown College

Okolona College

Saints Junior College

Shaw College at Detroit

Storer College

T. J. Harris Junior College

Pitney Woods County Life School

Prentiss Institute Junior College

Highland Park Community College

Natchez Junior College

Since the mid-1800s the toil and determination of numerous men and women resulted in institutions where African Americans can receive a quality education and ultimately enhance their lives and promote their odds of success. Numerous schools were closed and reopened during their early years; however, the dedication of the founders, the church, and the community generated a resolve that nearly always resulted in the maintenance of the institution. Sadly, the above-named institutions were not able to bounce back. For example, Bishop College was established in Tyler, Texas, in 1905 by the East Texas Baptist Association and offered vocational courses, including tailoring and secretarial sciences. Butler managed to survive throughout its early years but the already low enrollment of just over 300 students began to decrease in the 1960s. In the summer of 1972 the college was forced to close.

For most of these institutions, low enrollment and lack of financial support were the contributing factors in their demise. Sadly, these twenty institutions and their unique threads among historically black colleges and universities are almost forgotten. Although these institutions were unable to survive, they hold an important place in history because of their rich roots and visionary founders.

Historically black colleges and universities will continue to serve as beacons of hope for this nation, and the legacy of all these institutions, whether open or closed, will carry on in the hearts and minds of all who have come through their doors.

NOTES

Chapter 1: Shackled Minds

1. James E. Fraser, *Between Church and State: Religion and Public Education in Multi-Cultural Education* (New York: St. Martin's Press), p. 67.
2. Ibid., p. 11.
3. Ibid., p. 79.
4. http://www.cheyney.edu/newsevents/catalog.pdf, 6–7.
5. William G. Shade, William R. Scott eds., *Upon These Shores: Themes on the African American Experience, 1600–Present* (New York: Routledge), p. 123.
6. Fraser, p. 69.
7. Fraser, p. 75.
8. Fraser, p. 69.
9. Raymond Wolters, *The New Negro on Campus: Black College Rebellions of the 1870s* (Princeton, N.J.: Princeton University Press, 1975), p. 278.

Chapter 2: Books Before Freedom

1. "Abraham Lincoln, Sixteenth President 1861–1865." Viewed online at Americancivilwar.com, http://www.americancivilwar.com/north/abe_lincoln.html.
2. Willie Lee Rose, *Rehearsal for Reconstruction: The Port Royal Experiment* (New York: Bobbs-Merrill Company, 1964), 15.
3. Ibid., 12.
4. Ibid., 21.
5. Edward Pierce, *The Negroes of Port Royal* (Report of the Government Agent to Hon. Salmon P. Chase) (Washington, D.C.: U.S. Department of Treasury, 1862), 32.
6. Ibid.
7. Rose, *Rehearsal for Reconstruction*, 43.
8. Ibid., 55.
9. Ibid.
10. Ibid., 161.
11. Henry N. Drewy and Humphrey Doermann, *Stand and Prosper: Private Black Colleges and Their Students* (Princeton: Princeton University Press, 2001), 54.
12. Rose, *Rehearsal for Reconstruction*, 85–86.
13. Ibid., 88.

Chapter 3: Yearning and Learning

1. National Archives, "7th Semi-Annual Freedmen's School Report, January 1, 1869," RG____ file 40A-F10.9, 201
2. National Archives, "[0] Br. Maj. General J.J. Reynolds, Asst. Commissioner for Texas, in his report of the operations of the bureau in that state . . . Oct. 31st 1868," RG____ file 40A-A7.3
3. National Achives, "Report from Freedmen's Bureau Agent J.B. Ramsdill, Louisville, Kentucky, January 16, 1867," RG____ file 40A-F10.3.
4. National Archives, "Report from W. Syphax, Chairman of the Trustees of Colored Schools in Washington, D.C.," RG____ file 40A-F7.6.
5. Booker T. Washington, *Up from Slavery: An Autobiography* (Garden City, N.J.: Doubleday, 1901), 220.
6. Ibid.
7. Washington, *Up from Slavery*, 58.

Chapter 4: Voices of a People

1. W. E. B. DuBois, *The Souls of Black Folk* (Chicago: A. C. McClurg & Co., 1903), pp. 32–33.
2. W. E. B. DuBois, "Returning Soldiers," *Crisis* magazine, May 1919, p. 14.
3. From the papers of Fayette McKensie, box 1 of 11, Letter from B. J. Fernandez, March 14, 1918, Fisk University Archive.
4. Ibid.
5. Raymond Wolters, *The New Negro on Campus*, (Princeton: Princeton University Press, 1975), p. 34.
6. W. E. B. DuBois, "Diuturni Silenti," *Fisk Herald*, vol. 33, no. 1, 1924, p. 2.
7. Ibid. p. 5.
8. Henry Lee Moon, *The Emerging Thought of W. E. B. Du Bois*, (New York: Simon & Schuster, 1972), pp. 131–32.
9. Letter from Carl James Barbous, from the papers of Fayette McKenzie, 1924, Fisk University Archive.
10. Letter from L. D. Collins, June 22, 1924, from the papers of Fayette McKenzie, 1924, Fisk University Archive.
11. Raymond Wolters, *The New Negro on Campus*, p. 37.
12. "Testimony of a Former White Teacher," *Fisk Herald*, vol. 33, no. 2, p. 22.
13. Raymond Wolters, *The New Negro on Campus*, p. 45.

14. Henry Lee Moon, *The Emerging Thought of W. E. B. Du Bois,* (New York: Simon & Schuster, 1972), p. 132.

15. Raymond Wolters, *The New Negro on Campus,* p. 42.

16. Henry Lee Moon, *The Emerging Thought of W. E. B. Du Bois,* (New York: Simon & Schuster, 1972), p. 132.

17. Raymond Wolters, *The New Negro on Campus,* p. 48; also, "50 Police Quell Demonstration of Fisk Students," *Nashville Tennessean,* February 5, 1925.

18. Raymond Wolters, *The New Negro on Campus,* p. 48.

19. Ibid., p. 49.

20. Ibid., p. 49.

21. Ibid., p. 49.

22. "Fisk President's Offer Accepted with Amendment," *Nashville Tennessean,* February 10, 1925, p. 3.

23. Henry Lee Moon, *The Emerging Thought of W. E. B. Du Bois,* (New York: Simon & Schuster, 1972), p. 135.

24. "Memorandum to Alumni Charges," The Alain Locke papers, p. 1, Moorland-Spingarn Library, Howard University.

25. "Letter to Doctor Du Bois," Alain Locke, The Alain Locke papers, 1925, p. 1, Moorland-Spingarn Library, Howard University.

26. W. E. B. DuBois, "The Durkee-Turner Indident," *Crisis* magazine, May 1926, pp. 37–8.

27. "Durkee Reported in Brooklyn, NY, Seeking Call to Bleecker Pulpit," *Afro-American Newspaper,* January 9, 1926.

28. Raymond Wolters, *The New Negro on Campus,* p. 74.

29. "Student Council Makes Much Needed Recommendations," *The Hilltop,* March 29, 1924, p. 6.

30. Ibid.

31. "Howard Faculty Attacks Salary Distribution," *The Washington American,* December 22, 1924, p.1.

32. "Letter to Doctor Du Bois," Alain Locke, The Alain Locke papers, 1925, p.2, Moorland-Spingarn Library, Howard University.

33. "Howard Faculty Defies Students," *The Washington American,* vol. 7, no. 237, May 8, 1925.

34. "Durkee Tells Strikers Police May Be Called," *Washington Times,* May 11, 1925.

35. Ibid.

36. "Queer School Durkee H'ads [*sic*] Enrollment 37, Graduates 41," *Baltimore Afro-American Newspaper,* May 16, 1925.

37. "Howard Faculty Serves Ultimatum on Student Body," *The Daily American Newspaper,* May 13, 1925, p. 1.

38. Raymond Wolters, *The New Negro on Campus,* p. 128.

Chapter 5: The Art of Culture

1. "Journal of the 27th Quadrennial Session of the African Methodist Episcopal Church," May 5, 1924.

2. Charles S. Johnson, *The Negro College Graduate* (Chapel Hill: University of North Carolina, 1938), p. 81.

3. Ibid., p. 221.

4. Interview with Kathleen Redding Adams, p. 16, unbound copy *Black Women's Oral History Project.*

5. Ibid., pp. 169–70.

6. "Historic AKA: Overview." Viewed at Alpha Kappa Alpha Sorority website, http://www.aka1908.com.

7. Ibid., pp. 169–170.

8. "About the Seniors," *The Hilltop,* April 29, 1929, p. 1.

9. Juan Williams, *Thurgood Marshall: American Revolutionary* (New York: Times Books, 1998).

10. Ibid.

11. *The Athenaeum Newsletter,* November 1910, p. 31.

12. W. E. B. DuBois, "The Talented Tenth," in *The Negro Problem,* September 1903, p. 75.

13. Alain Locke, "Enter the New Negro," *Survey Graphics,* March 1925, p. 1.

14. Steve Watson, *The Harlem Renaissance: Hub of African-American Culture* (New York: Pantheon Books, 1996), p. 25.

15. Ralph Blumenthal, "Small University in Battle for Control of Billions in Art," *New York Times,* October 30, 2002. Viewed online at http://www.nytimes.com.

16. "Stylus Society Selects New Members," *The Hilltop,* March 28, 1928, p. 1.

Chapter 6: Season of Threat

1. D.O.W. Holmes, *The Journal of Negro Education,* "The Negro College Faces the Depression," January 1933, vol II, no. 1, p. 21.

2. Ibid., p.22.

3. Ibid.

4. Ibid., p.23.

5. Ibid., p.25.

6. Mordecai Johnson, Mordecai Johnson Papers, biography draft, Howard Law School chapter, p.1, Manuscript Department, Moorland-Spingarn Research Center, Howard University.

7. Ibid., p.2.

8. Ibid.

9. Ibid., p.3.

10. Ibid.

11. Jonathan Scott Holloway, *Confronting the Veil: Abram Harris, Jr., E. Franklin Frasier, and Ralph Bunche, 1919–1941* (Chapel Hill: University of North Carolina Press, 2002), p. 50.

12. John P. Davis, *The Journal of Negro Education,* "A Survey of the Problems of the Negro Under the New Deal," 1935, p. 12.

13. Ibid.

14. Viewed at Morehouse College website, http://www.morehouse.edu.

15. Ibid.

16. Ibid.

17. Ibid.

18. Taylor Branch, *Parting the Waters:* (New York: Touchstone Books, 1988), 62.

19. Coretta Scott King, *My Life with Dr. Martin Luther King, Jr.* (New York: Henry Holt, 1969), 83.

Chapter 7: Manifest Destiny

1. From the Papers of Mordecai Watts Johnson, Moorland Spingarn Special Collection at the Howard University Library.
2. John Hope Franklin, *From Slavery to Freedom* (New York: McGraw-Hill, 1998), 458.
3. William L. Patterson, *The Man Who Cried Genocide* (New York: International Publishers, 1971), 175.
4. NAACP, *Highlights of NAACP History, 1909–1979* (Baltimore: National Association for the Advancement of Colored People, 1980).
5. Joseph Harris, *Pillars in Ethiopian History* (Washington, D.C.: Howard University Press, 1981), 9.
6. Horace M. Bond, Alain Locke Paper, Invitation to Conference on African Affairs letter, by October 27, 1950, Manuscripts Division, Moorland-Spingarn Research Center, Howard University, p. 1.
7. *Journal of Negro Education* 17, no. x (1948).
8. Herb Boyd, ed., *Autobiography of a People: Three Centuries of African American History Told by Those Who Lived It* (New York: Doubleday, 2000), 360.
9. Viewed at the NAACP Legal Defense Fund website, http://www.naacpldf.org/welcome/timeline/1966_info.html
10. Branch, *Parting the Waters,* 131–32.
11. Rosa Parks with Jim Haskins, *Rosa Parks: My Story* (New York: Dial Books, 1992), p. 160.
12. Ibid.

Chapter 8: An Education in Protest

1. Juan Williams, *Eyes on the Prize: America's Civil Rights Years, 1954–1965* (New York: Viking, 1987).
2. Taylor Branch, *Parting The Waters,* New York: Simon & Schuster Inc., 1988.
3. Ibid.
4. Williams, 114.
5. Ibid.
6. Viewed at Shaw University website, http://www.shawuniversity.edu.
7. Barbara Ransby, *Ella Baker and the Black Freedom Movement: A Radical Democratic Vision* (Chapel Hill: University of North Carolina Press, 2003), p. 243.
8. Student Nonviolent Coordinating Committee (SNCC) paper, "Non-Violence Speaks to the Movement," Library of Congress, April 1960, Shaw Conference, p. 1.
9. Cherly Lynn Greenberg, editor, *A Circle of Trust: Remembering SNCC* (Piscataway, N.J.: Rutgers University Press, 1998) p. 40.

10. John Lewis, *Walking with the Wind: A Memoir of the Movement* (New York: Harcourt Brace and Company, 1998), p. 193.
11. Student Nonviolent Coordinating Committee (SNCC) paper, "Non-Violence Speaks to the Movement," Library of Congress, April 1960, Shaw Conference, p. 1.
12. Manning Marable, *Race, Reform and Rebellion* (Jackson: University of Mississippi Press, 1984), p. 112.
13. Aframerican News Service, April 10, 1967.
14. Marable, p. 112.
15. Terry Wallace, ed., *Bloods: An Oral History of the Vietnam War* (New York: Ballantine Books, 1992).
16. Taken from Dr. King's speech at Riverside Church, April 4, 1967, cited in *Brotherman: The Odyssey of Black Men in America,* edited by Herb Boyd and Robert Allen (New York: Ballantine Books, 1995), p. 393.
17. Alton Hornsby, Jr., ed., *Milestones in Twentieth-Century African American History,* (Detroit: Visible Ink Press, 1993), 89.
18. Robert Allen, "Black Awakening in Capitalist America," from *A Guide to Black Power in America: An Historical Analysis* (London: Gollancz, 1970).
19. Ibid., p. 92.
20. Ibid., p. 92.
21. Ibid., p. 92.
22. Marshall Frady, *Jesse: The Life and Pilgrimage of Jesse Jackson* (New York: Random House, 1996), pp. 246–47.
23. (History of the Sanders v. Ellington Case Leading to the Implementation of the Merger Between Tennessee State University and the University of Tennessee Nashville," Christopher L. Crowell, Tennessee State University, Nashville, Tenn., 1996), p. 48
24. Ibid., p. 66.
25. Ibid., p. 61.
26. Sonya Gyjuan Smith, "Stories from the Promised Land: Tennessee State University from Merger to Integration" (UMI Dissertation Services, 1994), p.39.
27. Ibid., p. 39.

Chapter 9: Calming the Storm, Healing the Cut

1. Alton Hornsby, Jr., ed., *Milestones in Twentieth-Century African American History* (Detroit: Visible Ink Press, 1993), p. 125.
2. Hornsby, p. 140.
3. Charles V. Willie and Ronald R. Edmonds, editors, *Black Colleges in America: Challenge, Development, Survival* (New York: Teachers College Press, 1978), p. 142.
4. Ibid., p. 23.
5. Ibid., p. 85.
6. Ibid., p. 12.
7. Ibid., p. 10.
8. Ibid., p. 133.
9. Ibid.
10. Ibid.

11. Ibid.,p. 64.
12. Ibid.,p. ix.
13. Mike Thelwell, *Massachusetts Review* (Autumn 1969), 701–12.
14. Hornsby, p. 288.

Chapter 10: New Day, New Challenges, New Hope
 1. Viewed at Livingstone College website, http://www.livingstone.edu.

2. "A Host of Black College Presidents Are Jumping Ship," *Journal of Blacks in Higher Education.* Viewed online at http://www.jbhe.com/news_views/38_HBCU_presidents.html.
3. Diana Jean Schemo, "Black Colleges Lobby Hard to Lure the Best and Brightest," *New York Times*, March 8, 2001.

BIBLIOGRAPHY

Books

Adams, Myron W. *A History of Atlanta University*. Atlanta: Atlanta University Press, 1930.

African Methodist Episcopal Church. *Journal of the Twenty-seventh Quadrennial Session General Conference*. Philadelphia: AME Book Concerns, 1924.

Aldridge, Daniel Webster, ed. *The Aldridge Historically Black College Guide*, Detroit: The Aldridge Group, 1984.

Amistad Committee. *Yale, Slavery and Abolition*. New Haven, Conn.: Amistad Committee, 2001.

Anderson, James D. *The Education of Blacks in the South, 1860–1935*. Chapel Hill: University of North Carolina Press, 1988.

Appiah, Kwame A, and Henry Louis Gates, Jr. *Africana: The Encyclopedia of the African and African American Experience*, New York: Basic Civitas Books, 1999.

Armstrong, M. F, and Helen W. Ludlow. *Hampton and Its Students*. New York: AMS Press, 1874.

Bernard, Emily. *Remember Me to Harlem: The Letters of Langston Hughes and Carl Van Vechten*. New York: Vintage Books, 2001.

Black, Isaac. *Twelve Things Students, Parents and Counselors Should Know About Historically Black Colleges (A Resource for Students of Color)*, New York: Black Excel, 1997–2003.

Butler, Addie L. *The Distinctive Black College: Talladega, Tuskegee and Morehouse*. Metuchen, N.J.: Scarecrow Press, 1977.

Davis, Hasan. *A. A. Burleigh, 1848–1939: Berea's First Black Graduate*. Lexington: Kentucky Humanities Council, 1998.

Drewry, Henry, et al. *Stand and Prosper: Private Black Colleges and Their Students*. Princeton, N.J.: Princeton University Press, 2001.

Foner, Philip S., and Pacheco, Josephine F. *Three Who Dared: Prudence Crandall, Margaret Douglass, Myrtilla Miner—Champions of Antebellum Black Education*. Westport, Conn.: Greenwood Press, 1984.

Fraser, James W. *Between Church and State: Religion and Public Education in Multi-Cultural Education*. New York: St. Martin's Press, 1999.

Hill, Ruth Edmonds. *The Black Women Oral History Project*, vols. 1 and 2. Westport, Conn.: Meckler Publishing, 1991.

Holloway, Jonathan S. *Confronting the Veil: Abram Harris, Jr., E. Franklin Frazier, and Ralph Bunche 1919–1941*. Chapel Hill: University of North Carolina Press, 2002.

Ingersoll, Thomas. *Mammon and Manon in Early New Orleans*. Knoxville: University of Tennessee Press, 1999.

Johnson, Charles S. *The Negro College Graduate*. Chapel Hill: University of North Carolina Press, 1938.

Lamon, Lester. *Black Tennesseans, 1900–1930*. Knoxville: University of Tennessee Press, 1977.

Lang, Willis Louis. *Black Bootstraps*, n.p., n.d.

Logan, Rayford W. *Howard University: The First Hundred Years, 1867–1967*. New York: New York University Press, 1969.

Moon, Henry Lee. *The Emerging Thought of W. E. B. DuBois*. New York: Simon & Schuster, 1972.

National Center for Educational Statistics. *Historically Black Colleges and Universities: 1976–1994*. Washington, D.C.: Government Printing Office, 1996.

Pierce, Edward. *The Negroes at Port Royal, S.C.: Report of the Government Agent*. Washington, D.C.: U.S. Department of Treasury, 1862.

Rhodes, Lelia Gaston. *Jackson State University: The First Hundred Years, 1877–1977*. Jackson: University of Mississippi Press, 1979.

Robinson, William H. *Indian Education at Hampton: Stony the Road*.

Rose, Willie Lee. *Rehearsal for Reconstruction: The Port Royal Experience*. New York: Oxford University Press, 1964.

Schall, Keith E. *Stony the Road: Chapters in the History of Hampton Institute*. Charlottesville: University Press of Virginia, 1977.

Scott, William R, et al. *Upon These Shores: Themes in the African-American Experience, 1600 to the Present*. New York: Routledge, 1999.

Sterne, Emma G. *Mary McLeod Bethune*. New York: Random House, 1957.

"The Port Royal Fact." *Harper's Weekly*, March 15, 1862, p.

Washington, Booker T. *Up from Slavery: An Autobiography*. Garden City, N.Y.: Doubleday Company, 1900.

Watson, Steven. *The Harlem Renaissance: Hub of African-American Culture, 1920–1930*. New York: Pantheon Books, 1996.

Wolters, Raymond. *The New Negro on Campus: Black College Rebellions of the 1920s*, Princeton: Princeton University Press, 1975.

Zikmund, Barbara B. *Hidden Histories in the United Church of Christ: Blacks and the American Missionary Association*. Cleveland: Pilgram Press, 1987.

Journals, Magazines, Newspapers, and Other Sources

"About the Seniors," *The Hilltop*, April 29, 1929.

"A Lowly Beginning," Mordecai Johnson Papers, Moorland Spingarn Research Center, Howard University, Washington, D.C.

"Alphas' Thirteenth Education Week Begins on May 6," *The Hilltop*, April 25, 1928.

Alumnus, "Another White President at Howard Would Be Blunder Says Alumnus," *Afro American Newspaper*, 1926.

Alumnus, "Durkee Reported in Brooklyn, N.Y. Seeking Call to Beecher Pulpit," *Afro American Newspaper*, January 9. 1926.

Alumnus, "Favoritism Is Ascribed to H. U. Prexy," *Afro American Newspaper,* June 27, 1925.

Alumnus, "Friends Seek to Call Off Fight Against Howard University Prexy," *Afro American Newspaper*, October 4, 1925.

Alumnus, "Howard Students on Strike, Durkee 500 Miles Away," *Afro American Newspaper*, May 15, 1925.

Alumnus, "Howard University Alumni to Seek the Intervention of Their Congressmen," *Afro American Newspaper,* November 21, 1925.

Alumnus, "Kelly Miller Hero as Howard Faculty Testifies Against Durkee Before Board," *Afro American Newspaper*, December 19, 1925.

Alumnus, "Professor Cook Ousted from Home on College Campus," *Afro American Newspaper*, May 30, 1925.

Alumnus, "Queer School Durkee H'ads Enrollment 37, Graduates 41," *Afro American Newspaper*.

American Missionary Association Archives Addendum: Historical Notes, American Missionary Association.

"And Durkee 500 Miles Away," *Washington Daily American Newspaper*, May 8, 1925.

American Missionary Association Archives Addendum: Historical Notes. The United Church Board for Homeland Ministries Archives [New] Addendum, 1869–1980. The Amistad Research Center, Tulane University, New Orleans, Louiisana.

Austin, Ben S., "The Fisk University Jubilee Singers." Viewed at Middle Tennessee State University website, http://www.mtsu.edu/~baustin/jubilee.html.

Barbour, Carl J., A Letter to Dr. McKenzie, June 22, 1924, Papers of Fayette A. McKenzie, Fisk University Archives.

Bayonton, Clara R., Western Union Telegram to Mrs. Addie Streator Wright, February 3, 1925, Papers of Fayette A. McKenzie.

Brooks, R. W., Letter to F. A. McKenzie, February 24, 1919, Papers of Fayette A. McKenzie.

Collins, L. D., Letter to My Dear Friends, June 22, 1924, Papers of Fayette A. McKenzie.

Committee on the District of Columbia, *Report of the Trustees of the Colored Schools,* The Bureau of Refugees, Freedmen and Abandoned Lands, Washington, D.C., 1869

"Daubers' Play, 'Bimbo,' a Success," *The Hilltop*, April 29, 1929.

Davis, E. P., "The Negro Liberal Arts College," *Journal of Negro Education*.

Davis, John W., "The Negro Land-Grant College," *The Journal of Negro Education*.

DeBerry, W. N., Western Union Telegram to Dr. F. A. McKenzie, March 14, 1925, Papers of Fayette A. McKenzie.

"Do Not Rock the Boat (and) No 'Hymn of Hate' by the United States: Two War Time Editorials," December 1917, *Fisk University News*, Fisk University Archives.

DuBois, W. E. B., "Diuturni Silenti," An Address Delivered to the Alumni of Fisk University at Fisk Memorial Chapel, June 2, 1924, *Fisk Herald* 33, no.1. (1924).

DuBois, W. E. B., "Editorial," *Fisk Herald* 33, no.2, 1925.

Dyett, Western Union Telegram to Alain L. Locke, March 1, 1926, Alain Locke Papers, Moorland Spingarn Research Center, Howard University.

Editorials, *The Athenaeum*, 13 no. 2 (1910).

Farnandez, B. J., Letter to Dr. McKenzie, March 14, 1918, Papers of Fayette A. McKenzie.

"Fifty Police Quell Demonstration of Fisk Students," *Nashville Banner*, February 5, 1925.

Fisk Board of Trustees, Western Union Telegram to President F. A. McKenzie, November 11, 1924, *Papers of Fayette A. McKenzie*.

"Fisk Students Stage a Walkout," *Nashville Banner*, February 6, 1925.

"Fisk President Rejects Request for Arbitration," *Nashville Banner*, February 8, 1925, p.____.

"Fisk President's Offer Accepted with Amendment," *Nashville Banner*, February 9, 1925, p.____.

Fisk University Student Body, A Statement of Grievances Against Fayette A. McKenzie as President of Fisk University, pub. date, Papers of Fayette A. McKenzie, Fisk University Archives.

"Fisk Wrangle to Be Discussed at Meeting Tonight," *Nashville Banner,* February 9, 1925.

Fisk Student Body, Is It Fair? (A Brief History of Fisk Trouble), February 1925, Papers of Fayette A. McKenzie.

Fleming, Richard S., Dr., Western Union Telegram to Dr. F. A. McKenzie, March 12, 1925, Papers of Fayette A. McKenzie.

Fultz, Michael, "A Quintessential American: Horace Mann Bond, 1924–1939," *Harvard Educational Review*.

Goodrich, Andrew L., "Jazz in Historically Black Colleges," *Jazz Education Journal,* November 2001. Viewed online at http://www.laje.org/article.asp? Article ID-79.

Holt, Shannone, "Black College Football," The Education Highway. Viewed online at http://www.eduhwy.com.

"Howard Faculty Attacks Salary Distribution," *Washington Daily American Newspaper,* December 22, 1924.

"Howard Faculty Defies Students," *Washington Daily American Newspaper,* May—, 1925.

"Howard Faculty Discusses Aleged 'Leak,' " *Washington Daily American Newspaper,* December 10, 1924.

"Howard Faculty Serves Ultimatum on Student Body," *Washington Daily American Newspaper,* May 13, 1925.

"Howard Strikers Refuse to Yield," *New Student Newspaper,* May 13, 1925.

"Howard Students Make Additional Demands," *Washington Daily American Newspaper,* May 11, 1925.

"Howard Trustees Exonerate Durkee of Alumni Charges," *Washington Post*, December 11, 1925.

"The Howard University Club of New York City, Resolution to Oust J. Stanley Durkee, June 17, 1925," Alain Locke Papers.

Howard University Board of Trustees, *An Official Statement from the Trustees of Howard University*. Washington, D.C.: Howard University Press.

"Howard's New Medical School Dedicated," *The Hilltop*, April 25, 1928.

Hurston, Zora Neale. Letter to Dr. Locke, June 5, 1927, Alain Locke Papers.

Jackson, Abigail, "Testimony of a Former White Teacher," *Fisk Herald* 33, no. 2, (1925).

Johnson, Marcia Lynn, "Student Protest at Fisk University in the 1920s," *Negro History Bulletin*, Nashville, Tenn, October 1970.

"Journal of the Proceedings of the Committee on Education and Labor of the House of Representatives During the Investigation of the Charges Proffered Against General O.O. Howard," *The Globe Newspaper*, April 8, 1870.

"Kappa Alpha Psi Guide Right Movement to Be Held," *The Hilltop*, April 25, 1928.

Letter to the Board of Trustees of Howard University, Date, *Alain Locke Papers*.

Lindsey, Donal Fred, "Indian Education at the Hampton Institute, 1877–1923." Doctoral dissertation, Kent State University, 1989.

Little, John Henry, *The Black Student and the Black College, 1880–1964,*

"Local Branch of Howard Alumni Committee to Investigate Student Strike," *Washington Daily American Newspaper*, Washington, D.C., May 8, 1925.

Locke, Alain, "Harlem," *Survey Graphic* 6, no. 6 (1925).

Locke, Alain, Letter to Doctor DuBois, Alain Locke Papers, Moorland Spingarn Research Center, Howard University, Washington, D.C., 1925.

Lowe, Alain, Letter to Professor A.O. Leuschner, January 26, 1926, Alain Locke Papers.

Locke, Alain, Letter to the Committee to Investigate Conditions at Howard, November 6, 1925, Alain Locke Papers.

McCoy, Frank, "Overturning the Court," *Howard Magazine*, 2002.

McKenzie, Fayette A., Letter to Mr. Farnandez, March 26, 1918, Papers of Fayette A. McKenzie.

McKenzie, Fayette A., Letter to Mr. R. W. Books, February 26, 1919, Papers of Fayette A. McKenzie.

McKenzie, Fayette A., Western Union Telegram to Dr. Richard S. Fleming, March 13, 1925, Papers of Fayette A. McKenzie.

McKenzie, Fayette A., Western Union Telegram to Mrs. James A. Myers, February 5, 1925, Papers of Fayette A. McKenzie.

McKenzie, Fayette A., Letter to Mrs. James A. Myers, February 11, 1925, Papers of Fayette A. McKenzie.

McKenzie, Fayette A., President's Report to the Board of Trustees, January 1, 1925, Papers of Fayette A. McKenzie.

McKenzie, Fayette A., Western Union Telegram to Mrs. J. Goodwin, Date, Papers of Fayette A. McKenzie.

McKenzie, Fayette A., Western Union Telegram to President J.

Stanley Durkee, March 13, 1925, Papers of Fayette A. McKenzie.

"Mazie Hubbard Wins Popularity Contest," *The Hilltop*, April 29, 1929.

Memorandum to Alumni Charges, 1925, Alain Locke Papers.

Memorandum re: Alumni Charges, Date, Alain Locke Papers.

Minutes of the Board of Trustees, October 19, 1921, Papers of Fayette A. McKenzie.

Minutes of the Meeting of the Executive Committee, February 11, 1924, Papers of Fayette A. McKenzie.

Mitchell, A. W., Letter to Dr. Charles R. Brown, August 18, 1925, Alain Locke Papers.

Mitchell, A. W., "The Case of the Howard Professors Decapitated by the Durkee Regime, August 8, 1925," Alain Locke Papers.

"M'Kenzie Will Leave Fisk," *Nashville Banner*, April 23, 1925.

Myers, James A., Letter to Fayette A. McKenzie, June 22, 1924, Papers of Fayette A. McKenzie.

Myers, James A., Letter to Our Very Dear, Dear Friends, June 1924, Papers of Fayette A. McKenzie.

Napier, J.C., Western Union Telegram to Mr. Paul D. Cravath, November 11, 1924, Papers of Fayette A. McKenzie.

"Negroes to Hold Mass Meeting on Trouble at Fisk," *Nashville Banner*, February 6, 1925.

Philippse, Alphonse D., "The Conditions at Fisk: Testimony of Alphonse D. Phillippse," *Fisk Herald*. 33, (1925).

O'Bannon, H., Letter to Fisk President, June 22, 1924, Papers of Fayette A. McKenzie.

"Putting a Question to Howard Students," *The Hilltop*, April 29, 1929.

Scott, Emmett J., Letter to Prof. Orlandao C. Thorton, June 16, 1925, Alain Locke Papers.

The Seventh Semi-Annual Freedmen's School Report. Washington, D.C.: The Bureau of Refugees, Freedmen and Abandoned Lands, 1869.

"Statements Give Various Angles of Trouble at Fisk," *Nashville Banner,* February 8, 1925.

"Striking Fisk Students Seek Removal of M'Kenzie," *Nashville Banner*, February 7, 1925.

Struggles at Fisk, *Fisk Herald*, vols. 43–46, 1949–1953, Fisk University Archives.

"Student Council Makes Much Needed Recommendations," *The Hilltop,* March 20, 1924.

"Students Strike to Eliminate Cut Rule," *New Student Newspaper*, May 16, 1925.

"Stylus Society Selects New Members," *The Hilltop*, March 28, 1928.

Thompson, Perry C., Letter to Dr. Fayette Avery McKenzie from the Editor of the *Chicago Whip*, November 22, 1924, Papers of Fayette Avery McKenzie.

"Time Line of African American History, 1852–1880." Viewed online at http://www.princeton.edu/~aares/chronologies.htm.

ILLUSTRATION CREDITS

ABOUT THE PROJECT TEAM

Dwayne Ashley

Dwayne Ashley is chief executive officer and president of the Thurgood Marshall Scholarship Fund. He leads the overall strategic direction for the national organization to raise funds for merit scholarships and provide programmatic and capacity-building support to the forty-five public historically black public colleges and universities (HBCUs). With more than 15 years of experience in nonprofit management and fundraising, he is one of the country's foremost experts in his field. Ashley comes from a long line of philanthropists and educators. His great-grandmother donated the land for the first colored school in Ringgold, Louisiana.

Ashley joined the Thurgood Marshall Scholarship Fund in 1998 as executive director and was appointed president the following year. He was recently named chief executive officer by the Board of Directors. His vision has moved the fund to the forefront of higher education authorities. He serves as the TMSF's spokesperson and, working closely with the Board of Directors, guides the company to its goals. During Ashley's tenure, TMSF's revenues have increased by more than 700 percent—under his leadership, more than 75 percent of the organization's total revenues since its founding have been raised, surpassing the $50 million mark.

Ashley has also spearheaded various studies for the TMSF, including the *Economic Impact Snapshot of the Thurgood Marshall Scholarship Fund: Member Colleges and Universities and Scholarship Evaluation Report* and the *Thurgood Marshall Scholarship Fund Demographic Report,* a study on public HBCUs. He created both the TMSF Leadership Institute, serving more than 500 HBCU students, and the TMSF President's Summit, which has served more than 700 public HBCU faculty and staff members.

Ashley's career includes more than 15 years experience as a fundraiser and nonprofit executive. Prior to joining TMSF, Ashley served as the national executive director and chief professional officer of the 100 Black Men of America, Inc., from 1996 to 1999. The 100 Black Men of America, Inc., is one of the nation's largest and oldest mentoring organizations. Under his leadership, the 100 Black Men of America, Inc., achieved unprecedented fundraising and organizational growth; its annual revenue grew from $250,000 to $6 million. He also launched the organization's first capital campaign to raise $35 million.

Before becoming national executive director of 100 Black Men of America, Inc., Ashley was area development director for the United Negro College Fund (UNCF) from 1991 to 1996.

Under his leadership, the Philadelphia region rose to new heights in its overall fundraising.

Prior to becoming a member of UNCF's executive team, Ashley was a campaign manager for the United Way. In that role, he realized record fundraising and programmatic results for United Way of the Texas Gulf Coast.

Ashley holds a master's degree in governmental administration from the University of Pennsylvania's Fel's School of Government and graduated cum laude from Wiley College (the oldest black college in Texas) with a bachelor of science degree. He is the third generation in his family to attend a historically black college. He was also awarded an honorary doctorate of laws from the University of the District of Columbia, a Thurgood Marshall Scholarship Fund member school, in May 2001.

He serves on the board of directors of the Gallup Organization, Newark Public Library and the New York–based Evidence Dance Company. Ashley has received numerous awards and honors and is a highly sought-after speaker and lecturer on leadership and nonprofit management.

Herb Boyd

Herb Boyd is an awarding-winning author and journalist who has published eleven books and countless articles for national magazines and newspapers. *Brotherman: The Odyssey of Black Men in America. An Anthology* (One World/Ballantine, 1995), coedited with Robert Allen, won the American Book Award for nonfiction. In 1999, Boyd won three first-place awards from the New York Association of Black Journalists for his articles published in the *Amsterdam News*. His book, *Autobiography of a People: Three Centuries of African American History Told By Those Who Lived It* (Doubleday, 2000), is currently listed on several best-seller bulletin boards. Among Boyd's most recent publications are *Race and Resistance: African Americans in the 21st Century* (South End Press, 2002) and *The Harlem Reader* (Three Rivers Press, 2003). He is currently completing a biography of famed boxer Sugar Ray Robinson (Amistad/HarperCollins), projected to be on the market in 2005, and working with world music composer Yusef Lateef on his autobiography.

Boyd is also a freelance journalist with several major black publications, including the *Amsterdam News*. He is a graduate of Wayne State University in Detroit and teaches African and African American history at the College of New Rochelle.

OLIVIA M. CLOUD, COPY EDITOR

Olivia Cloud, who provided editorial assistance to this work, has devoted nearly a quarter-century to the field of publishing as a writer, editor, and curriculum developer, primarily in the Christian arena.

An ordained Baptist minister, Cloud served for ten years as black church editorial and product development coordinator at the Sunday School Board of the Southern Baptist Convention, now LifeWay Christian Resources.

Cloud now serves as senior editor at the R. H. Boyd Publishing Corporation, a 108-year-old African American publishing company headquartered in Nashville, Tennessee. She is also owner of Guardian Angel Communications Services and has provided editorial and desktop publishing services to a variety of independent authors and publishers, including LifeWay Christian Resources, Focus on the Family, Urban Ministries, Inc., Thomas Nelson Publishers, Cook Communications, and Judson Press.

Cloud has published eight books, including: *Rules of the Road: A Guide to Spiritual Growth* (National Baptist Publishing Board, 1999), *Life Challenges for Teens* (Boyd Publications, 1999), *Bible Q &A for Kids* (MEGA Corporation, 2000), *Testify! Testimonies of the Faithful* (MEGA Corporation, 2000), and *Roadmaps for Living: More Rules of the Road* (R. H. Boyd Publishing Corporation, 2004).

She has a B.A. in journalism from the University of Kentucky, Lexington and a master's degree in religious education from the Southern Baptist Theological Seminary in Louisville.

ADRIENNE INGRUM, EDITOR AND PROJECT MANAGER

Adrienne Ingrum has twenty-five years of experience in book publishing. She has served as vice president at G. P. Putnam's Sons (now part of Penguin Putnam), Waldenbooks, and Crown, a division of Random House, publishing more than 500 fiction, nonfiction, and sideline titles and working personally with dozens of authors, including the best-selling Bebe Moore Campbell, national poet laureate Rita Dove, and screenwriter-turned-novelist Nelson George. Ingrum also developed and published the best-sellers *We Are the World* and *Million Man March*.

An independent publishing consultant for the past five years, Ingrum launched and oversees *Black Issues Book Review* for Cox, Matthews & Associates. She has served as lead consultant for Doubleday Direct (now Bookspan) in the development of Black Expressions Book Club and has consulted for such corporations as Urban Ministries, Inc. (the country's largest African American Christian publisher).

BOOKER T. MATTISON

Booker T. Mattison is an award-winning writer and director whose films and music videos have screened extensively in the United States and Europe. His film adaptation of *The Gilded Six Bits*, based on the Zora Neale Hurston short story, was televised nationally on Showtime cable network's *Ninth Annual Black Filmmaker Showcase*. According to the *Hollywood Reporter* it was the best of the films featured.

Films that Mattison has written and directed have screened at the Smithsonian Institute and the Library of Congress in Washington D.C., the Directors Guild of America in Hollywood, and Harvard University. Abroad, his work has been showcased on the television show *Sanostra* in Madrid, Spain, and MTV Europe. His music video for the Cross Movement's song "Know Me (Huh What?)" was in rotation on Black Entertainment Television, the Trinity Broadcasting Network, and the Word Network. He has served as an important reviewer of written works on film for *Black Issues Book Review* magazine. He recently wrote and directed the Cross Movement's music video for the song "When I Flow" from their latest album, *Holy Culture*, which is currently the fastest-selling gospel hip-hop album in history.

Mattison was featured as "a filmmaker on the verge" in *Vibe* magazine. His work has also been discussed in the *Christian Science Monitor, Black Issues Book Review,* and *Feed* magazines. He has received the prestigious Warner Brothers Pictures Production Award, the *Entertainment Weekly* Post-Production Award, and the Spike Lee Fellowship. He has taught film production at Brooklyn College, literary criticism at the College of New Rochelle, and apologetics at Tabernacle Bible Institute.

Booker T. Mattison received his bachelor of science degree in mass communications from Norfolk State University and his master of fine arts in film from New York University.

PRECIOUS ADDIE MATTISON

Precious A. Mattison is a veteran of the U.S. Army. After graduating from advanced training as a distinguished honor graduate and serving three years of honorable service and soldier support, she returned to college in pursuit of a B.A. in English. During her college studies, which included multiple composition, grammar, and technical writing courses, she acquired the necessary tools to proficiently edit a variety of works. She has also developed a working knowledge of Spanish.

Throughout her college career, Mattison has maintained employment at the prominent brokerage firm of Financial Security Group, where she continues to use her communication and personnel skills to assist a diverse clientele. Mattison is also pursuing her goals by sharing the beauty of language, reading, and writing as an English instructor for an adult literacy program.

SHAWN E. RHEA, RESEARCHER AND WRITER

Shawn E. Rhea is a journalist, essayist, poet, and fiction writer. She has been a contributor to *The Source* magazine, and has also penned articles for *Essence, Black Enterprise, Teen People,* BET.com, and the New Orleans *Times Picayune* newspaper. Her short fiction has been featured in the literary publication *Anansi,* and her poetry and essays in the anthologies *Speak the Truth to the People* (Runagate Press) and *Unheard Voices*.

Rhea has also taught English composition at Xavier University of Louisiana in New Orleans, an HBCU. Rhea received her bachelor's degree from Howard University and her master's from Columbia University's Graduate School of Journalism.

SUZANNE RUST

Suzanne Rust is a contributing editor at *Black Issues Book Review*. She also has written extensively for *Italian Elle* and *Variety* as well as for the Internet, where at one time she had her own entertainment column.

Rust, a graduate of Sarah Lawrence College, has an eclectic background. Fluent in Italian, she has been an on-air reporter for one of Italy's top radio stations, where she has interviewed celebrities and talked about trends and cultural events. While living in Rome, this native New Yorker worked in film production for several years before moving back to the United States.

She has been a photo researcher and editor for numerous projects, including the book *Harlem Style*. She is currently at work on a series of books for children.

JUAN WILLIAMS, COAUTHOR

Author of the best-selling book, *Eyes on the Prize*, Juan Williams has spent twenty-three years as a political analyst and national correspondent for the *Washington Post*. Currently the senior correspondent for National Public Radio News, he is also the author of the critically acclaimed biography of Justice Thurgood Marshall.

Williams has won an Emmy Award for his television documentary writing, and has contributed features to such periodicals as *Fortune, The Atlantic Monthly, Ebony, GQ, The New Republic,* and *Black Issues Book Review.* He is a regular panelist on *Fox News Sunday,* a host of *America's Black Forum,* and former host of NPR's *Talk of the Nation.* Williams lives in Washington, D.C.

INDEX